Mollie's Job

A STORY OF LIFE AND WORK
ON THE GLOBAL ASSEMBLY LINE

William M. Adler

A LISA DREW BOOK

SCRIBNER
New York   London   Toronto   Sydney   Singapore

SCRIBNER
1230 Avenue of the Americas
New York, NY 10020

SCRIBNER and design are trademarks of Macmillan Library
Reference USA, Inc., used under license by Simon & Schuster,
the publisher of this work.

Set in New Baskerville
Manufactured in the United States of America

1 3 5 7 9 10 8 6 4 2

Library of Congress Cataloging-in-Publication Data.

Adler, William M.
Mollie's Job: a story of life and work on the
global assembly line/William M. Adler.
p. cm.
Includes bibliographical references and index.
1. Working class women—United States—Interviews.
2. Assembly-line methods.
3. Industrial sociology—United States.
4. James, Mollie, 1931–
I. Title.
HD6068.2.U6 A33 2000
331.4'87—dc21
99-059825

ISBN 0-684-83779-X

In memory of Maurine Hedgepeth
and
In memory of Cliff Olofson

Mollie's Job

CONTENTS

Introduction: End of the Line   11

PART I: PATERSON

1. Dimples Takes a Ride   19
2. The Golden Land   32
3. High, Wide and Handsome   53
4. The World of Tomorrow   70
5. Eight Days a Week   81
6. Farrell Dobbs's Vision   99
7. "All Hell Broke Loose"   112

PART II: MISSISSIPPI

8. Biscuits and Bond Issues   139
9. Working for the Railroad   166
10. Handbills from Heaven   173

PART III: MEXICO

11. Border Dreams   207
12. Leveraged Lives   218
13. "On the Border, By the Sea"   253
14. The Lucky Ones   268
15. Sleeping with the Elephant   287

Epilogue: "Thank God for NAFTA"   305
Acknowledgments   315
Selected Bibliography   319
Source Notes   323
Index   353

INTRODUCTION

End of the Line

PATERSON, NEW JERSEY, JUNE 30, 1989. Mollie James sensed it the morning she came to work and noticed the hole in the floor. It wasn't a hole, really, in the sense of an opening; it was more of a void: a great yawning space of discolored concrete where just the afternoon before had sat a steel-stamping machine, a hulking piece of American industrial might. Before long, more holes appeared, each tracing the outline of the base of another machine, like chalk around a sidewalk corpse.

It is three o'clock on a warm Friday afternoon, and the second of the two washup bells has rung for the final time. Mollie James has been here, on the assembly line at Universal Manufacturing Company, since 1955. She was the first female union steward and among the first African American union stewards; hers was a self-assured presence any grievant would want on his side. She was the first woman to run a stamping machine, the first to laminate steel. And now, after thirty-four years on the line—nearly two-thirds of her life—she is the last to go. Her wide shoulders are hunched over the sink as she rinses her hands with industrial soap alongside the others. She is a big-boned woman of fifty-nine, with a handsome, animated face framed by over-size glasses.

At the end of every other shift for more than three decades, Mollie and her co-workers beat a quick path to the plant parking lot. On this day there is less sense of hurry. There are still children to feed, clothes to wash, bills to pay, errands to run, other jobs to race to. But as she and the others leave the washroom, no one seems pressed to leave. All about the plant entrance, and out in the lot, people stand in small clusters, like mourners at their own wake, talking, laughing, hugging, crying. Almost always Mollie James is outgoing and outspoken, her voice loud, assertive; her smile nicely lighted. She is a strong woman, her strength forged from a life of hard work and sacrifice and faith in God. She is not one to betray her emotions, but this day is different. Her bearing has turned to reserve, her normally quick eyes dull and watery. Her working life is over, and that is all she has ever known.

During nearly two decades of ownership by the company's founder, a Paterson native named Archie Sergy, and two decades more by absentee corporations that more or less allowed the Paterson plant to operate as if it were still a locally owned business, Universal had always turned a tidy profit. Its signature product, ballasts for fluorescent lights (the ballast regulates the flow of current into the lamp), attracted attention only when the ballast failed—causing the light fixture to hum or flicker. In the middle 1980s, however, the company was swept up in the gale winds of Wall Street's merger mania. Twice within eight months Universal was sold, both times to companies headed by disciples of Michael Milken, the Street's reigning evil genius.

It was not until after its latest sale, in 1986, to an electrical-components conglomerate called MagneTek, Inc., that workers began taking plant-closing rumors seriously. There had been several rounds of layoffs since, and even though the company had promised employees as recently as six months ago that the plant would not close altogether, few believed it. It was around then, in fact, that Mollie James had noticed the hole in the floor, that movers had begun pulling up the plant's massive machinery, much of which was bolted to the cement floor when the factory opened in 1950. Paterson then was thriving, reveling in the postwar boom. By this early summer day four decades later, vast stretches of the floor are uninhabited, bereft of all signs of the plant's and the city's former glory.

There were no valediction speeches from company or union officials, no farewell luncheon, no pomp of any sort. A week earlier the workers themselves held a dinner at Lunello's, an Italian eatery on Union Boulevard. They kicked in fifteen dollars apiece and celebrated their long years together at Universal.

Many of these people are more than co-workers; they are friends on whom Mollie has come to depend as she would members of her extended family. They ate together at work, attended weddings, baptisms, parties, funerals, together. On this afternoon, though Mollie knows many of her co-workers better than she knows some of her relatives—knows their mannerisms, ways of speech, strengths, flaws—on this afternoon their voices blend, their faces blur. The decades together on the line have done that: bound together the most varied of people. Black and white Americans. Dominicans. Russians. Italians. Indians. Puerto Ricans. Peruvians. They came to work for Universal—and stayed—because of the good wages and benefits their union had negotiated. Mollie earned $7.91 an hour; not so much in itself, but with all the overtime she put in, it came to about $30,000 a year. She also received company-paid health insurance, and the peace of mind that came from a secure job—a job she could raise a family on, buy a house, a car, borrow money against, count on for the future.

When there is no one left to say good-bye to, Mollie slumps behind the wheel of her rusting 1977 Dodge Charger and follows the procession out of the lot. From the corner of Fifth Avenue and East Sixth Street, she heads toward the hill up Lyon Street, south on East Sixteenth Street, east on Eleventh Avenue. It is not far, three miles or so, from the plant in the industrial Bunker Hill neighborhood to the three-story, three-family house she owns on the near East Side. Upon pulling into her customary space in the driveway, in front of the right door of the detached two-car garage, Mollie sits in the car a good long while, letting the heat of the summer afternoon settle her. By the time she fits the key into the lock of the back door and begins climbing the three flights of stairs to her bedroom, she has stopped crying.

MATAMOROS, TAMAULIPAS, MEXICO, JUNE 10, 1988. It is a year before Mollie James would lose her job. On this blindingly blue, hot and humid Friday morning in Matamoros, the booming border city across the Rio Grande from Brownsville, Texas, Hector J. Romeu Jr. is one frantic man, as harried as Chaplin's Little Tramp. Romeu, like the border region itself, straddles both worlds; he was born in Cuba and schooled in Texas, married a Mexican American, works in Matamoros, and lives in Brownsville. The thirty-four-year-old handles sales and public relations for the Finsa Group, a principal developer of industrial parks along the Mexican border. Its flagship park, less than a ten-minute drive from the International Bridge, occupies five hundred acres on what used to be farmland on the west side of Matamoros. Romeu has been chasing his tail for weeks, tending to the innumerable details of staging today's gala ribbon cutting: It's the grand opening of the first MagneTek plant here.

The Finsa Group's two years of gut-grinding work—from recruiting MagneTek to shepherding it through site selection and ground breaking to the manufacture of the first ballasts—all of that pays off today. Romeu has been rewarded with a splendid morning, and the MagneTek honchos, in from corporate headquarters in Los Angeles, are delighted with their gleaming plant and the enthusiastic welcome Romeu has orchestrated. There are city and state officials on hand to meet and greet the American executives, as well as government-approved union leaders, and a reporter and photographer from *El Bravo,* the Matamoros daily with long and deep ties to Romeu's employer, the powerful Arguelles family. And Romeu has even thought to outfit the visiting execs in natty going-native panama hats emblazoned with MagneTek's royal blue capital-M "power" logo.

Plant manager Charles E. Peeples, an affable Arkansas expatriate, leads the officials on a tour of the plant. They goose-step past equipment ripped from the shopworn floor in Paterson, machinery operated by a young, almost entirely female workforce. These women, primarily in their teens and twenties, have come north to Matamoros in search of work and a better future than the bleakness promised in the jobless farming towns of the interior.

It is the future to which Anthony J. Pucillo, the company's executive vice president, directs his remarks during the opening ceremonies. Pucillo applauds the way labor and management worked together to open the plant—the first ballasts came off the line here two months earlier, in April. "In order to be able to successfully compete in world markets and create jobs," Pucillo says, "one has to rely on this kind of team. Here in Matamoros, people have a vision for the future; if we can make quality products at competitive prices, the company grows. If MagneTek grows, we all grow."

If Pucillo's vision was not original, it remained compelling: that labor would prosper alongside capital. It was the very notion that had pulled a teen-age Mollie James out of her native rural central Virginia four decades earlier, and it was the reason another hopeful teen-ager would soon be drawn from her home in the placid high desert of central Mexico.

CIUDAD DEL MAÍZ, SAN LUIS POTOSÍ, MEXICO, APRIL 1991. On a cool spring night, a fresh-faced twenty-year-old named Balbina Duque Granados boards a bus near her picturesque but impoverished mountain village four hundred miles southwest of Matamoros, where she is bound for. With its comparatively low wages, endless supply of labor, lack of regulation, and proximity to the United States, Matamoros is a magnet for *maquiladoras,* the foreign-owned assembly plants that wed first-world engineering with third-world working conditions. The *maquilas,* in turn, are a beacon to tens of thousands of poor, young women such as Balbina (the industry prefers women, the younger, for their nimble fingers and compliant minds, the better), for whom a factory job trumps any other employment options.

But with the surplus labor force, there is no certainty of a job in the *maquilas.* After enduring a succession of odd and degrading jobs and weeks of travails in the *maquila* union's Dickensian central hiring hall, Balbina finally lands a *maquila* job. Her probationary pay is slightly less than twenty-six dollars a week, or about sixty-five cents an hour. It is difficult work, repetitive and tiring and mind-numbing, but it is a job she is thrilled to have—her "answered prayer." And although Balbina doesn't know it, it is not just any job. It is Mollie's job.

THIS IS THE chronicle of that single job as it passed from the urban North to the rural South (Universal opened an ancillary plant in Mississippi in 1963) to Mexico over the course of the past half-century and the dawn of the new one. The job in which Mollie James once took great pride, the job that fostered and valued her loyalty, enabled her to rise above humble beginnings, provide for her family—that job does not now pay Balbina Duque a wage sufficient to live on. Embedded in that core fact, and in the story of the intersecting lives and fates of Mollie and Balbina, is a larger story about fundamental changes in the economy—a story about the demise of unions and the middle class and the concurrent rise of the plutocracy; about the disposability of workers and the portability of work; about how government and Wall Street reward U.S.-based companies for closing domestic plants and scouring the globe for the lowest wages in places where human rights and labor rights are ignored; and about the ways in which "free trade" harms democracy, undermines stable businesses and communities, exploits workers on both sides of the border, both ends of the global assembly line.

"The movers came at night, like thieves, sometimes just taking one piece at a time," Mollie recalls when asked how she learned what Universal's new ownership had ordained for her future. "We'd come in in the mornings and there'd be another hole in the floor."

Part I / Paterson

ONE

Dimples Takes a Ride

Photo by Ellen Denato

Mollie James

RICHMOND, VIRGINIA, NOVEMBER 1950. Rolling into Broad Street Station on the daily northbound run, the conductor of the Silver Meteor does not bother to stop the train. Richmond is not a principal destination for the Meteor, the queen of the Seaboard Air Line Railroad's Florida to New York whistle-stoppers, and so the depot merits the train's slowing only enough for passengers to disembark and for new passengers to hop on.

At a few minutes before two on a cold, pitch-black morning, a father and his nineteen-year-old daughter wait anxiously on the platform of the ornate World War I–era station. The young woman is Mollie Brown, "Dimples" to the folks back home in Cartersville, in

Cumberland County, forty-five miles west of Richmond in the rolling farmland of central Virginia. Mollie is headed to Penn Station in Newark, New Jersey, to meet her fiancé, who would take her home, to Paterson, to her new life. She is dressed in her finest: a new navy blue suit, new shoes, new hairdo. She carries nearly everything she owns in a half-dozen sky blue suitcases her father has given her for the trip.

Mollie is traveling alone, but the "colored" train cars of the Silver Meteor, and indeed those of the other great northbound coaches— the Champion, the Florida Sunbeam, the Silver Comet—are full of Mollie Browns: black Southerners crossing the Mason-Dixon Line, heading for the promised land.

World War II was over, and the Great Migration to the urban centers of the North was in full swing. Southern blacks no sooner graduated from high school than they packed their bags for the inevitable ride on the "Chickenbone Special." The name appeared on no timetable; it was coined, apparently, by the passengers. They were disinclined or disinvited to patronize the Jim Crow dining cars, and so they sustained themselves during the long trip with box lunches, which nearly always included the staple from which the trains derived their nickname: fried chicken.

This was not Mollie's first trip north; two summers earlier she went to Brooklyn to stay with her aunt Lucille, her mother's only sister. She had had a terrific time, riding the subway, seeing movies, even saving some money. "At home I made only about six dollars a week babysitting," she recalls. "In New York I could make sixteen or eighteen dollars a week."

It wasn't only the wages she found so appealing. Jackie Robinson had broken into the major leagues with the Brooklyn Dodgers the previous season, and Mollie well recalls the pride and excitement it generated in places such as the restaurant in Harlem owned by the boxer Sugar Ray Robinson. "I couldn't believe he had his own place," she says, "that was just amazing to me. And everyone there just slapping each other when Jackie got a hit."

And it was not just at black-owned businesses that the teen-age Mollie was made to feel welcome. "Wherever I went in New York, I could go in for a cup of tea and a doughnut, and I could sit anywhere. You were not told to sit in a certain area. And when we shopped! The department stores were not segregated. Sears, Macy's, Gimbels—everybody tried on clothes in the same area." It wasn't like that at home. "In Farmville [the commercial center of Cumberland County] the stores had separate dressing rooms. And I heard a lot of blacks complain that the stores wouldn't allow them to try on hats. My mother always did, though. If they told her she couldn't try one on, she told them she couldn't buy it. That's the way my mother was."

Mollie's mother, for whom she was named, was fifteen when she married Renza Brown (his formal name was Lorenzo), six years her senior. For seventeen years the couple was childless. The elder Mollie had suffered two miscarriages, and it did not look to the Browns like they would fulfill their dream of becoming parents. And then, during the depths of the Depression, on October 24, 1931, came Mollie, and three years later, another daughter, Anna. "I guess that was one of those mysterious ways the Lord works in," Mollie says.

Mollie would learn much about the Lord. Her father was a minister, the assistant pastor at New Hope Baptist. "Church was my middle name growing up," she says. The church was next door to the two-room schoolhouse Mollie first attended, which itself adjoined the Browns' land. The family bought the land in 1934—after several failed attempts to buy property. It was not that Renza couldn't afford it; he had money stashed away for a down payment. But while there was a tradition of black landownership in Cumberland, the seat of the county, Cartersville, in the northeast portion of the county, had yet to embrace this radical idea; none of the landowners in town would sell to a black family. Several times Renza had attempted to buy property, and several times he had been rebuffed. Finally, the lumber mill owner for whom Renza worked as a sawyer, a Canadian who had married a local woman, purchased the house and the six acres of surrounding land, in turn selling it to the Browns. "We were the first black family on the road in that area," Mollie says. "There were families behind us, but not on the road, and the whites wanted to keep it that way."

It was not until that liberating summer of 1948, when Mollie went away to Brooklyn, that she more fully understood the deprivations of legal segregation at home—and how good freedom tasted. She was not yet sixteen, would not graduate from the all-black Cumberland Training School for two more years, but she already knew she would one day move to the North for good. "That's when I made up my mind I wasn't going to stay here, that it was *so* dark down here," she recalls years later, driving the winding roads of Cumberland County, through the deep green of rolling hills, tobacco plants, soybean fields, black walnut groves.

Millions of Southern blacks, of course, reached a similar conclusion. The first wave of the Great Migration had begun a generation before Mollie set foot in Brooklyn, during World War I, when European immigrants, who had comprised the bulk of the industrial workforce in America, were denied entrance to the United States. With the flow of European labor virtually evaporated, desperate Northern industrialists beckoned Southern blacks to their workforces. Come they did: A half-million blacks moved North between 1910 and 1920, eight hundred thousand more in the next decade.

Over the next four decades some five million blacks left the fields of the South for the urban life of the North and West. Many followed their elders and relatives. It gave them a place to stay, a possible job contact, a familiar face in a strange place. Those from Mississippi and Alabama and Arkansas commonly headed for Chicago or Detroit; Texans and Louisianans went to California; Georgians, Carolinians, and Virginians usually stayed on the eastern seaboard, migrating to Washington, Philadelphia or New York, or to smaller industrial cities such as Camden, New Jersey, or Newark or Paterson.

It was to Paterson that Mollie Brown's fiancé, Sam James, had moved. He, too, had grown up in Cumberland County, but he and Mollie did not meet until after he had moved up North. They were introduced on one of his return visits to the family farm, when he accompanied his brother Vivien on an outing with Mollie's sister, Anna, whom Vivien was dating.

Sam's family farmed tobacco and corn outside the town of Cumberland, some thirteen miles from Cartersville. He was the fourth of eight children born to Vivien and Florence James, who relied on their brood to help bring in the crops. Even when Sam was enrolled in elementary school, he often missed classes to work in the fields, and his formal education ceased altogether after sixth grade.

Sam was named for an uncle who had moved up North, to New York City, when Sam was young. Uncle Sam had made a name as a cook, and the impressionable youth decided he, too, would leave home for the big city as soon as possible. At first he thought he'd probably head to New York, but when, during the war, his firstborn sister,

Mozelle, and her husband, Turner Coleman, left home, they ended up in Paterson, where jobs were plentiful and where they found the small city (the population was 139,000) more manageable. (When their relatives from New York would ready to visit Paterson, they'd say, "We're comin' to the country.")

WHEN THE streamlined diesel-electric engine of the Silver Meteor finally came into sight, when they could hear the familiar blast of the horn, Renza handed Mollie the envelope containing her ticket. The one-way fare was eighteen dollars. Renza hugged his daughter good-bye and good luck, told her he loved her, and waited on the platform until the train pulled away. Mollie found a seat, waved to her father, and settled in for the long morning ride. "You are about to take a trip by train," the back of the ticket envelope read, "the most dependable, carefree, comfortable form of travel known."

"I thought I was *travelin'*, brother," Mollie says, marveling, almost a half-century later, at the wonder of the Meteor. She recalls with clarity the black satin interior of the coach, the plush reclining seats. But certainly the car Mollie rode in wasn't as "carefree" or "comfortable" as those in which the white passengers sat. "Our cars were filthy and the rest rooms dirty," Mollie says of the Jim Crow coaches into which blacks were directed.

Mollie arrived around ten A.M. at the Newark station, a magnificent Art Deco nod to the grandeur of train travel. Sam James had managed to leave his metalworking job to pick her up, but he hadn't had time to change out of his protective clothing. What he wore mattered little to Mollie; what mattered was that as sure as she watched the sun rise from her window seat on the Meteor, she would soon marry, find a decent job, start a family.

Sam drove his bride-to-be home in his new yellow two-door Ford, home to the second-floor one-room apartment he rented for twenty dollars a week above his sister and brother-in-law's apartment in their two-family house at 520 East Eighteenth Street. Although the accommodations were far from luxurious—Mollie and Sam shared a kitchen and bath with other upstairs tenants—her new life seemed as bright as Sam's shiny car.

All of them had steady work, Sam in the foundry at American

Light Alloy, one of several foundries that provided steady work to black men. Turner was employed at a rock quarry near Montclair, Mozelle at Spotless Laundry. Spotless serviced all the dry cleaners in the area; it was a principal employer of black women in the city. "They were the dirtiest, hottest, hardest jobs," recalls Arthur Holloway, a native Virginian who arrived in Paterson a few years before Mollie, "but we were still better off here than in the South."

When Mollie arrived in Paterson precisely at midcentury, she found a vibrant city pulsing with street life. "This was *the* shopping city then," says Vincent J. Cortese, president of the Greater Paterson Chamber of Commerce. FOLLOW ME TO DOWNTOWN PATERSON, read the slogan on city buses.

And people did. They flocked to the grand temples of retail, Meyer Bros. and Quackenbush's, the large department stores; Konner's Men's Shop; Charles W. Elbow, the haberdasher. On Thursday evenings, when the stores stayed open late, until nine, motorists circled around town searching for parking spaces. The holiday season and the January white sales, in particular, drew customers from throughout northern New Jersey, as well as from New York City and even Connecticut and western Pennsylvania. Downtown traffic was so choked that Paterson police implemented a plan to handle the sale period. "We put two to three officers at key intersections during and immediately after the holidays," says William Dolan, the city's current public safety director. "We needed one guy to direct traffic and two others to hold the pedestrians back on the green."

Meyer Bros. was the heart of downtown, at the prime corner of Main and Market streets, the city's main commercial thoroughfares. The store was diagonally across from City Hall, an 1896 neo-Renaissance stone replica of that of Lyons, the silk capital of France. With five stories of merchandise, Meyer's, as it was known, was the city's flagship department store. Rebuilt in 1925 after a fire, the store absolutely exuded elegance, from its interior acres of matched walnut and mahogany to the twin vestibules, at both entrances, covered in twenty-four-karat gold. Employees wore a black-and-white uniform to match the checkerboard marble floors. There was a fine restaurant in the basement, where the shopworn could dine on sandwiches or multicourse feasts. And there was an ornate ladies' room, for which the standard fee was a nickle (no tipping allowed). For an extra nickel, patrons would have access to a private changing room, with sink, toilet, mirrors.

There were also specialty shops: butchers on Washington Street, milliners on Church Street, shoe merchants on lower Main, and three high-end furniture stores on upper Main: Bograd's, Van Dyke's (which was also known for its basement gift shop), and Keystone.

It wasn't only the retailers that lured people downtown.

Hinchcliffe Stadium was the premier venue for sports. There were the Monday night stock-car or motorcycle races; it was the home field for the semipro Paterson Panthers football team and a couple of semipro baseball clubs, House of David and Wonder Bread. And during the summer months, the stadium hosted the Diamond Gloves boxing matches (a sort of minor league to the Golden Gloves fights at Madison Square Garden in New York), as well as traveling spectacles such as the Buster Crabbe water show. And for participants, there were bowling alleys in the basements of the firehouses.

There was a thriving cultural district that included a half-dozen theaters and an opera house, Lazzara's Music Hall. The theaters included the Regent, the U.S., the Rivoli, the Garden, the Majestic, and the Fabian. Several of the theaters had also showcased touring vaudeville and musical acts in the 1920s and 1930s. The Regent, on Union Street, a twenty-four-hundred-seat auditorium trimmed in gold leaf, hosted many acts who would go on to household-word fame: Edgar Bergen and Charlie McCarthy, Bing Crosby, Bob Hope, Jack Benny, Milton Berle, George Burns and Gracie Allen. They and other well-to-do visitors to the city stayed at the deluxe Alexander Hamilton Hotel, next door to the Fabian on the corner of Church and Market streets.

By the middle 1930s, though, with the widespread availability of a new medium, the Regent could no longer afford such talents. "Radio had a lot to do with our shutting down vaudeville," Joseph Lefkowitz, the theater's manager in its heyday, once recalled. "Burns and Allen played the Regent for six hundred and fifty dollars a week, then when they became stars on the radio circuit their asking price leaped to two thousand two hundred and fifty."

Well into the 1950s, downtown remained the cultural hub. Theaters continued to screen movies long after radio supplanted their live shows. The films were promoted as events, often playing to standing-room-only audiences, who crowded in not only for the feature but for the newsreel, the cartoon, and the coming-attractions trailer.

• • •

Not everyone enjoyed equal access to the big entertainments of the era: The Paterson of the early 1950s was a segregated city. Not in the rigid, codified Southern sense—there were none of the overt symbols of Jim Crow, the "Colored" and "White" signs that pervaded Mollie's homeland, for instance—but in ways that cut as deeply. At the Fabian, for instance, the city's premier movie palace, "it was known" that blacks were welcome only in the "peanut galleries"—the balcony and second balcony. Downstairs seating was reserved for whites. The city's only roller-skating rink, in the Paterson Recreation Center on Market Street, was closed to blacks, as was Circle Pool, a privately owned facility two blocks away. (Rather than yield to black demands to desegregate, the owners sold the swimming pool to the city.) Things were hardly different at the downtown YMCA, which also housed a swimming pool. The Y allowed blacks to swim—for an hour a week on Saturday mornings, and provided that they enter through the back door. The Y's other facilities, the bowling alley, pool tables, cafeteria, were off-limits to blacks.

Until the late 1940s, there had been one other swimming option for blacks in Paterson. On Garret Mountain Reservation, parkland on rocky heights overlooking Paterson with panoramic views of the city and its landmark buildings, the county maintained a pool and beach known as Barbour's Pond. Phil Chase, a black Paterson native, was a teen-ager during those years. He recalls the chain-link fence that ran the length of the dock at the pond. The fence divided both the waiting line for the sole diving board and the separate beaches for black and white swimmers. "We all got on the same board," Chase says, "but when we got up there, we dove left, and the white people dove right. Their beach was over there, and ours was over here."

Just as blacks in Paterson were herded to separate recreational facilities, so they were steered to low-paying, entry-level jobs: as broom pushers, seamstresses, washroom attendants, domestics, foundry workers. But even those jobs—at seventy-five or ninety cents an hour—paid nearly as much as field hands down South made for a whole day of picking tobacco or chopping cotton. The factory work *was* hard and dirty and hot and dusty and sometimes dangerous, but it wasn't nearly as merciless as the conditions to which they were accustomed. Industrial work paid overtime, provided annual wage increases, offered a sense of dignity and the possibility, however slim, for advancement—a concept wholly absent from the plantation culture down home.

And so people kept coming. During the 1940s, even as the city's overall population shrank slightly, the black population of Paterson more than tripled, from forty-two hundred to almost fourteen thousand. Driving the influx was the availability of defense jobs, especially at Wright Aeronautical Company, Paterson's largest employer and, during the war, the nation's largest airplane-engine factory.

In seven plants in and around Paterson, Wright's, as the company was known, employed some thirty-four thousand workers in round-the-clock shifts. Wright's bore the name of its founders, the famous pioneering aviation brothers. Their company came to Paterson in 1920, shortly after it incorporated. By the late twenties, with a growing interest in general aviation, fueled, in large part, by the success of Charles Lindbergh's epic flight, Wright's expanded in Paterson, adding three wings to its original plant and building a second facility.

As the threat of war engulfed Europe in the late thirties, Wright's swelled again, moving into three former silk mills and constructing a new plant in East Paterson to handle the orders from the French and British. During the war it would be renowned for producing engines for America's "giant super fortresses," the B-17s, B-25s, Helldivers, Avengers, Mariners.

Wright's was also renowned for its high-paying, unionized jobs. With all those defense orders for engines—the company would build more than 120,000 during the war—Wright's looked beyond its traditional workforce to fill the jobs. Women "dropped their aprons to don overalls," as a local newspaper put it, taking "swing shift" jobs alongside the men in the plant. And blacks fled Southern farms for jobs at Wright's—among the first large plants in the region open to them.

Neither Wright's nor its union, the previously all-white United Auto Workers, Local 669, however, desegregated without a fight. When the war buildup intensified in the summer of 1941, it took widespread, organized protest to impel equal treatment for blacks in the huge defense plants, their unions, and the military. Only after A. Philip Randolph, the head of the Brotherhood of Sleeping Car Porters, and other black leaders forced Roosevelt's hand by threatening to bring thousands upon thousands of blacks to Washington to rally against discrimination in civilian and military life did Roosevelt feel compelled to act. As a presidential aide explained it to Labor Department lawyer Joseph Rauh: "Some guy named Randolph is going to march on Washington unless we put out a fair employment practices order. . . . We got defense factories goin' up all over this goddamn country, but no blacks are bein' hired. Go down to the Budget Bureau and work something out." Rauh drafted Executive Order 8802, which Roosevelt promptly signed and which mandated a nondiscrimination policy for government agencies and contractors. Randolph called off the march.

He may have canceled it too soon. At Wright's, as in many plants across the country, management and union leaders basically ignored the executive order. Black workers, however, saw the order as a call to action. "Once FDR signed 8802," says Phil Chase, who would become a union and civil rights activist in Paterson, and who, interviewed a half-century later, recites the order number as if it were fresh in his mind, "that gave the people license to take action at Wright's." Walkouts were threatened and sit-ins staged until the company relented, Chase says, "because there was too much money at stake."

Wright's wholly transformed the standard of living for blacks in and around Paterson. "Everybody went to work there," Chase says. "My mother, father, aunt, sister-in-law. Everybody who could walk went to Wright's." (Chase himself later went to work at a Wright plant.) And they may have gone in pushing a broom, but they came out as machine operators. They ran lathes and grinders and millers. They worked in tool-and-die sheds. "The money was unbelievable," Chase adds. "They started off making about a dollar eighty-five, and were quickly making two-fifty and up. Before that, a whole dollar was almost unheard of. So it raised the scale of income by three or four magnitudes."

The increase in black economic power and population, the formation of a solid middle class, led to no increase in political power. When Mollie arrived in 1950, there were no elected blacks in municipal or county government. Nor were there any administrators or clerical workers, just the rare window cleaner or elevator operator. "For a black person to be employed at City Hall, even as a janitor, he was a celebrity," says Phil Chase.

No matter how bleak were the prospects for the new migrants in postwar Paterson, they seemed altogether rosier than did the future back home. Says Arthur Holloway, who arrived from Virginia shortly after the war ended: "We weren't integrated, we weren't advancing, we weren't participating in government, but it was still hard for us to recognize we hadn't arrived."

Holloway himself recognized that fact. "We had plenty of black professionals in town—doctors, lawyers, accountants—but none could hold political office," he says. Holloway and other activists in the Fourth Ward, a historically Jewish precinct that was rapidly changing to black, formed the Negro Committee for Participation in Government. Its mission, says Holloway, was to expose the "plight of the black community" to itself, and to educate and register the influx of potential new voters from the South, many of whom had never before cast a ballot.

The face of the Fourth Ward—a district that stretched from Hamilton Avenue and East Twelfth Street up to East Eighteenth Street, where Mollie and Sam lived—was changing by the day. Its houses were mostly tenant-occupied and crowded: Some accommodated up to six families. As Southern blacks moved in during and immediately after the war, Jewish descendants of immigrants from Eastern Europe, who had settled there a half-century earlier, moved out. Those who could afford to moved to suburban Wayne or Fair Lawn; those who could not moved from the four- and six-family homes into two- and three-family homes.

About the time Sam brought Mollie home to the Fourth Ward, Arnold Berger decided to vacate the neighborhood. Berger had grown up on Water Street, in the Jewish working-class section known as "Over the River." As a young family man, he moved to a four-family house at the corner of Twentieth Avenue and East Fortieth Street. Berger owned a liquor store downtown and wanted to buy a house in the neighborhood. He and his wife found one they liked, but he says they lost interest after eyeing the neighbors. "At the time we visited, there was a black family picnicking next door with lots of kids running around."

The Bergers headed for the split-level homogeneity of Fair Lawn, where "half the town" were self-exiled Jews from Paterson. "As much as I wanted to stay," Berger says, "it didn't pay to buy a house in Paterson. Blacks moved in and we moved out; that's just the way it was."

Mollie Brown saw the city differently. Where Arnie Berger saw blight, Mollie saw beauty. While walking toward downtown on Broadway (or riding the No. 50 bus), she marveled at the gracious mansions and offices that lined "Millionaires Row," the stretch of Broadway that ran west from East Eighteenth to Paterson Street (now known as Memorial Drive). The homes belonged to doctors (many of whom officed there), textile merchants, funeral-home operators. During the holidays, people came from throughout north Jersey to view the extravagant homes and their Christmas decorations. And on the morning of the Christmas parade, the street would be lined with tens of thousands of people. "I tell you, it was gorgeous," Mollie says. "Broadway was really Broadway."

Not only was Paterson a beautiful city full of gracious homes, it was a city that afforded Mollie new opportunities. It took her no time to find work. "I could have five jobs in the same day," she recalls. "And if I didn't like one, I could leave and get another, sure." She certainly didn't like the first, at Spotless Laundry, her new sister-in-law Mozelle's employer. "I worked one hour there and left," Mollie says. "I couldn't take it. Too hot."

She hired on as a domestic in a private home in Fair Lawn, but that position lasted little longer. The family's dog, a bitch, apparently was menstruating on the kitchen floor. The woman of the house asked her to clean up after the dog. "I got right back on the bus to Paterson," Mollie says.

She got off at a television factory on Market Street, where she found work installing reflection yokes—the round coil that housed the tangle of wires in the bowels of black-and-white sets. "It was piece work, and you worked hard," Mollie says, "but you made good money"—about $250 a week. She stayed nearly five years, until the next wave, color television, began sweeping the country. The factory attempted to convert to the new rage—her job shifted to installing *deflection* yokes—but the technology, apparently, passed it by. In 1955 the plant closed. Mollie and her four hundred co-workers received no warning and no severance pay.

Even with a big plant closing in town, there were jobs for the asking. She found work at a sewing plant on Getty Avenue, a maker of parachutes. The job paid better than a lot of others, $1.50 an hour, but the repetitive motion of operating a sewing-machine foot pedal all day long numbed her foot. "My foot would fall asleep with all that press and release, press and release, press and release." She didn't want to quit her job without another one in hand, but she knew she couldn't last much longer. She decided to take a couple of days off to look around.

Paterson was an entrepreneur's city, a town brimming with factories small and large, from textiles to machine shops to electrical components. "There were so many places to work," Mollie says. "You'd just catch the bus and go from factory to factory and see who was hiring." Among her first stops was a low-slung cement building in Bunker Hill, a newly industrializing neighborhood near the Fair Lawn bridge in northeast Paterson. The sign out front said, UNIVERSAL MANUFACTURING CO. Mollie knew no one there, nor had she heard of the company or understood exactly what it manufactured. "Something about a part for fluorescent lights," she told her husband that night.

But she understood there were openings. The owner himself showed her through the plant, explaining that the company made a part for fluorescent lights called a ballast that regulates the flow of electricity into the energy-efficient lights. "They showed me how it was made, the whole assembly line. I learned there's a lot to it, a *very* lot." Mollie wanted the job, but she audaciously told the owner she needed a better starting salary. "They wanted to start me at only ninety cents, and I was making one-fifty [an hour] at the sewing plant."

Mollie went back to the parachute factory, where she lasted less than another week before her foot problems proved too severe. She returned to Universal, where the owner, a gregarious man named Archie Sergy, warmly reiterated his job offer. He told her the company was doing well, and that it was about to implement a second shift, from three P.M. to midnight, and that she could earn an extra dime an hour on that shift. Those hours were ideal for Mollie. She and Sam had three children—Etta was four; Sam three; David a year old (and another daughter, Anita, on the way)—and if she were to work nights and he days, the couple could care for the children without hiring a sitter. She accepted the job on the spot. "Welcome back to Universal," Sergy told her. "I hope you'll be here a long time. I hope we'll *all* be here a long time!"

TWO

The Golden Land

PATERSON WAS BORN of dreamers and schemers. Almost three centuries before Mollie James arrived and Archie Sergy set up shop, what would become Paterson was "howling wilderness": green hills and dark forests on the banks of a pristine river known to the native Leni-Lenape Indians as the Passaick. Above their settlement was the Great Falls, a majestic waterfall that thundered over a seventy-foot-high cliff.

The first white settlers were Dutch farmers who in the 1670s ventured the seventeen miles northwest from their forts and trading posts established on Manhattan Island, more than half a century after the English explorer Henry Hudson sailed up the river that bears his name and that separates the present New York and New Jersey. In 1679 the Dutch obtained from the Indians the first tract of land within the present bounds of Paterson.

For a century the settlement remained small; in the late 1770s there were on the main street of Peace and Plenty Lane but ten houses and a tavern. Travelers occasionally dropped in, none more prominent than a party of four on July 10, 1778, led by General George Washington, the commander in chief of the Continental Army. The

Revolutionary War was raging. Washington and his entourage, including his aide-de-camp, Colonel Alexander Hamilton, were on the way to an encampment at nearby Paramus when they stopped for a picnic lunch at the base of the Passaic Falls.

It was then and there, beneath a "friendly oak" while "enjoying some excellent grog" with the future first president, that the precocious Hamilton—he had just turned twenty-three—gazed at the mighty falls and envisioned in the churning waters what America needed to survive its revolution. The new world, of course, had been a colony: Its natural resources and raw materials—pelts, precious metals, tobacco, and so on—had always been turned over to the mother country for manufacture—and for sale to the colonists at a steep price. The thirteen colonies were forbidden to make and sell their own textiles or convert iron into steel.

What Hamilton saw in the powerful falls was the means for self-sufficiency in postcolonial America: economic independence. And economic independence, he believed, required a plan to fundamentally alter the character and destiny of the new country. A postcolonial America could not rely on its agrarian roots. To achieve true freedom, Hamilton believed, required more than political freedom; it also meant independence from foreign industry. America needed its own "national manufactory."

And there on the banks of the Passaic River, staring up at the Great Falls, Alexander Hamilton had a vision: of "a great manufacturing center, a great Federal city, to supply the needs of the country," William Carlos Williams wrote in *Paterson,* his epic prose-poem. "Here was waterpower to turn the mill wheels and the navigable river to carry manufactured goods to the market centers: a national manufactory."

Hamilton's vision was at odds with that of not a few of his fellow framers and Founding Fathers. Madison, Jefferson, Adams, Franklin—all held the view that the new nation could prosper as a purely agricultural society, that the "power of the people" was rooted in the virtuous soil, and that an industrial economy would wither representative democracy. Their opposition was not wholly philosophical; they believed industry impractical. "America will not make manufactures enough for her own consumption these thousand years," John Adams noted in a 1780 letter to Benjamin Franklin. Thomas Jefferson's championing of agrarianism was based largely on his observations of industrial life abroad. (Prior to his position as Secretary of State in the Washington administration, he lived in Paris while serving as U.S. minister to France.) The foremost apostle of individual liberty, Jefferson saw that European industry and urbanization went hand in hand with vice, and believed that concentrations of people in America would "prostrate agriculture." "The mobs of great cities add just so much to the support of pure government," Jefferson said, "as sores do to the strength of the human body."

Hamilton, however, held that only through creation of a strong federal government could America forge a shared identity among the squabbling former colonies. Eleven years after the fateful picnic at the Great Falls of the Passaic, in April 1789, George Washington was inaugurated president and gave his young protégé an opportunity to test his economic theories. Washington appointed Hamilton Secretary of the Treasury.

Hamilton was a prodigy of thirty-two, with a boyish charm that belied his shrewd political instincts and keen financial mind. He had written the bulk of *The Federalist Papers,* the eighty-five numbered manifestos that laid out the case for the new Constitution and a strong central government. Once Hamilton became Treasury Secretary, he made clear in his writings that which he had only vaguely alluded to in *The Federalist:* his grand economic design for the new country. His proposals, delivered to Congress in a series of papers over a twelve-month period beginning in the fall of 1790, included the establishment of a national bank, federal assumption of state debts incurred during the Revolution, and the fostering of industry by government toward creation of a national manufactory.

Hamilton submitted his "Report on the Subject of Manufactures" in December 1791. Why would it not be better and cheaper, he asked Congress, for example, to spin and weave cotton near the fields where it grew rather than sending it to England and buying the manufactured product? Hamilton countered the Jeffersonians' argument that were the government to actively encourage industry, the support would come at the expense of agriculture. A diversified economy, Hamilton wrote, is "more lucrative and prosperous" than a purely agricultural one, adding that "the aggregate prosperity of manufactures, and the aggregate prosperity of Agriculture are intimately connected."

Hamilton proposed that the government spend a million dollars (at the time 2 percent of the national debt) to build a "national manufactory." Such an industrial complex, he maintained, would be an exemplar and would spur further manufacturing throughout the country. He announced in the report the embodiment of this plan: formation of a "society" for "prosecuting, on a large scale, the making and printing of cotton goods."

Hamilton had actually begun laying the groundwork for the Society for Establishing Useful Manufactures, or SUM, several months prior to releasing his report. Although he did not serve the SUM in any official capacity, he apparently drafted both its prospectus and chartering legislation, and recruited its initial stockholders and directors.

In his report to Congress, Hamilton did not reveal his proposed location for the venture, although it was clear where his intentions lay. "This [the Great Falls] was the finest site anywhere in the world for a manufactory," he remarked. He was struck by the beauty and water-power potential of the falls, its proximity to New York's major market and port, and the political warmth of New Jersey. The state's governor was William Paterson, an ally of Hamilton's from the Constitutional Convention of 1787 and the leader of the state's Federalist Party, whose national head was Hamilton.

It was to Governor Paterson and the New Jersey legislature that Hamilton turned for the political favors necessary to launch his grandiose experiment. On November 22, 1791, two weeks before Hamilton appeared before Congress, the New Jersey legislature granted the SUM a charter authorizing it as the state's (and perhaps the nation's) first industrial corporation and giving it extraordinary powers and privileges: governance of its own land, six square miles on the Passaic; the right of eminent domain to condemn other property for its use; and control of the water rights of the Passaic River. The legislature also provided the SUM the nation's first tax abatement: The corporation was exempted from all taxes for ten years, and thereafter from all but state taxes.

The SUM returned the favor. At a meeting of its board of directors on July 4, 1792, the corporation, at Hamilton's suggestion, named its new city for New Jersey's accommodating governor. Paterson was founded on the sixteenth anniversary of America's Declaration of Independence, not as a municipality but as a business: the home of the country's first industrial corporation, the cradle of American industry.

• • •

Although there was some opposition, the Treasury Secretary had a number of influential supporters, among them some of the country's leading financiers. One was William Duer, of New York, a resourceful stock speculator and crony of Hamilton's (they were related by marriage) whom Hamilton had named his assistant when the federal Treasury was organized in 1789. Duer was the original inside trader, a high government official who parlayed his access to sensitive information into great personal profit. He left the Treasury after only seven months, and thereafter continued to trade on his contacts by speculating in federal securities.

Hamilton tapped his old friend Duer, the ostensible epitome of means and power and influence, as governor of the Society for Establishing Useful Manufactures. Unfortunately, even as Hamilton was extolling Duer's financial wizardry, Duer, almost certainly unknown to Hamilton, was himself in a deep credit crisis brought on by borrowing huge sums to cover his speculative losses in the stock market. In March of 1792, months after he became governor of the SUM, William Duer went to debtor's prison, where he remained, insolvent, until his death.

The SUM never fully overcame the inauspicious start. Beyond the Duer debacle, Hamilton misgauged congressional support for his plan. With no major Northern interest group to offset the irreconcilable opposition from the agrarian South, Congress declined to allocate the funds for a national manufactory—the lone major piece of legislation denied Hamilton.

There were other blunders. Hamilton recommended that the SUM hire to design its new city and industrial complex the French architectural engineer Major Pierre-Charles L'Enfant, whom Washington had previously engaged to draw the elaborate plans for the new "federal city" on the Potomac. But L'Enfant had no industrial engineering experience. Despite lauding his design for Paterson as "far surpass[ing] anything of the kind yet seen in this country," his plans, including a series of Rube Goldberg–like raceways, or aqueducts, stretching seven miles to harness the water power, were halted in midcourse; completion would have bankrupted the SUM.

With the entire future of Paterson in jeopardy, one director of the Society took it upon himself to buck up Hamilton. "Do not let anything draw your attention from this great object," Elisha Boudinot wrote to the father of the enterprise, "but look forward to those tranquil days when this child will be a Hercules, you sitting on the beautiful and tranquil banks of the Passaic, enjoying the fruits of your labor."

Hamilton never enjoyed that vantage point. The ill-fated SUM had managed in 1793 to open a single cotton mill, only to close it a few years later; in 1796, the SUM discontinued manufacturing, concentrating instead on exploiting its legacy of real estate, water rights, and tax breaks. Over the course of the new century, Paterson would become an industrial epicenter, but Hamilton himself would not live to witness the transformation. At dawn on July 11, 1804, on the banks of the Hudson in nearby Weehawken, New Jersey, he was felled by a bullet fired by his great rival Aaron Burr in the nation's most sensational duel.

Though Hamilton's dream for the Great Falls never materialized, by the middle of the century Paterson had indeed become the bellwether for the new industrial age. There were small cotton mills at first, in the early years of the century, dozens of them, relying on the waters of the Passaic to power the looms and spindles to weave and spin the domestic raw cotton into finished cloth—cloth that could not be imported during the embargo of European manufactures during the War of 1812.

The success of the red-brick mills—Paterson earned the sobriquet "The Cotton Town"—attracted hordes of textile machinists to the city, and beginning around 1830, a host of other manufacturing interests: iron works, all kinds of machine-tool shops, transportation-equipment merchants. In 1860, one of every ten of Paterson's nearly twenty thousand residents was an "iron worker." The city's workforce won acclaim around the globe for its metal works. The J. C. Todd Machine Works exported its hemp and twine machinery throughout the world; Watson Manufacturing marketed its millwright products to Latin America; the iron beams that held aloft New York's first elevated trains in the 1870s and 1880s came from the Passaic Rolling Mill, as did finished iron for the drawbridge over the Mississippi at St. Paul, Minnesota, and the buildings for the 1876 Centennial Exposition in Philadelphia.

The city was also home to four locomotive factories, including Rogers Locomotive Works, which by the middle 1850s was likely the second largest such factory in the country. (Following the ceremonial pounding of a golden spike in the Utah desert in 1869, it was the Rogers-built "Engine No. 119" that ceremoniously bumped a Western-made locomotive to commemorate the nation's first transcontinental rail link.)

For all the city's international renown for its machinery and iron and railroad engines, it was for textiles—not cotton, which had begun to fail in the depression of the 1830s, but silk—that Paterson became best known. The mills had gradually shifted from cotton to silk production after 1840, when the superintendent of the Gun Mill (textiles had taken over the building from a failed revolver factory), John Ryle, an Englishman who emigrated from the silk center of Macclesfield, conceived a way of winding silk on a spool rather than in skeins. By midcentury, New Jersey produced more silk than any state but Connecticut, and Paterson was the heart of the new industry. As in Hamilton's day, the textile magnates found Paterson a sensible manufacturing location for its proximity to New York and Philadelphia, and for its abundant water, which was especially well suited for dyeing purposes. Paterson had a new moniker, "Silk City," and a Great Seal to fit: a worker planting a mulberry tree beneath the motto *spe et labore*— "with hope and hard work."

The hope and hard work would be supplied by the masses of impoverished and imperiled Europeans who emigrated from the traditional textile centers: the British Isles, France, Italy, Germany, Poland. Some were skilled weavers; many were farmers or peasants who had been forced off the land by the prolonged agricultural depression in Europe. Still others were fleeing all manner of persecution. "They pushed me into America," lamented one east European Jewish memoirist of the myriad forces of oppression he encountered at home.

Pulled and pushed, the newcomers during the last four decades of the nineteenth century comprised the greatest population movement in history: Ten million people overall, mostly Europeans, some Asians, immigrated to the United States during that period. And Paterson, its thirst for workers nearly insatiable, grew faster than any other city on the eastern seaboard, its population increasing an average of 50 percent every decade of the nineteenth century.

Writing near the end of the century, hometown booster William G. Fenner reflected on the "permanency" of the world's other great industrial centers, including Lyons, the "great silk manufacturing center of France"; Manchester, England, "noted for its cotton and wool dress goods"; Sheffield, England, "historically famous for her cutlery"; Paisley, Scotland, "the home of shawls"; and Birmingham, England, the "head centre of the iron industry." Armed with these examples of industrial perpetuity, Fenner foresaw for Paterson's silk trade a similarly glorious epoch.

"There is only one conclusion to be drawn from this array of historical data, viz: that no manufacturing center where the plant has been fully established has ever lost its industries or weakened in its industry." To underscore the "obvious advantages" of locating in Paterson, Fenner reminded his anticipated readership of prospective manufacturers of his city's proximity to New York. This, he deduced, was "virtually bound to give her an unsurpassed industrial position, the permanency of which is a foregone conclusion if the uniform experience of centuries the world over can be accepted as a guarantee of the future."*

The future indeed looked bright at century's turn. Paterson was a magnet for east European Jews. They came from shtetl and city, from the Russian Empire and Germany and Romania, some fleeing in fear for their lives, others searching for new possibilities for religious and economic freedom. In the third of a century between the assassination of the reformist Russian czar Alexander II in 1881 and the outbreak of world war in 1914, a third of east European Jews left home; over 90 percent sought refuge in the United States. "America," recalled one immigrant, "was in everybody's mouth. . . . People who had relatives in the famous land went around reading their letters for the enlightenment of less fortunate folk. . . . All talked of it, but scarcely anyone knew one true fact about this magic land."

One young man who possessed not a single fact about America but who harbored the common dream to see the "famous land" was a Lithuanian Jew named Samuel Sergy. His parents, Morris and Bessie, were bakers, and though they were disinclined to pull up stakes, they

---

*Fenner's enthusiastic prose rivaled that of his contemporary L. R. Trumbull, who breathlessly predicted that Paterson "is destined soon to beggar the chief centres of silk manufacture in Europe. . . ."

wanted a better life for their children, Sam and his five siblings. The Sergys baked bread and rolls and challah (the ceremonial egg bread eaten on the Sabbath, on Friday and Saturday nights) in Dorbian (or Darbian), a village of some six hundred persons in western Lithuania, fifteen miles from the Baltic coast. In the center of town was a synagogue, a church, a teahouse, and a little square where the Sergys brought their baked goods for sale. Sam, the second of the Sergys' children, was born in 1894 under czarist rule (pre–World War I Lithuania was part of the Russian Empire), a condition of extreme suppression— Lithuanian schools, for example, were barred from teaching the Lithuanian language, and all printed matter in the language was banned. For Jews, a small minority of the predominantly Catholic population, there was added to the cultural suppression relentless religious persecution. (Jewish students, for example, in addition to being force-fed the Russian language, were required to sit or stand in the back of the classroom.)

Any promise of a better life meant leaving home. For some in Dorbian, that meant trekking to the industrial centers of the Empire: Odessa or St. Petersburg or Riga. But for those who remained within Russia's elastic borders, there was also the constant worry of military conscription. For young Sam Sergy, who had heard stories of the *"Goldena Medina,"* the Golden Land, from his uncle Selig—Selig who had left Dorbian several years earlier—and then from his eldest sister, Annie, the first of his family to join Selig, the promise meant one word: *Paterson.* Paterson, America, where there was gold on the sidewalk, and where, the steady cry went, "there's no czar!"

Sam likely left home when he was sixteen years old, in 1910. He never again saw his parents. "When we said good-bye, [my mother] said it was just like seeing me go into my casket," recalls a fellow emigrant from Lithuania.* Sam made his way across western Europe to the port city of Hamburg, Germany, where he boarded a Hamburg-Amerika Line steamship bound for New York harbor. For Sam and his fellow passengers herded in the nearly suffocating crush and constant, pervading stench of steerage accommodations, the approximately ten-

*No naturalization or immigration records could be located for Sam, but such records were found for his sister Ida. Based on those documents and interviews with descendants, in all probability Sam left Dorbian for America in 1910.

day journey must have seemed an eternity. They passed the time in the bottom of the boat, in dark, filthy, cramped dormitories lined with triple bunk beds. "We could see a lot of water," remembers a voyager, "but we couldn't see the sky."

The provisions were equally miserable. However much water they saw, there was little for those in steerage to drink. "Sometimes they gave you a watery soup, more like a mud puddle than soup," Pauline Newman recalled. They were faced also with spoiled food and toilet facilities made ever more fetid by the chronic and widespread seasickness. "I tried to fall asleep," recalled one steerage passenger of his first night aboard the German steamship *Wieland*, "but the ship was rocking like a seesaw, and all the tin utensils kept banging against the wall in a musical rhythm that was simply deafening." Another passenger similarly noted the "clattering of the dishes, the groans and wailing of the men, women and children, the bad effects of nausea," which "could drive anyone insane."

Despite the incessant squalor and racket and illness, the younger passengers, like Sam, were unfazed. "Who cared?" wrote a fellow sixteen-year-old. "We were going to America!"

Sam Sergy and his shipmates disembarked at the heavenly gates of Ellis Island. There in the Great Hall amid the complex of red-brick buildings, he stood with no baggage to speak of save for clothes, in an interminable line, one of dozens and dozens of lines of bewildered, frightened, lonely, exhausted, and yet exhilarated aliens snaking through the hall, each awaiting a battery of medical tests: for tuberculosis, venereal disease, and other contagions. Sam Sergy was given a clean bill of health and received a certificate stating that he "has been vaccinated and unloused and is passed as vermin-free. . . ." (Those who failed the tests were hospitalized until they were cured, or they were deported. "I decided if they sent me back, I'd jump in the water," one emigrant from Russia said. "I never wanted to see it again.")

Then it was on to another line, where a Yiddish-speaking inspector (aliens were lined up by nationality) interviewed Sam about his personal habits and morals. Are you an anarchist? Polygamist? Criminal? And questions, as the writer Irving Howe recounts, such as: "You have a job waiting? Who paid your passage? Anyone meeting you? Can you read and write? Ever in prison? Where's your money?"

The ordeal took about a day. Once released, Sam caught a ferry to

Hoboken, New Jersey, and then a train to Paterson, where his sister Annie was settled. Annie had arrived a few years earlier at the invitation of Uncle Selig, who had begun his working life in Paterson as a peddler, but had worked his way up the pecking order to grocer. By the time Annie summoned Sam, she was married to a fellow Lithuanian emigrant, Nathan Zager. (By 1923, three of Sam's other siblings had immigrated to Paterson; the fourth, a sister, was engaged to be married at home, and elected to stay in Lithuania. She later died in the Holocaust.)

Sam joined Annie and Nathan Zager in their cold-water flat in the Riverside section of Paterson. The neighborhood, hard by the humming silk mills along the east bank of the Passaic, was in the main comprised of similarly situated folk: newly arrived east European working-class Jews. (Other working-class neighborhoods in town described the national origins of the residents: "Dublin," "Belgium Hill," "Little Holland," and so forth.) They were there, along the Passaic, because the mills were there, as Hamilton had planned a century earlier, and because where there were mills, there were rooming houses and dry goods establishments and saloons and junkyards.

Sam found no Paterson sidewalks paved with gold; the cobblestone streets were reminiscent of home, as was the lack of sewers and garbage collection and indoor bathrooms. Developers in the Riverside section and in "Over-the-River," its counterpart on the west bank, maximized profits by squeezing together the wood-frame tenements and row houses without regard for privacy or hygiene. Living conditions, said the city's leading rabbi, were "distinctly bad."

When the river flooded, as it did several times a year, Sam saw outhouses floating down River Street. And he saw countless neighbors die of diphtheria, measles, tuberculosis, and other infectious diseases, spread by the unsanitary conditions. Epidemics were so common that the Paterson Board of Health posted prominent signs—different colored signs for each of the well-known diseases—to alert parents to keep their children out of school.

Skilled immigrants, those, usually, from the larger cities of Europe, found work in the silk mills as spinners or dyers or warpers or winders or weavers, or better yet, as loom fixers—the highest-paying job. (Fixer jobs were for men only.) In 1910, more than twenty thousand Patersonians worked in the silk industry, processing the imported raw silk for dress material, hair ribbons, wall hangings, parachutes.* (Not all, of course, were east European Jews. Many experienced textile workers emigrated from England and Ireland, France, Germany, Italy, Belgium, Switzerland, Armenia, Syria, Lebanon.)

For the unskilled, job options were limited. Women and girls, some not as old as ten, worked in the mills as seamstresses or entry-level "bobbin girls." The mills also hired boys and unskilled men for their first jobs, for which they were rewarded accordingly: ten-to-twelve-hour days for which they received an average weekly wage of $9.60. (By comparison, Ford Motor Company in Detroit was offering $5.00 a *day*.) Others scratched out a living selling newspapers on street corners, caddying for the Jewish merchants and manufacturers at the golf clubs, peddling any and all wares door-to-door: seltzer (which was sought for the Sabbath), milk, linen, pots, clothing.

By the time Sam Sergy arrived, his brother-in-law, Nathan Zager, had advanced from peddling to the moving business with his uncle, Louis Paer. They operated a horse-drawn wagon to capitalize on the rapid turnover in the neighborhood. (There were frequent evictions for nonpayment of rent, and there were the upwardly mobile who were replaced by the steady stream of new arrivals.) Sam found some work with Nathan, and he also tramped door-to-door, hauling a heavy pack on his back of rags and dry goods. Soon he progressed to a horse-and-wagon equipped with bells. "He'd ring the bells and people would bring their cans and bottles and rags to him," remembers Arnold Berger, who grew up in Over-the-River, on Water Street, where Sam plied his trade.

A peddler's product line changed from season to season. In the summer, in addition to his junk business, he was an iceman, guiding his horse down the street, ringing his bell, hollering, in a singsong voice, "Ice, ice." When the weather turned, he would shout, "Hot coal, hot coal."

---

*In the 1790s, in probably the nation's first attempt at vertical integration, the Society for Establishing Useful Manufactures endeavored to grow mulberry trees, upon the leaves of which New Jersey–born silkworms were to feed and spin their delicate fibers. The scheme, however, proved as blighted as most of the Society's plans: Neither the worm nor the tree flourished in the local climate, and from then on the industry imported its silk from northern Italy and the Far East.

As energetic and industrious as the new immigrants were in eking a living out of their chaotic new urban world, they were also busy re-creating what they could of religious, cultural, and commercial life in their old-world villages. Judaism in the Riverside and Over-the-River sections revolved around the Water Street Shul, on Water between Arch and Clinton streets, and two other Orthodox synagogues on nearby Godwin Street, the "Little Shul" and "Big Shul." Membership, as it was at home, was based on economic standing, a division that within three years of Sam's arrival in Paterson would erupt into full-fledged class warfare. Working families belonged to the Water Street and Little shuls; the Big Shul was home to the Jewish elite—the professionals and merchants and silk manufacturers. Those Jews were predominantly German immigrants of the late nineteenth century who had moved up and out of Riverside and Over-the-River as the newcomers poured in from eastern Europe. The Jewish upper class settled in the Eastside neighborhood, south of downtown and east of Broadway, with wide, quiet streets filled with magnificent Victorian homes—mansions, even—of Queen Anne and Italianate and Colonial Revival style. The neighborhood rimmed Eastside Park, the recreational hub of Jewish Paterson. The beautifully landscaped sixty-six-acre park was noted for its handsome terrace leading down to manicured ball fields on the riverbank, picnic grounds, flower gardens, tennis courts, a playground, gazebo, and sheltered bandstand.

If Eastsiders at night were ensconced in their leafy, tranquil environs, their days were still spent on River Street, in the executive offices of Peerless Plush Manufacturing and Manhattan Shirt Mills and A. & M. Levy Silk Ribbon Mill and the mills of Altshuler Bros. and Kaufman Bros. and Secaucus Silk Company.

Others who had graduated to the Eastside, many of whom had begun in Paterson as peddlers, also spent their working lives in the flourishing commercial district on and around River Street. They owned competing drugstores, Jacobs's on Bridge Street near River, Kangisser's at River and Main; and competing fishmongers, Rosenbloom's, Weis's, Miller's. They operated a department store, Kitay's; and Agins's and Rosenberg's furniture outlets. There were two delis, Mandiberg's at the corner of Tyler and River, and Esterman's on Bridge, both of which stocked barrels of herrings and pickles outside.

There was a chicken shop at Washington and Fair, where customers would select and inspect a live bird for sufficient plumpness before it surrendered to the kosher butcher around back. There were two dairies, Rosenblum's and Mendinkowitz's. The latter was on Tyler Street, a half block off Bridge, next to the Purity Cooperative Association, a collective that operated a round-the-clock kosher bakery and butcher shop.

The YMHA, Young Men's Hebrew Association, operating in rented space downtown at 97 Broadway, was the bustling center of Jewish cultural life. (The Y and its sister YWHA were established early in the century in response to the Christian Y's anti-Semitism. The YMCA had traditionally slotted a few token memberships for Jews. The Jewish Ys countered their rival's exclusionism with a proud banner: "No Quota Here!")

The YMHA offered English classes for Yiddish and Russian speakers, organized sports leagues and Boy Scout troops, formed literary and musical clubs, even a symphony orchestra that performed at the Majestic Theatre. The Y also hosted Sunday afternoon "tea dances" for singles and couples. (Sunday was the only day the mills closed.)

It was at one such dance that Sam Sergy met his future wife, Rose Gutin. Rose had emigrated from Tzria, Russia, to Paterson about the same time Sam had arrived. Born in 1889, she was five years older than Sam. An aunt from her shtetl had settled in Paterson, married a junk dealer named Lipkin, and sent word home of the unfettered new world. Rose was the eldest of the four Gutchkin children (her surname was condensed at Ellis Island), and the first to emigrate. Her sister, Ida, and brother, Sam, who escaped from the Russian army, later joined her in Paterson. Her father, a peasant, died young, and her mother and sibling who remained in Russia would die in the Holocaust.

Rose settled with her aunt in the Over-the-River section and found work as a seamstress at a silk plant where her aunt had "spoken up" for her to a foreman. Working conditions were woeful: In the winter months she kept her overcoat on to ward off the chill of the drafty, unheated plant; in the summer she was indentured to the humidifiers necessary to create an environment sufficiently damp for silk weaving. Year-round she contended with poor lighting, and overwhelming noise and dust. The pay was no less wretched: Rose earned less than ten dollars for a six-day, sixty-hour week. But if the job was arduous, it also was secure: The future looked lustrous for the silk industry in Paterson.

Or so it seemed. By 1913, the year Sam and Rose married, Paterson led the nation in silk production. Some twenty-five thousand women, men, and children—more than a third of Paterson's labor force—worked in more than three hundred mills and dye houses, dying and weaving silks for the nation's garment industry, centered in New York City. (Conditions in the dye houses were even worse than the weave rooms. Dyers contended with noxious bleaches, acids, and fumes, brewing, as one writer put it, a "steam so thick you cannot see the worker opposite you.")

Paterson's mills were known worldwide for manufacturing silks of the highest quality and cost. Skilled weavers traditionally tended one or two Jacquard looms—complex looms that used a punch card to design patterns on fine silk. By the time Rose went to work, however, technological innovations were changing the workplace. High-speed, automatic looms were installed, looms that were so simple to operate, mill owners could replace skilled weavers with the unskilled. The consequences were monumental: Some mills established secondary plants— "annexes"—in rural areas, primarily in the mining country of eastern Pennsylvania, a state that, unlike New Jersey, had no law limiting the number of hours in a work week, and where manufacturers found the sort of workers, as the treasurer of the Silk Association put it, who "were less liable to labor troubles which are incident to Paterson." These less troublesome employees were women and girls willing to work for about $6.50 a week, little more than half the wages paid for comparable work in Paterson, to supplement the meager incomes of the male coal miners. These out-of-state branch operations, among the nation's first "runaway shops," would also be useful to the employers in the event of a work stoppage in Paterson—a looming possibility at the dawn of 1913.

The possibility evolved into a certainty in the very first month of the new year. At the end of January at Doherty and Company, the newest and one of the largest silk mills in the city, broad-silk weavers, who wove fabrics over twelve inches wide, primarily for dresses, drapes, and linings, and who formerly operated no more than two looms concurrently, were required to work four. The four-loom "stretch-out" was the last straw for Paterson weavers, who over the past half-dozen years had seen their piece rates slashed, ostensibly so the mills could remain competitive with those in states with lower wages and weaker labor laws. Doherty workers belonged to the United Textile Workers, an American Federation of Labor craft union. The UTW, however, was less interested in confrontation than accommodation; its local leaders counseled that there was no turning back from the four-loom system.

Into the breach stormed the IWW, the Industrial Workers of the World. The IWW was organized in 1905 amid the mining and logging camps of the Pacific Northwest. Its brand of unionism, "Socialism with its working clothes on," was a radical departure from the craft union-ism of the American Federation of Labor; its goal was to build "One Big Union"—regardless of craft or ethnicity. It would do so by spread-ing its militant, class-conscious message among destitute lumberjacks and miners, and then, as its founder and best-known organizer, the two-fisted, one-eyed William D. (Big Bill) Haywood, put it, by "[com-ing] out of the West to meet the textile workers of the East."

The "Wobblies," as they were known, came east in 1912, when they organized and won the celebrated "Bread and Roses" strike against the woolen mills in Lawrence, Massachusetts. Anxious to build on its suc-cess among immigrant textile workers, the IWW's "One Big Union" bandwagon rolled into Paterson. The time could not have been more ripe for the union's aggressive call for an eight-hour day and immedi-ate abolition of the four-loom system. As one IWW recruit later put it: "There was a fruitful and fertile soil when the IWW dropped its seed here . . . which rapidly took root and spread."

On the late January day Doherty fired four members of a workers' committee for protesting the company's four-loom system, eight hun-dred employees of the mill walked out in solidarity. The IWW spent the next three weeks preparing to call a general strike not only against the stretch-out but against wages, hours, and working conditions. The union organized strike committees in practically all the city's mills and dye houses, counseling workers, "It is far better to starve fighting than to starve working." The strike began on February 25, 1913; within a few days twenty-five thousand workers had walked out, and the Pater-son silk industry was nailed shut.

Mill owners refused to negotiate with the militant union, claiming its gifted "jawsmiths"—among them the forty-four-year-old Haywood,

Elizabeth Gurley (Rebel Girl) Flynn, just twenty-two, and Carlo Tresca, thirty-three—preached anarchism and violence.* "The IWW must go," was the bosses' battle cry. But it wasn't the IWW that practiced lawlessness in Paterson. The first time the IWW speakers tried to address the workers, Paterson police arrested them for "disorderly conduct" and "inciting to riot." And it was not only the union's famous leaders who were harassed (and beaten and clubbed); police arrested more than eighteen hundred hometown strikers. The night after the walkout began, police broke up a meeting at strike headquarters and arrested a speaker named Frederick Sumner Boyd for reading the free-speech clause of the state constitution. His crime? Sedition. At the police station, Chief John Bimson asked Boyd from what curious document he'd been reading. "Why chief," Boyd replied, "that was the Constitution of New Jersey. Never heard of it before? I thought not."

When repression and intimidation failed, the mill owners tried another tack, impugning the workers' patriotism by equating the strike with disloyalty to country—a cheap shot to the immigrant workers who had fled their homelands for a new life in Paterson. The owners declared Monday, March 17, as Flag Day. They literally wrapped their mills in the flag, and enlisted the city's merchants to decorate similarly. Paterson that morning was festooned with the Stars and Stripes and with streamers urging the strikers to return to work. Across the central shopping district of Market Street hung a large flag accompanied by a banner: WE LIVE UNDER THE FLAG, WE WORK UNDER THIS FLAG, WE WILL DEFEND THIS FLAG.

Hopes were high the workers would take the red bait. "The ending of the gigantic labor war was beautifully planned," the *Newark Star* reported. "The factory owners were going to forgive their erring workmen. Mayor [Andrew F.] McBride and the police saw the end of their trouble approaching. The ministers who had urged the workers to return understood that their exhortations were to be obeyed. It was a very successful end of the strike, marred by only one thing—none of the strikers went back."

---

*Flynn said Big Bill's speeches were like "sledge hammer blows, simple and direct." She credited Haywood with teaching her "how to speak to workers . . . to use short words and short sentences, to repeat the same thought in different words if I saw that the audience did not understand." (Lukas, p. 220.)

Instead, the workers countered the employers' public relations maneuver: They paraded down Main Street with their own huge American flag, along with a banner (and like signs all over town) reading: WE WOVE THE FLAG, WE DYED THE FLAG. WE LIVE UNDER THE FLAG. BUT WE WON'T SCAB UNDER THE FLAG.

The drama of the strike attracted the attention of New York's radical intelligentsia. John Reed, the young Harvard-educated writer and romantic revolutionary (who would later be hailed a hero of the Russian Revolution and buried, seven years later, at the base of the Kremlin wall), had learned of the strike from Bill Haywood, whom he'd met at a party in Greenwich Village. Reed went to Paterson to write a magazine story for *The Masses,* and was promptly arrested during an interview with a handful of strikers on the porch of one worker's house. After four days in a cramped, vermin-infested cell in the Passaic County Jail in Paterson, Reed returned to New York to write "War in Paterson" and with a determination to raise money for the IWW's depleted strike fund.

His idea was to stage a huge pageant at Madison Square Garden. The lavish event, a simply plotted reenactment of scenes from the strike, would meld Reed's twin passions of art and revolution. Among the scenes, all of which were depicted by a thousand or so of the Paterson workers themselves: the rattle of looms and the sound of protest on the morning of the walkout; a mass meeting at Botto House in the neighboring Socialist town of Haledon, where the writer Upton Sinclair and the fiery Bill Haywood (who played themselves as well) addressed twenty thousand strikers; the funeral of a worker shot by a private detective. On June 7, with the electrified ten-foot-high red letters I-W-W illuminating the night sky outside the Garden, the strikers paraded up Fifth Avenue, union banners aloft as they sang along to an IWW band's rendition of "The Internationale."

The atmosphere inside was similarly charged. The Garden, its balconies bedecked with red IWW flags, was packed to the rafters with fifteen thousand union members and supporters, including New York silk workers. As the brass band warmed up the boisterous crowd, radical pamphleteers and Reed's *Masses* colleagues hawked their goods among the crammed aisles.

The reviews were decidedly mixed. A *New York Times* editorialist found the performance a veritable menace to society. "Under the direction of a destructive organization opposed in spirit and antagonistic in action to all the forces which have upbuilded this republic, a series of pictures in action were shown with the design of stimulating mad passion against law and order and promulgating a gospel of discontent. . . ."

The critic for the *New York World,* however, praised the worker-actors for their "sincerity," and found in their propaganda piece something more poetic and less menacing. "As viewed by a spectator unbiased either from the labor or management standpoint, their pageant was rather in the nature of a tragedy than anything else."

The *World*'s critic was prescient. As successful as the pageant was at raising awareness of their cause, it failed to raise what the strikers needed most: money. Rather than turn a profit, the event lost two thousand dollars. (IWW cardholders were let in free, and much of the rest of the crowd was admitted for a quarter—not nearly enough per head to cover the night's rent, let alone other expenses.)

In the end, John Reed's fervent belief that art could affect history was not borne out; his pageant could not and would not alter the realities of an entrenched economic order. And in the end, no performance, even one so moving, nor any amount of publicity or goodwill from well-wishing New York bohemians, could compensate for the ever-dwindling strike fund, which could provide only fifty cents a month per worker.

Each mill established a General Relief Committee, which arranged for "war rations" and worked with retailers and landlords to extend credit to the strikers. The Purity Cooperative Bakery offered free bread; restaurants donated meals; barbers gave haircuts; doctors volunteered their care.

Most of the city's establishment, however, those who gathered for drinks and prattle at the genteel Hamilton Club and who belonged to the Paterson Board of Trade, whose roster included the silk manufacturers, were, naturally, hostile to the strikers. Such hostility affected not only the strikers' livelihoods, but their health as well. Even General Hospital, a charity-care facility that relied on workers' contributions through collections at the mills, refused to treat indigent strikers. "Go to Haywood and get the money," the administrator said, turning away a suffering woman.

As the stalemate dragged into July, its sixth month, the manufacturers showed no sign of capitulation. Many of the larger firms were able to fill their regular customers' orders by transferring work to their low-wage mills in Pennsylvania, which the IWW hadn't the resources to shut down. And the smaller mills, even those on the brink of bankruptcy, stuck together out of solidarity and pragmatism with the larger ones, refusing to capitulate. "The employers say they will go out of business before they will yield to the demands of the strikers," a writer for *Outlook* reported, "the latter fervidly declare that they will starve rather than return to the looms."

Some of the strikers *were* starving. The IWW's Elizabeth Gurley Flynn recalled meeting one man on the picket line, a father of eight, whose family "didn't have a crust of bread, didn't have a bowl of milk for the baby in the house." Within six weeks of the pageant, with the workers' families growing ever hungrier—a "hunger," Flynn wrote, "gnawing at their vitals; tearing them down"—there appeared, in the middle of July, an irreparable crack in the workers' unity. On July 18, the ribbon weavers—skilled, English-speaking members of the AFL's Textile Workers Union who wove silks less than twelve inches wide—broke from the strike committee, agreeing, on a shop-by-shop basis, to return to work.

The surrender shattered the IWW's hopes for an industry-wide agreement, and with it, any prospect for the union's continued growth and success, let alone for the dawn, ultimately, of a revolutionary new era. (By 1916, in fact, the IWW was effectively broken in the East, and, due in large part to federal repression and the Red Scare of 1919, would then shatter altogether.) And the surrender led to individual settlements with all three hundred shops, scattershot settlements that in the main provided neither gains in wages nor improved working conditions. During the last week of July, there was a virtual stampede back to work. "It was the stampede of hungry people," Flynn concluded, "people who could no longer think clearly."

Rose Sergy was more fortunate than many of her co-workers. Unlike many, whose spouses were also silk workers, her husband had worked through the long months of the strike. Nor did Rose and Sam Sergy yet have children, which eased their burden considerably. Sam had continued as a peddler and junk man, lugging scrap metal and crockery and socks and rags and fruit and coal and ice, all the while rising from backpack to pushcart to wagon. He had established himself with the two leading yards in the mill district: Riverside Iron & Metal, at 285 River Street, which his brother-in-law, Nathan Zager, owned; and Max (Grubby) Politinsky & Sons, whose yard was at nearby 263 Water Street.

Rose was twenty-four years old when the strike ended; Sam, nineteen. With Rose back at work, the time had nearly come to start a family. They had yet to trod over golden sidewalks, and they were as poor and overworked as everyone else in the Over-the-River section, living in scandalously overcrowded and disease-encouraging conditions. Nevertheless, at the end of the following year, 1914, as war at once swallowed their European homeland and brought a boom to industrial Paterson, the Sergys must have marveled at their fate: They had come so far, come from their hopeless, obscure shtetls to the promise of Water Street, the promise of survival and freedom and rising. They were making a new life, expecting a child.

THREE

High, Wide and Handsome

Courtesy of Sam Stein

Archie Sergy

ARCHIE SERGY, the first of Rose and Sam's three children, was born at home on September 2, 1915. From his mother he inherited smooth cheeks and large brown eyes that gave his face a reserved, almost mournful appearance. His father, no more than five-seven or five-eight, bequeathed to his only son his swarthy complexion and heavyset build. There was also in the Sergy genes a big, generous spirit, a quick friendliness, boundless energy—a nature that more often than not supplanted the doleful look, alighted his eyes.

Archie's world, the world of Water Street, was vibrant and self-contained, buzzing with the ambition of the striving and harried and driven sons of first-generation east European immigrants. The Sergys lived at 219 Water, they worshiped at 182 Water, and Sam worked out of the junkyard at 263 Water. And although most of the Jewish retailers were located across the Arch Street Bridge on and around bustling River Street, there were several small merchants in Over-the-River, including a shoe repair shop, a saloon across the street from the Sergys', and a grocer, to which parents would send their children for emergency provisions. "I'd tell 'em, 'I want a loaf of bread and three eggs, and put it on the books,' " recalls Arnold Berger, the Paterson liquor merchant who grew up at 269 Water, next door to Grubby Politinsky's junkyard. "We'd pay every week if possible."

The Sergys' two-family house abutted the Passaic River. It was of simple wood-frame construction, as were all the homes on the street, and, at the time of Archie's birth, was without indoor plumbing. Heat was supplied by the coal stove in the kitchen, which was where Archie did his homework, splayed on the floor under a gas light. (At bedtime during the severe winters, the family would heat bricks on the stove top, wrap them in towels, and place them at the foot of the beds. Even that measure was hardly adequate. "You put on two sweaters and three shirts and two pair of socks and you managed," says Arnie Berger, "but you froze.")

Except weekdays at School No. 4, which was across the river at Clinton and Temple streets and which he attended from kindergarten through eighth grade, most of Archie's waking hours were spent with the other neighborhood boys on Water Street, often in the vicinity of Miller's candy store. Other diversions included wading barefoot through the flooded streets, flipping baseball cards, and "scraps"—neighborhood boxing matches, with gloves, if available.

In the wintertime they'd skate at Westside Park or build mountainous snow piles and play "King of the Hill," where with his considerable girth and low center of gravity, Archie's reign as "king" was enduring. "He was tough to topple," says Arnie Berger. "One time, the only time," he recalls of a glorious day atop a snowdrift three-quarters of a century earlier, "I came along and knocked him on his ass!"

In the summer the gang played in the river. They fished near Bowers's Boat House, above the thundering Falls, for carp and eel and catfish, and swam, says Morris Paer, who lived on River Street, "b.a."—bare ass—"in the chasm" below the Falls.

Occasionally the boys' families would "vacation" at Coney Island, at the tip of Brooklyn. To do so without a car, which few Over-the-River residents owned, was a "complicated two-hour pilgrimage," recalls Stanley Kushner, whose family made the trek twice each summer and who later worked with Archie Sergy at Universal. The Kushners rode the Erie Railroad from Paterson to Jersey City, then the ferry to Chambers Street in lower Manhattan, then walked to the BMT Coney Island line to ride the subway to Stillwell Avenue. "We covered the entire distance schlepping suitcases and bags containing towels, bathing outfits, pails, shovels, and, most important, food—more precisely, lunch." For dinner they treated themselves to hot dogs and knishes at Nathan's, "where we fought through crowds four deep around the stand."

The twenties was a great time to grow up, "an easy, quick, adventurous age, good to be young in," the writer Malcolm Cowley put it. Certainly that carefree portrait of the era, the prosperous, fun Roaring Twenties, was recognizable: Unemployment had decreased from 4.3 million in 1921 to little more than 2 million in 1927.* It was the Jazz Age; anything was possible. The Over-the-River kids cheered Lindy's 1927 flight across the Atlantic to Paris as if America's golden boy were one of their own, and in a way he was: The Wright Whirlwind engine for his *Spirit of St. Louis* was built in Paterson.

Never before had the stock market soared so high; never had there been such feverish trading, such speculative frenzy. The value of all shares on the New York Stock Exchange rose from $27 billion in 1925 to $67 billion in 1929. In a three-month period that summer, industrial stocks surged 110 points, swelling in value by almost a quarter. The stock market was carrying the nation's economy; it had become, for the moment, anyway, "a roulette wheel at which no one lost."

Paterson, too, was on a roll. Little more than a decade after the

*Like that of other heavily industrial cities, Paterson's economy benefited greatly from World War I. The Du Pont Company, for example, in what would become the Passaic County borough of Wanaque, contracted in 1914 with the French government to manufacture eight million pounds of smokeless powder. The company expanded the plant to meet French demand, employing some 7,500 local men and women. (Smyk, November 7, 1993.) With the war's end, however, the Du Pont plant retrenched, as did much of American industry. In late 1920, 100,000 firms, many dependent on wartime government contracts, went bankrupt.

great strike brought the city to a virtual standstill, city fathers were declaring the late twenties an era of good feelings, a time to "Quit Knocking and Boost." To dramatize its point, the chamber of commerce commissioned a piece of art, a twenty-five-foot-long propaganda tool, which was paraded through downtown streets and then interred to well-orchestrated cheers. The tool was inscribed: THE HAMMER. BURY IT.

The public relations campaign and the ostensibly buoyant economy did spark consumer confidence. Many families were buying the newest gadgets and conveniences: cars, refrigerators, electric irons, washing machines, vacuum cleaners, radios. Patersonians tuned in to the city's first radio station, WODA, which signed on the air in April 1925 with greetings from Mayor Colin M. McLean and live entertainment by members of Elks Lodge 60. The station boasted a local newscast, anchored by a harried moonlighting reporter from the *Paterson Evening News*. Twice daily, recalls WODA's founder, Richard O'Dea (the call letters were derived from his surname), the *News* reporter would "rush down the street with his papers, red pencil the main items, read them into the mike, and that was it."

Two months after the station started broadcasting, Mayor McLean dedicated a new luxury hotel, the Alexander Hamilton. Paterson's smart set celebrated the opening of the 210-room hotel with a gala dinner-dance in the Hamilton's spacious, cream-colored ballroom. The brick Colonial-style showplace cost $1.5 million, all of which was raised from local businessmen, who, as the *Paterson Press-Guardian* put it, saw their investment as "something more than a commercial enterprise. . . . It is a monument to the great financial genius whose name looms so largely in early American history."

But the decade's fortunes in Paterson, as throughout America, were wildly uneven. For those hundreds of well-dressed Patersonians who waltzed away the early summer night under the Hamilton's crystal chandeliers, there were countless others, those, for example, whose "unsightly lot of shacks" were removed to make way for the "magnificent building," to whom the decade's heralded prosperity did not trickle down. And there were the thousands of ordinary Paterson families, like the Sergys, for whom the struggle for survival eased only marginally. These were the families for whom the happy clatter of the ticker tape machine meant nothing, who lived in drafty firetraps, who rose before dawn, who breathed toxic dust and fumes every day of their working lives, and whose wages were stagnant or driven down or who, by the close of the decade, were put out of work by new machinery that enabled manufacturers to produce more goods—industrial production nearly doubled during the twenties—with fewer hands.

The Age of Business, as the era came to be known, was built upon a "fundamentally unsound" foundation. It tottered, most precariously, on the uneven progress of soaring corporate profits and increased productivity, and on curtailed workplace rights—only 7 percent of workers carried a union card at the end of the twenties—and wages too low to enable workers to purchase the goods manufacturers were overproducing.

The silk industry had continued through the middle twenties to dominate Paterson's economy (although the organization of work had changed radically since the great strike: Many of the large plants were subcontracting their work to small family shops, some with no more than a handful of looms). Toward the close of the decade, though, silk fashions began fading; rayon, a cheaper synthetic, was in vogue.

By the summer of 1929, industrial corporations moved to trim their bloated inventories: They reduced production and instituted massive layoffs. Within a few months, the reality of the recession on Main Street would at last catch up with the easy credit and wanton speculation on Wall Street: On the morning of Thursday, October 24, prices on the New York Stock Exchange began plunging. By the closing bell the market had crashed, bringing the nation's economy down in the same heap: The Great Depression had begun.

If "Black Thursday" marked the start of the Depression in the popular imagination, for the Sergy family the crash began some four months earlier, on June 7. On that fine spring day, Sam awoke feeling feverish and sick to his stomach. He had generally enjoyed good health, although not long earlier he had fallen off his horse-drawn wagon and broken a leg. The leg never healed properly, and Sam was unable after that to make his peddling rounds. Sam was then working for Sender Bloom, who owned a junkyard on Circle Avenue. Bloom, a big, gentle man known for his philanthropic ways, reassigned Sam to office work, which did not pay as well but enabled him to continue to bring home a regular check. Rose, meanwhile, had lost her job at the silk mill and was operating a tiny candy store out of their home, where she could also care for Archie's two younger sisters.

The pain Sam felt would not recede. For some time, apparently, he'd had an inflamed and infected appendix. The untreated infection—like most people in his circumstances, he was reluctant to see a doctor—spread throughout his abdominal lining, or peritoneal cavity. On June 7, Sam Sergy died of general peritonitis. He was thirty-five years old. He left behind his forty-year-old widow, Rose, and their three children: Mary, six; Sylvia, eleven; and Archie, thirteen.

Archie was in the final month of eighth grade, and though he had recently celebrated his bar mitzvah—the symbolic Jewish ceremony for reaching the age of maturity—he was hardly ready for full-fledged adulthood. Only that winter he had extended his reign as "King of the Hill"; as his final summer before high school neared he wanted nothing so much as to hang out at the Y or loiter on his favored corners with his pals and maybe pick up a few dollars from some bootleggers the boys knew from the neighborhood.

It was the era of Prohibition, which had been effected with the passage in 1919 of the Eighteenth Amendment to the Constitution. And however uninterested Archie and his friends were in its political aspects, they cared about the upward mobility that illegal liquor sales and transportation could provide. Paterson's many saloons, including the one across Water Street from the Sergys' home, manufactured their own liquor. "Most of the cops looked the other way," recalls a retired police officer who was a contemporary of Archie's. "Most were on the payroll."

Paterson was overrun with rumrunners and bootleggers and racketeers, all of whom needed couriers and lookouts. One beer bootlegger named "Doc" owned a couple of saloons near the Eastside section of town. One afternoon Archie and his friends were hanging out on the corner of Carroll and Governor streets, not far from one of Doc's saloons, when Doc himself arrived at the corner.

"Hey, who wants to make a coupla bucks?"

Doc explained that he needed the boys to "ride shotgun" in a big black limousine, trailing his beer truck. The truck was headed to upstate New York, where it would unload a shipment. The bootlegger, says Arnie Berger, wanted the boys to "act tough": "make believe we were all gangsters who had plenty of ammunition to scare off anybody who might want to hijack the truck."

There were also employment opportunities assisting bootleggers in local transport. A brewery on the edge of Garret Mountain reputedly borrowed, from the Paterson Fire Department, fire hoses to pump beer through the sewer system to an ad hoc bottling facility in an abandoned spring-manufacturing factory. Not a few Over-the-River boys assisted in the tunnel operations.

But if Archie was seduced by the vague danger of bootlegging, the romance and easy money, the reality was that such job opportunities were fickle and far between. As his family's new breadwinner, Archie needed steady work, a chance for advancement. He would find it, of all places, on a golf course.

The Preakness Hills Country Club, in the outlying hamlet of Wayne, had opened the previous year. It catered to Paterson's Jewish professionals—doctors, lawyers, accountants, merchants, textile barons. "All the big shots belonged there—the wealth of the world!" says Morris Paer, who along with Archie would apply as a caddy at the prestigious new club.

The club hired them and many other Jewish kids from the Riverside and Over-the-River sections. The caddies would congregate in a small park at the corner of North Main Street and Haledon Avenue in Paterson, where, upon decree from the club's board of directors, the members would stop to pick them up. "They'd drive us up to the golf course, and we'd walk over to the caddy shack, and the caddy master would assign us to our member," says Paer, a short, fastidious man with a strong handshake and an easy smile. "You'd get a buck for a round of golf. If they gave you a quarter tip, that was a godsend."

It was the summer of his fourteenth year, 1930, and life for Archie and his family had been an unrelenting struggle since Sam Sergy's death. Archie had enrolled at Central High School the previous fall, mainly, he told his friends, to play football. He was still a big kid, about 190 pounds, but he was pretty quick for his size, and he was developing into a fine running guard. "He'd pull out and scamper across the line," recalls his teammate Charles Conti. "We played both ways"—offense and defense—"and Archie never got tired."

He tired more easily of academics. "He wasn't a great student," says classmate Ruby Goldstein, "mediocre." Like many hard-pressed students of his era, Archie dropped in and out of school. He played most of two seasons of football for the Central High Colts (the team was named for the prominent revolver-and-textile family, who had owned the land on which the school stood) before dropping out for good, probably toward the end of his sophomore year.

It was the spring of 1931, and the nation remained locked in the vise-grip of depression: Eight million people were out of work, double the figure of a year earlier. Growing numbers of families were without shelter and warm clothing and food and fuel. But little help was forthcoming from the administration of President Herbert Hoover. Federal aid, in fact, was antithetical to Hoover, who argued that state and local organizations could and should meet relief needs. The head of the President's Organization on Unemployment Relief (POUR), Walter Gifford, made clear the administration's position in testimony before a Senate subcommittee. "My sober and considered judgment" is that federal relief would be a "disservice" to the jobless; "the net result might well be that the unemployed who are in need would be worse instead of better off."*

It is difficult to imagine that relief would have created a more dire situation. In Paterson, homeless encampments—"Hoovervilles"—of tents and scavenged-wood-and-tarpaper shacks sprang up along the banks of the Passaic; downtown, competing apple sellers jockeyed for position on streets teeming with hungry people and failing businesses.† (There were so many apple sellers nationally that the Bureau of the Census classified them as employed. When this was pointed out to President Hoover, he argued that "many persons left their jobs for the more profitable one of selling apples.")

By the winter of 1931–32, what little relief the state and city could provide had all but vanished. In lieu of aid, New Jersey issued licenses to beg. Wrote a New Jersey man to Hoover: "Can not you find a quicker way of Executing us than to Starve us to death?"

If not for the generosity of Sam's former boss, the Sergy family might well have starved. For about two years after Sam's death, Sender Bloom made a monthly donation, a pension of sorts, to the Sergys. It is

---

*Gifford was also the chief executive of AT&T. In reply to similar remarks he made on a radio broadcast, a New Jersey man wrote: "You say wages have, and are being reduced only to correspond to reduced cost of living. Why haven't you reduced telephone rates?"

†The value of the city's manufactures would fall from $198 million in 1929 to $107 million in 1939, and wages during that period would drop by almost half, from $44 million to $26 million.

not known how much he gave, or whether it was always in cash. "They got a few bucks every month, or maybe food or shoes or medicine if one of the girls was sick," says Ruby Goldstein. By the winter of 1931–32, Bloom's junkyard was failing, too; he had no more to give. The Sergys went on relief, says Goldstein, "such as it was."

It wasn't enough. Archie was caddying as often as possible at Preakness Hills (even trudging through ankle-deep snow when members hit red golf balls), Rose was selling penny candy, and still ends were not meeting. Like nearly everyone, Archie tried any number of ways to bring home a little more. "You worked here, you worked there," says Goldstein. One place he and Archie worked was in a dye house owned by a club member, Herman Geller. Archie also scraped together a few dollars peddling junk, selling and buying scrap metal, hawking vacuum cleaners door-to-door, and selling ice and coal with his former teammate Sam Conti, who had captained the Central High team.

No matter what manner of odd job Archie performed over the next couple of years, he continued to work at Preakness Hills. He was rising in the ranks, from a part-time "B" to a full-time "A" caddy. To an "A," many of whom were older men, the caddy master gave the plum assignment of accompanying favored members: those whose business connections might be most helpful or who were known as generous tippers. Those caddies on the lower rung were assigned to less beneficent members, those known as "cheapies" or "chiselers."

It is unknown who the caddy master was in the earliest years of the club. By the 1934 season, there was a new one, an eighteen-year-old veteran caddy who had so impressed the club's teaching professional with his character and his golf game—Monday was "Caddy Day," when the club allowed the help to play the course—that he was offered the salaried position. The new master was Archie Sergy.

Having started at the bottom of the pecking order, he understood the omnipotence of the position, and tried hard to use his power judiciously. On at least one occasion, however, apparently at a time of desperation, he suffered an ethical lapse.

He needed some fast cash, perhaps to repay a debt, and so he devised a scheme to fleece the caddies. He proposed that each caddy buy a sweater emblazoned with the club monogram. The caddies were to advance Archie the money, $1.50 apiece, and he would order the sweaters in volume. Weeks and months went by without delivery. "Where's the money? Where's the sweaters?" the caddies asked him daily.

Archie had no answer. "Those dollars went south," says Ruby Goldstein. "We put a lot of heat on him and finally at the end of the season he found another avenue of green and refunded us the money."

On balance, Archie used his position wisely, parlaying his impressive golf game and gift of gab into any number of useful contacts with Paterson's Jewish establishment. This is not to suggest that opportunism alone informed his relationships with club members. It had been five summers since the death of his father; the loss, and the burden of supporting his family, seemingly suffused him with a need for paternal figures. Many members befriended him, took him in for a meal, offered advice; some, such as Herman Geller, hired him in times of extreme want.

In his time away from the caddy shack, Archie devoted most of his time to resurrecting his family's good name in the junk business. He and his family had moved across the river to a cold-water flat at 66 North Third Street, but the best available space for a junkyard was still near his boyhood home on Water Street, and so he leased a small fenced piece of land there. He began paying visits to the workplaces of club members who operated mills and machine shops—men like Al Goldman, a native New Yorker who owned a machine shop on State Street in Paterson. Archie had called on Goldman to see if he had any scrap iron or spare parts or any other junk for sale. Goldman mentioned he was looking for a used lathe. Archie told him he'd see what he could do.

Archie promptly found a lathe, as well as some other machine tools Goldman needed. The older man was impressed with Archie's moxie, and began to serve as a mentor, introducing him to men with whom he might do junk business. One was Frank Lesnick, a colorful entrepreneur who, despite—or because of—his famously grandiose lifestyle, was always on the verge, as one friend put it, of "either the poorhouse or the big house."

"The guy was a real wheeler-dealer, happy-go-lucky," says Abe Jaffee, a boyhood pal of Archie's who dealt with Lesnick in the late thirties. "He made more money and blew more money than anyone I knew."

Lesnick was born in 1910, five years before Archie, but he had grown up in neighboring Passaic and attended its schools and synagogues, and so their paths never crossed until Goldman introduced them. Lesnick was a gifted mechanic, able to fix all things motorized. As a young man, he worked in Passaic for Strauss Brothers, a leading auto-parts dealer in the region, building and rebuilding transformers, automotive generators, windshield wipers, brake shoes.

By the middle 1930s, Lesnick was itching to strike out on his own. In 1937, he and his new bride, Elsie, who had grown up in Paterson, moved to an apartment there, where Lesnick leased a small storefront on "Auto Row," the strip of dealerships and parts distributors at the end of Market Street near Lakeview Avenue.

He called his new business Automotive Necessities Company, or Anco. He bought, renovated, and sold all manner of automotive equipment—motors, generators, starters, windshield wipers, carburetors, fuel pumps, anything he could get his hands on. "Frank was always desperate for spare parts, and Archie had this uncanny ability to find hard-to-find parts," says Abe Jaffee.

Lesnick also dabbled in any number of small electrical-manufacturing endeavors, including producing ballasts for fluorescent lights. But the fluorescent fixtures were still in their infancy, and Lesnick did not believe he could score a quick hit, something he desperately needed. And like many entrepreneurs, he was as restless as he was creative. "Frank could get tremendously enthused about something new, often to the detriment of his current project," recalls his widow, Elsie Poppe. "He was always sure the next ship in would be his."

Lesnick's ship finally came in on December 7, 1941, when the Japanese sank several American war boats in Hawaii. Indeed, if not for the outbreak of World War II, countless small-business men, Frank Lesnick and Archie Sergy among them, might not have outlasted the Great Depression. But in the aftermath of Pearl Harbor, the U.S. Government's ravenous appetite for defense-related production and services was fed by anyone and everyone who could supply the raw materials and machinery vital to the war effort.

Among the equipment the government needed were inverters, the devices that convert direct current into alternating current. Frank Lesnick had heard that the U.S. Signal Corps, the War Department division charged with providing Allied troops with battlefield communications systems, was letting bids on inverter manufacturing for use on Allied aircraft, specifically Britain's Lancaster and Spitfire planes. Lesnick had never made an inverter, had never *seen* an inverter, but he was not about to let that inconvenient fact stop him from contributing to the war effort. "Frankie didn't know his backside from a hole in the wall as to what an inverter looked like," recalls Irving (Zeke) Bromberg, who initially kept the books for Anco and later worked as the company's purchasing director. "But he was probably the greatest salesman I ever saw, I mean an ice-to-the-Eskimos salesman, and he had a great mechanical mind, not an engineering mind, but a mechanical mind, and once he got his foot in the door of the general's office, and the general told him he needed three thousand inverters in fifteen months, and Frankie assured him that would be no problem, he had the contract."

He began, in the middle of 1942, by hiring engineers from Bendix Corporation, men who knew how to design and build the contraption. And he hired scores of new employees, about two hundred in all, and moved them all across Market Street into the more spacious quarters of a former Buick dealership his brother Jack had operated.

And Lesnick—"to everyone's surprise, including Frankie's," says Bromberg—made good on the $4.5 million contract. The Signal Corps rewarded Anco with a second, slightly more lucrative one. "He was riding high, wide and handsome," says Bromberg.

Lesnick was one of Paterson's great wartime success stories. He was of average build and height, about five-seven, but his full head of hair made him seem a bit taller. He was always well groomed and dressed, and encouraged his employees to be likewise. As his net worth accumulated, so did his reputation as a man who could make things happen, a fixer. That might mean offering a draftee a job at Anco, a government-designated "prime work" plant, to spare him from active military service. Or it might mean putting the arm on a bureaucrat to issue a marriage license on a Sunday to a young couple who couldn't wait another day—the prospective groom was to be shipped out for military service on Monday. Those were the types of gestures of goodwill for which Lesnick was renowned. There were other favors, or arrangements, for which he preferred to stay in the shadows.

About the time Lesnick renewed the government contract, for instance, a union started an organizing drive at Anco (which by then, in a nod to its good fortune, had changed its formal name to Aeronautic Necessities Company from Automotive Necessities). Lesnick, says Zeke Bromberg, who had become Anco's director of purchasing, was "an ardent foe of unions; he'd rather take a buck out of his pocket than sign a union contract." So Lesnick did just that, enlisting the help of organized crime to fight organized labor. Some reputed local mobsters began showing up at the plant; one, a one-armed former boxer named Mickey Gerard, became Lesnick's bodyguard. "We always heard it was the mob who took his arm off," Abe Jaffee says, but Bromberg offers a less engaging explanation: "He lost it in an auto accident." (Lesnick's widow, Elsie, says that she recalls Gerard's name, but that he was "never a bodyguard" for her husband. "Frank was a very free agent.")

Gerard and his "henchmen" broke the union, Bromberg says, and from then on, Lesnick was fairly surrounded with mobster "hangers-on." "Frank relished the company of these so-called Mafia boys. He liked power, and he liked their connections to the black market. And those boys liked Frank's money. They weren't on the payroll, exactly, but in those days you had a lot of money off the books."

In fact, much of the wartime economy was "off the books" and on the "black market." After Pearl Harbor, President Roosevelt established the War Labor Board, which set wage rates for all workers. At the same time, the president set up the Office of Price Administration (OPA), which formulated price ceilings for consumer goods and distributed ration coupons for the many items in short supply: canned goods, fruits, vegetables, meats, butter, sugar, cheese, coffee, even shoes. Life had become "a series of shortages," reported the *Paterson Evening News*. "The harassed retailer staggered under the burden of constant complaints from irate customers. Mrs. Average Citizen spent sleepless nights as she devised methods of 'stretching ration points.'"

The sale of gasoline, too, was strictly regulated. When rationing began in the spring of 1942, the average driver received a twenty-one-gallon allotment for forty-five days, or less than half a gallon a day. Even if gasoline were more plentiful, many would-be drivers would still have been rendered nearly immobile: Tires were almost impossible to come by—the government suspended tire manufacturing for civilians—and were sold only to those who demonstrated a vital need. In June, Esso dealers in Paterson joined a nationwide campaign urging motorists to recycle their old tires. The dealers displayed posters that read: RUBBER SCRAP WILL LICK THE JAP—LEAVE IT HERE!

Paterson, home to machine shops and engine builders and textile manufacturers, benefited from the nationalistic fervor like few other small cities. Nearly everyone in town—workers, industrialists, merchants, whites and blacks—prospered during the five-year-long war in Europe, the costliest, most deadly conflict in history. And then, on May 7, 1945, within four weeks of Roosevelt's death at the beginning of his fourth term in office, and seven days after Hitler's suicide, Germany surrendered unconditionally; the war in Europe was over. The following day, May 8, was proclaimed V-E (Victory in Europe) Day; wild celebrations erupted in cities around the Allied world.

Frank Lesnick's first reaction was more prosaic: "Now what?" With the government gravy train soon to grind to a halt, Anco and Wright Aeronautics and every defense-related industry in town had to come to terms with conversion to a peacetime economy. "We knew the Signal Corps was about to cancel us out," Bromberg recalls, "so the question became how do we stay in business." That was the question everyone, everywhere, asked. On August 12, 1945, three days after President Harry Truman dropped the second of two atomic bombs on Japan, killing seventy thousand in the major seaport of Nagasaki, a *New York Times* headline read: 5,000,000 EXPECTED TO LOSE ARMS JOBS.

Two days later, on V-J Day, within fifteen minutes of the news flash that Japan had surrendered, downtown Paterson was awash with revelers. CITY GOES WILD AT PEACE WORD, MOBS JAM THE DOWNTOWN, read the subhead of the *Evening News*'s extra edition. Celebrants joined impromptu parades down Market Street; effigies of Tojo and Hitler were burned and hanged from poles. And, as the *News* reported, "Lipstick-smeared soldiers and sailors proceeded to distribute kisses to young ladies with unprecedented generosity."

For Frank Lesnick, once the dancing in the streets subsided, the future was less giddy. He turned for advice to his general manager, John Constantine, one of his Bendix recruits, who astutely observed that more and more homeowners were converting their furnaces from coal to oil. The conversion required a small "oil-burner," or fractional horsepower motor. Electrical parts at war's end remained in scant supply, but as Constantine pointed out, Anco already owned the coil-winding machinery necessary to produce the motors; all it needed was a steady store of steel and copper wire. Wire, though, like all raw materials, was unavailable on the open market; it had to be procured through back channels—the "black market."

Price controls continued in effect in the immediate aftermath of the war. For Frank Lesnick that meant he could legally sell a fractional horsepower motor for no more than $13.80. But the government set that price based on the assumption that parts for the motor could be obtained at market price—an assumption that overlooked the central fact that virtually nothing could be obtained on the open market. "Everything was black market, so we'd always pay more for our copper and steel," says Bromberg. "We figured it was costing us fourteen ninety-five for a product the OPA told us we could *sell* for thirteen-eighty."

So Anco charged a price more in line with demand on the black market. "These guys"—the oil-burner furnace distributors—"were desperate," Bromberg says. "They would come around and say, 'Tell us what you want, we'll pay it.' And Lesnick would say, 'I want forty dollars a motor.' The distributors would agree to the price, but were concerned about how the transaction would look to OPA monitors. 'No problem,' Lesnick assured them. 'I'll bill you for a hundred motors and only give you forty or fifty.' And that's the way you did business."

But there were times when no matter how much business came its way, Anco simply could not obtain the materials—at any price—to fill the orders. Bromberg used to "beg" for every pound of copper wire he could get out of his primary distributor, Anaconda Wire & Cable Company. "Their salesman used to come in every Friday afternoon," he says, "and one Friday when we were completely out, I asked him, 'Tom, where the hell can I get some copper wire? Can't you help me out?' I mean, I was pleading."

"I can't get you any myself, Zeke, but there's an outfit in New York called United Transformer. They just bought [from government surplus] twelve thousand underwater mine-pole detectors," the apparatus that hangs from ships to detect underwater mines.

"What good is that to me?" Zeke asked.

The salesman explained that each detector contained twenty pounds of copper wound around a rod encased in rubber. "That means," said the salesman, helpfully doing the math, "that United

Transformer has two hundred and forty thousand pounds of copper wire among the twelve thousand mine-pole detectors."

Bromberg secured a few samples and brought them into Lesnick's office. "When I told him there's twenty pounds of copper wire on each, his eyes popped out." The two dissected one of the poles, slicing the rubber casing down the whole of the pole's fifty-four inches. And there, as advertised, was all this wire. They had only to figure out how to separate it from its housing. No one at either Anaconda nor at United Transformer thought it could be done. But Frank Lesnick knew how to do it.

He told his winding foreman to hang the rods up in Anco's furnace. Heating the rods at twelve hundred degrees, he explained, would cause the rubber casing to expand around the wire. Sure enough, Bromberg recalls, when the rods were removed from the heat, the rubber "slipped off like a glove." "And then you peeled off one strand of wire at the beginning and it unraveled like a ball of twine. We took that strand and kept winding it on coils, and pretty soon we had twenty pounds of wire on every coil. And then we took those five thousand or six thousand metal rods we didn't need and sold them for a helluva profit." Lesnick was so delighted with his purchasing agent's resourcefulness that he rewarded him with a year-end bonus: a new 1947 Chrysler New Yorker.

But that windfall of wire did not solve the company's long-term supply problems. It needed a more reliable source, and Lesnick hoped to find it through a small outfit in Paterson with a grandiose name: International Transformer Corporation. International was located across town from Anco, at 27 Kentucky Avenue. Its president and chief executive was Archie Sergy, the young man—he turned thirty the day Japan formally surrendered—to whom Al Goldman had introduced Lesnick before the war. Archie and Lesnick had become friends over the war years, had done a few deals, buying and selling from each other scrap iron and machinery. Not long after Pearl Harbor Day, Archie had purchased, for salvage, the contents of a Canadian-owned company on State Street called National Manufacturing. (The company was closing its Paterson plant due to wartime restrictions on international trade.) The National plant had been one of many from which Archie picked up scrap metal before the war. After war broke out, the company invited him, essentially, to clean out its building and to keep or sell whatever he wanted.

Among the machinery he found in operable condition were some coil-winders and a lone wire-making machine. Instead of scrapping the equipment, Archie proposed to Goldman that they enter into manufacturing themselves. They moved the equipment to the site on Kentucky Avenue, and consulted with Lesnick about how best to use their machinery. Lesnick suggested they could take up the ballast business, in which he had dabbled before abandoning it for the greener pastures of government-sponsored inverters. Lesnick pointed out that if they could add a few parts to the coils, they could make "sparkers," and that if they could make sparkers, they could add this and that and make a simple transformer, or ballast, for a new kind of energy-efficient lighting fixture known as a fluorescent light. The new light, and the ballast necessary to regulate its flow of electricity, would, along with the timely outbreak of peace and the postwar building boom, provide the spark for Archie Sergy's life's work, the business that would surpass International, in deed as well as name: Universal Manufacturing.

FOUR

The World of Tomorrow

THE SEEDS OF Universal's success and ultimate demise, and so, too, the fate of Mollie's job, were sown in seemingly unrelated events surrounding one of the most publicized days of the twentieth century. By midafternoon on Sunday, April 30, 1939, under gray, sullen skies and low clouds on the verge of bursting, nearly half a million people had poured through the turnstiles of what promised to be the greatest international exposition in history, the New York World's Fair. It was opening day, and though the weather threatened and not a few of the exhibits remained unfinished, there was in the gusty air of Flushing Meadows (on a site transformed from an ash dump) in the borough of Queens, a buoyant, expectant feeling, a feeling that for the first time in a long, dispiriting decade, America was renewing itself, emerging, at last, from the staggering grip of the Great Depression.

By three o'clock the winds had picked up and the skies had darkened. At the ceremonial Court of Peace plaza, at the far end of the long mall from the Mutt-and-Jeff structures known as the Trylon and Perisphere—the pointed Trylon was seven hundred feet high and the globe-like Perisphere two hundred feet in diameter—at the geographic and thematic center of the Fair, some sixty thousand fortunate souls, their coat collars turned up against the gusts, their souvenir programs shielding their spring hats from the raindrops, crowded the plaza to listen to their president, Franklin D. Roosevelt, officially open the World's Fair. The reviewing stand a few steps behind the president was filled with VIPs—entertainers and politicians and athletes and business executives. In the president's box, directly behind the podium, sat New York governor Herbert Lehman; Fiorello La Guardia, the mayor of New York City; and Grover Whalen, the president of the New York World's Fair Corporation.

These officials had already spoken, all bearing a sort of utopian message that sounded the theme of the Fair, a belief that the "American Way of Life" would prevail in "The World of Tomorrow." It was a message that resonated with the hard-bitten populus. The Great Depression that had begun with the stock market crash a decade earlier had not fully lifted; the country was stalled, the cities shabby, the people worn out. If the American present was dim, the Fair pronounced the American future dynamic and bright with democracy and technology.

At a few minutes past three, the Army band struck up "The Stars and Stripes Forever," and then President Roosevelt, doffing, for the moment, his familiar silk high hat and morning coat, was helped to the podium. He spoke for fifteen minutes, his huge head bobbing like a buoy in rough seas, his hands gripping the hidden, built-in handles of the podium, his voice booming over loudspeakers scattered throughout the fairgrounds. He told Fairgoers—and the world—that "the eyes of the United States are fixed on the future."

Not only was Roosevelt's speech covered by every newsreel, and beamed live via radio around the world, it was also the first commercial broadcast of the medium of tomorrow: television.

The most visited commercial exhibition was GM's Futurama. The site was designed by Norman Bel Geddes, a leading industrial designer, whose inspired confluence of architecture and engineering and propaganda made for, as GM's immodest but accurate brochure put it, "the number 1 hit of the Fair." Once inside, visitors were seated on plush chairs on a moving platform. Far below, under angled glass, was a huge diorama of GM's vision of the American landscape of 1960. Visitors to the exhibit were given a blue-and-white button on their way out. "I have seen the future," it read.

General Electric, the nation's—and the world's—dominant electric-lighting manufacturer, had also seen the future. And GE's future, at least its lamp division's, was in the brand-new realm of fluorescent lights. Its Fair building was located, along with those of Westinghouse and Consolidated Edison, the New York power company, at the Plaza of Light. The exterior of the building was distinctive for its towering stainless steel zigzag lightning bolt topped with an astrolabe*—a monument to GE's professed mission of harnessing energy to serve mankind.

Inside, the building's right wing flaunted GE's latest consumer gadgets, including a television, an FM radio, and a "magic kitchen" featuring a talking dishwasher and other newfangled appliances. The real draw, however, was in the left wing, in the House of Magic, the auditorium where the company demonstrated its new whiz-bang lighting.

Like GM's Futurama and the other corporate exhibitions, GE's House of Magic was designed not only to dazzle with ingenuity but to take advantage of its utility as a marketing tool. As *Business Week* reported, "Not many in the packed audiences understood the significance of the tricks they saw performed with thyratrons and stroboscopes. But they came away thrilled, mystified, and soundly sold on the company."

It wasn't only Fairgoers whom GE impressed. So, too, were the Fair's own lighting engineers, who had invited GE to design much of the Fair's dramatic nighttime lighting. Grover Whalen, ever the barker, prevailed upon the world's most famous scientist, Dr. Albert Einstein, to introduce the splashy lighting. As dusk settled over the fairgrounds on opening day, another huge crowd was convened at the Court of Peace to listen to Einstein explain "interplanetary" cosmic rays and their supposed connection to earthly illumination. The plan was for Einstein to chat for a few minutes about the rays, to shed some light on the structure of matter, and then to flip a switch "trapping" ten of the visiting rays and putting them to use to illuminate the night skies. All but Einstein's opening words, unfortunately, were garbled by the faulty sound system, and the electrical system, too, malfunctioned, leaving the great crowd in the dark instead of the advertised light "as bright as day."

The setback was mercifully brief; before long the vaunted night-

---

*A medieval instrument that was used to determine the positions of the sun and stars.

time lighting was in working order and being hailed as "one of the Fair's major contributions to American industrial design," and "as dramatic as science can make it." Or as the *Official Guide Book* waxed: "Visible for miles around, a flood of multi-colored light drenches the sky above the glowing spectacle that is the Fair at night. . . . The city of magic, it might well be called, an enchanting vision hinting at the future in artificial illumination."

This future was being charted by General Electric. It was, after all, GE engineers who perfected—or at least improved to the point of marketability—fluorescent lighting, the technology that made possible the "city of magic" that so dazzled critics and Fairgoers.

General Electric had reigned over the electric-lamp industry virtually since it began supplanting gas as the primary source of light in the late 1870s. The company's "cornerstone of control," as the felicitously named Arthur Bright put it in his fine history of electric lighting, was its breadth of patents—from Thomas Edison's incandescent lamp patents to innumerable lesser ones on design, parts, and lamp-making machinery. The famous inventor formed his Edison Electric Light Company in 1878 in Menlo Park, New Jersey, with a capitalization of $300,000, money raised by Grosvenor P. Lowrey, a New York lawyer and counsel to the Western Union Telegraph Company. In return for developing incandescent lighting (he was granted the patent in 1880), Edison received half the shares of his new company. As his biographer Matthew Josephson noted, the agreement "inaugurated a phase of increasingly close relations between big business and technology in this country."*

General Electric epitomized big business during the Gilded Age, a frenzied time of merger and acquisition, of trusts and combinations and consolidations. The company was formed in 1892 through the merger of Thomson-Houston Company and Edison's firm, which itself had expanded beyond incandescent lighting by acquiring several other inventors' businesses and was known then as Edison General Electric Company. General Electric grew rapidly into one of the coun-

---

*The *New York Herald* announced Edison's successful lighting system on December 21, 1879. Gas stocks soon fell precipitously while Edison Electric's own shares soared to $3,500. Edison unveiled his invention ten days later, when some three thousand observers flocked to Menlo Park for a New Year's Eve demonstration.

try's leading manufacturers. It was one of a dozen companies listed in the original Dow Jones Industrial Average of 1896 (and is the lone survivor on today's list), and by 1900, it and Westinghouse were the only major electrical-equipment manufacturers left standing. In the course of less than a quarter century, GE had grown from its entrepreneurial roots in a small research laboratory in Menlo Park to a workforce of fifteen thousand at its plant in Schenectady, New York, and eleven thousand at its factory in Lynn, Massachusetts.

After Edison sold out to GE, he remained associated with the company as a consultant and through his patents, one of which, granted in 1907, was for a fluorescent lamp. The patent covered a short vacuum tube coated on the interior with calcium tungstate and containing two electrodes at either end of the tube. Cathode rays excited the calcium tungstate to produce a light, which, Arthur Bright writes, "was supposed to be cold and like sunlight in appearance."

It didn't work out as planned. Edison's lamp was not commercially viable; it was "too small, too red, too hot," as his assistant told him.

It would fall to General Electric and its noted Lamp Development Laboratory in Cleveland to perform the research and development for fluorescent lighting suitable for general illumination. In Paris in 1933, Dr. William L. Enfield, the manager of the GE lab, had seen an example of a glass tube coated with fluorescent material. The following year a GE consultant in England wrote to Enfield of an improved lamp: "The coated portion gave off a yellowish green light and seemed to be highly efficient," he reported.

General Electric theretofore had been satisfied with its dominance in incandescent lighting. But the news from the European front (in addition to the French and English, German engineers were also reported to be making advances) sparked General Electric to devise its own low-voltage commercial fluorescent lamp. Dr. Enfield assigned a four-man team to the task. Within six weeks the team made significant breakthroughs. Their work consisted of mixing and matching lamp sizes and shapes and colors; attaching the colors to the tube's interior; and experimenting with different types of cathode construction and gas pressures, as well as the lamp's various auxilaries.

The first commercial rendering of the lamp employed the basic ingredients of earlier designs: a long glass tube, internally coated with powdered phosphors, and containing argon gas and a drop of mercury with electrodes at either end of the tube. (The lamp was made in four sizes, ranging in length from 18 inches to 36 inches, and in a diameter of 1 inch or 1½ inches.) When excited by electric current, the mercury vaporized and an arc struck through it, radiating some energy as visible blue light, but mostly as invisible ultraviolet energy. To make visible light, the powdered phosphors glow, or fluoresce, under ultraviolet radiation. The conversion of current to ultraviolet energy to visible light was so efficient that a fluorescent lamp of forty watts produced twice the light of an incandescent bulb of equal wattage, and emitted only about a quarter of the heat radiated by an incandescent lamp of the same light output.

There were some disadvantages, too, to the early "tin-knocker" models. There were only minimal standards for the fixtures, many of which were shoddy and large and expensive, and required special handling to install and maintain. And the auxiliaries, such as the ballast, which regulated the flow of current, were an added cost. And the early lamps were plagued by radio interference and hum.

Despite those drawbacks, the Fair should have been a golden opportunity for GE to introduce to consumers a reward for technological advance—a way to get twice the lighting for about half the cost. And yet: Even as Dr. Einstein was gamely elucidating cosmic rays to the masses, even as multicolored light "drenched" the heavens, as domes and sculptures glowed against the night sky, as steel lightning bolts flashed, towering "test tubes" bubbled, even as visitors to the House of Magic were rendered speechless, even as all that wattage burned bright, brighter, brightest, for all the world to see, General Electric executives were huddled in a conference room in faraway Cleveland, Ohio, conspiring to keep the new technology—not the theatrical pyrotechnics, but the low-cost, easy-on-the-eyes, energy-efficient lamps that would make a real difference in people's lives—off the consumer market. General Electric, in league with the second-largest lighting manufacturer and the nation's electric utility companies, was conspiring—literally—to keep the American people in the dark.

Here was a case of technological progress conflicting with economic self-interest in a way that could only stifle the ability of small but nimble entrepreneurs—people like Archie Sergy—to find their niches.

The fact that lighting existed that would use only half as much electricity was a secret the utility companies were determined to keep from the public. Astonishingly, they almost got away with it. Their ability to do so, to restrain trade, was grounded in an unholy alliance with the major manufacturers. At that time, the utilities bought much of their equipment through GE and Westinghouse and were the major retailers of lamps and bulbs. It was also the era of the "Better Light–Better Sight" program, a joint promotion of the utilities and the manufacturers to sell higher-wattage lighting. The more energy-efficient fluorescent lamps, therefore, posed a threat to the utilities' revenues; it was believed that wide acceptance would result in decreased lighting loads.

General Electric was torn between its marketeers, who were ready to proclaim the cool, bright, glare-free dawn of a new day, and its engineers, who were confident their brainchild was ready for colored and decorative lighting, but were less certain about its readiness as a replacement for general incandescent lighting. One thing was certain: The timing of the World's Fair had forced GE's hand. The Fair's lighting engineers, once they got wind of the magical powers of fluorescence, insisted on it to illuminate the night sky. And Grover Whalen had made it known that if GE or Westinghouse could not deliver the new lamps in time, he stood ready to call upon the manufacturers' European competitors. And so GE rushed into commercial production. Its first fluorescent lamps were added to its product lines on April 1, 1938. The new product caused an immediate sensation—and a panic among the utility companies.

In a confidential memo to the utility trade association, Ward Harrison, the general manager of GE's lamp department, candidly outlined the reasons GE expedited the product launch. "We didn't want to be open to the charge of trying to stop progress," he wrote. He said the company was anxious about competition from the neon-sign companies, which "found it quite easy to coat their tubing with fluorescent powder," and which, Harrison and his cohorts felt, would not likely "confine themselves" to outdoor lighting. Finally, he added, there was the Fair, which was "to be lighted almost entirely with the high-tension tube lighting if [it was] not supplied with some lamps of ours."

Those arguments hardly placated the furious utility company executives, who pressed GE for an emergency meeting on the eve of the Fair. On the Monday and Tuesday before Sunday's opening ceremonies, GE attempted to avert further hostilities by hosting a delegation of utility men at its lamp-department headquarters in Cleveland. At the meeting, dubbed the "Fluorescent Council of War," were delegates from power companies in Buffalo and Pittsburgh and Poughkeepsie and Pawtucket and New York and New Orleans. They were adamant that GE and Westinghouse cease and desist from promoting fluorescent lighting for general illumination. (The chairman of the U.S. Senate Patents Committee, Homer T. Bone of Washington, would later wryly suggest that the utilities took this hard stand to shore up the nation's economy. "If they could take away more of the consumer's money, he would not have so much money to spend, thus helping to hold down inflation.")

The utilities' displeasure was not unanticipated. Six months earlier, on October 28, 1938, shortly before GE planned to announce an improved product, H. F. Barnes of the company's sales department predicted in a letter to his colleagues that the latest innovations would anger the utility companies. "I am very, very much disturbed over the utility reactions which I am sure we are going to have as soon as we announce the longer, larger and higher wattage fluorescent lamps. With these lamps, it's going to be possible to produce the same or increased footcandles at a very practical installation cost and with a very decided drop in wattage."

Barnes was dead-on about the utilities' hostile reaction. At the Cleveland summit—in smoking-gun language—they insisted that the manufacturers' advertising omit any reference promoting fluorescent lighting for everyday usage. "[General Electric] should specifically state that fluorescent lighting is not now known to be applicable for any lighting purposes except colored or atmospheric lighting and certain phases of localized lighting such as wall cases, show cases, and display niches," declared C. T. Bremicker, chairman of the lighting sales department of the Minneapolis-based Northern States Power Company.

Both GE and Westinghouse issued statements of acquiescence. *"We will oppose the use of fluorescent lamps to reduce wattages,"* Westinghouse said. (The italics are the company's.) The GE release, issued the day after the Fair opened, said, in part: "The fluorescent . . . lamp should not be presented as a light source which will reduce lighting costs."

The statements were not released to the public but distributed only internally among GE, Westinghouse, their wholesale houses, and the utility industry. Were it known generally that the industry opposed fluorescent lights as a means of saving on electricity, the industry feared, the public might start buying the new lamps for that very reason. "There is an old saying . . . about giving the public light and it will find its way," said Creekmore Fath, the Senate Patents Committee's counsel. "General Electric has determined that it shall be incandescent lighting."

But while GE's engineering department sought peace with the utility boys, GE's marketing department was not about to let slip one of the great promotional opportunities in history; they would at least sneak a small fluorescent exhibit into their huge World's Fair building. Three weeks into the Fair, however, the jig was up. A utility company official from Buffalo, New York, Howard M. Sharp, who chaired the industry group's subcommittee on fluorescent lighting, wrote Ward Harrison, the general manager of the GE lamp department, to report that some "utility men" had complained to him about the portion of GE's display at the Fair that purported to show "dramatic differences" between equal wattages of fluorescent and incandescent lighting.

The utility man wrote that the exhibit violated the letter and spirit of the statement of policy hammered out at the summit meeting in Cleveland a month earlier. Within a week, Harrison reassured Sharp that it had not been GE's intention to demonstrate the amount of electricity that could be saved by the use of fluorescent lamps, and that the exhibit was already being withdrawn.

General Electric's skittishness about testing the waters at the Fair was not shared by the smaller lamp manufacturers, which had fewer ties to the utilities (they had largely been shut out of the purchasing agreements enjoyed by the majors) and little inclination to abide by their wishes. These manufacturers, notably Sylvania Hygrade, saw in the Fair a large and enthusiastic market, and every reason to plunge in, especially given the opening provided by the reticent GE and Westinghouse.

Sylvania's aggressive marketing—the company launched a nationwide advertising campaign for its "Miralumes"—paid off: Within a "fairly short time," it gained 20 percent of the American fluorescent lamp market, an impressive achievement for a company denied access to the entrenched marketing channels, and for a company that GE previously could not have considered more threatening than a gnat: Sylvania's share of the incandescent lamp market was less than 6 percent.

By the middle of 1940, with higher standards in place for the fixture manufacturers and with Sylvania's market share still on the rise and with the government beginning to crank up the machinery of war—a move that signaled an unprecedented demand for industrial lighting—GE struck back. In May it sued Sylvania for patent infringement in federal court in New York City.

While that case and a countersuit by Sylvania wound their way through the courts, the U.S. Congress entered the fray. In August 1942, the Senate Patents Committee held hearings into allegations that GE was at the heart of a conspiracy to restrain trade and monopolize the production and sale of fluorescent lamps, parts, fixtures, auxiliaries, and machinery. The war was raging, and Americans everywhere tightened their belts, contributing wherever possible to the defense effort, enduring shortages of food staples and gasoline and most other necessities, including electric power. "This is a time of power shortage all over the nation," said Creekmore Fath, the committee's counsel, "and we hear the Power Branch of the W.P.B. [War Production Board] howling constantly that we are going to have black-outs, when the development of this new technique would save a terrific amount of electricity just by the introduction of fluorescent lighting in the place of incandescent lamps."

Committee chairman Bone echoed the counsel's concerns: "We are threatened all over the country with the rationing of electric energy, and we are trying to encourage domestic consumers to cut down on their lighting load and perhaps to cut out some consumption for electric ranges and water heaters. Such a current saving would enable us to bring about a diversion of energy into the field of production. In the airplane industry, for instance, it would certainly be helpful. It might not be a very persuasive argument with gentlemen who are looking at the balance sheet of a power company instead of at our national balance sheet. I wish we could induce more to look at the balance sheet of national welfare in a life and death struggle like this."

•　　•　　•

Those airplanes, all the vast machinery of war, were produced in new or converted industrial plants, lighted, in the main, by fluorescent lamps. Wartime studies by the lamp manufacturers determined that long burning periods produced even longer lamp life than previously thought possible; lamps burned up to 6,000 hours, a huge improvement over the 750-hour to 1,000-hour life of a standard incandescent lamp. By 1942, although restrictions on sheet steel limited fixture production, and installations were limited to plants under defense contract, it was apparent that the new industrial lighting's higher efficiencies and longer life would soon spill over into any number of commercial and residential uses. By war's end in 1945, sales of the lamps had increased exponentially: from 200,000 in 1938, the year they were introduced, to 40 million.

And there would be no letup: In 1946 lamp manufacturers shipped almost fifty-one million units; a year later they sold seventy-nine million. Each of those lamp fixtures needed a ballast, a verity Archie Sergy well recognized. The years to come would be prosperous, the beginning of suburban expansion, of new schools and shopping centers and hospitals and offices, all of which would be lighted with fluorescent lamps, and if Archie Sergy had his way, into each of those fixtures would be mounted his fledgling company's modest but indispensable ballast.

FIVE

Eight Days a Week

Universal executives, shipping room, late 1950s.

PEACE CHANGED everything. Restriction and sacrifice were lifting, rationing was over, price controls disappearing. Unbridled energy, *contagious* energy, abounded. "Everything was in motion," Philip Roth has written. "The lid was off."

The war years, especially the earlier ones, had been bleak for Archie Sergy, bleaker even than the onset of the Depression, when his father had died and when, at the age of fourteen, he was called upon to support his family. Archie had not fought in the war. On Pearl Harbor Day, instead of steeling himself like his boyhood friends for assignment to a U.S. Army division in some distant land, he was confined to a cell in the New Jersey Penitentiary at Trenton. All of the

Over-the-River boys had felt the grip of the Depression; all had needed money badly. Unlike most, though, he had fallen into the bad habit of stealing.

In Archie's early days of delinquency, the Paterson Police Department started a rap sheet on him; its first listing was "Arrested 8-15-32" for "False Pret." The disposition of the case was left blank. The arrests mounted up, but in most instances the cases (primarily for writing worthless checks) were dismissed, the charges were dropped pending restitution, or he received a suspended sentence. "He was a wallpaperer, bounced checks pretty much," recalls Ruby Goldstein, a lifelong friend. "But that was a part of doing business." In September 1940, however, Archie Sergy was arrested on a charge of receiving stolen goods, and this time he would find himself in a legal mess that would haunt him for the rest of his life.

Although the existing police record is scant on details of the crime, Ruby Goldstein says the stolen property was textile printing machines. "He didn't steal them, but he did sell them." An employee of the engraving shop apparently sold the copper print rollers to Archie, who melted down the valuable copper to sell by the pound. "Listen, they're not worth nickels," Goldstein explains. "Each roller was worth a couple hundred dollars. And he [Archie] got twenty or thirty. Whether he knew they weren't a hundred percent kosher, I don't know."

In April 1941, in a Passaic County courtroom, Archie was convicted and sentenced to one to three years in the state prison.

He was twenty-five and married to a woman he'd dated while in high school, the former Pearl Eisman. Pearl, whose father operated a small textile mill until losing it in the Depression, was raised in the fashionable Eastside neighborhood and attended Eastside High; Archie, a year younger, was at Central High. They met through a cousin of Archie's who lived next door to the Eismans. By the time Archie and Pearl married in 1937, her father had relocated the business to Allentown, Pennsylvania. "They went broke in Paterson, and they found cheaper labor and a finance man there," says Sam Stein, who was married to Pearl's sister.

Archie was still, barely, in the junk business when he was sentenced to prison. He served about eight months and was released in early December 1941—within days of the Japanese invasion of Pearl Harbor. The timing was fortuitous. He picked up where he'd left off, selling and buying scrap, including the wire-making machinery of National Manufacturing, the Canadian company that was abandoning its Paterson operations to comply with wartime trade restrictions.

For the remainder of the war years, Archie and his partner, Al Goldman, doing business as International Transformer and operating out of the small leased building at 27 Kentucky Avenue, strung together from their wire business the manufacture of any number of electric-lighting products—sockets, switches, fixtures, ballasts. The product they made on any given day depended entirely on the raw materials available on the black market.

Just scrounging parts was a full-time job. Archie needed assistance, and he found it in Sam Stein, who cheated sleep to help: Stein's nights were consumed by a job as a postal clerk in New York City. Still, he spent his days scavenging for his wife's brother-in-law. "Here we were trying to make ballasts," Stein recalls. "And you had to mount the ballast inside the fixture with a screw and a nut, and half the time we couldn't find any screws and half the time we couldn't find any nuts. And when we *could* find both, then we couldn't even get a drill to make the holes for the screws."

And when Archie wasn't dealing with the finances or rooting around for parts, he was lending a hand on the assembly line.

Then as now, the ballasts and transformers were sealed with liquefied pitch. In those days the pitch was delivered to Kentucky Avenue in solid form in two-hundred-pound drums, which then had to be frozen in order to be chopped into quantities small enough to melt in the plant's pots and poured into the ballasts. In the winter, the pitch would be left outside to freeze; in the summer, however, it was necessary to store the huge drums in freezers. International had no freezers of its own; instead, it rented space in the walk-in freezer of a nearby ice-cream parlor. "Every day we'd haul a drum to Huff's in a pickup truck, and every night we'd take it back and chop it," says Joe Santelli, who started as a twenty-year-old in the plant's stockroom in 1945.

In those early years, Santelli and others—Archie included—were at the plant all hours of the day and night. "Archie was there with us chopping [with an ax] at two in the morning," Santelli recalls. "Then when we got a little bigger we hired guys to do it."

With the end of the war came the promise of the end of rationing and price controls. Nine days after V-E Day, on May 17, 1945, the founders of International Transformer signed papers of incorporation. It was Archie Sergy's company (by then he had bought out Al Goldman), but he was not among the signatories; it was felt that his felony conviction might complicate the incorporation process.

International grew rapidly after the war. By the late summer of 1945, Sergy employed some seventy-five workers in the basement plant on Kentucky Avenue. The rent on the building was cheap, but the site was ill-suited for electrical work. "The place was a work of art," says Armando DeMauro, who started there in January 1946, within days of his military discharge. (His brother, John, was plant manager.) "Everything was jerry-rigged down there, and whenever it rained the plant flooded. We had to put down skids"—wooden pallets—"for everyone to stand on. And we were working with wire and transformers—the kind of stuff you want to be careful with when it's wet. It's a miracle no one was electrocuted."

But even with the bargain rent and lack of creature comforts, Archie was having a tough go meeting an expanding payroll, which nearly doubled by the end of 1946. Meanwhile, his old friend Frank Lesnick, whose company's government contracts for inverters had long since been canceled, hungrily eyed Archie's wire-making capacity. Lesnick offered to buy International Transformer, provided Archie agree to a noncompete agreement. "He wanted Archie out of the ballast business for at least three years," says Zeke Bromberg, who had left Lesnick's company to work for International. In December 1946, they cut a deal and Archie closed the Kentucky Avenue plant.

Archie sold the business on a cash and note deal, the specifics of which are unknown. It is known that from the very beginning, Lesnick was unable to make a go of it. By the spring of 1947, Lesnick was well behind on his payments to Archie. He approached Archie with a new proposition.

"Look, I can't pay you what I'm supposed to, but I'll give you back your equipment."

Archie said he would be happy to repossess the machinery on the condition that they void their noncompete agreement. Lesnick was going out of business, anyway, so he saw no harm in tearing up the old contract.

Archie retrieved the equipment and searched for an inexpensive space to set up shop anew. He found it some twenty miles north of Paterson, in Westwood, New Jersey. He chartered the new corporation on March 31, 1947. By then, his former company's name could not describe his ambition. "He always thought big," says Morris Pashman, the attorney who filed the certificate of incorporation. "And I guess 'International' was no longer big enough. So he chose 'Universal'— Universal Manufacturing."

Almost from the beginning, the Westwood facility's shortcomings were obvious. For one thing, it wasn't in Paterson. This meant that Archie and his core staff—those eighteen or twenty employees who would follow him from Kentucky Avenue—would have to crowd into the few vehicles available for carpool. Archie and his sister Sylvia, who was the office manager, always rode together, and usually picked up two or three other relatives.* And Joe Santelli drove a pickup truck, a "rack job" that could accommodate several more, although it was sometimes so cozy that one rider might spill over into the driver's lap.

The plant was equally crowded. It was not a conventional factory space, but a rambling, narrow maze of connected storefronts. Somehow the ballasts got made and sold in ever-increasing numbers, but Archie once again was finding it difficult to turn a profit. He turned for advice to Paul H. Einhorn, whose Newark accounting firm had conducted industrial audits before the war. In the late spring or early summer of 1949, Sergy escorted Einhorn through the plant.

"After the tour I told him I'd like to see the contents of his scrap barrels outside," Einhorn recalls.

Archie had never met an accountant who wanted to see his plant— let alone his rubble. "What are you after?" he asked as the two walked back inside.

The reply was unequivocal. "Your plant's a shithouse," Einhorn said. "You called me because the plant's showing a consistent loss, and I wanted to see how efficiently it's operating."

Archie appreciated Einhorn's blunt manner. Here was a man who could bring stability and planned growth to a haphazard operation, he told friends. Archie had always operated by the seat of his pants, figur-

---

*Archie had hired his other sister, Mary, and her husband, Irving; his sister-in-law Henrietta; his aunt Ida and her sons; and any number of other cousins and their spouses, and their in-laws, and their in-laws' children.

ing it out as he went, and there were times, despite the company's growth, when he nearly missed his payroll and his phone was nearly shut off. He was great with people, gregarious, a natural conversationalist, but efficiency was not a word with which he was on speaking terms. No commercial financial institution would lend him money (due at least in part to his criminal record), so, Sam Stein recalls, Archie borrowed from any number of customers. "He'd go to a fixture manufacturer and say, 'Look, give me ten grand and every time we make a shipment I'll take ten percent off.' And that's how he kept the wolf from the door."

Archie began telling Einhorn about Kentucky Avenue, about the company's past. "I'm not interested in your history, Mr. Sergy. I'm interested in your future. What can we do to make the *future* better?"

Archie mentioned a problem he was having with an unreliable contractor, the firm that stamped out the steel core of the ballast. Einhorn asked him how Universal's competitors—principally GE and North American Philips—stamped their ballasts. He learned the bigger companies operated their own presses. "Why not find a way to do the stamping here?" Einhorn all but commanded. "Get rid of the middle man."

In the spring of 1950, Archie called upon Frank Lesnick to help find a way. Lesnick by then was enjoying another of his comebacks; he was operating a plant that made picture-tube parts for black-and-white televisions—the plant, incidentally, where Mollie James would briefly work. (Lesnick's success, as usual, would be short-lived—by 1955 the burgeoning color TV industry put him out of business.) Lesnick put Archie in touch with a fellow who knew a fellow with presses for sale. "We got them at ninety thousand [dollars], a ridiculously low price—a distressed price," says Paul Einhorn. "We didn't know how good a deal we got at the time, but when the Korean War broke out that summer, you couldn't get those presses at any price, they were worth a cockeyed fortune!"

Before Universal could exploit its new presses, it would need room to house them: It would need a new building. Even if expanding the labyrinthine Westwood facility across more storefronts had been an option, it made vastly more sense to Archie and the other managers to relocate to Paterson, where most of them lived and where there was a larger and more experienced labor pool. Archie called on a man named David Greenberg, who had repaired motors for him before the war and who was now in real estate. "I'd like to move back to Paterson," he told Greenberg. "Why don't you look around for some property."

Archie and Greenberg formed a partnership to purchase land in the largely undeveloped Bunker Hill section near the Fair Lawn bridge in northeast Paterson. Greenberg oversaw construction of the 129,000-square-foot plant, and in late 1950, the two of them leased the building to Universal.

Everything was in motion. Just as Universal was moving to a new, modern facility, so the entire country at midcentury seemed to be stirring. It was a time of unprecedented American prosperity: Unemployment was low, wages high. Returned veterans were marrying, starting families, deserting cities for suburbs.

Archie Sergy himself had recently joined the suburban exodus. Like many of his boyhood friends, he left Paterson for Fair Lawn, the heavily Jewish enclave situated just across the Passaic River east of the city. And not just his friends were leaving: The 1950 census showed for the first time a drop in Paterson's population, albeit a small one, from the previous census.

Fair Lawn, meanwhile, was growing as fast as any town in the state: From 1940 to 1950 the population swelled to almost twenty-four thousand from nine thousand. Its spectacular growth was fueled by economic and social forces flowing from Washington and Wall Street: federal housing subsidies, low inflation, abundant energy. Fair Lawn was but a five-cent bus ride away from the retailers and workplaces of downtown Paterson; it was said the town's growth was "on the nickel." Archie and Pearl bought a four-bedroom Cape Cod–style house with a picket-fenced yard on Summit Avenue, a quiet, leafy street off Broadway, and enrolled their eldest sons, Sam and Alan, in the acclaimed but recently overburdened schools. (A third son, Bruce, was a toddler.)

As Fair Lawn changed so did Paterson. The city still pulsed with activity—the downtown shopping district hummed, ten theater marquees glowed, most industrial and retail workers carried union cards (there were thirty-seven locals, from the Bakery & Confectionary Workers to the Window Cleaners)—but the very heart of civic life was starting to fail. "Paterson," wrote hometown poet Allen Ginsberg in the mid-fifties, "is only a big sad poppa who needs compassion."

By the time Mollie started at Universal in 1955, the graceful, noble department stores, Meyer Bros. and Konner's, were choking on their own suburban branches. They and the other once-invincible kings of Paterson retailing were either retreating from downtown or opening secondary outlets in the shopping centers sprouting on what until recently had been farmland. The Preakness Shopping Center in Wayne, a suburb to the west, opened in 1955. Two years later came both the Garden State Plaza and Bergen Mall. The region's new retail capitals, along Routes 4 and 17 in nearby Paramus in western Bergen County, were built on celery fields.

The outlying growth that strangled Paterson invigorated Universal. Suburbs, *Fortune* magazine reported, grew at ten times the rate of central cities in 1950. All those young families in their starter homes needed new roads and schools and houses of worship and those huge, sparkling shopping centers and supermarkets with giant parking lots and office complexes and industrial parks. And all of that construction needed bright, efficient fluorescent lighting. And all those fluorescent fixtures—a single supermarket used hundreds and hundreds of fixtures—needed ballasts.

There was a manic, boomtown quality to Universal's early days in Paterson. There were more jobs than people to fill them, so Archie recruited by cruising the streets of his old neighborhood. If he came upon a prospect on her front porch, he'd stop the car. "Hey," he'd yell, his voice practiced from his youthful tenure as an ice and coal salesman, "you looking for a job?"

If so, little time was wasted on the application process. "Well, come on!"

And he kept hiring more and more relatives and friends. In June, fathers of newly minted high school graduates would pay Archie their respects. "They'd inquire about a job for their kids, and Archie would always put them to work," says his son Sam Sergy.

Even as he added production lines, hundreds of employees, and a third, graveyard shift to keep up with the roaring demand, Archie operated as if he were running a corner store in the old neighborhood: He knew and greeted everyone by name, often by their street names—"Hey Munny! Hey Moishe!" Or it was like old times at the caddy shack: Archie dispensing favors like a benevolent overlord. Once he announced bids on a job to paint the plant, and when an old friend's offer sheet came in only third lowest, he gave him the job anyway. Countless were the employees who came to him with a personal problem—an unpayable debt, an abusive husband, a sick child. And almost always, he intervened, either with a loan or donation or a timely referral or phone call.

But Universal was no longer a mom-pop-and-the-cousins enterprise. Its growth was outpacing its founder's ability to manage the daily enterprise. Almost overnight, after its move to Paterson, Universal was bursting into the ballast business, unannounced and uninvited by General Electric and North American Philips, and it was ripping away sales from its established rivals. Archie needed help. He had his finance man, Paul Einhorn (whom Archie had cajoled into selling his accounting practice to work full-time at Universal), but he needed an operations man, someone capable of focusing on the minutiae *and* understanding the big picture. In Rube Pashman Archie found him.

Rube. Not Reuben, his given name, or Mr. Pashman. Just Rube. Everyone called him that, even those few who called Archie "Mr. Sergy." (Most everyone called Einhorn "Mr. Einhorn"—he neither sought nor welcomed informality.) Rube was of average height and ample paunch, but he had about him an outsized way, a *presence*. He was a man of considerable appetite and strong opinion. At his first lunchtime management meeting, he demanded to know who requested the platter of bologna-and-cheese on white bread. "Who ordered this shit?" Rube asked. He was gruff and profane and kind and funny—a jumble of contradictions enshrouded in a haze of cigarette smoke.

The only time Rube didn't smoke was when he ate. But the habit went with the era, and the work. "All of us smoked all the time," says Siegfried Steinberger, Universal's quality-assurance man. "I used to have a Panatella for dinner and a Pall Mall for dessert. But Rube smoked everyone under the table." Says his brother, Morris Pashman: "No one was more adept at talking and walking through the plant— *running* through the plant—while dangling a cigarette from the corner of his mouth."

Rube insisted that his managers familiarize themselves with all aspects of production. He instituted a two-week orientation program that required managers to spend a day in each department—one day in coil-winding, the next in metal-stamping, and so forth. Jules (Julie)

Schwartz went through orientation in 1956 as a new member of the service department. He remembers Rube telling him, "I want you to know this because one day when someone says to you the cream cheese is coming out of the ballast, you'll know they're full of shit because there's no cream cheese in these damn things."

It was Morris Pashman, the attorney who had filed Universal's corporate charter for Archie, who introduced Rube to Universal. Morris himself had met Archie in court in the early 1940s, when he represented a client who had sued Archie on a civil matter related to his scrap business. "I won the case," Pashman recalls, "and apparently he was slightly impressed with my work." Some time later, when Archie again needed legal counsel, he turned to Pashman. And in May of 1945, when Archie needed a lawyer to prepare the papers of incorporation for International Transformer and then, two years later, for Universal, he again hired Pashman, who would continue to serve the company as general counsel. (Pashman went on to a career in politics, serving a term as mayor of his hometown of Passaic and as a county judge; in 1961 Governor Robert B. Meyner appointed him to the Superior Court of New Jersey.)

Around the time Universal was moving from Westwood to Paterson, Rube Pashman returned to Passaic County. He had been away from the States for nearly eight years, working as a civilian budget officer for an Army contractor in the Virgin Islands. Although he never studied finance, Rube proved his business acumen during the Depression, when he owned and operated three movie theaters in the county: the Capital in Paterson, the Rivoli in Rutherford, and the Strand in Clifton. (He also booked the Rialto in Passaic, which qualified him for a discount distributors offered to chains of at least four theaters.) In the late thirties, however, the industry was consolidating, squeezing out the smaller owners. Rube sold his theaters to Sy Fabian, a second-generation Paterson mogul who had accumulated a vast chain of movie and vaudeville houses (and who himself would sell out to Warner Bros). Rube made some unfortunate investments with the proceeds from the deal, and very nearly lost everything. When the war broke out and the Army was undecided about drafting him, Rube signed on with the civilian construction company, building island airstrips and ports.

In 1944, he married Belle Cohen, a former Strand cashier, and the newlyweds lived in Army housing in Puerto Rico. It wasn't the life Belle had pictured. She wanted a baby, and she wanted to raise the child back home. But she dutifully toughed it out for five years. One night, though, she found a roach in the bed. The indignity was not received warmly. "Honey," she announced, "that's it. We're going home."

When they returned to Passaic, Morris Pashman put in a word about his brother with Archie Sergy. Rube knew nothing about the ballast business, but he was a quick study and started poring over the price and product lists at home and spending hours at the plant. Archie was dazzled by Rube's quick and firm grasp of the business, and hired him as head of operations.

Universal quickly became Rube's blood. He and Belle did have a child, a daughter, but Rube made little time for his family. "There was no such thing as hours, not for Rube," Belle recalls. "He told me, 'You want me home at five, I'll take a postman's job.' Even on vacation in Europe, he'd be on the phone with the company. When he was home he was constantly on the phone. And there were always after-hours meetings."

The late meetings, held at least twice weekly, began over dinner. On Thursdays, Archie, Rube, and Paul Einhorn dined at the Sergys' house, where Pearl cooked cabbage soup and pot roast or lamb chops. (On most other weeknights, the Sergys' twelve-foot-long dining room table functioned as a dessert buffet: Friends and relatives and co-workers dropped by steadily to sample Pearl's pastries, candies, cookies.) On Mondays, the ruling triumverate and any number of other managers ate at the Black Bear Grill & Restaurant at the corner of Belmont Avenue and North Eighth Street. (The place was noted for the large stuffed bear behind the bar. Its head was wired to a button under the bar, which the bartender liked to press for the benefit of newcomers. As one regular put it: "You would wonder if the head was actually moving, if it was your imagination, or what kind of beer [the proprietor] served.") The hearty German fare and thick steaks were not for the health conscious, an interest group to which Rube insisted he belonged. "He was on a diet," says Sig Steinberger. "So he wouldn't order—he'd sit next to me and eat off my plate."

After dinner, they often adjourned to Archie's house, where kitchen-table strategy and bull sessions continued late into the night, and not infrequently until one or two in the morning. Nor would the work slacken on weekends. "They were eight-day-a-week guys," says Morris Pashman. He was speaking of the company's top executives, but the long, frequently uninterrupted workday was contagious. Most all the managerial staff worked a portion of their Saturdays, and some, Rube included, worked all day. Others, such as Joe Santelli, who was officially the foreman of the stamping department, but who functioned as Archie and Rube's eyes and ears throughout the plant, seemingly worked all day and night.

In a plant full of loyal and dedicated employees, no one was more so than Santelli. He was a genial beat cop, patrolling the production lines, offering an encouraging word. If he spotted an infraction, though, recalls Milt Cohen, a salesman, "you'd get laid out in lavender." When Santelli was not at the plant, he could usually be found at the Sergys' house, baby-sitting the boys or sharing a meal. "I was like a fourth son to the Sergys," Santelli says. "I was around there all the time. I'm Italian, but I was more Jewish than Italian. I was always there for the holidays, the bar mitzvahs, everything."

Santelli was part of a foursome that routinely lunched on Saturday. He, Sig Steinberger, Rube, and Angelo Mancone feasted on hot pumpernickel bread from a nearby bakery, and big bowls of salad and spaghetti that Mancone prepared in his living quarters off the boiler room. Mancone was another case of devotion above-and-beyond to the company. A cigar-chomping Italian of an indeterminate, advanced age, he had been with Archie since the days on Kentucky Avenue. Mancone operated the ovens that impregnated the steel coils—baked varnish on them. The ovens ran all night, which meant that someone—Mancone—had to watch them. At Westwood, he made do with catnaps in an easy chair. When the company moved to its new plant in Paterson, it built Mancone a room of his own next to the boiler room. It was furnished with a bed, refrigerator, and hot pot, on which he cooked the noontime meal each Saturday. (Eventually he married the woman who once ran the employee cafeteria and moved out of the plant. He did not drive, though, so Archie sent a car for him each morning, and had him driven home nightly. He stayed with Universal until his death, supposedly in his nineties.)

It was the camaraderie that sustained Universal in those terribly difficult early years. "Everyone was in it together," says Sam Sergy, Archie's eldest son, "and if that meant everyone staying late to fill an order, that's what they did." (The devout Joe Santelli even left his wedding-night bed to check on an order; the marriage lasted less than a year.) "Everyone was always pitching in everywhere," says Michael Stein, a nephew of Archie's and an engineer who would spend his entire career with the company. "The clock never stopped."

For years and years, Archie and Rube made it a point to know everyone in the plant by name. "They never treated you as inferior, regardless of whether you cleaned the toilets or whatever your job was," says Mollie James. "They'd walk up and down the line and talk to us, joke with us, sometimes have their sandwiches with us right there on the line. Rube and Mr. Sergy both were the type that if you needed something, money or whatever, you could get it. If you needed a home loan, they'd give it to you, and you could make arrangements to pay it back."

At the holidays, Archie distributed turkeys for every employee (kosher for the Jews) and helped clear out the shipping room for the company's annual "Beefsteak"—the beefsteak being a New Jersey din-ing tradition at which huge platters of steak strips on thick slices of bread were passed around endlessly, and then again. "They'd open up the place," recalls Joe Santelli, "put long tables in there, and the caterer would line up cheeses, radishes, beefsteaks, corn on the cob. And Sergy would open his arms and invite everyone in."

The atmosphere of the plant resembled less a corporate office than it did the open street stalls of the old Jewish peddlers downtown. No one had a private office. Archie, Rube, Einhorn, everyone had desks in the long open room, the "bull pen," at the front of the plant that housed all the administrative employees—the engineers, the sales staff, and the purchasing, operations, and payroll departments. When Archie needed a word with, say, the head of purchasing, he would wail across the room: "Zeke, *Zeke*, gotta minute?" Archie's desk, which he kept clean save for three scratch pads, was next to the room that housed the stamping operation. Why he wanted to sit near the ear-pounding presses was a mystery Sig Steinberger once asked him about.

"That, Sig, is the sound of money!"

The sound was getting louder year by year. At the end of 1953, Archie invited everyone to a surprise beefsteak dinner at the plant to celebrate Universal's sales topping, for the first time, a million dollars. By the end of the decade, annual revenues exceeded twenty million dollars.

With that sort of spectacular growth, the burden of raising operating capital never ceased. One morning in the late 1950s, Einhorn received a long-distance phone call from Rube Pashman, who was with Archie on a sales trip in Texas.

"Paul," an obviously agitated Rube began, "I was just talking to [the bookkeeper], who tells me we only have two dollars in the bank."

"Rube, what day is today?"

"Thursday."

"If today's Thursday," a relieved Einhorn said, "we made payroll yesterday. When you left, I wasn't so sure we'd make it."

Make it they did. Certainly the company was in the right place at a time of tremendous demand for fluorescent fixtures and for its companion niche product. The problem for Universal was that its major competitor, General Electric, boasted one of the longest marketing arms and leading brand names in America. And in truth there was no difference between the two products; Universal engineers spent a good deal of their workdays dissecting GE ballasts, studying the components, and deducing how to build identical ones. It was cheaper and more efficient, the company reasoned. "Periodically, I'd settle with GE on patent-infringement cases," says Joel Steiger, a Universal attorney. "It made sense for Universal. We didn't have to spend money on research and development."

Because his products were indistinguishable from those produced by one of the nation's industrial blue bloods, Archie offered more than a ballast; he offered unparalleled customer service. The service involved two components: technical, hands-on help, and innovative salesmanship.

Archie was a man of natural charm and warmth, a plus for any salesman. And he had long since shed his youthful chubbiness, had his teeth fixed, his clothes tailored. Like all master salesmen, he sold not only his product but himself: He sold confidence. He had spent a lifetime in sales, since he was thrust into the role of family breadwinner at fourteen. He'd learned to read people, understand what they needed from his product, and from him. Universal's product was not glamorous; it wasn't sold in department stores or on television or in magazines. His customers were the lighting-fixture manufacturers and the men who ran electrical-supply houses, wholesale distributors, general contractors, men who generally were not closely acquainted with what Archie called "the red-carpet life."

So Archie rolled it out famously. He wined and dined them and their wives at New York's finest restaurants and in a catered hospitality suite at the elegant Essex House, overlooking Central Park, during the annual National Lighting Exposition at the New York Coliseum. (And he invited them to his regular beefsteak dinners in the shipping room of the plant.) He bought them orchestra seats for Broadway shows, box seats for Yankees games, ringside seats for prizefights; sent lavish gifts to their homes at the holidays. And not only did he indulge his own lifelong passion for the game by treating customers to rounds of golf, he also kept on the Universal payroll a golf pro, Frank Dalvito, who offered customers complimentary lessons in Palm Springs, Miami Beach, Las Vegas. ("Don't ask me about ballasts, because I don't know the first fucking thing about them," Dalvito used to say. "If you want to talk golf, I'll talk golf.")

Archie himself often played with Dalvito in Las Vegas. He routinely stopped there on sales trips to the West Coast. "We'd go to L.A. and San Francisco, great areas for sales," says Morris Pashman, who accompanied Archie on four or five such excursions a year. They always stayed in the finest rooms and always flew first class. "And invariably, on the return trip home, by Friday, we'd go to Vegas, stay two nights, play golf, gamble a bit, go to the midnight floor shows, gamble some more, and take the flight home on Sunday. Nobody ever slept."

While Archie wooed new customers, Universal's repairmen paid vigilant attention to current ones. Their diligence first became evident on the day that a gentleman working at his desk in a new office building in a new office park suddenly noticed a glob of oily liquid on the sleeve of his white dress-shirt. And then another. He glanced skyward— *"What the . . . ?"*—where he discerned the culprit: a leaking fluorescent fixture.

Upon investigation it was determined the leak came not from the fixture, precisely, but from the capacitor of the ballast. The capacitor contained the toxic compound PCB, or polychlorinated biphenyl. Only the capacitor was not containing much of it. Further investigation revealed the defect was no anomaly—leaks and soiled shirts were being reported wide and far. The PCB manufacturer, a St. Louis company, had apparently delivered a shipment of contaminated liquid to a GE plant in Hudson Falls, New York. That plant, in turn, had delivered a shipment of defective capacitors to Universal, which at the time bought that component from GE. The liquid wound up in the Universal ballasts installed in the shipment of fixtures under which sat the befuddled desk clerk.

Universal's phones rang mightily with the cries of contractors and wholesalers desperate to replace the faulty ballasts. Universal swung into action. "We set up a hot line to give immediate help," says Paul Einhorn. "We told our customers that if necessary, we would fly replacement ballasts out, and make a complete change-out, get their lights going again. Meanwhile, we kept detailed records of what our costs were, and sued GE for every penny. People were calling us because if you called GE you were hard-pressed to get anyone on the line. They were interested in sales, all right, but not service."

One day, recalls Julie Schwartz, he had just completed a service call on Long Island when the mobile phone rang in his car. (The phone was so heavy it weighed down the springs in the backseat.) It was the office calling to ask if he could service a customer at a nearby drugstore. "I happened to be right around the block," Schwartz recalled forty years later. "I walked in, told the guy I was from Universal, and all he could say was, 'You're full of shit.' "

As word spread among electrical contractors of Universal's attentiveness, the company continued to receive pleas for help. Einhorn: "It was not unusual to get a phone call from a brand-new shopping center saying, 'Hey, my next-door neighbor has Universal ballasts. He's got this problem, and you got him changed out. I got GE ballasts and nobody over there will help me.' We'd send our people down to help." Such hands-on service won Universal a loyal following. Around 1960, it further enhanced its reputation for service by pioneering the industry's first warranty, a two-year parts-and-labor guarantee.

Universal's customer-comes-first ethos extended well beyond repair and replacements. Unlike GE, the company was small and nimble, and therein lay its strength: When a customer needed a custom ballast—fast—he got one. If that meant breaking a production line, the line was broken. "Let's say a customer calls Rube and wants two thousand units of a 930-K ballast," Milt Cohen explains. "He checks with the foremen of all the departments that make the components for that unit. And they tell him, yes, we can have it this day or that day. And Rube puts all that information together, figures he can go into production in three days, and then calls the customer back: 'Give me five days and I'll have it ready for you.'

"At GE, meanwhile, they'd look up their production schedule, and they'd see that 930-Ks don't go on the line for, say, four weeks. They would never, ever, under any conditions, break a line. A customer could call up and order four thousand of a unit, but if that line isn't made, you'd get the date when it would be made."

General Electric ultimately abandoned the ballast business, selling that division to a midwestern competitor. "They figured out they were better off with the bulbs than the ballasts," Cohen says.

One other critical element of Universal's remarkable growth was its steadfast sales force. While Archie golfed and drank with the senior executives, Universal's sales force dealt with the hundreds and thousands of purchasing agents for malls and supermarkets and department stores and office towers. Angelo Mancone, the boiler operator who lived out his life at Universal, was hardly the only employee to spend his working life with the company. "Eighty percent of our growth was based on personal relationships, and on people who stayed there," says Harold Harris, who retired in 1991 after forty-one years with the company. "A lot of us would attend the National Lighting Expo every year and we'd meet and greet our key customers at our hospitality suite, and they'd see the same faces year after year. They knew we weren't going anywhere, not like some companies with great turnover. Not like GE, which didn't retain their salespeople for twenty or thirty years like we did."

By the early sixties, Universal employed a workforce of some twelve hundred. Archie and Rube, of course, no longer knew all the workers by name, but they continued to distribute holiday turkeys and hold the beefsteak dinners. All this, the communal meals and work space, the eight-day workweeks, the shared sacrifices, the managers' sincere interest in the employees' welfare, all this made Universal a company revered by its employees and admired by its customers and its community. It was as if Archie Sergy's own ambition, his determination to make something of himself, had seeped into the company water supply. "We used the best materials and we never took shortcuts and because of that we never had very many returns," Mollie James says. "We made *the* best ballasts—period." She recalls that whenever someone asked her where she worked, the response to her answer never varied. "You'd always hear, 'Boy, I sure would like to work for them.'"

SIX

Farrell Dobbs's Vision

GEORGE MEANY had heard enough.

He'd let the morning's proceedings—the gassy testimonials, the heartfelt if misguided appeals—defer the
inevitable long enough. He'd let them all tender their last rites—the
delegates from the Building Trades Department, from the construction unions, the carpenters. But it was too late; they knew it, Meany
knew it: The Teamsters were dead. Outside, on this snowy Friday
morning in early December, the chill ocean winds were whipping and
howling against the famed Atlantic City boardwalk. Inside the convention hall, the bluster was equally forceful, the air laden with heat and
bombast. It was the second day of the AFL-CIO convention of 1957,
and Meany, the bulldog president of the recently merged federation
(the American Federation of Labor and the Congress of Industrial
Organizations had reunited in 1955 after a split twenty years earlier),
was leading the charge to expel the International Brotherhood of
Teamsters (IBT), the AFL-CIO's largest, richest, and most powerful
union.

The resolution to expel stemmed from sensational U.S. Senate
hearings into allegations that the Teamsters was a sink of corruption.

The televised hearings had begun in February and were conducted by the Select Committee on Improper Activities in the Labor or Management Field—better known as the Senate Rackets Committee, or simply the McClellan Committee, after its chairman, John L. McClellan, Democrat of Arkansas. There was a fine undercard, featuring a who's who of America's foremost mobsters, murderers, shakedown artists, and blackmailers, who paraded before the committee long enough to plead their Fifth Amendment rights against compelled self-incrimination.

The main event was a heavyweight fight between two men who were then little known outside their small circles of influence: the committee's chief counsel, Robert F. Kennedy, and its chief target of investigation, James R. Hoffa. Kennedy, only thirty-one years old, had first heard allegations of malignance and racketeering in the Teamsters ranks a year earlier, during an investigation into corrupt government procurement practices. The trail led to Dave Beck, president of the IBT, and eventually to the union's powerful ninth vice president and Beck's rival for the union presidency, Jimmy Hoffa.

Hoffa, forty-five, first stood at the witness table before the McClellan Committee on August 20, 1957. The red-carpeted, marble-walled, high-ceilinged Caucus Room on the third floor of the old Senate Office Building was filled to capacity. Senator McClellan sat facing Hoffa on the elevated dais; flanking the courtly chairman were the committee's four Republicans and three other Democrats, including the young Massachusetts senator John F. Kennedy. Kennedy's younger brother sat to the chairman's left.

Bobby Kennedy and Jimmy Hoffa sparred all day, and all the next, and the day after that. The questioning centered on allegations that Hoffa mixed union funds with his personal business ventures, on the shady people with whom he was engaged in those ventures, and on the harm the ventures inflicted on the Teamsters membership.

Instead of resorting to taking the Fifth Amendment, Hoffa dodged most of his foe's jabs with artless but effective lapses of memory. In one typical exchange, Kennedy asked Hoffa about a conversation he'd had three months earlier with John Dioguardi, a mobster who was under indictment for blinding the newspaper columnist Victor Riesel with acid. Hoffa claimed repeatedly he could not recall such a meeting, even after Kennedy produced a surveillance tape recording of the discussion in question.

"To the best of my recollection, I must recall on my memory," Hoffa said, elaborating: "I cannot remember."

Chairman McClellan was sufficiently displeased with the witness's shoddy memory to interrupt the proceedings. Into the record he read a statement outlining forty-eight charges against Hoffa, along the lines of conflict of interest, misuses of union and welfare funds, consorting with known racketeers, stifling union democracy, and so forth.

The committee issued its first interim report in the middle of September—two weeks before the Teamsters' annual convention in Miami Beach. The report called Hoffa not only a "dangerous influence" on organized labor but "dangerous for the country at large" and found that "well-nigh incalculable power over our economy is wielded by this union." It also noted that a criminal background was a "prerequisite" for "advancement within the Teamster firmament."

The gamy revelations were enough to persuade George Meany to notify the executive board of the Teamsters that if Hoffa, as widely expected, were elected president at the upcoming convention, Meany would recommend that the AFL-CIO expel the union. (The federation's Ethical Practices Committee had issued its own report, drawing heavily on the McClellan Committee's, and finding "unrefuted . . . evidence . . . that the Teamsters Union has been and continues to be dominated, controlled, or substantially influenced by corrupt influences." It also criticized Dave Beck and Hoffa for using "their official union positions for personal profit and advantage, frequently to the direct detriment of the . . . membership.")

The AFL-CIO said it would give the Teamsters until October 24—three weeks after the union closed its convention—to rid itself of Hoffa and other corrupt leaders, or face suspension. And Meany specifically asked that the AFL-CIO's damning report be brought to the attention of the delegates.

Hoffa and his supporters were gleefully obstinate. He had no intention of stepping aside, and was happy to let the delegates hear the full text of the AFL-CIO's "indictment" against him. "I don't want anybody, from George Meany down," Hoffa told reporters, "to say that any delegate here voted in the election for president without knowing what the Ethical Practices Committee said. I'm not afraid of the outcome."

He needn't have been. From the moment convention delegates stepped into the lobby of the Eden Roc, the host hotel, they were engulfed in Hoffa campaign propaganda. The walls were plastered with life-size portraits. "Hoffa Hostesses" poured free coffee and orange juice for the delegates, and distributed buttons, pennants, fountain pens, and orchid leis flown in from Hawaii. Inside the hall, bedecked similarly with Hoffa banners and posters, the tone of the convention's opening session was one of "no appeasement" toward the AFL-CIO. John English, the Teamsters secretary-treasurer, received a standing ovation from the nineteen hundred delegates after his speech warning federation leaders they could "all go straight to hell" if they expelled the union.

On October 4, 1957, the Teamsters Union elected Jimmy Hoffa as its president by a margin of three to one over the combined vote of two rank-and-file reform candidates. In his acceptance speech, Hoffa painted himself and the union as innocent victims of a smear campaign. "From every side, inside and outside the labor movement, we have been subjected to accusations and charges of every sort and description."

After complaining about the lack of due process and the high-powered political weaponry trained on the Teamsters, Hoffa demonstrated his own political skills by wrapping his case in the flag and hoisting it above and beyond the relatively small audience in the Miami Beach auditorium. "And I want to say this to the whole country: the one and a half million working American men and women that make up this International Brotherhood of Teamsters are your next-door neighbors. They aren't gangsters. They aren't hoodlums. They are respected citizens who live next door to you; who go to the same churches and synagogues; whose children go to the same schools that your children go to; who serve the Red Cross and the Community Chest the same as you do. Our members belong to the same clubs and societies that you do. These people are Americans. I am proud to be one of these people."

Reaching full throttle, Hoffa portrayed George Meany as a dupe of "labor's enemies" and "union haters" in Congress and corporate boardrooms. "Something has happened to the labor movement in recent days. I am ashamed of what I see within labor's ranks. I see men who would betray principle to get a better headline. Samuel Gompers [the founding president the American Federation of Labor] did not formulate his program by reading the morning newspapers. . . .

"It is unfortunate that the AFL-CIO accepted unproven charges without full investigation as to their merits. . . . If these people succeed in forcing the Teamsters out of the federation," Hoffa warned, "and attempt to raid our organization, mark my words, and mark them well, we will be ready to defend ourselves with every ounce of strength we possess."

With the battle lines drawn, George Meany declared war: On October 24, as expected, the executive council of the AFL-CIO voted overwhelmingly, twenty-five to four, to suspend the Teamsters. The council declared that the suspension would not be lifted until the Teamsters met two conditions: remove Hoffa as president-elect and agree to a monitoring committee of the AFL-CIO to correct the "abuses" delineated in the report of the Ethical Practices Committee. To fail to do so promptly, Meany warned, would result in a recommendation of expulsion at the federation's convention forthcoming in early December.

How had the Teamsters come to be, in the words of Bobby Kennedy, a "conspiracy of evil," and "the most powerful institution in this country—aside from the United States Government itself"?* And how had it come to be that the AFL-CIO was on the verge of casting out the Teamsters as pariahs unfit to live inside labor's house?

The origins of the Teamsters date to 1898, twelve years after Sam Gompers convened unionists from across the country to "draw the bonds of unity much closer together between all the trade unions of America" by means of "an American federation of alliance of all national and international trade unions." Delegates from twenty-five labor organizations assembled in Columbus, Ohio, on December 8, 1886, to form the American Federation of Labor.

By 1902, there were two Teamsters organizations: the fourteen thousand–member Team Drivers International Union, an AFL affiliate of horse-drawn wagon operators chartered in 1899 and based in Detroit; and the Teamsters National Union, a splinter group of eighteen thousand horse handlers headquartered in Chicago. It was the

---

*In his 1960 book, *The Enemy Within,* Kennedy added: "In many major metropolitan areas the Teamsters control all transportation. It is a Teamster who drives the mother to the hospital at birth. It is the Teamster who drives the hearse at death. And between birth and burial, the Teamsters drive the trucks that clothe and feed us and provide the vital necessities of life. . . . Quite literally your life— the life of every person in the United States—is in the hands of Hoffa and his Teamsters."

AFL president Gompers who prevailed upon the rival factions to settle their differences, arranging for a joint convention in 1903 at Niagara Falls to found the International Brotherhood of Teamsters.

The union was beset with corruption from the beginning. Its first president, Cornelius P. Shea of Boston, was indicted for conspiring to extort money from team owners. Although he won acquittal, in 1907 he lost his bid for reelection to another Bostonian, Daniel J. (Big Dan) Tobin. Tobin would endure as president for forty-five years, during which the Teamsters would grow into the AFL's major power, with a net worth of thirty million dollars and a membership of more than a million.

But the union was anything but big and strong when the young man who would become its most celebrated and infamous member signed his first union card. In the midst of the Depression in 1932, the Teamsters was still a small, motley craft union comprised primarily of men who delivered ice, coal, milk, and bread; its membership shrank that year to seventy-eight thousand from a high five years earlier of eighty-eight thousand.

In its founding city of Detroit, there were two Teamsters locals in 1932. The Commission House Drivers, Warehouse, Produce and Fish Employees Local 674 was destitute and facing eviction from its office. Few of its two hundred members could afford the ten-dollar initiation fee or two-dollar monthly dues. The larger General Truck Drivers Local 299 faced even more problems: Not only was it without a single labor contract for its three hundred members, but it was ridden with scandal. The local's first president and secretary-treasurer were alleged to have fixed their election and "misused" the local's finances. The international union removed the officers and appointed a receiver for the local.

Apart from their internal troubles, unionists in Detroit in the early thirties faced daunting obstacles to organizing. Detroit was known as the "open shop capital of America." "It was tough days for the union," a Local 299 member recalled to the writer Dan Moldea. "You couldn't even wear your union button where it could be seen."

Virulently antiunion employers, epitomized by Henry Ford, retained their own strikebreaking "security forces." During the Communist-led Ford Hunger March of unemployed workers in March 1932, Ford's men shot to death four workers at the gates of the huge River Rouge complex. After more than seventy thousand sympathizers attended the funeral march, Ford and other employers responded by purging and blacklisting thousands of suspected radicals from their plants.

Hoffa's bare-knuckled politics, and indeed the brash and muscular international union he transformed, was forged in the raw and brutal Detroit of the early 1930s. Hoffa himself arrived in Detroit in 1924, at the age of eleven. His father, an itinerant coal driller, had died when Jimmy was seven, leaving his mother to fend for Jimmy and his three siblings in the mining town of Brazil, Indiana. The family moved elsewhere in Indiana, and then, during a boom in the auto industry, to Detroit. Hoffa quit school at fourteen and soon enough found work on the loading dock of the Kroger Grocery & Baking Company. For thirty-two cents an hour, he unloaded boxcars full of produce.

After leading a work stoppage to protest conditions on the dock, Hoffa and his fellow warehousemen won a union contract and a raise of thirteen cents an hour. The union, an independent affiliate of the AFL, in time merged with Teamsters Local 674, and in early 1936, when the receiver took over troubled Local 299, he folded 674 into Local 299. It was not long thereafter that Kroger rid itself of the outspoken Hoffa, and the local's head man hired the twenty-two-year-old rabble-rouser as its business agent.

The middle 1930s was a time of tremendous growth for the Teamsters. In part this was due to progressive labor legislation enacted by Congress, including the landmark Wagner Act of 1935, which created a federal agency, the National Labor Relations Board, to enforce workers' rights to organize unions and bargain collectively; and the Fair Labor Standards Act of 1938, which mandated a minimum wage, banned child labor, and established the forty-hour workweek.*

But the union's growth spurt, as Steven Brill pointed out in *The Teamsters*, was "more directly" attributable to the strategy of a single small local in Minneapolis, Minnesota. In May 1934, Local 574 called a citywide strike of all Teamsters. The strike turned violent; a volunteer "deputy" from an upper-crust family was killed during a riot. The following day, police opened fire on unarmed strikers, killing two. The governor declared martial law.

*Both acts had gaping loopholes. Excluded were farmworkers, service workers, public employees, and anyone not involved in interstate commerce.

The strike dragged on all summer before employers began relenting in September. Out of the union's victory emerged an idea that would create an entirely new pattern for Teamsters organizing, and would fundamentally change the character of the union. And not only would the implementation of this idea alter the Teamsters, it would turn the union into one of the nation's greatest economic and political entities.

The idea belonged to Farrell Dobbs, a Trotskyist* whose politics the IBT president, Dan Tobin, abhorred and from which he distanced himself. (Tobin was a full-bore Roosevelt man and chief labor consultant to the Democratic Party.) Hauling freight had previously been the exclusive province of the railroads, but trucks were beginning to compete for the business. What Dobbs understood before anyone else was the unrealized power of the Teamsters: their place as an indispensable cog in the nation's economy. Dobbs's vision for tapping that power was to organize not only local delivery men and warehousemen but the long-haul truckers who drove between cities. Dobbs announced he would see that "every driver pulling into our terminals has a union button." Barring that, he decreed, deliveries would be disallowed.

Local 574 capitalized on its strike victory by immediately expanding beyond Minneapolis to start organizing over-the-road drivers. Dobbs and his brethren believed that it was not possible "to have an island of truckdrivers, isolated in one place like the workers of a coal tipple or a woolen mill." And they understood, better, certainly, than Dan Tobin, that with "the trucking industry rapidly replacing the railroads in the handling of freight, the truckdrivers union becomes the dominating factor in labor organization."

Dobbs called it "leapfrogging": first organizing a terminal, then its incoming drivers, then teaching those drivers to organize the next terminal they enter, and the ones after that. And Dobbs's disciples did not stop there: Not only did Teamsters warehousemen refuse shipments that were not delivered by fellow Teamsters, but they began refusing goods that were not union-made. The technique brought in many

*The wing of the Communist Party that supported Leon Trotsky against Joseph Stalin in 1928.

thousands of new members to the Teamsters and spawned imitative efforts across the country—the union's membership leapt to 277,000 in 1937 from 75,000 in 1933.

Dobbs's inventiveness also helped bring to the fore industrial union-ism—a concept anathema to old-school AFL leaders like Dan Tobin who favored the traditional practice of segregating unions by craft or occupation, instead of welcoming all workers in a single industry, regardless of skill. But federal law now said that an employer *had* to bargain collectively with unions, and millions of unorganized Ameri-can workers in the mass-production industries were determined that employers would do just that. The AFL could no longer ignore all those unskilled workers—autoworkers, rubber, textile, mine, shipyard, packinghouse workers.

The fire Dobbs helped light had sparked intense debate among the federation's leadership as to whether and how to organize beyond craft boundaries—on a broad, industry-wide basis. The dispute erupted into fisticuffs at the AFL national convention in October of 1935. Early in the convention the executive council's stolid defenders of craft union-ism rejected repeated resolutions to organize the unorganized. Dan Tobin, for one, described as "rubbish" all workers who joined industrial unions.

Toward the end of the convention, John L. Lewis, the president of the United Mine Workers, brought matters to a head—the head of William Hutcheson, president of the Brotherhood of Carpenters and a leader of the AFL's Old Guard. Hutcheson had been engaging in par-liamentary-procedure shenanigans, interrupting supporters of indus-trial unionism with points of order.

"This thing of raising points of order all the time on minor dele-gates is rather small potatoes," Lewis declared. The two had had their run-ins before.

"Bastard," Hutcheson muttered.

Lewis's temper flared. He leapt to his feet, bounded over a row of chairs, and punched William Hutcheson "square on the nose."

Lewis's dramatic right jab struck a decisive blow for the partisans of industrial organization. Within a month, Lewis and the presidents of seven other AFL unions met to form the Committee for Industrial Organization under the banner of the AFL. When the CIO rejected the Old Guard's order to dissolve (and renamed itself the Congress of Industrial Organizations), the AFL in August 1936 suspended and later expelled the dissident unions.

The Teamsters under Tobin remained in the AFL fold. And even as Farrell Dobbs was finding it increasingly difficult to abide by the International's reactionary policies, he had one other brainstorm that would accomplish nothing less than upending the very balance of power between labor and capital. He grasped that no matter how many members his and the other Teamsters locals in the Midwest enlisted, until they had joint bargaining power—a master contract—the employers could continually shift their terminals to the lowest-wage cities. In 1937, Dobbs confederated the twelve-state region's seventy locals into a sort of supralocal: the North Central District Drivers Council. The following year, he negotiated a regional uniform contract for all over-the-road drivers. By decade's end, the Teamsters had grown to 420,000 members—most of them in Dobbs's Midwest and in the Pacific Northwest, where Dave Beck, who would succeed Tobin as Teamsters president, successfully emulated Dobbs's organizing tactics.

Watching with great interest the developments emanating from Minneapolis was Jimmy Hoffa. He had met Dobbs in 1934, when Hoffa was sent from Detroit to lend a hand during the bloody strike. Four years later he again worked with Dobbs, then as a member of the Detroit committee hammering out that first region-wide master contract. (Dobbs lauded Hoffa as "eager to learn and quick to absorb new ideas.")

Despite his trailblazing organizing, Farrell Dobbs was forced to quit the Teamsters in 1941, when his outspoken opposition to Roosevelt's war preparations proved too embarrassing to FDR's close friend Dan Tobin. Dobbs thereafter devoted himself to the Socialist Workers' Party (he would three times be its presidential candidate), and Jimmy Hoffa took over as negotiating chairman of the renamed Central States Drivers Council.*

---

*In a final ignominy, at Tobin's prompting, the government indicted Dobbs and a handful of the Minneapolis-based local's other officers under the 1940 sedition law known as the Smith Act. They were charged with conspiring to overthrow the U.S. government and creating insubordination in the armed forces. Dobbs and a co-conspirator were found guilty and were the first people imprisoned under the act.

• • •

In the fifteen years between the start of the war and the start of the McClellan Committee hearings, the International Brotherhood of Teamsters nearly tripled its numbers. And Jimmy Hoffa's star was rising as fast as the membership figures. Farrell Dobbs had forged the first rough master contracts; Hoffa set about burnishing, strengthening, broadening them. He rose in those fifteen years from business agent to president of Local 299 in Detroit to the International's ninth vice president to the heir apparent to the presidency of the union.

Much has been written about Hoffa's quick clamber on the Teamsters ladder, much of it concentrated on his ties to the crooks who facilitated his climb: Moe Dalitz and his Purple Gang in Detroit; Paul Dorfman of Chicago, a former associate of Capone's, and Dorfman's stepson, Allen; and, on the East Coast, members of the national crime syndicate (founded by Charles [Lucky] Luciano and Meyer Lansky), including Vito Genovese and Frank Costello. As intertwined as were Hoffa's Teamsters and organized crime, and as important as understanding these multilayered connections are to the sway the union held over the nation's economy, one other often overlooked factor weighed heavily: It wasn't only the threat of gangsterism upon which Hoffa built the union's power; it was the contracts he negotiated. Hoffa delivered. So long as he did so, so long as he kept delivering fatter pay envelopes, bigger pensions, longer vacations, safer working conditions, his membership, unlike the U.S. Senate and the executive council of the AFL-CIO, seemed to forgive him of any moral shortcomings. "Treat 'em right," Hoffa once explained, "and you don't have to worry."

But now, on this wet and wintry Friday morning in early December of 1957, the Teamsters president-elect had plenty to worry about. Not only was the AFL-CIO readying to vote in Atlantic City on the union's proposed expulsion, but Hoffa himself could not be there to plead its case. He was ninety miles away in New York, on trial on a wire-tapping charge. (Nor were those the only venues in which the Teamsters were under siege. In Seattle Dave Beck was being tried for grand larceny on a charge he had helped himself to $320,000 of union funds to build his home and swimming pool, and to pay off personal debts. In Washington, D.C., meanwhile, another battalion of Hoffa's lawyers was defending him in federal court in a suit brought by thirteen dissident

Teamsters who claimed that Hoffa's forces had rigged his election at the IBT convention in Miami Beach two months earlier. And also in Washington the ever-vigilant McClellan Committee was back on the case, questioning Hoffa's brethren from Tennessee about a $20,000 payoff with Teamsters funds to a state judge for fixing a criminal charge against union leaders.)

In Hoffa's stead to plead the Teamsters' case at the AFL-CIO convention was Einar Mohn, the union's vice president, and John English, the secretary-treasurer. Mohn spoke first, reminding the delegates in a dry, dispassionate voice of the Teamsters' "strategic importance" to the labor movement. "Nothing can change [that]," he said.

The tall, dour English neither asked for nor expected mercy. Instead, as one reporter put it, he "dispensed with supplication" and spoke emotionally, defiantly, about the labor movement's debt to his union. "How many times in your lives," he asked the delegates representing the 127 member unions, "if it hadn't been for the Teamsters would you have lost strikes and maybe you would not be here?"

Why, then, he persisted, were the Teamsters being punished?

"Some people don't like us because we are a big organization, and they are afraid we are going to be overpowerful," he said, pointing from a floor microphone to the dais, where George Meany and Hoffa's other avowed enemies—Walter Reuther of the United Auto Workers and James Carey of the International Union of Electrical Workers, in particular—returned English's flinty stare.

He softened his tone. "Oh, it makes my blood run cold," the venerable Teamster continued. "I am coming near the end of my days. I never thought I would live to see this."

When English sat down, not a single delegate rose from the floor to speak in favor of expulsion. Nor did any member of the executive council. "No one," reported one observer, "would bell the cat."

And so it was up to Meany. He allowed a few final tributes from Teamsters allies and then he himself rose to bury the body. Walking with a heavy limp due to a chronically sore heel, he crossed the dais to the lectern. Punching out short, plain sentences, the former plumber cut angrily to the heart of the matter. He sarcastically described the scene at the Teamsters convention when Hoffa ordered the reading of the federation's Ethical Practices Committee report. "They went through a performance, and they read . . . the report in an atmosphere of hilarity. They had quite a nice time doing it."

Then Meany told of one Teamsters vice president who was convicted of the cardinal sin of accepting bribes from an employer in return for breaking a strike. The man remained a vice president, Meany said.

"We have to free the membership from these men, from this dictatorship," Meany concluded. "The Secretary will call the roll. You vote yes or no."

Meany got far more than the two-thirds majority he needed. The vote was five to one in favor of expulsion.

Jimmy Hoffa heard the news in New York, where his wiretapping trial was under way. The AFL-CIO "didn't build us," he scoffed, "they won't weaken us."

SEVEN

"All Hell Broke Loose"

I T DIDN'T TAKE Mollie James long to feel the impact of the Teamsters expulsion. Mollie and her twelve hundred co-workers at Universal belonged to Teamsters Local 945, which had organized the plant in 1950, when Archie Sergy moved the company back to Paterson. Universal had been nonunion at its earlier sites, but by the time he opened the new plant, it was apparent to Archie that that was a luxury he could no longer afford. "Union electricians would install only union-made ballasts," Paul Einhorn recalls, "and so we basically invited the union in. I'm not even sure there was ever an election."

Local 945 then was an independent union chartered by the CIO; it would not affiliate with the International Brotherhood of Teamsters until April 1955. It was known in New Jersey as the "garbage local"— that is, its members worked primarily for concerns that collected trash and hauled waste. Universal had been Local 945's first big foray into industry. Mollie believed in the union, in the principle of collective action. "I had worked nonunion jobs in places where the boss would do whatever he wanted," she says. "A union gave us some protection, made him answer to us." She became a shop steward on the night shift, the first woman at Universal to hold that position. Representing grievants, filling out the paperwork, briefing union officials, was an added responsibility to her already demanding day—the youngest of her three children was an infant, and she also held down a second job—but she enjoyed the advocacy (and the perquisite of free dues) and she welcomed the opportunity to learn about her union. The more she learned, however, the less she liked.

By the summer of 1961, as Local 945's latest three-year contract with Universal was nearing expiration, she and others on the shop floor were upset with the Teamsters. Their dissatisfaction was not so much with their contract as with how their union allocated its resources. Instead of expending funds and time on supplemental bargaining or new organizing, the local was pouring money and muscle into a jurisdictional fight with a union affiliated with the AFL-CIO.

The problem of turf battles was thought to have been solved by the 1955 merger of the AFL and the CIO. A provision in the constitution stated that its president and executive council "shall seek to eliminate such conflicts and duplications through the process of voluntary agreement or voluntary merger between the affiliates involved." But that was before the Teamsters Union was sent packing.

If among George Meany's aims in banishing the Teamsters was to curb Jimmy Hoffa's power, in that regard he failed miserably. No longer did the Teamsters have to play by the AFL-CIO's no-raiding rules, and no longer did the union have to pay some $800,000 a year in dues to the federation; the money could be deployed toward raiding the jurisdictions of AFL-CIO unions. Even as an affiliate, the union was notorious for its strong-arm approach to jurisdictional disputes. Hoffa's Teamsters saw waging war on other unions as its passport to growth. "What we want we try to get," Hoffa once explained about his union's swelling membership. "What we get we keep."

Among the jurisdictions Mollie's own local "tried to get" was a factory called Duralite in Clifton, New Jersey, the Passaic County town that borders the southern limits of Paterson. The company made lightweight aluminum outdoor furniture—the inexpensive folding chairs with waterproof woven seats and seat backs suitable for the beach or patio. She knew her union played hardball. She'd followed the newspaper accounts and heard the shoptalk about the International's sordid reputation. And she knew her own local was teeming with dark secrets. Two years earlier, a garbage contractor in East

Orange, New Jersey, had testified before a state Senate committee that he signed a contract with Local 945 under threats to his children. The president of the local at the time, John V. Serratelli, received any number of kickbacks and favors from garbage contractors who wished to "keep on his good side." The New Jersey Municipal Garbage Contractors Association, for instance, purchased a thirty-thousand-dollar mortgage belonging to Serratelli's brother-in-law; the association hired Serratelli's son as counsel; and it made a point of recommending that association members buy their truck tires from a close friend of Serratelli's in Paterson.

Serratelli declined an invitation from the state Senate committee to tell his side of the story; by mid-April of 1959 he was under indictment for failing to answer the subpoena. Serratelli by then had also been indicted for conspiracy to rig a municipal garbage contract and for accepting a four-thousand-dollar bribe (payable to his wife in ten monthly installments) from a garbage hauler to guarantee labor peace. But all those charges were no longer of concern to him. In early March, state police had found his new black Cadillac abandoned at a rest stop on the Garden State Parkway. John Serratelli, who was fifty years old, was declared missing and presumed dead. His body was never found.

In June of 1959, Jimmy Hoffa transferred control of the local to the international union, placing it in trusteeship. The move was "necessary," the Teamsters secretary-treasurer said at the hearing on trusteeship, "for stability and security." To clean up the Local 945 mess, Hoffa appointed none other than Anthony (Tony Pro) Provenzano, a *caporegime,* or lieutenant, in Vito Genovese's crime family, one of New York's five Cosa Nostra organizations. Provenzano also served as president of Local 560 in Union City and Joint Council 73, the Teamsters umbrella organization for north Jersey. He was an accomplished strikebreaker, racketeer, murderer. He ran Local 560, and indeed the whole of north Jersey Teamsterdom, as an appendage of organized crime. During the two years Local 945 remained under his watch, Tony Pro was indicted for precisely what John Serratelli had been accused of—taking bribes for labor peace.

When the trusteeship expired in March 1961, Tony Pro named as incoming president Michael A. Ardis, whose career in the labor movement began in the silk mills of his native Paterson. Ardis, born in 1914, was one of eight children. His parents were Italian immigrants who settled on Mill Street in the Dublin section of Paterson. His father ran a grocery store, above which the family lived. "Too often there was nothing to eat," Ardis once told a reporter. "My mother went without shoes and my father cut the kids' hair to save what little money they could."

Ardis left school at the age of fourteen to hire on at a silk mill. It was 1928. The Depression blew through the following year, wiping out the mill, and Ardis took to scraping a living off the streets, shining shoes, selling newspapers, like most every young man in Paterson, Archie Sergy included. In 1931, at the age of seventeen, Ardis was hired as a hospital attendant. The AFL had just launched a health-care organizing drive in that field in New York and New Jersey, and Ardis pitched in. He evidently impressed someone on the field staff, who later recommended him for an organizing job with the Furniture Workers Union, which affiliated with the CIO after the split from the AFL in 1936. In 1939, Ardis was named the union's eastern seaboard representative.

After a stint as a sergeant in an armored division during the war, Ardis joined Local 945 as an organizer in 1947. Fourteen years later, he emerged at the top of the heap when Tony Pro blessed him with the presidency.

Ardis had developed a loyal following during his long, slow ascent to the presidency. "Mike was terrific," Mollie James says. "Very likable guy. And in the beginning, anyway, he would push for us. But when the troubles began over at Duralite, that's when we decided to try and make a change."

The troubles would not erupt until July of 1961, two months before Duralite's three-year contract with Local 485 of the International Union of Electrical Workers—the IUE—was to expire. But the company had had union-busting stars in its eyes for at least a year. Duralite was originally located in The Bronx, New York. In September 1960, as the company made its final preparations to relocate across the Hudson to an abandoned textile mill in Clifton, it simultaneously prepared to shed itself of the IUE.

The company hired a management consultant, one Edward Rohrbach, who approached the vice president of the Textile Workers Union of America, Sol Stetin, to feel him out about representing the

Duralite workers. Rohrbach told Stetin, who had been a dye-house worker and local union leader in Paterson, that Duralite would soon open with five hundred employees in a Clifton plant that had once been under contract to Stetin's union. Rohrbach said that Duralite was "having trouble" with the IUE local and "that the company was very unhappy with that union and could not continue doing business with it." He made it known the company was "shopping around for another union to do business with."

Stetin told Rohrbach he would get back to him. He immediately called an IUE lawyer, who apprised Stetin of the facts: that the plant ran away from New York City to escape the IUE. "Thank you very much," Stetin informed Rohrbach, "the Textile Workers Union of America is not interested in raiding a fellow AFL-CIO affiliate."

But the company was hardly ready to call off the search.

In the middle of March 1961, the very month Mike Ardis took the helm of Local 945, Duralite president Bert Lesser summoned his personnel director to his office. Lesser reiterated his "unhappiness" with the IUE local, and asked the personnel man, Joseph Opilla, "whether there was any other union they could bring [in]."

"I told [him] that in view of the AFL-CIO no-raiding policy, that it would be difficult to interest any union in this situation," Opilla later recalled.

But would a nonaffiliate be interested? Lesser pressed.

Opilla replied that "if they were going to bring another union in, they were asking for trouble."

They were asking for the Teamsters. They were asking for Tony Pro.

By late June, Local 945 organizers were loitering at the plant gates to induce IUE members to sign Teamsters cards calling for a representation election. When not a single Duralite worker signed a Teamsters card, the union and the company cooked up an astonishing scheme: Duralite ceded the right to hire to Local 945, instructing the union to recruit its members for employment.

The summer months were slow for the outdoor-furniture business. The season's orders had been filled, and it would not be until fall that production would gear up for the following year's orders. Duralite had recently laid off three hundred employees. And so it came as no small shock to the IUE when it learned that not only was the company about to hire fifteen workers, but they would come from the ranks of the rival Teamsters local.

On the morning after the Fourth of July, five carloads of Local 945 members arrived at the plant gates to provoke an IUE walkout. The Teamsters set up a picket line, they said, to help Duralite workers secure their independence from the tyrannical IUE, and to help the company's displaced workers in The Bronx, most of whom were Hispanic, win back their jobs.

While these self-styled freedom fighters picketed the plant, their accomplices were in The Bronx rounding up guileless union-busters. They found them via advertisements they placed that morning and the next in *La Prensa,* a Spanish-language newspaper in New York. The ads, signed by two Local 945 representatives with Hispanic surnames, were directed to "All Employees of Duralite."

ALL THE EMPLOYEES OF DURALITE COMPANY WORKING IN 120 EAST 144TH STREET, BRONX, AND NOW IN PASSAIC [ACTUALLY, CLIFTON], NEW JERSEY, SHOULD GO TO CLAIM THEIR JOBS WHICH THE COMPANY TOOK IN CONNECTION WITH LOCAL 485.

NEXT FRIDAY, JULY 7, 1961, AT 6:30 A.M., ALL THE EMPLOYEES WILL LEAVE TO THE DURALITE COMPANY IN PASSAIC, N.J. . . . TRANSPORTATION WILL BE AVAILABLE FOR EVERYBODY—ROUND TRIP.

Sure enough, that Friday the Teamsters arrived with fifteen recruits from The Bronx in tow. The company put them to work immediately, causing the intended effect: a work stoppage. The company announced that the plant was being shut—indefinitely. Duralite's IUE members took to the picket line, where they would remain for the balance of the summer.

Efforts at mediation failed, as did the intervention of the mayor of Clifton and the governor of New Jersey. Duralite apparently intended to conserve its cash during the slack season and maintain the lockout long enough to starve the IUE local out of existence.

By Labor Day, however, not a single Duralite worker had crossed the picket line. The fight turned to the local newspapers. The company placed ads in the Paterson papers for permanent replacement workers; IUE Local 485 placed ads urging prospective workers not to become strikebreakers. The union also aired radio spots and distributed twenty thousand leaflets explaining its position. The leaflet unflatteringly pictured three leaders of Local 945, Mike Ardis among them, with the headline: NOT WANTED . . . DEAD OR ALIVE. "No decent man or woman would touch them with a ten-foot pole," the text continued. "They would do anything for a buck and the Duralite Co. and bosses everywhere can rely on them for their dirty work. They are a disgrace to the whole Teamster union. They are a blot on the labor movement. They are agents of the bosses. They are enemies of the people."

Paterson was a proud old industrial union town, a CIO town, and union locals in the area, as well as the state labor federation, joined the IUE in denouncing the "scab-herding" of the company and the Teamsters. Duralite would have no luck recruiting local replacements.

That's when Tony Pro stepped in. Two days after Labor Day, the boss of Teamsters bosses in New Jersey dispatched seventy members from his headquarters at Local 560 in Union City to the Duralite plant. He had learned at the knee of some of the more notorious thugs in the metropolitan area about the potency of mixing organized crime with organized labor.

Tony Pro was born in 1917 to Italian immigrants living on the Lower East Side of New York City. He started driving a truck at eighteen, and befriended the family's next-door neighbor, a mobster named Tony Strollo who oversaw some Teamsters locals and who instated Tony as shop steward at the trucking company. Strollo (aka Tony Bender) was a *capo* in the Genovese family. In 1950, the year Universal opened in Paterson, Strollo reassigned his protégé to an organizing job at Local 560 in Union City. Over the next decade Tony Pro prospered in a mutually beneficial dual career track. He rose through the ranks to business agent and then president of Local 560, and from "soldier" to *capo* in the Genovese family.

Pro was short, stout and notoriously hot-tempered, with a barrel chest and "the puffed eyelids of one who used to fight," as the columnist Jimmy Breslin described him. His persona was as much gangster as Teamster, and he contributed greatly to melding the two lines of work in the popular imagination. He was, as Steven Brill wrote, "capable of atrocities that were right out of grade-B" movies—"like having one of his loan sharks killed but remembering to send his widow a Christmas card three weeks later."

When Pro was elected president in 1958, almost fourteen thousand members belonged to Local 560, which made it one of the largest of the Teamsters' 920 locals. It also made Pro an invaluable Eastern ally to Jimmy Hoffa, who had ascended to the general presidency the previous fall. Pro solidified the ranks in New York for Hoffa (in part by creating "paper locals"—locals with few or no members—to vote in elections to determine control of the region's joint councils), and Hoffa in turn facilitated Pro's lucrative and nefarious grabs for power and money. Tony Pro's appetite for both was as insatiable as his addiction to violence. It was said that he was "one of the few people on earth—and possibly the only one—whom Hoffa himself feared."

By Labor Day of 1961, Tony Pro was, after Hoffa, among the most powerful two or three officers of the International Brotherhood of Teamsters. He held three offices concurrently: president of Local 560; president of Joint Council 73, the union's north Jersey federation of some thirty-five locals; and a vice president and member of the executive board of the International union. Hoffa had appointed him to fill the vacant seat on the executive board at the International convention in July, at a time Pro was under indictment for extorting money from trucking companies in New Jersey in return for ending their labor troubles. (The three jobs together paid him a total of more than $100,000 a year—more than any other union official, including Hoffa, earned legally.)

Extortion was the least of Tony Pro's crimes that summer. A month before the Teamsters arrived at Duralite, Pro ordered the murder of Anthony (Three Fingers Brown) Castellito, the secretary-treasurer of Local 560 and a former ally of Pro's who planned to run against him on a "reform" ticket. On the night of June 3, Castellito was lured to a meeting at his own summer home in upstate New York. What he met was his death: Two of Tony Pro's associates, one from the union and one from the Genovese family, beat, strangled, and buried Castellito.* (Two years later, during Pro's extortion trial, another Local 560 dissi-

---

*Provenzano was indicted in 1976 for conspiring to murder Castellito. In 1978, he was convicted and sentenced to life in prison. He also was a prime suspect in the 1975 disappearance of Jimmy Hoffa, with whom he had had a falling-out. Provenzano died of a heart attack in 1988.

dent, Walter Glockner, whom the government had recruited as a witness, was murdered before his scheduled testimony. He was shot three times in the back. Tony Pro told reporters Glockner was "accident-prone.")

THE CONVOY Tony Pro dispatched to Duralite arrived at nine A.M. at the Barbour Avenue entrance, where they were met by resistant IUE picketers hell-bent on maintaining their jurisdiction. Within minutes, some two dozen police officers were on the scene, witnesses to the Teamsters' taunting and the IUE's counter-chest-thumping.

By early afternoon, the picket line had yet to be crossed; members of both unions and the police were milling around, waiting, interminably, it seemed to one participant, for someone to throw the first punch. "We knew they [the Teamsters] were getting ready because one of our guys saw them paying off the [police] captain on the scene," recalls Wallace Eisenberg, an IUE Local 485 organizer. "But we were determined to hold the line." Phil Chase, the civil rights veteran and Teamsters organizer, confirms that his union bought police protection. "We paid off the cops," Chase admits. "We thought that if they were going to take sides between us and the IUE, we wanted 'em on our side. Like when we fought with the IUE, we wanted to make sure our guys didn't go to jail."

Over the next week, the explosive situation detonated. With the help of daily police escorts of the strikebreakers' three chartered buses (and regular arrests of picketers, including Wally Eisenberg, who failed to clear the way), the Teamsters and Duralite management had succeeded in reopening the plant. But the IUE persisted, remaining on the line in full force, enduring the daily indignity of watching replacement workers imported from outside the region filling their jobs.

Late in the afternoon of the following Wednesday, September 13, a Teamster inside the plant gate spewed some obscenities at a woman on the picket line. Someone outside the gate returned the vile language with a stone aimed at the Teamster's vocal chords. Then, in the words of Clifton Police captain Joseph Nowak, "all hell broke loose."

Suddenly the months and weeks of frustration and anger and hunger blew up. From every direction and angle, inventive weaponry nearest at hand filled the air. Bottles, tools, chair legs, stones, spare parts, bricks, metal objects, nails: all in flight. From inside the plant, up on the roof, outside the gate, atop the fence, a firestorm of debris was raining on Duralite.

For more than an hour the no-holds-barred riot raged, and it was only when firefighters arrived to douse the participants with high-pressure hoses did the violence subside. In the end, sixteen persons were arrested and at least twenty injured, eight severely enough to warrant admittance to hospitals, including four police officers.

The Clifton chief of police declared a "state of emergency." He ordered a special detail of twenty-five officers to remain at the plant around the clock and requested backup from the state police. He also banned "all unauthorized persons" from the area of the plant gate, which effectively put an end to the picket line. "I will not tolerate mob rule," the chief explained.

"He literally read me the riot act," Wally Eisenberg recalls nearly four decades later. "We had labor law on our side, but the Teamsters had the powers-that-be in their hip pocket."

Just when Eisenberg thought he'd seen most of the malice in the allied Duralite-Teamsters' arsenal, there came one last time-honored dirty trick: red-baiting. Bert Lesser, the company president, charged in a statement printed in the *Paterson Morning Call* that the IUE was "Communist-dominated." The local union's lawyer, Irving Abramson, refused the bait. "There is only one issue in the Duralite strike," he told the newspaper. "That is whether the company will get away with firing all of its Passaic County employees and displace them with Teamsters from outside the county and state and who never worked for the company before."*

Meanwhile, the IUE's District 4, which represented eighty thousand members in northern New Jersey and New York, sent telegrams to all Teamsters locals in the region asking them to "repudiate the strike-

---

*There was rich irony to the charge that the IUE was a "Commie front" organization. A decade earlier, the IUE itself had engaged in a lengthy campaign to defame its rival United Electrical Radio and Machine Workers of America (UE) as "the Communist Party masquerading as a labor union."

breaking" of Local 945 on behalf of Duralite. Although it could not be determined whether any Teamsters locals formally replied to the IUE's request, it is known that at least one camp of Teamsters disavowed the rogue local. That camp were themselves dues-paying members of none other than Local 945—the rank-and-file at Universal Manufacturing. (Ultimately, however, Duralite rewarded the Teamsters for their inglorious activities with the mutually desired sweetheart contract.)

Throughout the summer of 1961, Mollie James and her co-workers had kept a close eye on their local's shameful activities. Their own contract with Universal was due to expire on October 3 and they had made it known to the IUE that they were open to its overtures, that they resented Local 945's diversion of their monthly five-dollar dues to bust another union. Plus, IUE Local 485 seemed to be everything Teamsters Local 945 was not: It had a reputation as a democratic union and it was in good standing with the AFL-CIO.

So when organizers for IUE Local 485 started whispering in the ear of Universal workers in mid-July, during the early stages of the lockout at Duralite, they found receptive, willing listeners. "We decided to challenge Teamsters shops in the hope they'd leave us alone," says Burt Caplan, who at the time was a thirty-four-year-old IUE organizer from Brooklyn whom the union had planted as its "eyes and ears" at Duralite. "So we quietly went after Universal, and the initial response was terrific." And when the IUE's wooing soon turned into a public flirtation, the Universal workers, forsaken for so many years by the Teamsters, embraced their new suitors with a passion reserved for the lovelorn.

The courtship began with a mimeographed one-page typewritten leaflet divided down the middle in half: The left-hand column was headed "IUE News"; the right, *"Noticia de IUE."*

"That was something different we noticed right off the bat," Mollie recalls. "We had a lot of Puerto Ricans in the plant and they [the IUE] made an effort to reach everyone. I think the people really appreciated that." Mollie did. She resigned as a Local 945 shop steward and pledged her support to the IUE.

The leaflet highlighted the IUE's strength: that it specialized in representing workers in electrical-components companies such as Universal. "We would not expect competent medical advice from a shoemaker; by the same token, workers in a manufacturing industry will always be treated as 2nd class citizens if they remain members of a 'catch all' branch of a truck drivers union."

Attached to that and subsequent daily leaflets were pro-IUE representation cards, which workers were asked to sign and return. After enough were collected to document sufficient interest, the IUE planned to petition the National Labor Relations Board (NLRB) for a certification election.

Teamsters leaders, publicly anyway, were initially so dismissive of their rivals that their response was no response—no leaflets, no organizers, no shop meetings. Its organizers were busy wreaking havoc at Duralite. "They figured the Universal thing was a bird in the hand, and they were going after the bird in the bush," says Nicholas Kourambis, who belonged to another Teamsters local and who would later that year be assigned as lead organizer on the Universal campaign.

So the IUE continued its barrage, its leaflets growing more incendiary by the day. "Workers tell us that 945 is the bosses' union; you don't dare open your mouth in the shop. You never see your union representative, and many workers don't even know what union they belong to. Grievances never seem to get settled, and Local 945 usually sides with the company against the workers."

It was a matter of faith and record that Local 945 was a "sweetheart" union at Universal. The company, after all, had *invited* the union in a decade earlier, and no substantive issues had arisen in the intervening years to sully the relationship. Employees received occasional wage increases of 2½¢ an hour, and sometimes as much as a nickel an hour; elsewhere in the electrical industry, the IUE was negotiating 10¢ to 15¢ increases. Wages at Universal ranged from $1.55 an hour to $3.75. There had never been a strike or slowdown at Universal, nor even, as best as could be determined, a *threat* of a work stoppage.

Had the IUE not reared its head, there is no way of telling how long the tidy arrangement at Universal would have lasted. But once the upstart union had the workers' ear, Local 945 needed to do *something*, anything, to show it was (even if it wasn't) something other than what it was being branded: a "do-nothing dues-collection agency." But like an incumbent officeholder, Local 945 needed to address its opponent's criticisms while appearing to remain, somehow, above the fray.

This required a bit of dramatic tension—tension orchestrated by the company and the union. And so Mike Ardis met privately with Archie Sergy to lay out the strategy.

"One day one of Ardis's underlings was raising hell with me, saying I was too hard on the workers," recalls Sig Steinberger, who was then a foreman. "Archie called me in and told me not to worry about it. 'He's just putting on a show for the workers.' "

The show wasn't very persuasive. By August 1, the IUE had collected enough workers' signatures to petition the NLRB for an election. A week later, an IUE leaflet helpfully informed Universal workers how their Local 945 organizers—the men whose salaries the workers paid—spent the previous day.

"Were they in Universal taking care of your grievances and problems? NO, they were in Clifton, trying to help Duralite bring in a scab. . . .

"Is this a union that can be trusted? We say a union that tries to bring in scabs for one employer will do this for any employer. Yes, maybe even Universal."

As Labor Day passed, and with it the increasingly more militant efforts of Duralite to resume production, the IUE ensured that Universal workers were kept abreast of developments at Duralite. "Again today [Tuesday, September 6], Local 945 Teamsters brought many strikebreakers to Duralite," reported the IUE's afternoon update from the front. "With the aid of the Clifton police, 945 was able to sneak some of their scabs into the plant." It was the following day that the company opened its arms to the seventy Teamsters on loan from Tony Pro's Local 560. "Using hoodlum tactics, these miserable creatures have bullied their way into Duralite, where they sit playing cards all day," the IUE reported.

As the Duralite lockout reached a boiling point, the IUE could not remind Universal workers enough times of their forced contribution to the woes of their union brethren in Clifton. "YOUR DUES MONEY IS USED TO BREAK STRIKES," one leaflet stated. "These animals draw their pay and get new cars from YOUR dues money. Are these strikebreakers, who use your dues money against working people, the kind of union you want to represent you?"

The question would be answered on October 26, the date the NLRB set for the election at Universal. In the week or so immediately preceding the election, the Teamsters and the company jointly waged a whisper campaign in a last-ditch effort to slow the IUE's momentum. Foremen and supervisors passed on "rumors" that if the IUE won, the company would refuse to negotiate a contract and lock out the workers as Duralite did; that it would discriminate against or even fire IUE supporters; that it would consider moving away from Paterson, as Duralite did from The Bronx.

The scare tactics probably worked. Although the IUE announced a "$1000 Reward" for anyone who could prove those rumors were true, and emphasized that the vote would be conducted "by secret ballot under the supervision of the United States Government," the murmured threats intimidated some wobbly IUE supporters. The ballot offered three choices: Teamsters Local 945; IUE Local 485; neither union. The IUE polled 392 votes, 45 more than the Teamsters, but the IUE's margin of victory fell far short of the majority needed, and so the NLRB called a runoff election, to be held twenty-one days later, on November 16.

After their near first-round knockout, the Teamsters came out swinging—with fistfuls of cash. Tony Pro, who had miscalculated the IUE's strength, took a more hands-on approach, loaning Local 945 three of his best organizers. Their orders were to buy the election—to spend whatever it took to persuade workers and management alike that the Teamsters ought to remain Universal's union.

    The first organizer to sign on for the furious three-week campaign was Nick (The Greek) Kourambis. Kourambis was an ebullient, outspoken man possessed of strong democratic values, a trait that sometimes put him at odds with the New Jersey Teamsters leadership. He'd had his ups and downs with the union since the middle 1950s, when as chief steward for Local 863 at a Grand Union supermarket in Carlstadt, ten miles southeast of Paterson, he challenged the local's discriminatory hiring practices. "The local didn't want to respect the seniority of black workers when it came to upgrading jobs," Kourambis says. "And I fought it on principle, plain and simple: This guy's got the seniority, he's next in line for the job."

    Neither the Teamsters nor the company saw it that way, and Kourambis found himself out a job. "I became trouble for 863, I became trouble for Grand Union, and I was forced out of the picture." He was blackballed from the union for his stance on civil rights. His courage endeared Kourambis to the Passaic chapter of the National Association for the Advancement of Colored People, which honored him for his work on behalf of the black Grand Union workers, many of whom lived in Passaic.

But Kourambis could not pay rent with a plaque, and with a wife and three children at home, he was having a hard time making it. He asked his Teamsters friends to keep an eye out for jobs, and in the meantime could find only weekend restaurant work. He waited tables, a job without benefits.

He eventually was hired as a trailer driver for a freight hauler based on the Clifton-Passaic border. It was a Local 560 job, with good pay and benefits, but no guarantee of steady work. He and the other drivers had to appear every morning at the "shape-hall"—the hiring hall. "You had to be there at six A.M. and you might or might not work."

There, too, Kourambis encountered the same exclusionary policies over which he'd lost his supermarket job. He would usually drive at least two or three days a week, but his black friends were routinely denied the high-paying drivers' jobs. This time, though, instead of simply raising hell about the racist Teamsters, Kourambis and his friends came up with a "gimmick." Their idea was to piggyback on the government's postwar Marshall Plan, which appropriated huge sums for the reconstruction of western Europe.

"We sat around talking about how the Army was moving personnel all over Europe, into this country, out of that country, and how somebody had to move all those soldiers' furniture," Kourambis says. "Which meant the trucking industry." A little research determined that many of the trucking concerns right under their noses in northern New Jersey were delivering furniture to an Army installation in the Bushwick section of Brooklyn. "So we said, OK, who's paying for all this? The government. Us. Our taxes. Then how come the union isn't putting qualified black drivers into those jobs?"

With that insight, Kourambis and his friends approached Tony Pro through an intermediary, Mike Ardis of Local 945. Ardis was known as a progressive on civil rights and as someone to whom Pro listened. Pro himself was a reactionary on racial issues, but his political instincts were sound. Kourambis: "Mike went to Tony and convinced him it would be to his benefit to break the Jim Crow door down, that he'd have a lot of people in his corner for reelection if he supported this."*

Not everyone rejoiced at the breakthrough. Notably angry were some members of the executive board of Local 560. Their ire was directed at Nick Kourambis, whom they accused of pandering to blacks and to President Kennedy, who remained a vilified figure for his and his brother's persecution of Hoffa. But Tony Pro, who himself was under indictment on the extortion charge, was less concerned about heat from his own executive board than he was about the relentless scrutiny from the Robert Kennedy–led Justice Department. If a concession on civil rights sent a signal to the Kennedys, so much the better. So Tony watched Nick's back. "Plenty of guys were pissed at me, *really* pissed," Kourambis says. "So I had to be careful." But he also had "godfathers" who would tell him, "If you need help, Greek, just let us know."

Kourambis had clawed his way back to a rarefied if precarious position with the union. He championed minority rights in a Teamsters joint council that was notoriously hostile to social change, and he did so by winning the support of Tony Pro, the only ally who truly mattered.

Here was just the man Mike Ardis needed to inject life into the Teamsters' moribund campaign at Universal. Kourambis had street smarts and charisma and energy and tenacity. And unlike his own Local 945 team of organizers and business agents, whom the IUE had done such a fine job of demonizing, Kourambis had credibility with rank-and-filers. No sooner had the labor board counted the ballots at Universal than Ardis dialed Kourambis's number. "Nick, I need your help." Ardis explained that he had three weeks to right a sinking ship, that he wanted Kourambis at the helm, and that Tony Pro would arrange for Kourambis to take leave-time from his job at the freight hauler.

Kourambis took the assignment and brought with him two orga-

---

*Pro and Ardis later fell out over jurisdictional disputes. "They had overlapping organizing areas," says Ardis's son, Michael Jr. "Pro was the power in the area and he didn't like it when there was someone on his turf."

nizing dynamos he knew from the Local 560 shape-hall, Phil Chase and Richie Sergeant. Both were black, and both were well known in Paterson for their civil rights work. Chase chaired the Labor and Industry Committee of the Passaic County NAACP; Sergeant would go on to head the local chapter of CORE, the Congress of Racial Equality. (In a display of solidarity the previous February with the students who were sitting in at the Woolworth's lunch counter in Greensboro, North Carolina, Chase and Sergeant were among those who picketed the Woolworth's on Main Street in Paterson.)

Tony Pro issued the new Local 945 team a mandate: "Mike [Ardis] must win this election." With the mandate came an unlimited budget for the campaign. "Where it came from, how it got there, we didn't know and we didn't care," Kourambis says. Pro did not disclose why the Universal election was so critical, but Kourambis knew the reason must have transcended the union's bitter rivalry with the AFL-CIO and its affiliates.

He was unsurprised to learn the reason: numbers-running, a lucrative and difficult-to-trace mode of gambling that produced suspiciously few winners. "We picked up a rumor that there was a million dollars of numbers being played [in the plant] every year," Kourambis says. "Somebody controlled it. The numbers played by the workers went to somebody." To Tony Pro, Kourambis suspected. "We knew Tony's right-hand man collected the numbers. There was a diner he'd meet you at every day." The payoff was determined by the last three numbers in the last race at whatever New York–area track was operating. If the amount, for example, wagered in the last race at Aqueduct was $3,280,120, as reported in the *Daily News,* the winning numbers were 1-2-0.

Among the first persons Kourambis contacted was the fellow in the plant who carried the numbers to Tony Pro's bag man. "We got to the main numbers carrier early, and he was on our side, of course. And he had a lot of influence over the people because he was also a little bit of a loan shark. He worked in the shop, but he didn't do a damn thing because even some of the foremen were playing numbers. And so we won the foremen over, because we found out a couple of them owed our guy a lot of money, too."

Unions normally begin organizing campaigns with basic research. They look over the plant: the location of the doors, the bays, the time-clock. And they check the neighborhood: the diner and bars where workers eat and drink. They note working conditions and shop-floor grievances and investigate where management's (or a rival union's) pressure points are. They study the plant's demographics. Most of the Universal members were black and Hispanic, save for the higher-paid machinists, who were predominantly whites. Like skilled workers elsewhere, the machinists at Universal were not strong union supporters, and so the issue of racial inequity in those jobs was ripe for exploitation. "We had nothing to lose, so we suggested to Tony [Pro] that he make a commitment to opening some of these jobs to minorities, and that he allow us to say that in our leaflets," Kourambis recalls.

That single leaflet signaled that this organizing drive would be ordered on a style vastly different from the union's traditionally imperial approach. Normally, a Teamsters business agent, clad in sharkskin suit and pinky ring and smoking a fat cigar, would cruise to the curb of the plant gate in his Cadillac, roll down the window, and hand out pro-union cards to the workers at shift change. "And people did sign up," Kourambis says, "because they were impressed with the Cadillacs and the suits and the cigars. And that's the way it was done—easy. In and out."

But this would not be easy. The IUE organizers were aggressive and effective and unintimidated; they had embarrassed the Teamsters into dressing down and abandoning their Cadillacs. One IUE leaflet praised Universal for its "terrific showing" of eleven million dollars in sales the previous year but criticized the Teamsters for failing to ensure that the workers shared in the bounty. "All we got in 1960–61 is a measly $2 a week raise . . . [while] the company enjoyed high profits and the boss drives around in a big Cadillac. And the big shots of Local 945 Teamsters who made the $2 deal with management, they're doing all right for themselves, too. . . ."

Never had the Teamsters been so attentive. Organizers bought rounds for the house at the nearby Fifth Avenue Tavern; they lingered at the diner before and after shift changes. "If we saw ten or fifteen people eating their lunches," Kourambis says, "we'd pick up the tabs. And we'd leave a 945 card or a button or leaflet with them." They threw a "Member-Appreciation Dinner" and Saturday night dance parties. And they were up early on Sundays to make the rounds of churches. "I gave witness from my own experience with the Teamsters," says Phil Chase.

Chase could not recall whether the Teamsters paid off any pastors in exchange for delivering their flocks to the polls, but given their deep pockets and the fact that payola was standard operating procedure for securing votes, it would seem likely that that was the case. Like a desperate politician in the eleventh-hour throes of a tight race, the Teamsters kissed a lot of babies and promised the moon.

But unlike most politicians, the Teamsters did more than promise the moon—they delivered it. They set up a file-card system, one card per voter, and visited as many members as possible, hundreds and hundreds, at their homes. (Some 850 Universal workers belonged to Local 945.) "House calls" were par for gauging support during union campaigns, but the Teamsters had in mind a different purpose for the visitations. What they had in mind was sheer bribery; they would size up a worker's tattered finances and mend them on the spot. "We took care of people's rents," Kourambis says. "We took care of their payment on their refrigerators, of their lighting bills."

That's where the bottomless bank account Tony Pro provided paid off. Kourambis and his organizers were weighted down with pockets overstuffed with cash, and they made it known that when they dropped by a member's house, all the member would have to say was something like, "Gee, I like the Teamsters, can they help me out?"

"Boom," says Kourambis. "We'd take care of 'em."

The IUE was aware of the payoffs, but it had neither the inclination nor the resources to match the Teamsters. "The workers told us time and again they were taken care of," recalls Burt Caplan. "One guy told me he really needed the money. I said, 'Fine, but you can still vote for IUE.' But he was scared the vote would not really be a secret ballot."

Other workers who took advantage of the Teamsters' philanthropy felt a moral obligation to vote for the Teamsters. "It was as if once they accepted the bribe, the honorable thing to do was vote for the Teamsters," Caplan says.

The Teamsters complemented the back-room maneuvers by matching the IUE leaflet for leaflet at the plant gate. The Teamsters' lackluster record of representation at Universal was nothing to boast about, and the Teamsters rarely did. Instead, they depicted themselves as toughs who never backed down from a fight. This was most evident during the daily confrontations with the IUE over position at the gate during shift changes, when the time came to distribute the day's leaflets. "We'd be on one side, the IUE on the other," says Phil Chase.

"It made so the workers almost walked a gauntlet and we'd watch which pamphlets hit the ground."

There were usually about six or eight organizers on either side of the gate, and if workers emerged from the plant expecting to see a brawl, they were rarely disappointed. "We used to show them our fists," Kourambis recalls, "and we'd get into catcalls back and forth, filthy language, real bad stuff: 'You fuckin' raiders, you're causing trouble for the people here; they don't want your fucking ass around.' We put them on the defensive, since they were the raiders.

"They'd come in with their thugs, we came in with our thugs. And we used to pass around bank coin rolls, two for each guy, one for each fist, and we had baseball bats, and it became a little violent. We had to show the people the Teamsters will fight for your rights, and will protect you. We used to say, 'See these guys? They don't belong here, they're outsiders. We live here in Paterson.' "

What Kourambis meant was that the Teamsters again resorted to branding the IUE as agitators come to paint the plant red. "**The False Victory,**" the Teamsters called the first election. "Through false promises, lies and unfounded accusations—the Red tactics of the Brooklyn Boys [the IUE district office was located there] have set brother against brother, neighbor against neighbor, and worker against worker. . . . They have used every Red-tainted trick in the book—trying to divide and rule."

The Teamsters' demagoguery knew no bounds. They portrayed the election as an explicit loyalty test: that a vote for the IUE was a vote against the American Way. A leaflet titled "**LEARN THE TRUTH!** FACTS vs. COMMUNIST LIES" spelled out "ONE DOZEN GOOD REASONS TO KICK THESE LEADERS OF LOCAL 485 BACK TO RED RUSSIA!!!!!" Among them: that the president of Local 485 had twenty years earlier attended a meeting in New York City of the American Peace Mobilization—"a subversive organization!!!!"—and that the meeting was covered by the *Daily Worker*; that the local's business agent had pleaded the Fifth Amendment in questioning before the infamous House Committee on Un-American Activities; and that the local's lead organizer, Wallace (alias "Wally") Eisenberg, "has been working with these recorded **Reds** for a long time."

These are facts from official government records!!!!
These are facts which put the Red, Communist Noose

firmly around the necks of these so-called leaders of Local 485!!!!

The loyal American workers of Universal now have their eyes open!!!—they will not be fooled anymore by Red lies!!!!! They will not be misled by Commie sympathizers!!!

The loyal American workers of Universal don't want any part of Communists or Red-led unions!!!!!

The Workers of Universal will go forward with Local 945 International Brotherhood of Teamsters—a union of, by, and for loyal American workers!!

The IUE countered by invoking the memory of Franklin D. Roosevelt. "In the labor movement, Local 485 IUE finds itself in the same position as FDR," intoned a leaflet headed "An Honor to Be IN GOOD COMPANY."

Throughout the electrical and machine industry in New York and New Jersey, Local 485 is beloved by thousands of workers who have been brought out of sweat shop conditions through the ceaseless efforts of our Local Union. . . .

But like President Roosevelt, Local 485 has incurred the wrath of many enemies of the working people—. . . people who would destroy decent labor unions. These forces also try to smear Local 485 as being communistic because we refuse to let up on our program to improve the conditions of the working people and demand equal treatment for all Americans.

The warnings about the un-American IUE, the jingoistic drums the Teamsters beat incessantly, struck a chord among Universal's many first- and second-generation immigrants, whose patriotism had been heightened by the ordeal of war and the rhetoric of Cold War. And so the IUE was forced to issue statement after statement defending its record of democratic unionism.

"CAN'T SUBSTITUTE RED FOR BREAD," one retort began.

"Are good wages and working conditions RED?

"Is it RED to want to be with the rest of the workers in the largest union in the electrical industry?

"Is it RED to want to put an end to Universal-945 back door deals?

"The Teamsters have too much 'housecleaning' to do before they can call anyone else names. Working people want homes, decent union-ism, not name calling. That's why Universal workers are joining the IUE landslide."

In addition to its main theme that the Teamsters were corrupt and out of touch with the membership, the IUE also sought to portray its opponent as unconcerned about the black and Hispanic workers at Universal. The Teamsters answered with a shrewd ploy.

On Saturday, November 4, twelve days before the election, Local 945 threw a "friendship dinner dance gala" at a rented hall. In a shameless attempt to ingratiate themselves with the many Puerto Rican members, the Local 945 leadership invited as "special guest" the Puerto Rican middleweight boxer Jose Torres, upon whom they bestowed honorary membership in the local. Torres, in turn, accord-ing to a Teamsters press release the *Paterson Morning Call* must have printed verbatim, "lauded [Mike] Ardis for . . . his deep concern and understanding for the many Puerto Ricans represented by Local 945." The appearance fee Torres earned is lost to history. Says one Teamster who witnessed his performance: "You can bet it was more than he ever made for a fight." The blatant—and potent—pandering to Hispanic voters was reiterated the following weekend in the pages of *El Obser-vador,* the Spanish-language weekly for Paterson. In a paid message masquerading as an unsigned editorial, *El Observador* observed that the AFL-CIO was founded to organize the unorganized, "but that up until now they have only succeeded in disorganizing the organized." (A month earlier, the AFL-CIO had rejected a proposal to readmit the Teamsters.*) Following a few heroic paragraphs on Teamsterism, the "editorial" arrived at its destination: the Universal election. "The workers at Universal know what they have now, but besides promises what is IUE offering? . . . Common sense dictates that a bird in the hand is worth 100 in the bushes. . . . Don't gamble with your wages! Don't gamble with your jobs! Protect your families! *El Observador* strongly urges the support of . . . Local No. 945. . . ."

The morning after *El Observador* hit the streets, the *New York Times* published a front-page story Local 945 thought so timely it photo-

---

*George Meany remained firm in his resolve that the Teamsters would remain in exile as long as Jimmy Hoffa headed the union. Hoffa could never hope for read-mission, Meany declared, "unless he did what Saul or Tarsus did—go off into the wilderness for a year and repent."

copied and distributed it as a companion piece. Headlined NEGRO UNION HEAD SCORES AFL-CIO, the article reported a speech by A. Philip Randolph, the distinguished black labor leader, condemning the AFL-CIO for its "do-little civil rights record." Randolph, president of the Brotherhood of Sleeping Car Porters, was the lone black on the AFL-CIO's executive council.

Local 945 attached the story to a leaflet titled "WHO'S SOFT ON CIVIL RIGHTS???" The leaflet quoted more remarks disparaging of the AFL-CIO from other well-known civil rights leaders, including Roy Wilkins of the NAACP and Martin Luther King Jr. of the Southern Christian Leadership Conference. "Any impartial observer watching the Universal workers streaming in and out of the plant would never think of accusing the Union which has represented you for many years of being soft on the rights of minority groups.

"Yet Local 485 IUE, AFL-CIO has again tried to confuse workers by raising this issue, patting themselves on the back and giving Local 945 TEAMSTERS a slap in the face. Surely they must think that the workers at Universal can't see for themselves, can't think for themselves."

Nick Kourambis and his crew had managed to shift the momentum to the Teamsters. They had worked hard, if scurrilously, and shown themselves to be accomplished propagandists. In the words of Kourambis himself, "what we did was, I must say, very clever, if unscrupulous." He was referring specifically to the payoffs made to members during the home visits. It wasn't only the Universal workers who profited from the Teamsters' largesse. As election day neared, the union also reputedly bribed the regional office of the labor board, based in Newark, which was to conduct the runoff election. "They were crooked," Kourambis says. "They could be bought." Were they? "Sure, that's what I was told. The Teamsters loved the Newark office. At that time they were our best friend."

In the end, their best friend appeared to look the other way when, according to the IUE's lead organizer, the Teamsters slipped in "fifty or sixty" *former* employees to cast ballots. If this was so (and no corroborating evidence could be obtained), it would go a long way toward explaining the outcome: The Teamsters received 435 votes; the IUE, 375—a difference of 60 votes. "We fought hard and we were honest to a fault, and that's why we lost," says Wally Eisenberg, still disturbed about those events of 1961. "There was no way to beat the collusion between the Teamsters, the labor board, and Universal."

On the Sunday afternoon after their win, the Teamsters' organizing team gathered in Mike Ardis's office for a final debriefing—and for an anticipated cash reward for the stunning victory. "We expected a bonus from Mike," recalls Nick Kourambis. "After all, he's flashing all kinds of money during the election, and we saved his million-dollar operation. We figured maybe a thousand dollars apiece."

Ardis indeed congratulated Kourambis and his men for a job well done. "You guys take a paid week off," Ardis directed, "and I'll tell Tony you'll go back to work after that." And, he added, "here's a little extra for your hard work."

Ardis reached into his left pants pocket as the organizers watched expectantly. "He couldn't get his hand out because it was stuffed so full with hundred-dollar bills," Kourambis says. "He finally pulls out, and it must have been this big"—Kourambis pushes together his ten meaty fingertips—"and he leafs through it and couldn't find any fifty-dollar bills. So he puts the roll in his jacket pocket. Then he goes to his right pants pocket and pulls out the fifty-dollar wad. 'Here's fifty dollars for each of you guys.' "

Though he was pleased with the outcome, the election shook Archie Sergy. The IUE would disappear for now, but for how long? Would they be back come contract-expiration time? And what of the Teamsters? Would the mud slung at them stick? Could they return to backroom business as usual, or were the members so agitated, so fed up with the years of sellouts and the latest perversion of their dues money, that they would have no choice but to enter into legitimate contract negotiations?

In fact, the Teamsters did display a new verve. Following a holiday cease-fire, in mid-January Mike Ardis presented Archie with a list of sixteen demands, among them an across-the-board wage increase of twenty-five cents per hour (a rate the IUE had proposed); overtime after eight hours; severance pay of a week's wages for each year of employment; more vacation days; a pension plan; and pay retroactive to October 4, 1961, the day after the contract expired. Ardis backed up the demands with some heated and unprecedented rhetoric. He even uttered a word he used disparagingly during the campaign against the IUE to warn members what could happen if the IUE were allowed to introduce its "red" and reckless confrontational tactics. Local 945 will "get these benefits for our workers," Ardis declared, "even if it takes a strike."

No strike was called, but on Saturday, January 20, the membership did overwhelmingly pass a resolution calling for a walkout unless Universal agreed within seventy-two hours to "bargain in good faith." With the help of a federal mediator, the company and the union came to terms on an eighteen-month contract providing for a wage increase of sixteen cents an hour. Most of the other demands were tabled.

Early in the morning of Saturday, February 24, 1962, one month after she had voted to ratify the new contract, Mollie James picked up her newspaper, the *Morning Call,* to catch up on the adventures of astronaut John Glenn, "America's Lindbergh of the Space Age," who the previous day had returned to Florida after his three-orbit flight around the earth. Alongside President Kennedy at Cape Canaveral, and under the banner headline, SPACE TRAVEL 'PLEASANT'—GLENN, the hero-astronaut flashed his broad grin and a double thumbs-up sign as his motorcade rode through a "tumultuous welcome."

As Mollie excitedly scanned the coverage (as well as a top-of-the-page teaser, 'FRANKLY, MY HUSBAND'S A BORE!' WIFE SAYS, SEE PAGE 18), her eyes widened on a one-column item in the lower-left quarter of the front page. Suddenly, John Glenn's description of spectacular sunsets and sparkling oceans was as remote as the dark side of the moon.

UNIVERSAL TO BUILD DIXIE PLANT, Mollie read, her jaw dropping like a space capsule reentering the earth's atmosphere. The story began:

"The Universal Manufacturing Co. of 29 East Sixth St., confirmed . . . reports that it will build another plant about 35 miles south of Jackson, Miss.

"Archie Sergy, president of the firm, said there are no plans to move the local plant—which employs 1,200 workers—outside Paterson. 'I have lived in Paterson all my life,' he said, 'and if we have no problems we don't intend leaving.' "

Part II

Mississippi

EIGHT

Biscuits and Bond Issues

T HAT MORNING'S edition of Mississippi's statewide newspaper, the *Clarion-Ledger*, bumped aside the major national story (CAPE, ENTIRE NATION IN ORBIT FOR GLENN), for a leader on a tornado that had touched down in Vicksburg, about forty miles east of Jackson. The editors also found space above the fold (though not on a level with the photo of a beaming Glenn) for a headline echoing that of the morning's Paterson paper: TWO INDUSTRIES COMING SOUTH.*

The *Clarion-Ledger* reported that Universal would ultimately employ up to a thousand people in Simpson County, which would make it "one of the largest employers of the state." The story quoted Governor Ross Barnett, who "wish[ed] to thank all Mississippians who have worked so hard to bring Universal . . . into the state." He continued: "The plant will add greatly to the further diversification of Mississippi industry and is another milestone in the [state's] industrial development."

• • •

*The other was a textile manufacturer from Chicago, heading to Shaw, Mississippi.

Twenty-two months later, on December 14, 1963, most everyone—everyone who counted—was there. And not just from Mendenhall and Magee, the rivalrous siblings anchoring the northern and southern ends of Simpson County, but from the outlying villages: Pinola and Sanatorium and D'Lo and Braxton and Harrisville and Merit. And they came despite the terrible weather—it didn't merely sleet in the middle of the night; it poured what seemed like fully formed sheets of ice. They came to this strange, sprawling mecca of corrugated metal and brick plunked down on a former gravel pit on U.S. Highway 49, smack between Mendenhall and Magee in the piney woods of south central Mississippi, to celebrate the grand opening of their county's first industrial employer: Universal Manufacturing.

Following the invocation, the day's festivities commenced with the playing of the national anthem by the combined high school bands of Mendenhall and Magee—itself no small feat of diplomacy—and ended with box lunches and guided tours of the shiny plant. In between there was all manner of speechifying and bow-taking by local politicians, plant managers, and state economic-development officials. Also appearing was governor-elect Paul B. Johnson Jr., an ardent segregationist who was swept into office the previous month on a wave of support from Ross Barnett, his notorious predecessor. It was Barnett himself who had led the negotiations with Archie Sergy. And on this Saturday it was Barnett and Archie who jointly cut the ceremonial ribbon.

Archie had flown down from Paterson to Jackson the previous afternoon, in time to attend a celebratory banquet at the Jacksonian, the city's best restaurant. And earlier on this Saturday morning he was treated to a traditional Southern breakfast in the elegant whitewashed Governor's Mansion. But Governor Barnett's hospitality extended beyond eggs and bacon, grits and biscuits and gravy. Archie was there sopping up the state's cheap, nonunion labor and its tax-free benefits to new industries, as well as a million-dollar-plus bond issue floated by the voters of Simpson County. Near the conclusion of the opening ceremonies, Archie rose to speak. He expressed his "gratitude for the cooperation Universal had received since its inception" and predicted a "long and prosperous relationship between Universal and Simpson County."

●　　●　　●

What brought Archie to Mississippi was the state's industrial-recruitment program, known as Balance Agriculture with Industry, or BAWI. Although by the early 1960s all the Southern states had established similar incentive programs, the concept was formulated in Mississippi a quarter century earlier. The state's Depression-era governor, a bushy-browed lumberman named Hugh L. White from the small southern Mississippi town of Columbia, had seen his own business fail during the late 1920s. Several years before the Depression rendered the same scene in every town in America, White's eight hundred sawmill employees were out of work and facing foreclosure or eviction. White was forced to close his mills when the forests disappeared; he and the other lumbermen had failed to retain enough trees for reseeding and were left with land so eroded it would take a generation or more to restore.

Hugh White, who was elected mayor of Columbia in 1929, took blame for the demise of his town's economy and sought to reverse its fortunes through diversification. He contacted a plant relocation consultant in Chicago, who found a textile manufacturer willing to move to Columbia if the town could collect eighty-five thousand dollars to construct a building. The company, in turn, vowed to put three hundred people to work, mainly women, and pay out a million dollars during its first ten years in business. Once those obligations were met, the company would own the building.

The plan worked from the start, reviving Columbia, pumping life into its commercial district, attracting other industries. Hugh White began spreading the gospel of industrial subsidies to other chambers of commerce around the state, and in 1931 declared his candidacy for governor. He lost, but ran again four years later. That time he won, on a pledge to "Balance Agriculture with Industry."

Governor White formally introduced his BAWI plan at the convention of the Mississippi Press Association in June 1936. As he saw it, the state had much to offer new industry, principally its "lowered manufacturing costs" and abundance of "efficient and intelligent labor," a "high percentage" of which was "our native Anglo-Saxon citizenship, with an absence of disturbing elements so common in larger industrial centers."

But Mississippi was not unique in that regard: All the Southern states could boast of similar attributes. Mississippi needed an edge to distinguish itself from its competitive neighbors. What Hugh White came up with was a bill to authorize the state's counties and municipalities to "erect, build, purchase, rent or otherwise acquire industries [and] factories . . . and to conduct and manage these on behalf of the citizens of such counties and municipalities."

White also proposed that local governing bodies be allowed to issue bonds to finance construction of factories. The bonds would be backed by the full faith and credit of the county or city, and the interest paid would be tax-exempt. The governor anticipated opposition from those who were concerned that local debt burdens were already too high. This was no time for timidity, he declared, "something must be done." "If your community could invest Fifty to Sixty Thousand Dollars and secure an average payroll of $200,000.00 a year, do you not think that would be a real investment for the general public welfare?"

Building to a dramatic finish, White offered the roomful of newspaper moguls a recent history lesson. "When we hear that our state has lost within recent years over two percent of its population; when we observe that agricultural development is paralyzed; we know that our present industries will soon close down by reason of the passing of the natural resources used by such industries, I believe that the great public interest demands the enactment of this plan for bringing immediate and lasting prosperity to our people." Just because nothing of this sort had ever been attempted was no reason not to try it, he argued. To the contrary, White argued, if this plan is "a step further than has heretofore been taken, than I, for one, urge the taking of that step to the end that our commonwealth may be saved, may prosper and may continue to shine as one of the brightest stars in Old Glory's field of blue."

White's BAWI plan, which the legislature passed late in 1936, probably did save Mississippi. Between 1937 and 1940, the Mississippi Industrial Commission oversaw construction of twelve plants built with BAWI funding. The most successful of these early BAWI plants was in the Gulf Coast city of Pascagoula, which passed a $100,000 bond issue in 1938 to build a plant for the Ingalls Ironworks Shipyard. When the war buildup began soon thereafter, government orders necessitated rapid expansion; at its peak the yard employed some twelve thousand workers.

After the war, other Southern states hopped on Mississippi's band-wagon. Tennessee, Kentucky, and Alabama, to name a few, all passed laws authorizing the creation of public industrial-development corporations that could issue bonds to finance and build manufacturing plants for lease to private business. By 1962, the year Universal announced its plant in Mendenhall, nine Southern states had established such programs.

These programs had their critics. Within the South, farmers decried the loss of their field hands to factory jobs, while others protested that public support of private industry smacked of socialism. Up North, the most vocal critics were union members, who saw their employers deserting them for a region where organized labor was taboo. What compounded labor's irritation was that Mississippi's BAWI and its Southern brethren's counterpart industrial-recruitment programs were given federal blessing to extract Northern jobs—by way of a tax policy that bestowed exempt status for the interest on securities the cities and municipalities issued.

Labor's complaints—the AFL-CIO resolved at its 1952 convention to condemn public subsidies to industry—eventually provoked members of Congress from the Northern precincts to call for restrictions on the use of industrial-development bonds. In May of 1953, Senator John F. Kennedy of Massachusetts informed his colleagues about the consequences of Southern "raiding." "Instead of utilizing their municipal bonding privileges for public works and the protection of the people from disaster and disease," Kennedy said, "the southerners put up streamlined mills which various cities and towns rented for almost unbelievably small amounts to bargain-hunting individuals from up North. This naturally enabled the fugitives to pare down their tax bills and to slash their operating costs so drastically that they could undersell their Northern competitors in the domestic and foreign markets."

The competition for new industry among the Southern states was intense. In the end, the incentive programs looked pretty similar—all used some combination of state and local credit to build the factories; all boasted of their right-to-work laws and microscopic wages—and so often it came down to the states' most visible salesmen: their governors. In the early 1960s, when Universal began looking at sites for its ancillary plant, no Southern state could boast a governor who took to selling more naturally and energetically than Ross Barnett of Mississippi.

Barnett was one of ten children born to a Confederate veteran and his wife on a farm in Leake County, in east central Mississippi. He worked his way through college and law school as a barber and janitor, and became one of the most successful personal-injury lawyers in Mississippi, earning upwards of $100,000 a year. He mesmerized juries with his bluster and his piety—he was a veteran Sunday school teacher—and figured he could do the same with voters. But even his considerable oratorical skills and personal wealth were insufficient the first two times he ran for governor; he lost in 1951 and again four years later.

When he won in 1959 on his third try, no one hailed him as a celestial wonder of the Southern political constellation. One critic wrote that his was "a mind relatively innocent of history, constitutional law, and the processes of government." A less charitable observer noted that the "kindest and most accurate thing that can be said is that he is bone dumb." When he was running for office, he promised jobs to so many people that following his inauguration the line of applicants was said to stretch forty yards from his office. One story has it that when a reporter asked Barnett what he thought of Matsu and Quemoy—the Taiwanese islands mainland China had bombed recently—the governor replied: "They're good men, and I'm sure I can find a place for them in Fish and Game."

Ross Barnett won the only way a candidate could: on a platform of unreconstructed bigotry. "The Negro is different because God made him different to punish him," Barnett explained during the campaign. "His forehead slants back. His nose is different. His lips are different, and his color is sure different." He was catapulted into office not by the strength of his stated convictions (which differed only in shading from those of his opponents, all of whom pledged to defend segregation then and forever), but by the backing of the Citizens Council of America, the militant white-supremacy organization that preached "racial integrity" and "massive resistance" to civil rights law and had been gaining hurricane-like strength across the Deep South in the years since the United States Supreme Court's landmark 1954 school desegregation decision in *Brown* v. *Board of Education of Topeka*. The court had called for integration not at once but with "all deliberate speed," a cautious phrase that gave solace to white segregationists and set the stage for the monumental decade-long campaign of mass protest and civil disobedience that would realign American politics.

In the aftermath of *Brown,* Barnett had impressed the Citizens Council with his vigorous legal defense of a group of vigilantes in Clinton, Tennessee, whom federal marshals arrested for attempting to block school integration through force. When he ran for governor of Mississippi again in 1959, he did so as the Citizens Council candidate. Soon after his inauguration, he established, "to no one's surprise," as the University of Mississippi professor James Silver wrote, "what amounted to an office of prime minister for racial integrity" and conferred it upon William Simmons, the chairman of the state Citizens Council.

For his infamous defiance of the Kennedy brothers and a federal court order to admit James Meredith as the first black student at Ole Miss in the fall of 1962, Barnett would become a Jim Crow folk hero. But before he gained worldwide notoriety for obstructing justice in the schoolhouse door, Governor Barnett devoted much effort and many miles to flying around the country, scheming to lure industry with the same promises of semi-slave labor and free land and buildings that Hugh White had employed a quarter century earlier.

Among the businessmen who took Barnett's bait was a Brooklyn, New York, native named Murray Reiter. Before the war, Reiter and an uncle had operated a retail lighting-fixture business in New York. By war's end, the business partners had had a falling-out, and in 1946 the twenty-eight-year-old Reiter and his wife decided to make a fresh start. The couple, who had met in college in the middle 1930s, at Washington University in St. Louis, moved south to her hometown of Marvel, Arkansas, a farming crossroads sixty miles or so across the Mississippi River from Memphis. The Brooklyn boy tried his hand at his in-laws' business, farming, but didn't have the aptitude for it. He turned once again to lighting, this time to the manufacturing end of the business. Fluorescent fixtures were flying off the shelves, and Reiter thought he could carve a niche for himself producing fixtures for the Southern market. By the early fifties, he was operating his own plant on Firestone Boulevard in Memphis.

Like most successful entrepreneurs, Reiter was an indefatigable promoter. He beat every bush he could: served on the board of the industry's trade association, sponsored an award of the Illuminating Engineering Society, attended all the lighting expositions. At one exposition he met Frank Smith, the man in charge of community and industrial development for Mississippi Power & Light. The state's utility company worked hand in glove with the Mississippi Agricultural and Industrial Board, the agency that administered the BAWI program. MP&L's interest, of course, was sparked by the heavy-use industrial customers new jobs would bring.

Murray Reiter mentioned to Frank Smith that he was running out of space at his plant in Memphis and was thinking about relocating. Smith called his attention to the BAWI program, and eventually located a suitable site for Reiter only twenty miles south of the outer reaches of Memphis, in Olive Branch, Mississippi. The voters of Olive Branch passed a bond referendum, and the plant opened in 1960.

At the gala opening was an array of dignitaries, including Governor Barnett and representatives of Reiter's major suppliers, among them Archie Sergy. Reiter had known Archie from his days up North, and had suggested that Archie take a look at establishing a Southern beachhead from which to supply ballasts to the fast-growing region. The idea piqued Archie enough to come see the state.

He apparently liked what he saw. "Can you locate me down here?" he asked Frank Smith at the opening.

"Sure," Smith replied. "I've got a staff of eight, and they'll be happy to take care of you."

"No," Archie said, "I want you."

Smith said that that would not be possible, that he was busy with other projects. Archie persisted, appealing to Smith's boss, Baxter Wilson, the president of Mississippi Power & Light, who also was in attendance. "I can promise you we'll have sixteen hundred people working in our plant," Archie told Wilson. Wilson agreed on the spot to relieve Smith of some of his other obligations to enable him to personally attend to Universal's needs.

When Archie returned to Paterson, he told only Rube Pashman and Paul Einhorn about his blueprint for expansion. Soon, however, word leaked throughout management as the recruiters from Mississippi began the courtship ritual of phone calls and letters, including sets of twin testimonials from satisfied Yankees who had relocated to the state and municipal officials who were glad they did. Archie maintained the file, but he treated it like the other maybe-someday solicitations with which he was inundated; the notion of actually sinking roots into what amounted to foreign soil seemed far-fetched—at least until the IUE-Teamsters labor war erupted at Universal in the summer of 1961.

It was sometime after the Fourth of July, after Local 945 had muscled its way into Duralite and set the stage for the fight at Universal, that Archie dusted off the file marked SOUTH? and dialed up Frank Smith at Mississippi Power & Light. "He made it known he was serious about his intentions and wanted me to get right on it," Smith recalls. "I found out what he wanted and then went to work to find an area that could and would support it. He wanted labor that was in sympathy with what he was trying to do, not union-type labor."

Unknown to Smith, however, Archie decided to cast a net wider than Mississippi: He contacted Fantus Factory Locating Service, a consulting firm with offices in New York and Chicago, to scout other Southern states for sites. After two or three months the Fantus consultant returned with a towering stack of data—"six- or eight-feet high," Rube Pashman once recalled. Fantus had surveyed a half-dozen states: the Carolinas, Virginia, Florida, Arkansas, and Mississippi. It studied the price of land and utilities, the availability of water and electricity, the cost and availability of labor, especially female labor, which Universal had indicated it preferred on the production lines. Ultimately Fantus recommended considering sites in just two of the states, two in Mississippi and one in Arkansas. Fantus explained to Universal's Paul Einhorn that although it believed Mississippi's BAWI program "almost certainly" offered the best terms for Universal, it wanted to offer the company the alternative of Arkansas, "given the situation in Mississippi."

The situation, in the summer of 1961, was that busloads of "Freedom Riders"—Northern college students, black and white—were streaming into Jackson in an all-out assault on Mississippi's segregation laws. They had absorbed earlier mob beatings and mass arrests in Montgomery, Alabama—where Rosa Parks had touched off the bus boycott six years earlier—and, beginning in late May, had set their sights on the Jackson air, bus, and train terminals. The *Jackson Daily News* "welcomed" the Freedom Riders with a mock advertisement:

ATTENTION: RESTLESS RACE-MIXERS

WHOSE HOBBY IS CREATING TROUBLE

GET AWAY FROM THE BLACKBOARD JUNGLE. RID YOURSELF OF

FEAR OF RAPISTS, MUGGERS, DOPEHEADS, AND SWITCHBLADE

ARTISTS DURING THE HOT, LONG SUMMER.

FULFILL THE DREAM OF A LIFETIME

HAVE A "VACATION" ON A REAL PLANTATION

HERE'S ALL YOU DO

BUY YOURSELF A SOUTHBOUND TICKET VIA RAIL, BUS OR AIR.

CHECK IN AND SIGN THE GUEST REGISTER AT THE JACKSON

CITY JAIL. PAY A NOMINAL FINE OF $200. THEN SPEND THE

NEXT 4 MONTHS AT OUR 21,000-ACRE PARCHMAN PLANTATION

IN THE HEART OF THE MISSISSIPPI DELTA. MEALS FURNISHED.

ENJOY THE WONDERS OF CHOPPING COTTON, WARM SUNSHINE,

PLOWING MULES AND TRACTORS, FEEDING THE CHICKENS,

SLOPPING THE PIGS, SCRUBBING FLOORS, COOKING AND

WASHING DISHES, LAUNDERING CLOTHES.

SUN LOTION, BUNION PLASTERS, AS WELL AS MEDICAL SERVICE

FREE. EXPERIENCE THE "ABUNDANT" LIFE UNDER TOTAL

SOCIALISM. PARCHMAN PRISON FULLY AIR-COOLED

BY MOTHER NATURE.

Two hundred and sixteen Freedom Riders were arrested at the Jackson bus depot and fined two hundred dollars each for "breach of the peace." Instead of paying the fine, many chose prison and were indeed sentenced to "destination doom," as William Faulkner labeled Parchman, the state's fabled penitentiary. They served thirty-nine days—one less than the maximum one could serve and still file an appeal.

The nationwide headlines gave further pause to Northern industrialists considering a move to Mississippi but already skittish about the possibility of being pinned down in the civil rights crossfire. The Mississippi legislature had begun to address those concerns, not by complying with federal law, but by funding a public relations campaign to sell its segregationist ways to the rest of the country. It created the Mississippi Sovereignty Commission, which, in addition to its propagandizing duties, was also charged with spying on suspected civil rights activists and sympathizers. "You go into the North and say you're from Mississippi, and they want to know how many Negroes you killed before breakfast," a Sovereignty Commission official lamented.

The state's Agricultural and Industrial Board, meanwhile, left the overtly racist rhetoric to Governor Barnett, the Sovereignty Commission, and the Citizens Council (to which the Sovereignty Commission channeled money). The board officials instead dangled the evergreen lures of BAWI incentives, cheap labor, and the state's right-to-work law, which outlawed compulsory union membership, whether or not a majority of the workers in a shop voted for it. This made (and makes) for tepid unions, since the nonmembers were entitled to the same wages and benefits as the voluntary dues-payers.

The industrial recruiters who telephoned and wrote Archie Sergy in Paterson would point out that while the average manufacturing wage in New Jersey in 1960 was $2.29 an hour, in Mississippi it was but $1.49. And they would mention that the state's pay scale compared favorably with those of its neighboring competitors. A Mississippi Power & Light pamphlet cited figures that Mississippi workers earned 20 percent less than Alabama's, and 30 percent less than Louisiana's. "Don't look at the Mississippi worker in terms of production per man hour," another brochure counseled. "Consider him instead in terms of production per dollar spent."

Archie certainly was considering his costs—the cost if the violent dispute between the IUE and the Teamsters at Duralite was to spread to and disrupt production at Universal, the cost if the less agreeable IUE local won the election, the cost to build a new facility in the South, and whether the price of all that strife in Mississippi was too great to pay for labor peace in his own shop.

While he sorted his options in the fall of 1961, and while the war intensified between the union rivals in Paterson, Archie received a call one morning from Joe Bullock, the executive director of the Mississippi A&I Board. The two had exchanged pleasantries at Murray Reiter's plant-opening ceremonies the previous year, but had not spoken since. Bullock was calling on a tip from Frank Smith that Universal was a red-hot prospect. "Time to roll out the heavy artillery," Smith had recommended to Bullock.

Bullock told Archie he'd just been talking to Governor Barnett about Universal; if it would not be an imposition, he said, the governor himself would very much like to visit Archie in Paterson for an hour or so to further explain the benefits of BAWI, and could an appointment be arranged for the following week?

A week later, Ross Barnett and Joe Bullock, along with two plain-clothed Mississippi state troopers, strolled into the Universal plant. For security reasons—the governor received alp-like stacks of hate mail bearing Northern postmarks—Barnett sometimes preferred to travel pseudonymously. He asked Archie to introduce him around the plant as "Mr. White"—the stab at humor was lost on no one.

Barnett was riding high that fall. Several weeks earlier he had helped Pascagoula reel in a $125 million oil refinery. But while reveling in the catch, the governor nearly hooked himself in the eye. In a speech before the Citizens Council, Barnett boasted that Mississippi attracted the Standard Oil of Kentucky plant because the state had become "a symbol of successful segregation." "Any Southern state would have been eager to secure such a project," he declared. "Many of them tried actively to get it, and yet it's coming to Mississippi. Who says segregation doesn't pay?"

It was the sort of pronouncement that yielded yips and howls from Northern editorial writers. An editorialist for the *Chicago Daily News* opined that a businessman looking to relocate to Mississippi should consider more than its advertised specials of low taxes, compliant labor, and liberal financial assistance to new industry. "He needs to be concerned about climate—and we are not talking about sunshine or mean temperatures. Thanks in considerable part to Barnett's unenlightened leadership, there prevails in Mississippi a climate of hate, of seething, subsurface unrest; of repression and bitterness and potential violence. A prudent businessman thinks twice before plunging into that kind of situation."*

Within a week after the mid-November runoff election at Universal, Archie convened his brain trust for final deliberations on Mississippi. The Teamsters had barely managed to hang on, but Local 945

---

* Some businessmen took such advice to heart. Wrote one textile executive: "We won't consider expanding in Mississippi again until the state and its people join the Union again." And another plant formerly located in Mississippi moved across the state line into Louisiana to erase the stain of a Mississippi mailing address.

president Mike Ardis had signaled Archie that he, Ardis, would be under pressure to deliver a meatier contract when negotiations began after the first of the year. In meeting after meeting—over late-night steaks at the Black Bear and midnight dessert in the Sergys' kitchen— Archie and Paul Einhorn and Rube Pashman hashed out the pros and cons of the move.

"There were three reasons we had to move," says Paul Einhorn, the chief financial officer. "One was to avoid work stoppages"—a second facility would take away the union's leverage. "Two was that with the growth we had projected, it was obvious we would need more space. And three, it was obvious we didn't have the funds on our own to pay for additional space."

The company's triumvirate decided it was worth a closer look to see if Governor Barnett could help Universal surmount these issues, and so they agreed to a visit. The governor began his presentation by outlining his state's "rapid industrial development," including the big Standard Oil refinery at Pascagoula. He then described Mississippi's "Bill of Rights for Business and Industry," which included recent legislative acts to restrict organized labor as well as a newly passed amendment embedding the state's right-to-work law in the Mississippi Constitution. As he concluded his boilerplate remarks, he invited Archie to visit him in the Governor's Mansion and he handed him a formal letter of invitation enclosed in a leatherette folder. Engraved in gold lettering on the cover was ARCHIE SERGY, along with the seal of Mississippi. Within a few days of the visit, Archie received a personal letter from the governor, thanking him for his "time and interest in our presentation."

Although the particulars would not be worked out until the middle of February—Archie wanted to keep the lid on the deal until the members of Local 945 ratified their new contract in mid-January—the pieces of the Mississippi plan then fell quickly into place. The principal issue to be resolved was location: Where would Universal build? Many of the state's eighty-three counties touted themselves as industrial paradises housing vast surpluses of "native-born, intelligent workers." Fresh off the farm, these would-be factory workers were accustomed to a minuscule prevailing wage; the state's per capita income was $1,173. Nor were they used to unions. As an easily decoded A&I Board brochure put it, "Strongly ingrained in their character is an attitude of individual liberty and resourcefulness and an unshakable belief in the rights of private ownership, free enterprise and individual initiative."

Archie would rely on the counsel of Frank Smith and the A&I Board, who recommended a site based at least as much on sound politics as sound policy. Their choice was Mendenhall, a farming town of twenty-four hundred residents that served as the seat of Simpson County. For a poor county, Simpson was well connected politically: Among its influential boosters-in-residence were a member of the state Highway Commission; a state senator who also sat on the A&I Board; a banker who was a key ally of Governor Barnett's; and the governor's former college roommate, a prominent minister whose son published one of the two weekly newspapers.

Frank Smith says that Mendenhall's strategic location, only thirty miles southeast of Jackson and on the major artery, U.S. Highway 49, from the capital city to the ports of the Gulf Coast, made it attractive. In 1962, Highway 49 was but a two-lane road. But the interstate highway system, begun during the Eisenhower administration, was about to reach Jackson, and the highway commissioner who lived in Mendenhall assured Frank Smith that if Simpson was selected as the site for Universal, he would expedite plans to widen Highway 49 to four lanes and to connect it to Interstate 20.

The original proposal called for the plant to be located near downtown Mendenhall, in the northern portion of the county. But that plan failed to account for the contentiousness between Mendenhall and Magee, the county's southern anchor, and Mendenhall's archrival in everything from retailing to politics to high school football. "We used to knock heads for the championship of the Dixie Conference every year," says G. O. Parker Jr., the longtime editor of the *Magee Courier.*

The towns of Simpson County had knocked heads for their share of the spoils for the whole of the twentieth century. Until the turn of the century, the village of Westville had been the county seat. In 1900, though, when the tracks were laid through the county for the Gulf & Ship Island Railroad, the nearest depot was built some eight miles away. The following year the board of supervisors ordered the county records moved to the site of the depot, at Edna, which the supervisors renamed in honor of a recently deceased clerk of the circuit court, Thomas L. Mendenhall.

Mendenhall enjoyed a boomlet: A two-story courthouse sprang up; hotels, a newspaper, a grocery, and a mercantile company all opened to support the railroad employees and mill hands moving to town. With its survival at stake, Westville was not about to take its loss quietly. It sued Mendenhall and the county, and in 1905 it won: The seat of government reverted to Westville. Mendenhall appealed, claiming that a surveyor (hired by Mendenhall) had determined that it was a mile closer to the center of the county than Westville and that therefore Mendenhall should be the seat. In 1906, the state supreme court agreed.

Westville disappeared, and Magee, itself home to a railroad depot, took its place as Mendenhall's chief economic threat. Mendenhall reigned supreme until midcentury, when Magee experienced a growth surge: Its 1950 population of 1,738 marked the first time the number of residents exceeded that of Mendenhall, in which lived 199 fewer souls. By the early sixties, when Universal arrived in Mendenhall, Magee's population had surged past 2,000, enabling the town to maintain bragging rights with a lead of 93 residents.

The 1962 referendum on the million-dollar bond issue was to be county-wide, and the city fathers of Magee made it known they would not support a plan that favored Mendenhall. And so a compromise was struck: The plant would be built on Highway 49, five miles south of Mendenhall, five miles north of Magee.

During the first week of March, Archie paid a visit to the county to start drumming up support for the bond issue. Before a gathering at the Simpson County Courthouse of the power elite, including the governor, Archie heaped praise on his audience. "I would like you to know that it was the leadership and guidance of Governor Ross Barnett, the Mississippi Power & Light Company, the Simpson County Board of Supervisors, the people of Simpson County, and so many civic-minded men in Mississippi that persuaded Universal Manufacturing to come here. With the support of such interested people and particularly those gathered here, the success of this undertaking is assured."

But Archie was not taking success for granted. The board of supervisors set the date of May 15 for the bond election, and in the meantime Archie was planning his own campaign to win over any skeptics. He invited the county's elected officeholders as well as officials from both towns' chambers of commerce to Paterson to tour the flagship and to spend a few days as his guest on the town in New York City. Many of these men had hardly been outside the South, and some had never flown; an all-expense-paid trip could hardly be refused.

Archie treated his guests like royalty, sending them first-class tickets for the flight to La Guardia, and meeting them at the airport with stretch limousines and a photographer to record the event. From there they were whisked to one of New York's finer hotels, the Essex House, where their rooms overlooked Central Park. That evening they were driven to the exclusive Four Seasons, where dinner was served in a private room. "I had never seen carrots priced so high," says Archie Magee, then the Simpson County Chancery Clerk. Afterward they passed around cigars, recalls Frank Smith, who accompanied the group. "None of these country guys had ever seen a two-dollar cigar, they were used to Roi-Tans."

The following day they toured the plant in Paterson and were later treated to a night on Broadway, where they took in "How to Succeed in Business Without Really Trying" from seats in the second and third rows, center, and dined at Trader Vic's. On their last night they sat in a field-level box at a Yankees-Indians game at Yankee Stadium. If there were any skeptics in the bunch before landing in New York, by the time they boarded the DC-3 for the return flight to Jackson, the Mississippians to a man were bent double with enthusiasm for their prospective new employer.

INDUSTRY IS KNOCKING AT OUR DOOR, G. O. Parker Jr. gushed in his posttrip editorial in late April. "This is the greatest opportunity Simpson County has ever had to provide job opportunities. . . . This is our opportunity to open the door to the greatest period of development Simpson County has ever enjoyed. . . ." That week's *Simpson County News*, published in Mendenhall, featured a page-one editorial cartoon depicting a smokestacked "BAWI PLANT" from which dollar signs radiated to a half-dozen stick-figure drawings intended to represent these interest groups: a farmer, a housewife, a secretary, an executive, a merchant, and a farm laborer. "Industrial payroll dollars benefit everyone," the caption read.

Most of the news hole for the next few editions of both papers was devoted to exhorting voters to the polls on May 15. (For the bond issues to pass, a majority of registered voters needed to cast ballots, and two-thirds of those needed to support the measures.) There were two propositions: One would authorize the board of supervisors to sell bonds in the amount of $1 million to purchase land and construct a building for Universal; the other called for the supervisors to sell $200,000 worth of bonds for land preparation and installation of water, sewer, and gas lines.

On May 1, two weeks before the election, the Magee and Mendenhall chambers of commerce held an unprecedented joint rally at the county courthouse. State representative Alton White called Universal a "blue chip" business that would "provide jobs here to permit our young people to remain at home instead of going somewhere else to work and live." The mayor of Magee reached back to the pre-Depression days to recall the county's last industrial heyday, when the sawmills of Finkbine Lumber Company in rural D'Lo whined around the clock. "I can remember when that mill was in operation that anybody who wanted a job could find one . . . and now it will be the same way with Universal Manufacturing Corporation."

The week before the vote, the newspapers could no longer contain their editorials to an inside page. The lead story in the *County News* for May 10 was headed: DON'T FORGET TO VOTE IN SIMPSON COUNTY'S FIRST BAWI BOND ISSUE ELECTION NEXT TUESDAY. A page-one sidebar, DECISION TIME IS NEAR, pulled no punches, beginning: "Tuesday, May 15, is certain to go down in history as the most important day in the history of Simpson County."

The public relations campaign was wildly successful: Simpson Countians voted 4,158 to 59 in favor of the bond issue. "This is only the beginning," the *Magee Courier* noted, "but what a wonderful beginning. WOW!" In a telegram he sent to the mayor of Mendenhall, Archie Sergy said he was "overjoyed" and that plans for construction of the building were "progressing rapidly."

Back home in Paterson, not all were overjoyed at the prospect of the new Southern plant. After Archie signed the contract with Simpson County, he informed his managers about the deal. "We're gonna open up in Mississippi," he told Zeke Bromberg, Universal's head of purchasing.

"Mississippi?" Bromberg replied. "Where the hell are you going down there?"

Archie unfolded a map and pointed to Mendenhall.

"Archie, if I look at a map of the U.S. and think of it as a person's body, Mendenhall is the asshole. How the hell am I going to get copper and steel and all the things we need into a place like this?"

"Don't worry, Zeke," Archie assured him, "we'll have railroads coming in there and you'll get it just the same."

Bromberg's attitude typified that of the company's salaried employees, whose consensus held that Mississippi was a place apart, if not the heart of darkness. None would have been inclined to raise his hand had Archie and Rube Pashman asked for volunteers to head south to set up operations. But Archie and Rube never asked. Instead, Rube one day invited Siegfried Steinberger, the former quality-assurance man who had since been promoted to head of manufacturing, out for a chat in his car parked in front of the plant.

"If—*if*—we go to Mississippi, would you be willing to go?" Rube asked him.

Sig Steinberger and his wife, June, had a nice life in New Jersey. With their three children—the oldest was twelve—they lived comfortably in rural Washington Township, a twenty- or thirty-minute commute by back roads from Paterson. But moving south would give him the opportunity to run his own show, to try something new. "Rube had a lot of confidence in me," Steinberger recalled not long ago. "He knew I'd been in combat [during World War II] and I guess he figured if I could handle that, I could handle Mississippi."

Sig Steinberger, a German émigré, had handled pretty much everything thrown his way. His mother died on the day he was born, in 1922, shortly after giving birth. The newborn was sent to live with his father's sister, who raised him until he was seven, when he was returned, involuntarily, to his father and his new wife. In 1938, when he turned sixteen, they sent him to New York to live with a first cousin, the daughter of the aunt who had mothered him. That was the last he would see of his father, who in the fall of the following year happened to be in England buying material for his Frankfurt fabric shop when war broke out. The English authorities rounded him up, as they did all Germans in the country, and sent him to a detention camp, where he caught pneumonia and died.

Young Sig arrived in New York via Dutch steamer from Rotterdam. He spoke no English, but his cousin helped him obtain a work permit.

He quickly found a job on an assembly line in a downtown button-manufacturing plant. He earned thirty cents an hour, the minimum wage. After work, he gulped dinner at a hot-dog stand—two hot dogs, a slice of apple pie, and a drink, all for twenty cents—and then hurried off to night school to study English.

Around the time of his eighteenth birthday, in October 1940, Steinberger sought to enlist in the U.S. Coast Guard. He got the idea from a German friend who had immigrated to America in 1928 and who belonged to an auxiliary unit of the Coast Guard on Long Island. But the guard was not receptive to Steinberger, who suspects it had to do with his citizenship status: The government classified him as a "friendly alien."

Then he tried the Navy. Same response. Finally he walked into an Army recruiting office, which initially also told him no thanks, but ultimately decided it needed all the "cannon fodder," as Steinberger says, it could muster. He was sent to basic training in Spartanburg, South Carolina—his first trip south.

After the long troop-train ride, his first order of business was to find a men's room. "I saw two signs: white and colored," recalls Steinberger, whose grasp of the language's colloquialisms was tentative. "And I thought, Oh, they're getting fancy down here, I'll try the colored one." Before he could unzip, however, he met Jim Crow for the first time: Fellow soldiers yanked him outside.

"You don't belong in there!" he was admonished.

Of his introduction to Jim Crow, he remembers, "I was scared to death. I knew the Army was all white, but I didn't understand that race ran through everything down South. I hadn't heard of the segregation laws until someone explained them to me later. I was never exposed to anything like that."

He never even *saw* a black person until after his transatlantic crossing, when he disembarked at the port of entry in Hoboken, New Jersey. On board the ferry for the quick trip across the Hudson, he laid eyes on the boat's shoe-shine boy. He had heard blacks existed—"My aunt used to scare me by saying if I wasn't good, the black man—the bogeyman—would come and get me."

It was in South Carolina that Steinberger became a U.S. citizen. It would normally have taken him five years in the country to qualify, but federal law required the Army to send only soldiers who were citizens overseas, and so it asked for and was granted a waiver for Steinberger. He and some nine hundred other foreign-born soldiers in Spartanburg were jointly administered the oath of citizenship. By late 1941, he was a staff sergeant stationed in Hawaii, a member of the Twenty-First Infantry Regiment of the Twenty-fourth Infantry Division of the Sixth Army. On a quiet Sunday morning in early December, he was eating breakfast in the Schofield Barracks, some thirty-five miles from Pearl Harbor, when Japanese machine-gun bullets peppered his scrambled eggs.

His division was dispatched first to Australia, then to New Guinea, and in October 1944, to Leyte Island in the Philippines. It was there, on November 16, that Steinberger took three bullets in the left leg and put an end to his active-duty military career. He made it back to the States in January 1945, spending the next two years in military hospitals, shuttling in and out of surgery: Army doctors in Atlantic City, New Jersey, operated on his leg five times. When he was released in January 1947, he went to work in a Bendix Aviation wire and steel plant in Teterboro, New Jersey.

He stayed at Bendix for a year, during which he lived with his cousin's family, who had moved during the war from New York City across the Hudson River to Englewood, New Jersey. His cousin's daughter was working as a secretary at a fluorescent-fixture company called Robert Manufacturing. She put in a word there for Steinberger and in 1948 he was hired as the firm's supervisor of manufacturing. Over the next couple of years, he would assume nearly every job in the plant, including purchasing director. Among his favored suppliers was Universal Manufacturing.

Steinberger's cousin eventually left the company and was replaced by a vivacious woman named June Wilke. He and June married in June 1950. When they returned to work following their wedding, Steinberger found a note on his desk informing him that his services were no longer needed; it seemed the owner had decided to bestow upon his brother-in-law Steinberger's job.

After collecting unemployment for one week, Steinberger called on Archie Sergy about a job. On July 5, 1950, Steinberger went to work for Universal on the assembly line in Westwood. He earned a dollar an hour, or forty dollars a week. He was trained by Meyer Horwitz, Archie's first cousin, and one of countless family members on the payroll.

Steinberger's stint on the line was short-lived. After about two months, Archie promoted him to foreman of the laminating department and raised his salary to sixty dollars a week. He later ran the winding department and then the one-man quality-assurance department. In the late 1950s, he was named supervisor of manufacturing, the job he held until the day in late March of 1963 that he and June and their three children piled into their just-purchased Chevrolet station wagon for the twelve-hundred-mile trip to their new home amid what they thought would be the tranquil pinelands of Mendenhall.

They arrived in Mississippi on Monday, April 1. That night, as Steinberger jiggled with the rabbit ears on his small television, he and June tuned in a newscast from Jackson. As Steinberger recalls it, the anchorman introduced the top story, the civil rights demonstrations in the Delta town of Greenwood, this way: "Let me show some pictures and let's see what the niggers are doing today."

What the demonstrators were doing was marching to the Leflore County Courthouse to attempt to register to vote. (Of 13,567 blacks of voting age in the county, only 250 were registered to vote.*) Though the 42 marchers were unarmed and peaceable, local police, aided by almost 100 officers from surrounding counties, unleashed their K-9 corps of German shepherds. Firefighters were also on the scene, positioning a fire truck in front of the courthouse. The threat of high-pressure hoses only emboldened the marchers, one of whom announced to the fire chief: "There's a fire going on inside of us, baby, but you can't put it out."

That afternoon, a federal judge in Mississippi had turned down a Kennedy administration request for a temporary restraining order barring Greenwood city officials from interfering with black registration efforts. He said the Justice Department's request was not "sufficient to warrant trampling on the rights" of local officials. One of the few faces in the state Sig Steinberger recognized appeared on television to cheer the ruling. "The election of the Kennedys does not amend the Constitution," Governor Barnett declared, "and I shall stand by the officials of Greenwood to assist them in the exercise of their lawful rights."

The newscast reported that protesters in Greenwood, led by the

---

*This contrasted with the county's voting-age white population of 10,274, of which 9,800 were registered.

"hired outside agitators" of SNCC, the Student Nonviolent Coordinating Committee, were marching for a fourth consecutive business day, and noted that eight protesters (including Robert Moses, the field director of SNCC's voter registration drive in Mississippi) had been imprisoned since Friday in the Greenwood jail on charges of disorderly conduct.

Although Greenwood was more than a hundred miles north of Mendenhall, the activities there were also chronicled closely in the two Simpson County weeklies. The theme of the coverage was remarkably consistent: that federal tyranny, in the person of the brothers Kennedy—JFK in the White House and RFK in the Justice Department—was trampling states' rights; that Yankees could not understand the Mississippi way of life; that blacks liked things the way they were; that Communist-inspired agitators were the cause of the troubles.

For newcomers such as Sig and June Steinberger, the simmering rancor raised a recurring question. "We kept asking ourselves what the hell did we get ourselves into?"

It was a question the entire nation seemed to be asking, along with the corollary: How do we get ourselves out of it? One answer that appealed to Sig Steinberger and to many Americans was suggested later that spring by President Kennedy: a comprehensive civil rights bill. Protests against downtown segregation and demonstrations for voting rights had continued to spread since the series of marches in Greenwood in late March and early April. In Birmingham, Alabama, police commissioner Bull Connor loosed the dogs and turned the fire hoses on nonviolent demonstrators, and thousands of demonstrators triumphantly filled the city's jails. (Among them was Martin Luther King Jr., who during nine days in custody drafted his twenty-page "Letter from Birmingham Jail.")

Emboldened by the international attention the direct-action campaign in Birmingham garnered, movement forces in Jackson believed the time was right for mass demonstrations to demand desegregated facilities and fair employment practices. On the hot, muggy morning of Tuesday, May 28, a handful of black Tougaloo College students took seats at the downtown Woolworth's lunch counter on Capitol Street. As word of the sit-in spread, radio and TV broadcasters recorded a mob of some three hundred whites, yelling and whooping, swarming the store, beating and kicking the demonstrators, pouring ketchup in their hair and sugar in their eyes, emptying the shelves of ashtrays and other throwable bric-a-brac.

The sit-in galvanized young blacks in Jackson. Over the next couple of days, hundreds of students were arrested for walking on picket lines across the city; on Friday, May 31, alone, 450 youths were hauled off in garbage trucks to a makeshift detention facility at the state fairgrounds. Nonviolent demonstrators in Jackson and across the South continued over the next couple of weeks to face beatings and billy clubs and police dogs and high-pressure hoses—in Danville, Virginia, 48 blacks were admitted to the hospital that Friday after authorities borrowed a page from Bull Connor's tactics book.

In the wake of the Danville incident, on June 11 Martin Luther King sent the Kennedys a noontime telegram beseeching the administration to seek a "just and moral" solution to "the nation's most grievous problem." King had also sent signals (via a story leaked to the *New York Times*) that the civil rights leadership was preparing to issue a call for a national march on Washington.

Facing the threat of a march, the president took immediate action. Eight hours after receiving the telegram, President Kennedy commandeered the nation's radio and television networks for a live, fifteen-minute address on civil rights. "We are confronted primarily with a moral issue," he said. "It is as old as the Scriptures and it is as clear as the American Constitution. The heart of the question is whether all Americans are to be afforded equal rights and equal opportunities, whether we are going to treat our fellow Americans as we want to be treated."*

It was a question that resonated with Sig Steinberger, this question of equality. He believed deeply in the American ideal of equal opportunity for all, had fought and nearly died for his adopted country in defense of such ideals. He appreciated democracy as could only one who had lived under totalitarianism. "It's hard to explain if you didn't

---

*The march, featuring King's "I have a dream" speech, took place on August 28. The following day's *Clarion-Ledger* documented the event with a photograph portraying the litter of a quarter-million marchers and a story headlined: WASHINGTON IS CLEAN AGAIN WITH NEGRO TRASH REMOVED.

live through it. But you have to understand that America was a free country and that I grew up in a police state. If you wanted to move from one street to another three blocks away, you had to go to the police station and report it. They always knew where you were.

"And then I came to New York, and you could ride the subway and sit next to a guy in a tuxedo who was going to a party, or go up to Harlem on a Friday night and have a great time with everybody. In my naïve way of thinking, everybody was equal. You could do what you wanted, go where you wanted."

And even though on his first trip south in 1940 he swallowed a dose of reality, his belief was never shaken, not to this day, that all Americans ought to be treated equally—no matter the color of their skin, or country of their origin, or thickness of their accent.

And yet Steinberger was a company man; Universal had given him a place in the world and he was determined to do right by it. And in the frenzied, self-destructive time and place he found himself in when he arrived in Mendenhall, that meant learning and abiding by local custom and ritual—the "Mississippi way of life." He was an outsider all over again, but as the chief executive for what would soon be the county's largest employer, he was also an insider. The two perspectives generally served him well, but in racially polarized Simpson County, it occasionally put him at odds with the power structure. "I was always having to bite my tongue because there was plenty I wanted to say as a private citizen that I couldn't say. I felt no matter what the circumstances, I had a job to do for the company."

One of the particulars he found most repugnant was the plant's initial policy of a whites-only workforce. Archie Sergy had struck an off-the-record deal with Governor Barnett, as many BAWI industrialists did, to allow the state Employment Security Commission (ESC) to screen job applicants. The governor's unstated but clear reason for this was to ensure that white applicants were given preference. Universal began hiring in the middle of June, during the latter stages of plant construction, when the Hazlehurst division of the ESC set up a satellite office in Mendenhall City Hall. Prospective employees were screened and given both a manual dexterity test and a reading and writing test. The latter effectively excluded blacks, whose separate and unequal schooling had yet to be remedied by the Supreme Court's *Brown* decision nearly a decade earlier.

The plant began training its first employees, ten whites, on June 24, two weeks after the president's impassioned plea for racial justice and five days after Medgar Evers was buried at Arlington Cemetery. Evers, the field secretary of the Mississippi NAACP, was murdered several hours after Kennedy's speech, felled by a sniper's rifle as he stepped from his car in the driveway of his home in Jackson. He collapsed clutching a handful of sweatshirts intended for sale at a fundraising event. Emblazoned on the sweatshirts was JIM CROW MUST GO!

In the summer of 1963, Jim Crow showed no sign of imminent departure. It had survived the Freedom Rides, James Meredith's admission to Ole Miss, the assassination of Medgar Evers, and with the August victory of Paul B. Johnson Jr., the most devout segregationist in the Democratic gubernatorial primary* (he routinely referred to the NAACP as an acronym for "Niggers, Alligators, Apes, Coons, and Possums"), it seemed that segregation would continue for the foreseeable future as the cornerstone of Mississippi society.

In Simpson County, though, there were signs that the old way of life, the Mississippi way, could not hold up under the weight of industrialization. It was a different world from that of the Delta, where the state's noisiest racists held fast to the remnants of their plantation economy. In Simpson, trees dominated the landscape; small dirt farms rather than endless stretches of cotton fields dotted the countryside. And there were fewer blacks in Simpson than in the Delta counties, where whites constituted a minority and where the planters depended upon large sharecropping and tenant-farming families of uneducated, nonvoting blacks to bring in the crops.

If white resistance was more subtle in Simpson County, it was only a matter of volume: The county was as staunchly segregationist as the rest of the state. There was no civil rights movement activity to speak of in Simpson County, where life for blacks had not changed appreciably since Reconstruction and not at all since the *Brown* decision in 1954. The Citizens Council controlled local politics; the two weekly papers, if not hate sheets like elsewhere, were stridently Jim Crow. (Blacks were

---

* Mississippi, like the rest of the South, was a one-party state. As one adage had it, Mississippi farmers put their faith in God, next year's crop, and the Democratic Party.

banished from their front pages, except in cases of criminality or violent death: NEGRO KILLED FRIDAY NIGHT, read a *Simpson County News* headline.) Blacks endured substandard schools and inequitable city and county services. These affronts to freedom, to full citizenship, were made possible by one denial of rights above all others: the right to vote.

There was no mass voter-registration drive in Simpson County. Nor were blacks who attempted to register turned away from the courthouse or threatened, implicitly or explicitly, with arrest or loss of job or residence if they tried to meddle in "white folks' business." Instead, as F. M. (Crip) Harvey, the circuit clerk and registrar of the county, explained to a State Sovereignty Commission investigator in July 1960, he simply kept on hand two distinct application forms: a "short" form for whites, a "long" form for blacks. The short form consisted of one page of basic biographical questions: name, age, occupation, address, length of residence in Mississippi, criminal record, and so on, followed by a page reserved for the signatures of the applicant and the registrar. The Sovereignty Commission investigator quoted Harvey as saying he "helps the whites if they can't answer this correctly."

The long form employed the same first page of questions. On the second page the applicant was asked to copy and interpret a section of the state constitution—of the registrar's choosing. On the following page the applicant was required to write a short essay "setting forth your understanding of the duties and obligations of citizenship under a constitutional form of government." As the Sovereignty Commission investigator noted, "I doubt if very many whites or negroes could answer this correctly."

Few blacks even tried. While 6,600 whites in Simpson County were registered to vote in July 1960, only 75 blacks were on the rolls. And not a single black had sought to register since February.

OBTAINING THE financing and the voters' authorization for Universal had been easy. (Governor-elect Paul Johnson would later joke that "Mr. Sergy got a better vote in Simpson County than I did, and Simpson County has always been one of my leading counties in any campaign I have ever run.") And the several stages of opening—from construction to training the first coil-winding operators in June to shipping the first completed ballasts in mid-August—had gone smoothly enough. The year was capped with the grand-opening celebration and dedication ceremony in December. OPEN HOUSE AT UNIVERSAL'S PLANT IS 'DREAM COME TRUE' FOR MANY PEOPLE, the *County News* reported.

Indeed, Sig Steinberger's first year in Mendenhall, his first as a plant administrator, was all he could have hoped for. Certainly there was a steep learning curve, both for him and his family, new to the ways of a rural, sleepy town in the most Southern of states, and for his employees, few of whom had performed industrial work. "People here had never been in a factory," Steinberger says, "so they'd take bathroom breaks or cigarette breaks every thirty minutes. We had to teach them about working on production lines."

Steinberger was a gifted teacher. Indeed, he had spent his life bridging cultural and linguistic differences, finding common ground with disparate people. That was certainly one reason Archie Sergy and Rube Pashman selected Steinberger as their chief executive in Mississippi, their missionary of sorts. But as Steinberger marked his first year in Mississippi in the spring of 1964, what neither he nor his bosses could have anticipated was just how complex the job would become—and how right a man he was for the job.

Universal's workforce had surpassed 150, all of whom (with the exception of two janitors), per Ross Barnett's design, were white. From Washington came word in March that Congress was on the verge of passing an omnibus civil rights bill. Among its portions was a fair-employment section, which would bar racial discrimination in the workplace. Soon Sig Steinberger would face a truly difficult challenge. He was going to try to bring peaceable integration to Simpson County.

But even that monumental task would be eclipsed, for the time being, by a more imminent threat. On a Wednesday afternoon that very month—indeed, only two days after the Senate opened debate on the civil rights bill—Steinberger heard a loud knocking at the entrance to the plant. Organized labor was at the door.

NINE

Working for the Railroad

STEINBERGER WAS not the only one to hear the knocking. The sound reverberated north toward Paterson, of course, and then east across the Hudson River to the Park Avenue headquarters of Philadelphia & Reading Corporation, the new owners of Universal.

Archie Sergy had turned forty-eight years old in September of 1963. He was in the prime of his corporate career, but he was not in the best of health. He had suffered a heart attack in 1957, and although he had since adhered to a healthful diet and regular exercise, his sons and associates believe he was thinking of estate planning.

And there was the matter of succession. His oldest son, Sam, was a lost soul at twenty-one—the "family troublemaker," he puts it. After Sam left school at sixteen, Archie employed him in a variety of capacities—in the plant, as a truck driver, operating a golf driving range Archie purchased for him. Alan, nineteen, had never shown much more than a passing interest in Universal, and was away in college in California. And even if Alan had found appealing the thought of one day running the company, he says Archie effectively discouraged the idea. "My father saw how much money people on Wall Street were making, and how hard he had to work to run his plant. He used to say, 'What kind of schmuck am I? Don't ever get into manufacturing.' " (Archie would give his youngest son, Bruce, who was only fourteen, the same advice.)

And there was the ever-present need for capital. The new Mississippi plant would alleviate the problem of insufficient capacity in Paterson, and although the company had received extremely generous incentives to move, the expansion into a distant state nevertheless raised the stakes considerably. "We either did something to finance our growth, or we stopped growing," says Paul Einhorn. "And if you stopped growing, there's only one way to go—backwards."

Weighing all these factors, Archie decided to explore the market for a sale. He sought counsel from his friend Bernard Aronson, the head of Continental Copper & Wire, a New Jersey–based company from which Universal bought copper for its wire mill. Aronson lived a double professional life; he was fluent in finance as well as in manufacturing. Every day, recalls his son-in-law, Aronson would leave his New York home before dawn, take care of the copper business in New Jersey, and return by nine A.M. to his day job at Bernard Aronson & Associates, the Manhattan stockbrokerage he founded as a young law school dropout in the summer of 1929—some three months before the crash.

Aronson studied the public companies that he thought might find Universal appetizing and placed his first call to a young wheeler-dealer named Howard A. (Mickey) Newman, whose father, Jerome, had been Aronson's summer-camp counselor in 1917 at Camp Paradox in the Adirondack Mountains of upstate New York. Jerome Newman and his partner, the noted stock-picker Benjamin Graham, ran the Wall Street investment firm of Graham-Newman Corporation. It was their inspiration to search for and invest in undervalued companies; in 1952 the firm bought a big stake, sixty thousand shares, in Philadelphia & Reading. The stake earned Ben Graham a seat on the board of directors.

Philadelphia & Reading dated to 1871, when it was formed as a wholly owned coal-mining subsidiary of the Philadelphia & Reading Railroad. A 1923 U.S. Supreme Court ruling split the coal company from the railroad. The coal company did well enough on its own until midcentury, when users of hard coal were changing to other fuels. The company, however, continued to mine its increasingly unsaleable product. By 1954, P&R's ledger was as deeply red as its mines were black—it booked a loss that year of seven million dollars.

By the beginning of 1955, Graham-Newman and an allied investor owned or spoke for nearly 30 percent of P&R's outstanding stock—enough for two more seats on the board. One of those seats went to the ally, the other to Jerome Newman's son, Mickey. In early 1956, the Graham-Newman forces won complete control of the P&R board and installed a new president, the thirty-four-year-old Mickey Newman.

The younger Newman was born to the world of high finance. After graduating from Cornell University and serving in the Navy during the war, he returned to New York City, where he ran his own export business for a few years before moving over to his father's firm and then on to P&R. Newman was intent on diversifying the aging company and building P&R into what was popularly known as a "conglomerate"—a corporation whose primary purpose was to maintain a precipitous rate of growth, and which did so by "ingesting whatever companies swam within reach." By 1963, Newman had dug P&R out of its unprofitable coal business—he sold the last piece of it in 1961—and transformed it into a holding company that earned a net profit of almost eight million dollars.

Starting in the mid-fifties and lasting through the sixties, conglomerates were all the rage. The stock market was a raging bull, surging to record-high levels; cash on Wall Street was flowing like cheap champagne. The legal climate was also hospitable. Antitrust lawyers in the Justice Department and Federal Trade Commission, who looked askance on mergers *within* industries, did not flinch when companies in disparate lines of business married. And so it was not unusual for firms in, say, weaponry and greeting cards, or hearing aids and snowmobiles, or, for that matter, underwear and ballasts, to find themselves huddled under the same corporate roof. "It will be our policy to continue seeking favorable opportunities for expansion and diversification in areas which may or may not be related to the business of our present subsidiaries," Mickey Newman declared to P&R shareholders in 1963.

The spending spree was on. Public corporations gobbled almost any line of business they thought could run profitably, provided the right terms and the right people were included. The men who ran these companies were financiers—conglomerateurs—not manufacturers. They might not know a ballast from a beehive, but they could read a balance sheet and an income statement, could assess an acquisition target's sales and earnings potential, could plot how to offset losses in one division with profits from another.

When Bernie Aronson called Mickey Newman early one evening toward the end of the year, Newman was unsurprised to pick up the phone to the recitation of words he had heard hundreds and hundreds of times: "I got a deal to show you." "I was always getting those calls," Newman remembered not long ago, "and probably forty-nine out of fifty of them were not of interest."

But Aronson knew how to rouse his old friend.

"Do me a favor," Aronson said. "Take a look outside your office." Newman puffed his pipe and gazed out his fourteenth-floor window at 400 Park Avenue, his view overlooking the landmark Pan Am Building next to Grand Central Station.

"See those zillions of lights sparkling out of all those office buildings?" Aronson asked. "Those are fluorescent lights, and every one of those lights needs a couple of somethings called ballasts, and you multiply that times all the cities throughout the country and you've got a helluva market."

In a very short time, the deal was done. Philadelphia & Reading insisted that Archie and Paul Einhorn and Rube Pashman stay on, and told them, Einhorn recalls, "that they'd leave us strictly alone as long as we met our budgeted targets." By December, when Archie and Einhorn attended P&R's holiday party, the Universal executives got their first real glimpse of the diversity of their new corporate parent. (The deal would not close until December 31, but they had reached a handshake agreement.) As they milled about with cocktails, the ballast makers met executives in underwear (Union Underwear), cowboy boots (Acme Boot), toys (Deluxe Reading), textiles (Fruit of the Loom), work clothes (Blue Ridge Manufacturers), and dress shirts (Imperial Shirt).

The sale barely registered amid the frenzy of corporate acquisitions; it merited but a single sentence in the *Wall Street Journal*: "Philadelphia & Reading Corp. disclosed acquisition of Universal Manufacturing Corp., a manufacturer of electrical components, for an undisclosed amount of cash and notes." The sale did not immediately change the lives of Universal employees, save for that of Archie's, who became an overnight multimillionaire—P&R paid Universal $8.7 million (of which $2 million was in notes to be paid out of Universal's future earnings). And Archie made no big deal about the new owners. He didn't even bother to inform most of his senior management. Down in Mississippi, Sig Steinberger heard of the sale from Sidney Davis, Universal's well-connected banker in Mendenhall. "I hear you're working for the railroad now," Davis remarked.

Mickey Newman's corporate empire was run like a feudal kingdom: The chief executive officers of P&R's operating companies were like medieval barons, with omnipotence in their own far-flung fiefs. Archie, along with Paul Einhorn and Rube Pashman, presided over Universal's day-to-day operations. Archie announced there would be no changes in personnel or policies and that Universal would continue to operate autonomously. "Our joining the Philadelphia & Reading family will not involve any change in the operating policies of Universal," he told the *Simpson County News*. "Present management will continue to operate Universal . . . and present personnel will be retained in accordance with previous policy."

Universal would never be the same.

The winds of change blew subtly after the sale, at least toward the hourly employees. Paul Einhorn felt the first currents, when the vice president of finance for P&R telephoned him to say he'd hired a new accounting clerk for Universal. Her name was Chestina Hughes and she had been the star of the finance department at Deluxe Reading, the P&R toy subsidiary based in Elizabeth, New Jersey. In the previous couple of years, though, Deluxe, a maker of low-end toys sold primarily through supermarkets, had failed to keep up with market trends; earnings had plummeted from $1.3 million in 1961 to $70,000 in 1962. Philadelphia & Reading responded, in part, by "strengthening the organizational structure"—it fired the toy company's entire finance department, save for Chestina Hughes. Hughes resigned in protest and moved to Florida, where she planned to repose awhile and rethink her career options.

In early 1964, though, she was wooed back to work by the honeyed words of P&R's vice president of finance, Paul Weir. "We just purchased this beautiful little company and they don't know it, but they need you." Weir begged Hughes to call Paul Einhorn, who, as instructed, invited Hughes to come work at Universal. Weir was concerned that however proficient Einhorn was at accounting, he was inexpert in the art of budgeting for manufacturing. "He didn't know what expense-absorption was," Hughes recalls by way of example, "or how to cost a product." Hughes worked alongside the company's comptroller, a somewhat dim bulb who seemed to brighten the moment Hughes came to work. "Eventually I found out that the answers to the questions I was asking of my comptroller were being funneled to him by Chestina," says Einhorn. "So I asked myself what do I need the comp-troller for? And I got rid of him and made Chestina vice president of finance."

Hughes set about revamping the company's organizational struc-ture. She began by dismantling Archie's quirky bookkeeping system. Archie's jury-rigged accounting had worked well enough while Univer-sal's books were open only to a privileged few, but could not pass the muster of a public company. Hughes wrote budgets, monthly and yearly, and set up company-wide controls for the first time, consolidat-ing its various businesses—the wire mill, the capacitor plant, the bal-last operations—under one accounting roof.

In Mississippi, too, the change of ownership would be quickly apparent. Major decisions—decisions the Universal executives were utterly qualified and often in a better position to make—were not to be made without P&R's advice and consent. This decree was initially most conspicuous in terms of labor relations. Where Archie and Rube had enjoyed a convivial, even collegial, relationship with the Teamsters local in Paterson (other than during the IUE war, when the Teamsters affected militance), P&R's vice president of personnel, Robert C. Courboin, radiated no warmth toward organized labor. He made clear that no longer would labor-policy decisions at the Simpson County plant rest with Sig Steinberger and top management in Paterson. When word of labor's presence in Mendenhall reached Courboin, he ordered Steinberger to "fight 'em."

Steinberger could be tough, but he was not reflexively antiunion. When he worked for Bendix Aviation in New Jersey after the war, he was a union member, and during his years in Paterson he became friendly with Mike Ardis of the Teamsters. Courboin had come to P&R

from St. Regis Paper Company, where he had been involved in several bruising union disputes. "He was a pure hardball player," Steinberger says.

Courboin does not disagree with that assessment. "Our posture was to keep our businesses as union-free as we could. I wasn't about to roll over and play dead."

TEN

Handbills from Heaven

O N A MARCH AFTERNOON hinting at spring, two men appear on the shoulder of Highway 49, at the foot of the entrance drive to the plant. One is thirty years old, the other a few years older. Both are white, dressed casually in blue jeans and sport shirts, and bearing a stack of leaflets. It is shortly before three-thirty, and the men are preparing to handbill Universal's four hundred employees as they head home at the end of the workday. The two men have been in Mendenhall for a couple of weeks, working stealthily, as stealthily as possible, at any rate, in a small town where new faces stand out like Mount Rushmore. They are union organizers, representatives for the International Brotherhood of Electrical Workers, AFL-CIO. They have spent their evenings calling on individual Universal workers at their homes, gauging their support for union representation, seeking to put together an in-plant organizing committee. Until this afternoon they had yet to appear in public, had yet to understand just how fruitless was their attempt to remain inconspicuous.

About the time the washup bell sounds inside, six men emerge from the plant to inquire of the strangers their business. The organizers give each a leaflet, tailored to address the primary concern expressed during the house calls of the preceding weeks.

"Dear Fellow Employee," the self-designated leader of the six men reads aloud,

> By Filling Out and signing the attached card and <u>Mailing it Today</u> in the Postage Free Envelope it will be your first step to Have Union Representation which we know many of you desire But Fear that Company knowledge of your desire may perhaps lead to your dismissal.
>
> By Filling Out and signing this card in the <u>Privacy of your Own Home</u> and <u>Mailing it</u> There is <u>No</u> possible way [Universal] can gain knowledge of your doing so . . .

At this point, even before he reaches the inflammatory part, the paragraph that explains that the cards will eventually be submitted to the National Labor Relations Board, "an agency of the Federal Government"—the very same government that was intent on ramming integration through their workplace—the leader of the plant committee wordlessly digs a matchbook out of his pants pocket. Moments later his and the others' leaflets are aflame, fluttering to the ground.

"Well, that's real smart," said Wallace Wickliff, one of the union men. "Did you learn anything before you burned it?"

"By God, no," he is told, "but you better not be here tomorrow or you're dead."

Due in great measure to the state's stringent right-to-work law, organized labor had never achieved a foothold in Mississippi. Despite this fact, whenever and wherever labor knocked, the state sounded the alarm. "The plan of the AFL-CIO to take control of politics in Mississippi will succeed" unless counterattack is taken, the head of the Mississippi Economic Council had warned. "The danger is real, the time is now."

It is Wednesday, March 11, 1964. The U.S. Senate had opened debate on the civil rights bill on Monday, a month after it cleared the House. Besides the future of race relations, on this day the rulers of Simpson County are most distressed about the union menace at their door. To them a successful invasion of organized labor would represent a harbinger of "even further liberalism than has been manifested by the national government." Money and organization would be required, the Economic Council advised, to avert "domination by those who are unfriendly to us and our way of life."

The unfriendly faces at Universal's door belong to Wallace G. Wickliff and E. C. (Red) Fiering. The IBEW had dispatched the pair to scout Simpson County after learning that several Southern lighting-fixture manufacturers under contract to the union were installing non-union-made ballasts from the new Universal plant. At the end of February, they checked into a motor court in the village of Sanatorium, in the shadow of the state tuberculosis hospital, and quietly went to work. (The motel was well located: near the plant and between the two metropolises, Mendenhall and Magee.) Fiering was himself a Southerner, a Floridian who had worked on many organizing campaigns in his native region. Wickliff was a native of Ohio who had hopscotched around the country for the IBEW, often landing jobs inside nonunion factories to scout organizing possibilities.

On March 17, six days after the organizers' aborted attempt to distribute union literature, Robert Courboin, the hard-boiled labor-relations man at Universal's parent company, Philadelphia & Reading, instructed Sig Steinberger to call a plant-wide meeting, otherwise known as a "captive-audience" session. At the meeting, held in the cafeteria, Steinberger read a speech coauthored by Courboin and a P&R labor lawyer from Atlanta. According to the union, the speech implied that "Universal left Paterson to get away from the union and that Universal then employed four hundred and ten employees and that if the union came in they would never employ the four hundred and eleventh."

Two days later, the *Magee Courier* chimed in with a front-page editorial, the first of many in the county's two weeklies denouncing the interlopers.

> [T]oday, with 400 plus people gainfully employed at Universal, outside organizers are camping with Universal employees in an effort to get them to join up with labor unions, who through their liberal policies, have helped promote many problems throughout the nation and have caused many employed to become unemployed.

For such a service they require the employee to pay a dues fee of $60 per year out of their earnings in order that their labor union bosses might have more padding on their office chairs and thicker carpets on their floors.

Simpson County is proud of the industrial benefits which have come inside her boundaries and looks forward to future industrial expansion and development.

However, if Simpson County industry is to become "hamstrung" with labor union agitators, it could mark the end of, not only present industry in Simpson County but all future industrial development. . . .

The citizens of Simpson County can well afford to resist the efforts of these outsiders who HAVE NOT and WILL NOT contribute anything to the progress of Simpson County. They are just looking for a free slice of cake after the baking.

Nearly thirty-five years after he wrote those words, G. O. Parker Jr. was asked why he was so virulently antiunion. "We worked hard trying to locate that industry here," Parker replied. He had been a member of the county delegation that toured the Paterson plant at Archie Sergy's invitation. "We had all spent a good deal of time and energy and so had the governor and the A&I Board, and then here came the union."

Parker says the Universal executives in Paterson "made it plain they were interested in our labor supply. They told us they liked the fact that our people had worked in cotton fields and had good hand dexterity. And that the people were used to hard work and not high wages—many of these people had picked cotton for a nickel a day." He adds: "I didn't want to see the union prematurely kill the goose that laid the golden egg."

Parker was a driving force behind formation of the Universal Citizens Advisory Committee, a group of business and professional men, elected officials, Parker himself, and his counterpart at the *Simpson County News*, Royce Coughman. At the behest of Universal's Rube Pashman, the company's Mendenhall banker invited some two dozen Simpson Countians to dinner at the Jackson Country Club. They dined in late 1963, around the time of the grand opening. Pashman told the assembled he was concerned that the company was on alien ground and could use some extra eyes and ears in the community. "We recognized that we, perhaps, didn't know too much about the South," he later recalled saying. "We were just kind of greenhorns down there, you know."

The Advisory Committee was formed shortly before the plant opened in 1963 but was mostly dormant until the threat of unionization surfaced. Then it sprung into action with such ferocity that not only would it be impossible to conduct a fair representation election but the union organizers had cause to fear for their lives. The Advisory Committee's constant theme was that the success of the union would mean economic doom—for Universal employees and their families, and for the whole county. This was horsewhipped in the editorial and advertising columns of the newspapers, in leaflets given to antiunion employees to distribute, in the captive-audience sessions.

Under the page-one headline WHO WANTS TO DESTROY SANTA CLAUS? Parker wrote in late March that "it's not Christmas, that's true, but it is truly the dawning of a new day and new era for Simpson County with our future developments resting chiefly on our personal behavior, our desire to cooperate with existing enterprise, and our willingness to keep our county free of inside and outside interference and turmoil."

In the same week's edition of the *County News* appeared a full-page advertisement, paid for by "Citizens of and for Simpson County," portending economic disaster if the union were victorious. "TRIUMPH COULD TURN INTO TRAGEDY if this happens. There is a serious threat that this plant would be completely closed if the employees should affiliate themselves with a union. This would be a tragedy for the employees and for every taxpayer in Simpson County." The ad included two photographs: of the full parking lot at Universal, and of an empty aluminum-company plant "for sale or lease" in Sheffield, Alabama, where "union demands forced the plant management to completely close and liquidate their operations. There is the vacant building—EMPTY, NO JOBS, NO PAYROLL, NO BENEFITS, NO FUTURE!"

The IBEW replied to the charges by producing a full-page camera-ready ad for both papers. Neither the *Courier* nor the *News* would accept the union's money; they refused to run the ad. So the union reproduced it as a leaflet, which they distributed at the plant gate and through the mail to all Simpson County residents.

"WHO'S KIDDING WHO???" it began.

While it is hoped the company WILL NOT RUN AWAY if its employees form a labor organization, IT IS INCONCEIVABLE THE BOARD OF SUPERVISORS . . . WOULD ENTER INTO ANY AGREEMENT WITH UNIVERSAL . . . WHICH DID NOT CONTAIN SAFEGUARDS TO PREVENT THE COMPANY FROM MOVING AWAY, FOR ANY REASON, LEAVING THE TAXPAYERS . . . SO DEEPLY INDEBTED AND WITHOUT ANY RECOURSE. IF THIS HAS BEEN DONE, THEN WE HAVE ERRED IN OUR JUDGMENT THAT THE BOARD OF SUPERVISORS ARE RESPONSIBLE MEN DEDICATED TO THE WELFARE OF SIMPSON COUNTY.

Closing ranks with the editors and the Advisory Committee were local law enforcement officials, who, if they themselves did not participate in vigilantism, certainly looked the other way in the face of it. At eight-thirty on the morning of May 24, for instance, Red Fiering heard a knock at the door of his motel room. Opening it, he encountered eight men who greeted him with six-inch knives. They told him and Wally Wickliff they had twelve hours to leave the county. Ignore the warning, they were told, and "you'll be hurt, or if you're lucky, killed."

The organizers placed a call to their boss, Paul Menger, the IBEW's director of organizing, in Washington. Menger spoke with a union attorney, who recommended they notify the FBI and the Simpson County sheriff. Later that morning, an FBI agent arrived to interview the shaken Fiering and Wickliff. The events also unnerved the motel manager, who asked the men to check out. That evening, as they were packing for a move to Jackson, local law enforcers arrived. It was six-thirty, ten hours after Fiering called the sheriff's department. Highway patrolman Frank Thames recalls that the mob was still in the area, but a hundred yards or so up the road. "One man was still muttering that he was gonna cut the guy's blankety-blank head off," says Thames, who confiscated the man's knife. When the unionists asked Sheriff Howard Varner if he could protect them if they remained in the county, the sheriff replied that there was nothing he could do "until trouble actually started."

Trouble started anew in the fall. The organizers had taken the summer off from the Universal campaign to let things cool down and to await word of an unfair-labor-practice charge the IBEW had filed with the NLRB over the captive-audience session in March. Wickliff and Fiering did not go far, however. They spent the summer canvassing for support at a wire-cable plant in neighboring Rankin County. Following the union's election victory there in late August and their work on the resulting contract, Wickliff and Fiering revived the Universal campaign, hoping to point to their experience in Rankin County as illustrative of the potential in Simpson County for a civil relationship between labor and the community.

It was not to be.

No sooner had the duo set foot once again in Mendenhall than their foes resurfaced. By late October, Wickliff recalls, he and Fiering were under constant surveillance, as were their key supporters in the plant. And all job applicants were being questioned about their attitude toward unions, according to an IBEW report. (Steinberger says he was unaware that the state Employment Security Commission, which was still screening Universal applicants, administered such questions.) By then, word in the plant had it that the union was running scared. In truth, the union *was* running scared; Fiering and Wickliff returned to the plant gates—the "gates of hell," they joked—only after assurances from Washington that reinforcements were on the way.

One other development helped, too. In October, the trial examiner for the NLRB ruled that the captive-audience speech Sig Steinberger read violated federal labor law by threatening employees with discharge and plant closure if the IBEW became their bargaining representative. The trial examiner ordered the company to refrain from such practices, to post a notice to that effect on the bulletin board, and to read the notice aloud to the employees.

On the afternoon of October 28, Wickliff and Fiering, bearing armloads of leaflets, returned to Universal for the first time since the mob had forced them out of the county five months earlier. When they arrived at the plant a few minutes before the shift ended, they were met by several highway patrol cars and Sheriff Varner. Before a single employee had left the plant, a patrolman told Wickliff, "If a mob of guys shows up out here, I am going to ask you to move." Just then, four carloads, including at least one car driven by a highway patrolman, pulled up to the plant entrance. As the men milled about, the patrolman ordered Fiering and Wickliff to leave the county. He escorted them to their van and followed them north to the county line, toward Jackson. Behind the trooper's car were the four other vehicles.

Again the organizers called headquarters in Washington for advice, and this time they were directed to sit tight in Jackson, while the legal department researched some options. It was several months in the making, but the rejoinder the IBEW developed would pack quite a punch.

On January 20, 1965, Lyndon Johnson took the oath of office for his full term. He had routed Senator Barry Goldwater in November by nearly 16 million votes, garnering a record 61 percent of the vote. Goldwater carried his home state of Arizona (by half a percentage point) and five Deep South states, Mississippi included. In the lily-white precincts of Simpson County, Goldwater positively buried Johnson, winning 4,872 votes to only 270 for the president. There, as throughout the nation, the election could be seen as a referendum on civil rights. (Nationally, no member of Congress who had voted for the Civil Rights Act of 1964 was defeated, while half the Northern members who opposed the bill faced defeat on election day.)

The rulers of Simpson County received twin blasts of cold air from Washington on Inauguration Day. Besides having to witness "the first Inauguration where every operation was integrated from the church to the ballroom" (Leontyne Price, the black soprano and a Mississippi native, sang "America the Beautiful" at the swearing-in ceremony), they also received word they had been sued. The IBEW that morning filed a federal lawsuit charging some thirty-two individuals in Simpson County with conspiring to deprive its union representatives of their civil rights in violation of the Fourteenth Amendment. Named as defendants were Universal Manufacturing Corporation, Sig Steinberger and his assistant, five county supervisors, the mayors and ten aldermen of Mendenhall and Magee, Sheriff Varner, a state police official, and thirteen other county officials and private citizens, among them the two newspaper editors. The plaintiffs were the two union organizers, Wickliff and Fiering, along with two Universal employees who were active in the in-plant committee.

The suit, filed in federal district court in Jackson, alleged that the "prime objective" of the Citizens Advisory Committee was the "prevention—by all possible means, lawful or otherwise"—of a union at Universal. The three-count complaint listed numerous acts of alleged conspiracy and "discrimination" against the plaintiffs, and charged the defendants with depriving the unionists of their right "to be free from mob violence and terror . . . to disseminate and receive information . . . and to assemble peaceably. . . ." In addition to damages of half a million dollars—$100,000 in compensatory damages and $400,000 in punitive damages—the suit asked for an injunction enjoining the defendants to cease "their anti-union terror campaign."

Certainly the lawsuit spoke to the union's resolve; the IBEW was not going meekly. But the federal courthouse in Jackson was hardly the lone battlefield; the union needed a show of strength on its opponents' home turf. It needed a spectacle in Simpson County.

The idea was Wally Wickliff's, and it came to him out of despair. For all the splash the lawsuit would make, he believed he was risking his life to return to Simpson County. (It was hardly a delusional thought: It was in August that the three civil rights workers in Neshoba County—Goodman, Schwerner, and Chaney—had turned up murdered.) And yet, Wickliff also believed that the union stood a chance to gain what so far it had been denied: a means to get its message out, unfiltered, to the people who mattered—the Universal workers. Certainly the lawyers could help with that, but the judicial gears ground slowly, and Wickliff felt the union needed to bolster its efforts with a swift tactical strike at the plant. On the Monday after news of the suit led the local papers—UNION REPRESENTATIVES CHARGE ANTI-UNION CONSPIRACY IN SIMPSON—Wickliff revealed his new stratagem.

The Universal workers heard it before they saw it: a faint skyward murmur. Then the noise grew louder, and as it grew louder, it grew more distinctive—a rushing, whirring, rhythmic sound. And when finally the noise grew so loud the sky above Universal was fairly roaring, so loud, one worker recalls, "we thought we were being invaded," the entire plant emptied to search the skies. And there it was, "swoop-swooping right out of nowhere," directly above the Universal parking lot: a helicopter. And as the people on the ground pointed and shouted in disbelief, there came raining down a blizzard of paper—"handbills from heaven," one employee put it. And then the helicopter dipped lower, so low that the people on the ground could recognize the man in the passenger seat grinning and leaning out of the glass-bubbled chopper. He was Wally Wickliff, the union man, the man who had been run out of town. Now, on the afternoon of January 24, 1965, Wally Wickliff was back, and so was his union. "**IBEW**," the fluttering leaflets proclaimed in bold, block lettering, "**HERE TO STAY**."

Word of the union's sensational return to the premises touched a raw nerve at Philadelphia & Reading. From the holding company's headquarters in New York, Bob Courboin instructed Sig Steinberger to return fire—with a toy machine gun. In a bow to corporate synergy, he sent Steinberger a "Johnny Seven O.M.A." (One Man Army), a three-quarter-size authentic-looking machine gun manufactured by the P&R toy-company subsidiary, Deluxe Reading.

Courboin ordered Steinberger to mount the machine gun on the roof of the plant and to cover it with a tarpaulin. "When the helicopter comes around again," he instructed, "get a bunch of guys, go up there, take the tarp off, and point it at 'em." The tactic may not have startled the union supporters (none recalls the gun), but what truly terrified them was the live ammunition some antiunionists fired one month later.

By the middle of February, the organizers had quietly held a series of meetings of pro-union employees in private homes. The first was way out in the country, at the home of a coil-finishing worker named Annie Mae Traxler. She lived in the New Zion community, a settlement of some seventy-five houses outside of Braxton, itself a snug hamlet a dozen miles or so northwest of downtown Mendenhall. Six people attended the first meeting, recalls Mildred Andrews, who also lived in New Zion. Unlike most of her co-workers, Andrews was familiar with unions. She had spent six years, from 1952 to 1958, working as a telephone operator in Jackson for Southern Bell, where she belonged to the Communications Workers of America.

"I knew what a union could do for you," Andrews says. "And at that first meeting I started talking about how low our wages at Universal were, and [that] we had no retirement or medical insurance or seniority, and how good our benefits were at the telephone company." Andrews quit her job at Southern Bell when she and her husband moved from Jackson to Simpson County. "Universal started me at a dollar-fifteen an hour," Andrews recalls, "with no benefits—absolutely nothing. And I wanted to get us hospital insurance. I knew a union could help us get that."

The small group became a dozen, and then twenty, and it became necessary to rent a meeting space. But no one who controlled the county's public buildings or halls or restaurants would rent to the union. So they traveled the long miles to Jackson for meetings. Eventually, the Simpson County branch of the American Legion broke ranks, granting its hut to the union. After one meeting there, Jewel Roberts, a member of the organizing committee, recalled, "we never got the hut again." Like her fellow members of the in-plant committee, Roberts was unprepared for the vitriolic response to their organizing efforts. "We were scorned, shunned by our neighbors and fellow employees, called Communists and put down to earth with the cold red clay of Simpson County," she would later write.

Words were not the sole weapons their opponents employed. On February 20, fifty or sixty union supporters crowded into the banquet room of Arnold's Restaurant in Sanatorium, near the motel from which the organizers had been rousted. After the meeting, and after Arnold's closed for the night, "several carloads" of night riders sent the building owner a forceful message that his decision to let the hall to the IBEW was misguided: Shotgun blasts shattered the three plate-glass windows at the front of the café. As a further reminder that the owner should think twice about to whom he might rent his hall, the vigilantes played yet another trick derived from the Kluxers and such who were riding roughshod over civil rights gatherings elsewhere in the state. They spread roofing tacks across the parking lot. The sheriff's investigation reached as far as requesting of the union a list of names of those Universal employees present at the meeting.

To the safe haven of Jackson the union meetings returned. Despite the inconvenience, attendance kept rising, and by early March the organizers believed they had enough support and had collected enough union authorization cards to stage their own show of force: On March 5, they filed a representation petition with the National Labor Relations Board. The board set the election date for Friday, April 23. The last, crucial phase of the campaign had begun.

The company fired an early salvo by announcing it was going ahead with an oft-requested and much-needed improvement in the plant: air-conditioning. "That was one of the things the union was bitching about," Sig Steinberger says, "and they were right—it *was* hot in there."

The proclamation led the news that week in the *Magee Courier,* which took the occasion to remind readers that "Simpson County can boast of an industrial facility second to none in the United States as to equipment, building and working surroundings." The story quoted Archie Sergy, who described his workforce as "industrious, faithful and attentive to their work." He said the installation of air-conditioning was a show of "faith in the future development of this fine facility for the mutual benefit of all concerned. . . ."

Archie's point was that Universal expected loyalty in return for its benevolence. If the point needed underscoring, the *Courier* was pleased to oblige. In a front-page editorial adjoining the news story, editor G. O. Parker Jr. laid out anew the case against the union.

"From whence do benefits come?" he asked. "When we needed jobs for Simpson Countians, no outside group of agitators or organizers came forward to offer one whit of sympathy, suggestion or work. . . .

"One cannot help but recall the story of the little red hen who could find no one to help make the bread, but, once made, many stood ready to eat. Beware of the 'Johnny come lately' who promises something for nothing, while at the same time siphoning money from the pockets of those he promises to help."

As election day neared, the war of leaflets and charges and counter-charges intensified. The union established a telephone "Truth Line"—daily recorded messages excoriating the opposition. The IBEW's lawsuit against the company and the Universal Citizens Advisory Board, filed three months earlier, had moved along to the discovery stage, and so Wally Wickliff provided callers to the Truth Line—telephone number 6965 (local numbers were only four digits)—with an analysis of the previous day's depositions of company officials. One message began: "Your Truth Committee can now reveal the betrayal of you, the workers of Universal, by company officials in sworn testimony at the Federal Building in Jackson yesterday."

The message itself, however, was hardly truthful; it was instead a collection of half-truths and gross distortions calculated to assuage fears that the union was a bunch of race-mixing agitators: It refuted the newspapers' charges that the union was "soft" on civil rights by demonstrating its own unequivocal stand against integration in the workplace.

> [Company officials] . . . testified under oath that the majority of the workers of Universal, Paterson, New Jersey, are Negroes and Puerto Ricans [who] are being paid an average of thirty cents more an hour than you, the workers of Universal in Simpson County. The company officials testified, under oath, that [you] are not mature enough to compete with the Negroes and Puerto Ricans of Universal in New Jersey. . . . Big question is Universal going to hire the Negroes and Puerto Ricans in the Simpson County plant if they are laid off at the New Jersey plant?
> Vote yes for IBEW contract to safeguard you, the workers of Simpson County.
> This is your international representative, Wally Wickliff, hoping that you have a good day every day. Thank you for calling your Truth Committee.

Upon hearing those words read aloud more than three decades later, Wickliff paused momentarily and said that despite his public line, he well understood at the time that the real enemy to the union was the Citizens Advisory Committee—the editors, the Simpson County Board of Supervisors, and those who did their bidding in the plant and in law enforcement—who were convinced any future industrial prospect would pass the county by when it learned of the presence of organized labor. "I knew this was about class and not race," Wickliff says. "But talking class to white workers in Mississippi was a no-winner. No one wanted to hear that the pillars of the county didn't have their best interests at heart. So we race-talked about the quote unquote nigger problem. That was the one thing in the plant everyone agreed about: 'protect our jobs, keep the blacks out.' "

But if the Advisory Committee was the driving antiunion force, its members also formed the bedrock of Simpson County—a force much harder to chip away at than the unfamiliar, absentee owners from New Jersey. Given that fact, the union put itself in the awkward and unfortunate position of making claims as false and outlandish as those of the Advisory Committee—like its "Truth Line" charge that without benefit of an IBEW contract, hordes of dark masses from Paterson could displace the Simpson County workers.

The company, too, found itself in an uncomfortable position, caught between its desire to avoid conflict with both the union and the county's power brokers. Most of Universal's ballasts were sold and installed in urban areas in regions of the country well populated by union electricians. In that regard it made good sense for Universal ballasts to carry a union label, as did those it produced in Paterson. And until the turf war in 1961 between its long-standing Teamsters local and the IUE, Universal had enjoyed the smoothest of labor relations. As Rube Pashman made clear in a deposition he gave nine days before the election in Mississippi, he was not at all opposed to unions. While he did say, "I don't think that we ought to roll out the red carpet for them," he also said he would brook no tactics that were not "strictly kosher." "I can't, in honesty, object to unions," he added. "We have had unions in Paterson for fifteen years. I don't dislike unions, not by a long shot."

But Rube knew signing a union contract would mean increased costs, especially in wages—a supposed plague on future Simpson County development and one that Universal had hoped to avoid by moving there in the first place. (In fact, as Wally Wickliff accurately pointed out on the Truth Line, the company paid its Mississippi workers some thirty cents an hour less than it paid its Paterson workforce.) Ballast manufacturing, as Rube once explained, is a low-profit, high-volume business. "Slight variances in cost can eat up your profit very quickly." Universal's most costly product sold for three dollars, so even a nickel increase in labor costs, Rube said, "would have a substantial effect" on profit.

There were other interests in play as well. Many merchants who were formerly allied with the Advisory Committee were publicly silent in the weeks immediately preceding the vote. "The retailers discreetly supported the union," Steinberger says. "They thought the higher wages would mean more to spend in their stores." And there were the farmers, who were losing field hands to Universal's higher, steadier wages and better—indoor—working conditions. Some farmers supported the union; they believed the Advisory Committee's propaganda that organized labor's "exorbitant" wage demands and its propensity to strike would indeed force the plant to close—and give them back their workforce.

Caught in the maelstrom of misinformation were the Universal employees. With all the leaflets and accusations and commotion, it was a wonder they continued to stamp out any ballasts. In truth, production did suffer, according to Rube Pashman, who closely monitored events from Paterson through regular phone calls—often six or eight a day—to Steinberger. "We're very unhappy with what we're getting production-wise," Pashman said in the heat of the campaign. "There is much too much confusion in the plant. . . . Girls sitting next to each other, talking about the pros and cons of unions. . . . There [is] a hard time getting a day's work done." Steinberger, for his part, agreed fully. He was tired of serving as the union's punching bag. "What do you want me to do here, Rube?" Steinberger asked his boss. "Fight unions or make ballasts? I can't do both."

The very day Pashman was giving a deposition in Paterson in the IBEW's lawsuit, the *Magee Courier* was stirring the mud ever thicker with a front-page civics lesson titled IT'S TIME TO THINK! The editorial alluding to the Teamsters' president was as irrelevant as it was frank in its base appeal to racism.

"Recently, the news headlined the fact that Mr. Hoffa, head union official, contributed $25,000 to Martin Luther King at the funeral of the lady killed in Alabama. WHOSE MONEY WAS THIS THAT WENT INTO THIS CONTRIBUTION? . . . LET'S STOP AND THINK . . . and while we think, ask a few simple questions. . . .

"Do I want part of my earnings to help support the forces of Martin Luther King?"

In the same edition, for Thursday, April 15, identical full-page advertisements appeared in the *Courier* and the *County News.** The ad spoke directly to Universal employees, warning in eleven numbered paragraphs of the devastation a union victory could bring. One paragraph threatened blacklisting. "If you should become a union member and later terminate your employment with the union plant, could you

---

* Although the ad stated it was "prepared and paid for by friends and neighbors of Simpson County," the NLRB later determined the editors had lifted the copy from various other antiunion ads in newspapers around the state.

expect to find employment with other industry in this area?" Another warned of the irreparable damage, as wage earners and taxpayers, they would suffer. "If any union is successful, all hope of industrial expansion will be lost. You will have placed a heavy tax burden on yourselves, and others who were willing to help the County and to help you."

The ad concluded with a reminder that "Even Though You Signed a Union Card, You Can Still Vote '**NO.**'"

Both papers, meanwhile, continued to reject the IBEW's requests for printing jobs and for advertising space to rebut the charges. (Nor would a local radio station sell the union airtime.) "They told me to name my price," recalls the *Courier*'s Parker.

The union representatives instead shuttled back and forth to Jackson for their printing needs, and relied on the in-plant committee to see that the leaflets hit their target. To the newspapers' frequently cited claim that job security would be tenuous in a union plant, the IBEW countered with a handbill describing job security "Universal Style."

First they hire some men and women, give them a pat-on-the-back, shove an extra nickel or dime in their pocket and call them Supervisors. We think that some of them should be called "Pushers," because all they do is push people around. If they can't find anything wrong with their work, it has been alleged that they deliberately ruin coils and blame it on the workers. **Watch the faces turn red when they read this.** Ziggy [Steinberger], it might be a good idea if you check up on some of your Supervisors. After they find something wrong with the work, or even if they can't find anything wrong, they have the right to say (just because they are supervisors) you are fired, and don't go to the office because they don't want to see you.

The lower portion of the leaflet reprinted a section of a "typical IBEW contract clause" regarding the grievance procedure, which allowed for the dismissed worker to present his side of the story to a shop steward before having to leave the premises and to have an airing of the grievance within three working days.

The oversize leaflet also took a few swipes at company brass, slyly suggesting that a supposed affair between the assistant plant manager and a supervisor was coloring personnel decisions. It also deviously implied that the union had the goods on the criminal past of Universal's founder and president. "**As for Mr. Sergy,** you can tell him for us that he had better stay in New Jersey, and buy a good **stiff back brush and a lot of lye soap.** Because if he keeps pushing, **we will help him try to wash clean a few records!!**"

The bare-knuckled campaign grew even uglier in the waning days. On the two days prior to the election, a two-page mimeographed handbill, paid for by "Taxpaying Citizens of Simpson County," found its way onto the windshields of cars parked in the Universal lot. On one sheet was reprinted an editorial cartoon from the pages of an IBEW local newspaper in New York City. The drawing depicted an interracial group marching, arm-in-arm, under a banner emblazoned with the familiar civil rights battle cry, "WE SHALL OVERCOME!" Beneath the cartoon the antiunionists posed their own question for Universal workers to ponder: "Where Did the Above Slogan Originate?"

Concerned, perhaps, that their point was too cryptic, the "Taxpaying Citizens" attached a page of unsubtle explanation:

> Have you asked the union why all the unions are pushing the Civil Rights Movement? Is it because all unions are infiltrated with Communists? Here are just a few examples: We all remember the $25,000 to *Martin Luther King*; we remember that George Meany, who is National President of the AFL-CIO said that the voter registration bill was not strong enough. . . .
>
> Wickie [a reference to Wally Wickliff], what did one of your STOOGIES by the name of *Lois Maygors* [a pro-union employee] have to say about the Negroes? She said that she didn't give a *damn* if her kids went to school with the Negroes, and she didn't give a *damn* if she sat right beside them to work, and that the Negroes were better than what she was working with NOW. . . .
>
> YES, LET'S KEEP UNIVERSAL SIMPSON COUNTY "PROFITS" IN SIMPSON COUNTY, NOT IN OHIO, FLORIDA, [the home states of Wickliff and Fiering] NEW YORK, CHICAGO, or the COMMUNIST PARTY.

The day before the election, the *Courier* again devoted the entire top half of its front page to its campaign. Alongside yet another antiunion editorial, WHO AIN'T TELLING THE TRUTH? G. O. Parker provided his own answer under a banner headline: MAGEE COURIER EDITOR FILES DAMAGE SUIT AGAINST UNION. Writing in the third person, Parker said that Parker had filed a suit against the IBEW alleging the union's representatives had "willfully and deliberately" engaged in unspecified "slanderous, libelous, false and malicious acts" against Parker. He said that *Simpson County News* editor Royce Coughman had filed a similar suit and that each was seeking $110,000 in damages.

The page-one editorial and report of the libel suit was hardly all the antiunion ink the *Courier* spilled in its final preelection edition. Directly under the banner headline announcing his lawsuit, and adjacent to the editorial, Parker published the "WE SHALL OVERCOME!" cartoon. (The *County News* also ran the cartoon but instead of the caption, "Where Did the Above Slogan Originate?" chose the snappier "Just a Reminder!")

On an inside page was one last election-eve bit of artistic inspiration—an urgent full-page memorandum "FROM Interested Simpson Countians" "TO Workers & Management at Universal": "DON'T LET AN OUTSIDE UNION INJECT FRICTION IN SIMPSON COUNTY." Below the admonishment was a cartoon: a crudely drawn dandy in top hat and tails with a smirk on his face and a spring in his step—a union organizer—bounding away from a dazed-looking man: a Universal employee. The organizer is brandishing a giant syringe labeled "job-killer syrum, [*sic*]" which he apparently injected in the worker's left arm, from which radiated three harmful aftereffects: "friction, conflict, violence."

Election Day, Friday, April 23. All day long workers streamed into the cafeteria to cast ballots. At shift's end, some 567 employees—clerical workers, production-line workers, maintenance workers—had voted, a turnout of all but 11 eligible voters. "I knew it would be tight," recalls Mildred Andews, a mainstay of the union, "but I was hardheaded and determined and sure we were going to win."

At the end of the day, however, the courage and determination of Andrews and her fellow union supporters could not surmount what the NLRB would later term the "outrageous interference" of many community leaders. Universal workers rejected the IBEW by 15 votes,

287 to 272. (Eight other ballots were challenged, a number insufficient to affect the results.)

Based on the charge that "laboratory conditions which should attend a representation election" were wholly contaminated, thereby denying Universal employees "their right of free choice," the IBEW appealed the results to the Southern regional office of the NLRB. The regional director, based in New Orleans, issued his report promptly enough, in early August, finding the appeal groundless and recommending to the full Labor Board that the union's objections be "overruled in their entirety."

The full Board disagreed with many of its regional director's findings. The regional director, for instance, concluded that the "WE SHALL OVERCOME" cartoon and its attached handbill distributed at the plant linking the union campaign to the civil rights movement and Communism "was truthful and could reasonably be evaluated by the employees." The Board found otherwise, stating that it would not condone linking those movements "as if they were aspects of a single pernicious entity," and "further impl[ying] that IBEW union dues would end up in Communist Party coffers."

The Board also criticized the newspapers for spreading racist propaganda and word that a union victory would "spell *only* economic hardship" for the county. "By appealing to the employees' sentiments as civic minded individuals, injecting the fear of personal economic loss, and playing on racial prejudice, the full-page ads, the editorials, the cartoon, and the handbill were calculated to convince the employees that a vote for the union meant the betrayal of the community's best interests." Faced with this sort of pressure, the Board wrote, the employees were indeed "inhibited from freely exercising their choice in the election."

In an opinion handed down on February 14, 1966, the five-member Board unanimously set aside the election and ordered a new election. By then, however, ten months had passed since the election, and events in Simpson County had overtaken the Board's actions in Washington.

The company had discreetly been looking for a way to recognize the union as bargaining agent. Universal's salesmen and distributors were hearing complaints that their Mississippi-made ballasts were worthless without a union label; union electricians considered it a critical component. But how was Universal to rectify this? That the Labor Board would eventually overturn the tainted election was no certainty.

And if it did order new balloting, *when* would it do so? And what guarantee did the company have that the union would win a new election? Would not members of the Advisory Committee, no matter how much Universal sought to distance itself from them, resort once again to their outlaw behavior? And finally, Universal was now answering more directly to its corporate parent, Philadelphia & Reading, whose chief labor-relations man had instructed Steinberger to "fight 'em." Would P&R be willing to capitulate?

It was up to Rube Pashman, the company's operations manager and master strategist, to forge a way. In a series of wildcat discussions held in late 1965 with IBEW officials in Washington, Pashman proposed that Universal recognize the union on the basis of a card check—that is, it would negotiate a contract if a majority of the union-eligible workers signed authorization cards. By the first days of the new year, the NLRB's forthcoming order of a new election at Universal, to be issued in mid-February, was rendered moot: A retired mediator from the Federal Mediation and Conciliation Service had certified the overwhelming majority of pro-union cards. On February 5, 1966, the members of IBEW Local 2198, Mendenhall, ratified their first contract. The three-year agreement covered some 950 workers and provided for wage increases up to forty-six cents an hour, three additional holidays, longer vacations, insurance, and other benefits.*

The new union merited no immediate attention from the local press. It was not until the NLRB released its decision two weeks later that either paper reported the contract agreement. Both the *Courier* and the *County News* published straightforward news stories gleaned from the Labor Board's press release. But the *County News* could not leave it at that. Like a twitching muscle in a lifeless body, the paper's editorial knee jerked one last time: "The NLRB," the editor's column summarized, "is not in business to be 'judicial' or 'impartial.' Its only purpose is to extend the power of [the] federal government by granting special coercive powers to union leaders." And while the *Courier* saw fit to give the story its due, printing it on the front page, the *County News* buried its four-paragraph account inside the paper, sandwiched

---

* As a part of the deal Pashman struck with the IBEW, the union agreed to drop its lawsuit. U.S. District Judge Harold Cox signed the order of dismissal on December 29, 1966.

between announcements of a first birthday celebration for Jim Giles III and the death of Harmon F. Fortenberry, a sixty-year-old retired farmer from Magee.

IF, AS THE newspaper editors and their cadre of antiunionists charged, organized labor and the civil rights movement marched in lockstep, there was no sign in Simpson County of such orchestration. Indeed, during the whole of the union campaign—from the first days of leafleting in the spring of 1964 through the election thirteen months later—Universal employed not a single black in the production lines. That would not change until after President Lyndon Johnson signed the civil rights bill into law on July 2, 1964—and even then not immediately.

Dorothy Carter

Though ten titles of the omnibus Civil Rights Act of 1964 barred segregation in schools, public accommodations, and federal programs, and another title outlawed both racial and sexual discrimination in employment, the stroke of the president's pen initially triggered advances more symbolic than real. For one thing, although the job-

discrimination barrier may have been lowered, there was an overwhelming gap in education to be overcome. Yet even in Mississippi,
once the act passed, the question was no longer *whether* the law would
be complied with, but *when.*

The segregationists' tone changed almost overnight from defiance
to resignation. The city of Greenwood closed its public swimming
pools rather than comply with the public-accommodations section of
the law. In downtown Jackson, the landmark Robert E. Lee Hotel made
a similar decision: Ten days after the bill became law, management
posted a sign on the hotel's front door: CLOSED IN DESPAIR—CIVIL
RIGHTS BILL UNCONSTITUTIONAL. And days after the law passed, the
editor of the *County News* could only write: "Frustration reigns supreme
in Mississippi over the Civil Rights Law. . . . But we are proud that as yet
there have been no causes for incidents in Simpson County."

For more than a year, race relations in Simpson County would be little
affected by the momentous law; there would be no "incidents." Blacks
were still routinely denied the right to vote, "White" and "Colored"
signs were affixed to the drinking fountains in the courthouse,
the schools remained wholly segregated. As a state Sovereignty Commission investigator reported in a 1965 memorandum, "Even though
the civil rights legislation regarding integration of the schools has
passed and is in effect in many counties in the [state], not one Negro
student has applied to attend a white school in Simpson County." Nor,
he might have added, was there an Urban League or NAACP chapter
in the county, and the more activist movement organizations—CORE
and SNCC and SCLC—were present only via television, radio, and out-
of-town newspapers.

But in July 1965, word did filter down that the last of the major
provisions of the Civil Rights Act of 1964 was going into effect. Title
VII, better known as the Equal Employment section, prohibited discrimination (by firms with twenty-five or more employees) on the basis
of race, color, religion, sex, and national origin, and created the Equal
Employment Opportunity Commission to investigate charges of discrimination in the workplace.

When word reached Louis Carter, he figured his worrying days were
over. He had grown up in the country, on his family's farm outside

Harrisville, about twenty miles from Mendenhall near the Simpson-Copiah county line. "My grandfather had bought his forty acres and a mule during the thirties," he says, adding that owning their land was no ticket to easy street. "We had to eat the damn mule." Like most members of the class of 1961 at New Hymn, the black school in rural Simpson County, he had left home soon after receiving his diploma. He joined the Army, which sent him to Fort Riley, in Kansas. In the fall of the year, he returned home to marry a classmate, Dorothy Black.

Dorothy, too, was born and raised in the country; her parents farmed cotton and corn and some cucumbers. The family also raised hogs and dairy cows. "Even if it was nothing but a biscuit every day, we never went hungry," Dorothy says.

Her parents had been denied a formal education; neither had made it past eighth grade. But they saw to it—"demanded"—that Dorothy and her five sisters (she was a middle child) finish high school. And even though Dorothy's parents needed her in the fields, keeping her and her sisters out of school every September and October to pick cotton, Dorothy always managed to attend school when the books (handed down from the rural white school) were distributed, and always kept up with her studies. On graduation day her hard work was recognized: She was honored as salutatorian of the New Hymn class of 1961.

There would be no immediate payoff for her academic prowess. Like Louis, she could find no job worth taking at home, and after his stint in the Army, they decided to follow the path of most of their classmates: They moved up North. They headed to Indianapolis, where opportunities were little better. In the spring of 1963, as construction was under way on the Universal plant, Dorothy and Louis came home, moving in with Louis's parents. Louis found occasional work cutting pulpwood (there was no work when it rained); Dorothy went to work as a maid in Jackson, some thirty-five miles from home. She earned three dollars a day, one of which went to her carpool driver.

In December of 1963, when Universal celebrated its grand opening, both of the county's weekly newspapers, the *Magee Courier* and the *Simpson County News,* heralded the event with special advertising sections. Various of Universal's contractors purchased ads extolling themselves—WE PROUDLY ANNOUNCE THAT WE WERE RESPONSIBLE FOR THE PAINTING OF THIS NEW PLANT—and Universal as good neighbors and good corporate citizens. Walter Chevrolet of Magee made known its belief that Universal was "one of Simpson County's finest assets," and that it, Walter Chevrolet, carried "a honey of a used car selection!"

Among the larger ads was one for Mississippi Power & Light, whose director of community and industrial development had served as matchmaker for Universal and Simpson County. Under a photo of an assortment of electrical products—a lawn mower, power saw, hi-fi, coffeepot—and the headline ON THE GO WITH MP&L ELECTRICITY, the company boasted of its role in helping the state's "industrial inventory" grow to include "everything from automatic submarines to zippers." "This week," it added, "MP&L joins with all Mississippians in welcoming to our state the Universal Manufacturing Corporation. Important new plants like this mean economic growth and increased opportunities not just for the citizens of Simpson County but for the entire area."

But not all in Simpson County would reap the benefits of the gleaming new plant. Not only, for example, had nearly half the county's voting-age population been denied the right to vote on the bond issue, but they were now being denied the opportunity to work in its industrial showcase. Says Louis Carter: "When they floated the bond issue, they wouldn't let me vote, but don't you know they taxed me the same as they taxed white people? So then I'm paying for their place to work, but yet I can't work there."

One morning in the summer of 1965, Louis's father-in-law told him and Dorothy of a news report he'd just heard. "The government is making them hire black folks, so you need to go up there." Dorothy did not go right away, but Louis and a friend made a beeline for the plant gate, where a guard matter-of-factly informed them the company would not be taking their applications: "We don't hire niggers here."

It was not long, however, before the Carters heard through the grapevine that Universal had hired a handful of black applicants. In August, Dorothy decided to try her luck. This time the guard showed her in. She was hired the day she applied. She was assigned to first shift on the final-assembly line, a soldering job, and was told she would earn $1.10 an hour. It may have been the minimum wage, but it was a hefty raise above the $2.00 a day she brought home as a maid. In September, Louis, too, was hired, assigned to the coil-cutting department.

Dorothy and Louis Carter were twenty-two years old, and life was looking rosier.

Theirs was a view that differed from that of the whites on the job. For many of them, the coming influx of black workers—Dorothy was the fifth or sixth hired—constituted too radical a change in the social order. Blacks in Simpson County had always worked *for* whites—as maids, woodcutters, tenant farmers, cooks. "The women worked inside, the men were field niggers," says Louis Carter. "We fixed your fences, hauled your chicken manure." Integration, moreover, led to a bit of a panic over the scarcity of domestic help. "You simply couldn't get a maid," recalls Archie Magee, the former chancery clerk. "We had a maid who left for the company."

The Magee family was not alone in their deprivation. "Every white woman in Mendenhall had a maid, because you could get one for twelve dollars a week," says Lenon Smith, who in 1969 would become Universal's first black supervisor. "And when Universal started hiring [blacks], all of a sudden not only did you have a shortage of maids, but you had white women working alongside the ladies who used to scrub their floors and wash their dishes."

If Universal's white workers thought integration spelled doom, it represented a whole other variety of agony to their boss, Sig Steinberger. As much as anyone in Simpson County, he was caught in the middle of the old order and the new; as chief executive of the largest employer in the county, he had to navigate through any number of divisive social issues—in and away from the workplace. It was with him that all plant matters rested—from allegations of race and sex discrimination to the invasion of organized labor. These were issues that did not stop at the plant gate, that affected everyone in Simpson County. For Steinberger, the agony was in trying to strike a balance between his beliefs and values and what he judged to be in the best interest of Universal.

"You live a double life as a plant manager here," Steinberger said not long ago. "You have your personal feelings, sure, but you have to keep peace in the plant." By way of example, Steinberger said that on November 22, 1963, Steinberger was "horrified" when his wife June called the plant with word of the news bulletin from Dallas. "I got on the loudspeaker and announced the president just got killed." Instead of muted reaction, he says, the workers "hooted and hollered and celebrated. I kept quiet, because I was always a company man and I felt no matter what the circumstances, I had a job to do. But I'll tell you, it sure caught me by surprise."

Despite efforts to keep his opinions to himself, Steinberger says that to many whites in Simpson County he was known as a "nigger-lover." "You know why? Because I treated blacks as human beings with a job to do, same as I did the whites." He recalls stopping at a filling station once and overhearing a conversation between the proprietor and another man about the low rate of pay at Universal.

"How much are you paying that gentleman who pumped my gas?" Steinberger asked.

"You mean that nigger?"

"I didn't say that."

"Well, I pay him a dollar a day."

"Well," Steinberger said, "we pay more than a dollar an hour."

That attitude earned him some scrutiny from a local Klansman, who was so concerned that Steinberger might be Jewish that one Sunday morning the Kluxer arranged for his son, a Universal employee, to ride with Steinberger to Steinberger's house of worship—an Episcopal church in Jackson. (Steinberger found out later the boy's father was in the Klan.)

There was a strong Klan presence in the plant, primarily in the high-paying maintenance department, where most of the white men worked. But according to many employees, Steinberger made it understood that he would tolerate no intimidation or harassment of the black workers. That stance earned him enemies, made him cautious. He had heard about the manager of a Westinghouse plant in Vicksburg who was blown up by a car bomb. Every morning, for some six months, Steinberger checked the hood of his car, where he kept a piece of Scotch tape, for signs of tampering. "The truth is that the hatred and tension down there was so thick you could feel it," recalls Lenon Smith. "But Mr. Steinberger did a tremendous job leading the plant. His stance on certain principles of fairness nipped a lot of stuff in the bud. He used to say, 'I'm gonna run my plant this way and if you don't like it, you can simply hit Highway 49.' "

●　　●　　●

For many whites, middle-aged women especially, the indignity of working alongside their former maids was too much to bear. "A few were very nice," Dorothy Carter says of her white co-workers, "but some just wouldn't even *look* at you." Others quit. "At first," Steinberger recalls, "for every black who walked in the front door, two whites walked out the back." Still others protested by refusing to share rest-room facilities and drinking fountains. (Archie Sergy had nixed a Jackson architect's original blueprint for the plant, which included separate bathrooms and water fountains.) Says Steinberger: "Some of the white women came to me, 'We can't drink out of the water fountains.' I told them you're welcome to bring water from home, but those are our only fountains." Nor would the company yield on the request for segregated rest rooms, which resulted in vile acts of protest: Some of the women defecated on the bathroom floor. "I wouldn't ask the black janitors to clean up after those women," Steinberger says. "I cleaned it up myself."

Even the parking lot was a steady reminder of white resistance. Says Louis Carter: "You'd see all these cars with their front tags"— license plates—"with, say, a caricature of a black woman, barefoot, pregnant, big lips, nappy hair, saying: I WENT ALL DE WAY WITH LBJ. Or they'd have tags with a picture of a dog chasing a barefoot black guy in overalls with an old hat and big lips and big eyes and the saying: GOIN' COON HUNTIN."

By the beginning of 1966, five months or so after Dorothy and Louis Carter were hired, the union and the company were negotiating their first contract. In addition to bargaining over wage increases and vacations and seniority and other benefits, the all-white union leadership wanted to revisit the question of segregated facilities. On this matter, management made clear, there would be no negotiations. "Steinberger hit the damn ceiling," Louis Carter recalls, "and some of us did, too. *This* is what we're paying dues for?" (Mildred Andrews, a member of the union's bargaining team, says she does not remember asking for separate facilities. She does say a lot of the "older women" resigned because they "didn't appreciate" some of their younger black co-workers—the "smart-alecky ones.")

After nearly three years in coil-winding, Louis Carter decided to test the seniority clause in the union contract. Sometime in 1968, a mechanic's job came open in the all-white maintenance department, which had remained a good-old-boy province. But the job paid better than any other, and Louis figured he had "the seniority and experience" to obtain it. The other main contender, however, was a white man who came from "one of the [prominent] families." The union intervened in behalf of Louis's rival, and the job went to the white man. Louis "raised hell with the union," but the officers ignored his grievance—"just sat on it." So Louis went directly to Sig Steinberger, who took it upon himself to find another job for Louis in maintenance.

His new co-workers made Louis's life hell. All day long they bombarded him with all manner of racial epithets and taunting. It was worst in the men's room, he says, which afforded a certain amount of privacy, and, therefore, a license to rant. "They'd go on about niggers and coons and spooks, and sometimes it would scare the shit out of you. It would really piss you off, but there was always like three black guys and maybe twenty or thirty white guys, so you'd just go in there and take a piss and get the hell out."

Not long after Louis integrated the maintenance department, Steinberger toppled another domino by hiring Lenon Smith as Universal's first black supervisor. The thirty-one-year-old Smith was one of eleven children—all of whom attended college. After graduating from Jackson State in 1960, he took a government job in El Paso, Texas. In 1968, when his father, a retired employee of the Illinois Central Railroad, and his mother were "becoming ageable," Smith returned to Mendenhall to help care for them. Some of his friends were working for Universal, Dorothy and Louis Carter among them, and Smith took a job in the shipping and receiving department. In 1969, Steinberger promoted him to supervisor of impregnation.

Impregnation was the step between the ballast's lamination and its final assembly. After it was laminated, the ballast's coils needed to be demoisturized, which was accomplished by baking the ballast in a 350-degree walk-in oven. From the oven the ballast was put in an impregnating vessel, a pressure cooker. The process sealed the unit, which enabled it to withstand great heat in the fluorescent fixture and to function quietly. The electric ovens were famously cranky, prone to blowing fuses. But the maintenance crew was negligent more than vigilant, figuring, Smith deduced, that if they threw a metaphorical wrench in the impregnation works, Steinberger would back away from his reckless decision to allow a black man to supervise white workers.

"Those guys were old hillbillies who'd done nothing but saw logs and pick cotton, and they'd give 'em a crescent wrench and a socket wrench and let 'em sit on their ass," Smith says. "They'd do everything they could to slow me down," Smith says. "I could page the maintenance boss-man to fix machinery broken down, and he'd be in the cafeteria just drinking coffee and bullshitting—and I'd *see* him in there, through a window, and he *still* wouldn't move. We moved a hundred thousand units a day through there and if we held them up, we held up the money. It was like a car with everything but the wheels."

Smith says he eventually stopped calling maintenance and learned to fix most of the machinery himself. He also complained to Steinberger, who summoned the maintenance foreman to a meeting. "The guy comes running in pointing his finger at me," Smith recalls. "But Mr. Steinberger backed me up. He took a lot of heat for it, too."

By the early 1970s, black workers outnumbered whites. The old guard, however, remained at the helm of Local 2198. Mildred Andrews, the first financial secretary, had been appointed president in June of 1969 to fill the unexpired term of her predecessor, who had moved out of state. In June 1973, Andrews stood for election for a full term. Her opponent was the chief steward on the second shift, Louis Carter.

To the dwindling but boisterous white racists who still dominated certain pockets of the plant, the maintenance department mainly, Louis's candidacy represented the final affront: the coming of black leadership. He was an exemplar of everything they were not: bright, ambitious, and black. And even if Louis's election was inevitable, his enemies, embittered by and frustrated with the changing demographics, were not going to surrender without one more show of intimidation.

The crusade to convince Louis Carter that serving as president would be detrimental to his health began during the campaign, when someone scratched the letters KKK on the side of his pickup truck. "I was pretty sure it didn't stand for Kool Kolored Kat," he says. On election night, as the candidates and their supporters awaited the ballot count outside the union hall, some of the maintenance men spouted Klan-like threats. "They talked about hanging me, hurting my family [if I won]," Louis recalls. The invective provoked skirmishes—"people pushing and shoving"—but, Louis says, it was not until one Saturday soon afterward that he felt truly endangered.

Louis won by a margin of better than two to one of the fourteen hundred votes cast, and faithful to their election-night thundering, his co-workers on second-shift maintenance launched a terror campaign intended to discourage him from taking the oath of office. On the Saturday morning immediately after the election, Louis and the rest of the second-shift mechanics were leaving work after pulling their regular Friday double shift. (Every Friday the second-shift maintenance workers, who normally worked from three-thirty in the afternoon until midnight, stayed overnight to clean the machinery.) As Louis headed north toward home on Highway 49, he noticed a couple of "maintenance buddies" alongside him in a pickup truck. "I was looking at them," he recounts, "and all of sudden this old shotgun pops out the passenger side. I jam on the brakes and the shot goes right across the windshield." Asked many years later if he reported the crime to the police, Louis dismisses the question as hopelessly naïve. "The law around here was about as useless as tits on a bull." But Louis was not without his protectors, black and white, and they organized a postwork midnight caravan of at least five cars to escort him safely to his and Dorothy's isolated country home, "way back in the woods," some twenty miles outside Mendenhall.

Universal escorted Simpson County into the late twentieth century. The company provided an alternative to pulling up stakes after high school or eking a living out of the Simpson County dirt. "I don't know anything for the poor whites and poor blacks that would have done as much good as Universal did for this county," says Lenon Smith, who put in twenty-six years, retiring in 1994. The job had enabled Smith to return home; it allowed so many others to stay, to make a decent living, keep their families intact, contribute to their schools, churches, communities.

Louis Carter: "This plant took people who lived in sharecropper shacks and gave them the means to buy land, an acre, ten acres. People bought their own homes because of this plant. And many of these people when they started work there didn't have a way to get there; they had to ride with somebody else. And now they're driving new automobiles. Or they worked in someone's house washing and ironing, putting that big old heavy iron in the hearth to heat it, and now they have a washer and dryer of their own, and a nice light iron that steams."

Louis Carter and Sig Steinberger shared a vision of equal opportunity. Together they ensured that black women and men and white women were offered management positions—"not just first-line jobs," Louis explains, "but as department heads, decision makers. And because more people could identify with the people in leadership, the company did better, too. It gave us all tremendous pride to work for Universal."

Nor were the Universal workers alone in their new prosperity. Although under the BAWI agreement Universal would pay no taxes during its first decade in Mississippi, the plant created, in the well-worn phrase of many a chamber of commerce official, a "ripple-effect": Numerous local vendors—electrical-supply houses, carton manufacturers, food-service providers—all were given a huge boost. Retailers, too, rode the wave: Womack Ford and Collins Furniture & Upholstery and the Jitney Jungle grocery store, and the Mendenhall Hotel, where Universal housed its traveling executives and fed them "family-style" in its revolving-tables restaurant. Says Lloyd Stephens, the second-generation proprietor of a Mendenhall clothing store that billed itself "The Poor Man's Friend": "We went from a hundred and twenty-five thousand [dollars] a year in sales [before Universal] to over a million."

One thing everyone in Simpson County could agree on, maybe the only thing in those divisive years of the middle sixties through the middle seventies, was how inextricably linked was the community with its largest employer. With so much riding on one horse, it is no wonder that people speculated about what would become of them were Universal ever to close the barn doors. "I remember when everyone was buying a new trailer," says Dorothy Carter, "and someone said, 'Boy, if that plant ever shuts down, they're gonna hook 'em up like a wagon train.' "

Part III

Mexico

ELEVEN

Border Dreams

IN THE SPRING OF 1965, some six months before Dorothy Carter celebrated her first paycheck from Universal by splurging at the grocery store, a high official of the Mexican government, the Secretary of Industry and Commerce, led a delegation of his countrymen on a tour of Far Eastern manufacturing plants. The Asians were working for foreign firms, American electronics and apparel companies mainly, assembling labor-intensive goods for export. In Korea and Taiwan, in Singapore and Hong Kong and Japan, the Mexicans' eyes were opened wide to the possibility of replication. Here was a solution to their own great domestic problem: an abundant labor supply and few jobs.

Though the consequences of the trip would ripple almost immediately through the corridors of international finance, it would be decades before the aftershocks rumbled into Universal, into the lives of Dorothy Carter in Mendenhall and Mollie James in Paterson. For Mollie, Paterson in the spring of 1965 remained full of promise. She was thirty-three years old, in her tenth year with the company. With four children at home—the eldest was fourteen, the youngest nine—and a husband who more often than not drank his paycheck, she also held down a second full-time job, at Popular Merchandise in nearby Passaic. She worked first shift in the shipping department at Popular, a mail-order fulfillment house, from seven A.M. to three P.M. and then went directly to Universal, where she punched in at three-thirty for her second-shift job as press operator, and punched out at midnight. Not even then, after sixteen hours of work, was the day done. "Then I'd come home and take care of my home life," Mollie recalls, "laundry, fixing the kids' meals for the next day." After a few hours of sleep, she would wake Etta, her fourteen-year-old, who "was old enough to do for the other children," and be out the door at six-thirty. Mollie's husband, Sam, could not be counted on for much of anything, not even helping Etta feed the younger children dinner while Mollie was at Universal.

Sometime in 1964, though, Mollie devised a way around that problem. She made a purchase that changed her life: a brand-new Sears double oven equipped with gas and electric stoves and timers for both ovens and the stove-top burners. For slightly under a thousand dollars, she had peace of mind that the kids would eat a hot evening meal, whether or not their father made it home on time. "Before I went to work in the morning, I would put everything on the stove and set the timers. You could set separate temperatures for the top and bottom, and for the eyes [burners], and it would automatically cook everything and shut itself off when it was done. So when they got home from school, the whole meal was already cooked, and Etta would know how to serve it."

Those nonstop days were aimed toward saving enough for her life's ambition: a home of her own. She would reach her goal in September of 1966, when she made a down payment of five thousand dollars on a seventeen-thousand-dollar three-family house near the intersection of Madison and Eleventh avenues.

Down in Mendenhall, too, Mollie's counterpart had reason to be hopeful. Says Dorothy Carter of the company's transcendent impact on her life: "It just changed everything—*everything*. We never had anything of our own before, and before long that first year we bought our first new car—a sixty-five Plymouth with zero miles on it. And then we bought an old house, tore it down, stacked the lumber, and rebuilt it on Louis's parents' place."

Whether in Paterson or Mendenhall, the outside world rarely intruded on the circumscribed lives of Universal workers. When it did, as when the battle erupted in Paterson in the raiding war between the Teamsters and the AFL-CIO, or when the federal government pried open the closed society of Simpson County by certifying the IBEW as the bargaining agent or by mandating desegregation in the plant, it generally intervened for the greater good of the workforce. Notwithstanding those fundamental changes fostered by events and circumstances seemingly far removed from their workplace, Universal in 1965 was an industrial safe-haven seemingly light-years removed from the burgeoning global economy. When many years later both Mollie James and Dorothy Carter would at last feel the tremors of the Mexicans' sightseeing junket to Asia, it was as if their company had gravitated to the fault line of globalization. No longer would Universal seem so remote, so disconnected. It would feel instead for all the world like the epicenter of an economic earthquake.

Due to an act of the U.S. Congress, Mexico's chronically high unemployment rate had spiked even higher in the months immediately preceding the journey abroad of the Secretary of Industry and Commerce, Octaviano Campos Salas. For the previous few years, there had been a pitched battle in Washington over employing Mexican nationals as farmworkers in the United States. The issue pitted agribusiness interests, primarily from the border states of California, Arizona, and Texas, as well as Florida, against organized labor, which maintained that the cheap-labor contracts with Mexican workers—known as *braceros* (translated, loosely, as strong arms)—undercut domestic farmworkers.

That big farmers depended on Mexicans to bring in their crops was nothing new; the United States had relied on Mexican farmworkers for the whole of the century. Mexico, for its part, had relied on the United States to provide jobs for its surplus laborers, for whom their own country "did not have enough work to hold" them. And while there were laws restricting undocumented immigration, the laws were enforced selectively, depending, it seemed, on the current state of the economy. Early in the Great Depression the new Secretary of Labor, William Doak, proposed that "one way to provide work for unemployed Americans was to oust any alien holding a job and to deport him."

But during the Second World War, when the defense effort emptied vast and fertile fields from the Rio Grande Valley of Texas to the Imperial Valley of California, the U.S. and Mexican governments instituted a large-scale contract-labor program for temporary Mexican migrant workers. Although the agreement expired at war's end, the first in a series of new "bracero" agreements was reached in 1946, agreements that would continue uninterrupted through the end of 1964.

At first the bracero program was administered jointly by both governments, which ordained certain requirements: that employers provide a written contract covering wages, hours, working and living conditions; that employers hire Mexicans based on "need"; that they not be used to displace domestic farmworkers nor lower domestic workers' wages; that the migrants leave the United States after the harvest; that there be no racial discrimination against Mexicans in public accommodations. (If a farm community was found to violate the antidiscrimination clause, Mexico could refuse to recertify the locale for bracero labor.)

Over the years contract compliance lapsed, and the employment process devolved from one of close governmental supervision to one in which the braceros were hired through growers associations, with little or no enforcement of federal wage, hour, and housing laws. And more and more frequently, employers sidestepped even the lax regulations by simply hiring undocumented Mexican field hands. Though the Border Patrol sporadically undertook mass deportation drives— most notoriously its 1954 "Operation Wetback"—it was understood that there was room for flexibility. One Border Patrol officer near El Paso, Texas, testified in 1950 that he "received orders" from his superior each harvest to "stop deporting illegal Mexican labor." And a senior officer in south Texas reportedly kept his patrolmen "away from certain farms and ranches in his district."

The Border Patrol's tendency to walk the beat with a blind eye virtually sanctioned the exploitation of Mexican workers. And with the growers allowed unfettered reign to dictate wages and working conditions, abuses of the program became commonplace. In a 1956 study of braceros in California, researcher Ernesto Galarza found that "in almost every area covered by the International Agreement, United States law, state law, and the provision of the work contract, serious violations of the rights of Mexican nationals were found to be the norm rather than the exception."

By the early 1960s, unions, religious groups, and community organizations had mobilized nationwide opposition to the bracero program. Their objections centered on a powerful argument: that if, as the growers maintained, there was a shortage of available domestic workers, it was a shortage perpetuated by the failure of the growers to offer Americans adequate working conditions. The growers were abetted by their potent farm-state allies in Congress, which had yet to extend the federal minimum-wage and collective-bargaining laws to farmworkers. As the *New York Times* editorialized, "When wages and working conditions in the fields approach some minimal level of decency, there will be no shortage of American workers available to harvest the crops."

In spite of the grassroots lobbying effort and unassailable moral arguments, Congress voted in 1961 to extend the program for two years. In 1963, despite opposition by the Kennedy administration and Congressional-hearing disclosures of civil rights violations and wage-reporting fraud by growers, Congress granted the program one final reprieve. It did so only after an eleventh-hour appeal from the Mexican government, which pleaded that given the country's severe unemployment problem, it would need more time to "stave off the sudden crisis" that would accompany the imminent return of some two hundred thousand citizens. Congress acceded to the request; the bracero program would expire, for good, on December 31, 1964.

At the end of May 1965, Secretary Campos returned to Mexico City from his Far Eastern junket determined to match the Asians' industrial successes by liberalizing his country's protectionist trade and investment laws. But Mexico was unready to cede the whole of its emerging industrial economy to American manufacturers. Its turbulent history of state-run development and strictly controlled foreign investment can be traced to the turn of the century, when a popular uprising against the dictatorial president Porfirio Díaz climaxed with the Revolution of 1910. During more than thirty years in power, from 1877 until he was forced from office in 1911, Díaz sought to bring Mexico into the industrial age by "embracing" foreign investment. With the slogan "order and progress," the president oversaw building and public-works projects throughout the country. Railroads, mines, and oil wells were built, banks established, telephone and telegraph lines strung.

The progress came with a price. With the exception of the president and his inner circle, whom foreign investors richly rewarded for their munificence, most Mexicans suffered greatly under the *Porfiriato,* as the era came to be known. Political opposition was squashed, free elections and a free press banned. Large-scale agriculture prospered, but at the expense of peasants who lost their land, mainly to foreign concerns who by 1910 owned fully a quarter of the country's acreage. Indeed, President Díaz granted nearly total control of the country's "modernization" and its resources to foreign corporations. Mexico under Díaz became the world's second-biggest oil exporter, but the industry was owned almost entirely by seventeen British and American firms.

By century's turn, the forces of rebellion were gathering. Some of the rebel leaders were forced into exile in the United States, where they repaired to St. Louis. From there they issued calls for mass strikes in Mexico. Díaz's army crushed the uprisings, and in the 1910 elections he staved off certain defeat only by jailing the opposition candidate, a landowner from the northern state of Coahuila named Francisco Madero. Within the year, however, Madero was out of jail and the anti-Díaz forces had issued a call to arms. In May 1911, when Francisco (Pancho) Villa and his band of revolutionaries took control of Ciudad Juárez, the border town across from El Paso, Texas, Díaz fled the country. In November, Francisco Madero was elected president. He would not serve his full six-year term. In 1913, Díaz's old allies, acting with the complicity of the U.S. envoy to Mexico, assassinated Madero by firing squad.

Following more years of warring between insurgents of varied political stripe (among them the populist Villa and the more radical Emiliano Zapata) and assorted counterrevolutionaries, a new government was formed by a coalition of former Madero loyalists. Though reformists hammered out a new constitution in 1917, the constitution did not end the violence—there would be no peace until 1920. And although foreign capital would continue to play a major role, the Revolution and Constitutional Convention veered Mexico toward a U-turn in economic development, and infused the country with a strong sense of economic nationalism. Succeeding administrations subordinated foreign to domestic interests, and enacted restrictive laws against foreigners owning property and majority shares of Mexican corporations. "Mexicanization" was most vividly demonstrated in 1938, when President Lázaro Cárdenas boldly expropriated the entire foreign oil industry and formed PEMEX, the state-run Mexican Petroleum Company. In the wake of the ouster of such industrial titans as Standard Oil of New Jersey and Royal Dutch/Shell, many other investors retreated, setting their sights elsewhere on the developing-countries horizon. By the time Cárdenas retired in 1940, only 15 percent of Mexico's economy was foreign owned, a decline of fully 50 percent from 1910.

Even as Cárdenas was nationalizing the country's economy and solidifying the ruling party's hold over workers, peasants, and government employees through mandatory membership (via incorporating the mass memberships of their respective unions), the president continued to court foreign, mainly American, capital. Just as Díaz had built the railroads, Cárdenas undertook massive highway-construction and other public-works projects, in great part to open new markets for business and lower transit costs. Much of the loan money to build his great public works came from U.S. banks. As historian Dan La Botz has written, Cárdenas's entire economic program was "intended to promote capitalist development, but development supervised by the revolutionary state."

Cárdenas retired just as Mexico was about to endure a wartime shortage of imports, his handpicked successor (Cárdenas established the practice of the outgoing president recommending his political heir, who in turn became the sole candidate of the ruling PRI—Institutional Revolutionary Party) devoted his administration to promoting domestic manufacturing. And though the Mexicanized economy grew steadily in the postwar years, it could not keep up with the rapid population growth. By the time the U.S. Congress ended the bracero program in December 1964, the country's hallowed resistance to Yankee economic imperialism was no match for its hundreds of thousands of unemployed farmworkers come home to roost in the borderlands.

In his inaugural address that month, President Gustavo Díaz Ordaz pledged his six-year term to improving living standards among Mexico's nineteen million peasants. The *campesinos,* who comprised nearly half the country's population, had a per capita income of less than a hundred dollars a year. "The farm problem," the new president declared, "is Mexico's number one problem. Our attention will be dedicated . . . to the needs of the weakest, the most destitute, among whom the farmworkers are the most numerous."

Díaz Ordaz also signaled he would make the country safe for capitalism, that he would encourage private investment, both domestic and foreign, and that foreigners would no longer have to worry about the threat of expropriation. The president's plan was to establish a new kind of bracero program. Instead of exporting cheap labor to the United States, which was no longer legal, why not invite U.S. manufacturers to bring their assembly work to Mexico? Not only would this reverse-bracero program help provide a solution to Mexico's oppressive unemployment problem, it would appeal to American companies ever eager of finding ways to cut costs of production.

This was not the first time in recent years efforts had been pledged to address the underserved border. In 1961, President Díaz Ordaz's predecessor, Adolfo López Mateos, established the *Programa Nacional Fronterizo,* or PRONAF, to promote border redevelopment. Rather than industrial in scope, PRONAF focused mainly on beautification, vice eradication, and public relations; it sought to clean up the "sin cities," or at least their sordid reputations, in order to bolster the family-tourism trade from the United States. By looking north, however, PRONAF officials failed to address the border cities' principal problem: crushing poverty. Nor did the government commit sufficient funds to the program to provide for more than window dressing: new port-of-entry buildings, widened roadways, some retail and sporting developments, and occasional, well-publicized vice-squad busts. What border citizens needed were jobs, schools, basic amenities: adequate housing, sewers, electricity, potable running water. What PRONAF would give them was Americans come to shop and play golf and watch greyhounds chase mechanical rabbits. "All that most of the North Americans coming here seem to want is a meal, a girl, a souvenir, or a bottle of whiskey," a Juárez businessman complained in 1964.

By the following year, though, American capitalists would pick up the scent of an aroma in the Mexican air even more arousing—an aphrodisiac no night in Boys Town nor the finest tequila could match. The first traces of the sweet smell of money came wafting across the border in May of 1965, when Secretary Campos announced that the industrialization effort would center on the border facing the United States, a remote and historically neglected region spanning some two thousand miles, from Tijuana on the Pacific to Matamoros on the Gulf of Mexico. In July, the Secretary convened a commission of three dozen Mexican power brokers—bankers, developers, industrialists—to prospect for foreign investors for his ambitious plan, which he termed "a new phase of our industrialization." "Our idea is to offer an alternative to Hong Kong, Japan and Puerto Rico for free enterprise," Campos Salas later explained. "There's a need for us to find an outlet for workers with no jobs."

Campos Salas told the assembled the key to success would be "cordial cooperation" between the government and the private sector. What set the pulse of corporate America racing was his declaration that the private sector included the *American* private sector, that after the long winter of Mexicanization, the government was not only liberalizing its restrictive investment laws but offering tax and land concessions and other "new stimulants" to foreign investment.

It was called the Border Industrialization Program (BIP) and it essentially created an insulated parallel economy: an export-driven free-trade zone that permitted foreign manufacturers to assemble goods without having to abide by existing import-export duties and regulations. The free-trade conditions applied to foreign plants located anywhere within 12½ miles of the border. If the plants imported all their raw materials and components, there would be no sales or corporate income taxes to pay—provided all finished products were exported.

The United States, too, provided a key incentive for businesses to establish "export-platforms" in Mexico. The government permitted the duty-free entry of U.S.-made components shipped abroad for assembly and then reimported to the United States. Under a provision of the U.S. Tariff Code, duty payments were required only on the value added in the foreign assembly process—meaning on the value of the low Mexican wages. This tariff item (806.30) had existed since 1930, when the U.S. government sought to promote the assembly of automobiles in Canada, but it was rarely put to use until the newly footloose capitalists of the middle 1960s rediscovered it concurrently with the advent of the Mexican border program. (The industrialists also seized on a more recent companion tariff item, 807.00, which was implemented in 1963 and which further broadened permissible duty-free imports.)

But for all the arcane tax and tariff incentives both countries dangled like a piñata, the most compelling reason for American business to pull up stakes was as it has always been: cheaper, compliant labor. In a speech in Tijuana in August of 1965, Secretary Campos Salas acknowledged as much: The Border Industry Program, he said, would benefit not only the citizens of the border region but "foreign consumers as well, who will be able to obtain products of the highest quality at the lowest prices using the cheap labor—*obra barata*—of the new Mexican workers that this program will create."

In the middle and late 1960s, the wages American companies paid in Mexico were *muy barata*—as low as two dollars daily per worker—less than Universal paid *hourly* in Paterson. "I'm convinced that the potential of cheap labor makes a border operation a natural for any labor-intensive manufacturing," an executive of one of the first American companies to participate in the Border Industrialization Program said in 1967.

The perennial enticement of low wages and weak or nonexistent unions was why Paterson silk makers opened ancillary plants in Pennsylvania at the dawn of the twentieth century; why Archie Sergy planted the Universal flag in Mississippi sixty years later; and why, just a few years after that, some visionary industrialists were rushing past the rural South, all the way across the Rio Grande. "Inexhaustible labor supply, 30 cents an hour," one come-hither pamphlet advertised in the late 1960s. American manufacturers, it continued, "don't have to go to Hong Kong, Taiwan, South Korea or Japan for low-cost, easily trainable foreign labor. . . . It's available right here in North America along the Mexico border for as low as 30 cents an hour in virtually inexhaustible numbers."

The BIP took a couple of years to establish operational, promotional, and application procedures. By 1967, the program was up and running with 72 American-owned plants. The plants would become known as *maquiladoras,* a derivation of *maquilar,* which in turn is a popular form of the verb *maquinar*—roughly, "to submit to the action of a machine."* The number of plants doubled within two years, and

---

* Mexican peasants speak of *maquilar* in relation to corn taken to a mill for processing. The miller grinds the corn, returning all but the portion he keeps, the *"maquila,"* as payment, just as the border factories return their processed goods to the producers for sale.

would double again within five: In 1972 there were 330 plants operating along the border. It would be another fifteen years before Universal itself, or rather its corporate successor, heard the Mexican siren song, but the conditions were ripening for a mass exodus of U.S. corporations. Already such brand names as RCA and General Motors and General Electric had been lured by the mouth-watering tax and wage treats and the lack of burdensome U.S. workplace and environmental regulations. And where they went, others, Universal among them, would surely follow.

TWELVE

Leveraged Lives

ON THE MORNING OF Monday, November 4, 1968, Archie Sergy awoke as usual around seven and padded out to the converted garage off the family room for his ritual calisthenics session. He seemed the picture of health: trim and vibrant, with a lean, handsome face kept tan year-round from regular golf outings. His looks belied a history of heart trouble—he had survived a heart attack eleven years earlier, at the tender age of forty-two. And he had just endured a turbulent, draining fall. One month earlier, on October 4, after two months of fruitless bargaining, more than eight hundred members of Teamsters Local 945 in Paterson had walked off the job at Universal the day their three-year contract expired. They made known that their grievances had as much to do with their bargaining agent as with their employer; the Teamsters, many believed, were selling out the membership yet again. They struck for twenty-five days, demanding not only substantial wage and benefit increases but also a new union.

When the dust settled at the end of October, the Local 945 leadership once again had prevailed. The Teamsters had defeated an attempt by the International Brotherhood of Electrical Workers—the

AFL-CIO affiliate that represented Universal workers in Mississippi—to hold a representation election at the Paterson plant. And the leadership had prevailed upon the rank-and-file to ratify a new contract providing for a forty-cent-an-hour raise—a dime less than the membership sought, but a nickel more than the company offered. The union also won two additional paid holidays, a more liberal vacation policy, and a new severance-pay benefit.

The strike took its toll on Archie. It was only the second walkout in Universal's two decades, but the first had occurred just a year earlier, in late September 1967, when a small group of workers walked off the job one Tuesday morning to protest their own union's inattentive, even traitorous, representation. Two dozen or so members organized a picket line in front of the plant, and after the lunch break they were joined by nearly every hourly employee—a thousand workers—who streamed outside to swell the line and shut down production. Among the primary demands was replacement of their chief shop steward, who, they claimed, plausibly, generally sided with the company in grievance hearings.

In a face-saving assertion surely few believed, Local 945 president Mike Ardis announced that the company had provoked the wildcat strike as an excuse to shut down, claiming he had heard rumors for months that Universal was "planning to leave Paterson anyway." He said the company was moving to Mississippi, "where the union is weaker." "I don't think the company wants to open," Ardis told a reporter. "We heard they were going to fold. . . . Their plant in Mississippi has twelve hundred employees and is big enough to absorb every type of work they do here."

The workers stayed out for three days, returning only after the mayor of Paterson, Lawrence F. Kramer, met separately with representatives of the three factions—the union, the company, and the insurgent strikers—and then jointly to mediate a settlement.

The acrimony of the past year was behind Archie on this Monday morning. The employees were back on the job as of Wednesday, the Teamsters local (and, truth to tell, Universal management) was happy it had once again staved off an AFL-CIO poacher. For the first time in three months, Archie had enjoyed a restful, relaxing weekend and looked forward to a resumption of normalcy. A few minutes into his routine of sit-ups, push-ups, and knee bends, Archie went into cardiac arrest and died. He was fifty-three years old.

The next afternoon's funeral was one to which everyone came. Alongside his wife, Pearl, their three sons, a large extended family, and a lifetime's assemblage of friends, many dozens of Universal employees crowded into the Robert Schoem Memorial Chapel in Paramus. Some had been with Archie for twenty years, since the business was known as International Transformer and operated in the flood-prone basement on Kentucky Avenue. Others he had hired at the maze-like plant in Westwood later in the 1940s; others still joined the company not long after Archie moved the business back to Paterson in 1950. Among the employees were many whose lives Archie had touched—with a hospital visit or an emergency loan or simply by acknowledging their daily presence at the plant. "In the early years Mr. Sergy knew all our names," Mollie James recalls. "I don't know how he did, but he did."

Although Universal would remain in business for years to come, many at the grave site on that clear and mild November afternoon in 1968—the day, incidentally, Richard Nixon would be elected the thirty-seventh president of the United States—may have sensed they were burying with Archie Sergy the end of an era in American business.

Sergy's Universal was no social-service agency; it venerated the bottom line as much as any self-respecting capitalist enterprise, but it also maintained a steely-eyed focus on high quality and customer service, probably to the degree that it hurt profit margins. Archie saw the world as an industrialist, not a financier, a view that put him at odds with conventional corporate thinking in the go-go years of the late sixties. His was a life filled with duty—to his company, to Paterson, to his family, to his faith. From his habit of hiring distant cousins and cousins of distant cousins, to doling out kosher turkeys at the holidays, to insisting that he and all the executives work in the "bull pen" rather than in private offices, to keeping a golf pro on the payroll, Sergy's Universal was a singular company, peculiar to its founder's values.

As all start-up companies must, Universal grew less characteristic of its founder as it grew larger. In the nearly five years between the company's sale to Philadelphia & Reading and Archie's death, he had remained Universal's titular head. But he no longer called the shots. That much was clear during the protracted fight with the union in Mississippi in 1965 and 1966, and was most evidently revealed anew when he announced to the employees in April of 1968, seven months before his death, that P&R itself had been swallowed whole by another conglomerate. "We're all working for a company out of Chicago. The name is Northwest Industries. Who they are I have no idea."

Northwest Industries, Inc., was the brainchild of Ben W. Heineman, a Chicago lawyer who headed the Chicago & North Western Railway, a commuter railroad. Heineman had taken over the C&NW in 1956. A decade later he caught the conglomeration bug. "We want to offset the weaknesses of the railroad," he said in the spring of 1967, "with the strength of other companies." (The railroad had suffered a loss of $1.4 million in the first quarter of the year.) Heineman began with the $90 million purchase of two chemical companies and then set his sights on Essex Wire, a Fort Wayne, Indiana–based company that operated fifty-four plants in the United States and Canada and was itself busy acquiring other companies. But certain of Essex's major shareholders apparently balked at the terms, and in August the deal collapsed. Soon after, Heineman received a phone call at his summer home in northern Wisconsin.

On the line were two well-known and highly regarded New York businessmen: Mickey Newman, the chairman and chief executive of Philadelphia & Reading, and Laurence A. Tisch, a member of the executive committee of the P&R board and chairman and president of Loew's Theatres, Inc. They told Heineman they would be interested in discussing a merger.

"Who or what is Philadelphia & Reading?" Heineman replied.

Newman laughed, explaining that living in New York gave them an inflated sense of self-importance.

"I'm sorry," Heineman told them, "but I've never heard of you."

The P&R pair asked to meet with Heineman in Chicago at his earliest convenience. Heineman explained that once ensconced in Wisconsin, he never forsook his summer home for business. "This can wait until fall as far as I'm concerned." Larry Tisch pressed him, and he agreed to meet with them in New York when he flew there to meet his son, a Rhodes scholar who was returning to the States from England.

To acquire Philadelphia & Reading, the fifty-three-year-old Heineman created a holding company, Northwest Industries, to bring the railway and its chemical subsidiaries under one corporate roof with the six operating companies of P&R. Under the terms of the agreement, Northwest issued a new convertible preferred stock in exchange for some three million shares of P&R common stock on a share-for-share basis—a deal valued at more than $300 million. It was further agreed that Heineman would serve as chairman and chief executive officer of the holding company and that Mickey Newman would become its president—a demotion Newman found so difficult to digest he ended up opposing the merger when it came to a vote of the P&R board. But the deal was a good one for P&R shareholders, and as Heineman insisted to Newman, he would veto it unless Newman agreed to play second fiddle. "I understood Mickey's reluctance," Heineman says. "He had founded the company, and at that point was the principal stockholder, and it became very clear to him that there was only one way in which the merger was going to be accomplished, and that is if I were going to be the chief executive in fact as well as in name." However cold their feet were, the corporate newlyweds were all smiles in public. In a joint statement, the two men said the merger was an "excellent reflection of the diversification objectives of each company."

Heineman and Newman also agreed to leave day-to-day control of the operating companies in the hands of their respective managements, and would intervene only in matters of "broad policy" and to review budgets and forecasts and financial performance. "They let us do what we wanted to do—up to a point," says Chestina Hughes, who would be promoted to treasurer of Universal during the Northwest era. "Like if we needed a piece of equipment that cost up to, say, ten thousand dollars, we'd just go ahead and buy it. But if it were a thirty-five-thousand-dollar piece of machinery, for that we'd have to write up a request. Then Northwest would give it to their analysts for a second opinion. 'Do you really need it? What savings would you get in return?' So while they gave us great latitude, they made sure controls were in place."

Day-to-day control fell to Paul Einhorn, who moved into the president's office upon Archie's death. (Archie had steadfastly refused to occupy the secluded office, preferring the rattle and din of the more collegial "bull pen.") By then, early November of 1968, Einhorn was the lone survivor of the original triumvirate. In March, the company had lost Rube Pashman, its beloved and profane operations manager and Archie's alter ego, to lung cancer. Einhorn would remain in office until he retired on his sixty-fifth birthday in August 1980. The company performed consistently well in those dozen years. It continued to expand, acquiring a plant in Bridgeport, Connecticut; opening a wire mill in Gallman, Mississippi (in Copiah County, adjacent to Simpson County); and building a new plant for the manufacture of capacitors in Totowa, New Jersey (the town bordering Paterson to the west); and a plant for fluorescent ballasts in Blytheville, Arkansas, a small town on the Mississippi River northwest of Memphis.

Numbers, too, tell the story. Universal posted record sales every year from 1968 to 1974. Though earnings dipped a bit in the early 1970s, by 1977 Universal had more than doubled in size from 1968, to sales of nearly $100 million, and was almost three times as profitable. In 1979, Einhorn's last full year at the helm, the ledger recorded yet another banner year, posting new highs for sales and earnings.

About a year before Einhorn was due to step down, Northwest engaged an executive recruiter—a headhunter—to scout for a replacement. Sometime in the summer of 1979, the headhunter, a Chicago man named Don Williams, phoned Otto Payonzeck, a lighting-industry executive. Payonzeck, then forty-five years old, was a lifer with ITT, the superconglomerate that owned everything from hotels (Sheraton) to rental cars (Avis) to bakeries (Wonder bread and Twinkies) to insurance companies (The Hartford) to fluorescent-fixture plants. He had joined the company in 1962, bouncing around its universe every couple of years. He'd started with a wire-and-cable subsidiary in his home state of Massachusetts. From there it was on to Rhode Island and two tours in Canada before reassignment to headquarters in New York City. In 1974, ITT sent him to Memphis as general manager of a lighting-fixture manufacturer. From his base in Memphis Payonzeck also oversaw an outdoor-fixture manufacturing plant in London, Ontario, and an indoor-fixture plant in Vermilion, Ohio. Those plants were some of the largest buyers of fluorescent ballasts, and so Payonzeck became well acquainted with that industry's three major suppliers: Advance, GE, and Universal.

So when Don Williams called to ask whether he knew anyone who might be a candidate for the job of chief executive officer at an unnamed ballast company, Payonzeck had a pretty good idea whose job he was talking about. "Why would Universal want to hire someone?" Payonzeck wondered. "I think Paul Einhorn's doing a good job."

Toward the end of the summer, Payonzeck took another call in his Memphis office from Williams.

"Have you thought any more about that job we discussed?" Williams wanted to arrange a meeting, but that would require catching the peripatetic Payonzeck in some airport between flights. "When and where is your next trip?"

"Cleveland," Payonzeck told him, playing along. "I'm going up Tuesday, coming back Wednesday night."

"Which airline?"

"Delta."

"First or coach?"

"First."

"Fine, I'll see you next Wednesday."

Sure enough, Williams flew in from Chicago and was waiting for Payonzeck at the Cleveland airport, his own first-class ticket in hand with a seat assignment next to Payonzeck's for the flight down to Memphis. Over apple pie and ice cream in a coffee shop near the gate, the men conversed while Williams took notes on a napkin. "He didn't get on the plane," Payonzeck recalls. "I guess he had enough information."

Williams reported to his contact at Northwest, the vice president of personnel, that he had found a solid candidate. Solid but uninterested. "I had moved around a lot with ITT, but I'd also moved up salary-wise," Payonzeck recalls. "I was in pretty good shape there."

About that time, however, ITT decided to shed some of its lighting businesses, including the plants in Canada and Ohio with which Payonzeck had been working. ITT offered him another position, with its lighting company in Pawtucket, Rhode Island. While he was debating the ins and outs of the ITT offer, he agreed to hear the pitch from Northwest Industries. After meeting the vice president of personnel in Payonzeck's office in Memphis, and after interviewing with another vice president in the Northwest offices in Chicago, Payonzeck was invited to breakfast with Ben Heineman. From there he was whisked by company plane to tour the Universal plant in Paterson and to meet Paul Einhorn. In the skies over New Jersey, Payonzeck's escort took a call from his boss. "You just got blessed by Heineman," he was told.

Payonzeck started at Universal in March 1980. As he tells it, the plan called for him to "sit quiet" for two months while observing

Einhorn. "Then we'd work two months side by side, and then for two months Paul would help me run the business while he phased out." The mentor-pupil arrangement lasted all of a week. Einhorn was already phasing out, marking time until his August retirement. "Paul wouldn't get in until about ten o'clock and he'd leave about three," Payonzeck says. "Meanwhile, I was there at seven, doing all sorts of things, busy making decisions."

Among the first decisions he had to make was how to deal with the union. This was never a simple question at the Paterson plant, where the employees' grievances more often than not continued to be against the Teamsters rather than the company. Little had changed in that regard since the 1960s, when Local 945 twice beat back insurgent movements—in 1961, when the IUE nearly prevailed, and in the 1968 strike, when the IBEW briefly gained a toehold.

Little had changed, that is, other than the local's leadership, who played musical chairs every few years due to disappearances and indictments. Mike Ardis was gone. He had replaced as head of Local 945 John Serratelli, who had not been heard from since disappearing in 1959 while under indictment. Ardis, too, was missing and presumed dead. He was last seen on June 18, 1971, at the local's sumptuous new union hall in West Paterson. His car, left in the parking lot, and his eyeglasses, nearby on the grass, were all that was found of him.*

Since Mike Ardis's presumed murder, the head of Local 945 had been Joseph Campisano, a protégé of Tony Provenzano's. Campisano was unusual in one regard: He had "no criminal record," according to a union reform group's 1978 report." The same could not be said of his second-in-command, secretary-treasurer Vito Cariello, whose conviction of conspiracy while a bookkeeper with another Teamsters local in 1964 apparently well qualified him for the top financial job at Local 945. After serving an eighteen-month prison term and a federally mandated hiatus from a position of union leadership, Cariello joined Local 945 in early 1972.

Cariello was hardly the lone felon in the local's pantheon. His

---

*Theories abounded in the wake of Ardis's disappearance: He was hiding from the IRS, which reportedly was investigating him; he was ducking mobsters, who wanted him silenced—or who silenced him.

cohorts included a business agent named Ernest Palmeri, who "came from a long line of organized crime figures," and who was appointed to his job by Peter LaPlaca, a *capo* in the Genovese crime family, according to an intelligence report of the New Jersey State Police. The police believed LaPlaca was the man running the mob's garbage operations. The diminutive Palmeri was often accompanied by a large man named Flen Chestnut, another Local 945 business agent, who had several arrests and at least one conviction for assault and battery.

Palmeri replaced John (Johnny Coca-Cola) Lardiere as director of the local's major unit, the sanitation department. (Some five thousand of its eight thousand members worked in the garbage and waste-hauling business.) Lardiere was imprisoned in August 1971, two months after Mike Ardis disappeared, for refusing to cooperate with the New Jersey State Commission of Investigation. Lardiere was thought to have named names anyway, and if being in prison spared *his* life, it offered no protection for his wife. In July 1972, the mob sent Lardiere a "not-so-subtle reminder," as a dissident Teamsters organization's report termed it, of its displeasure. Someone offered his wife a bottle of Fresca. After one sip, she "ran into her driveway, clutching her throat." The soft drink had been laced with enough arsenic to kill fifty people, the medical examiner determined.*

As for the local's president, the untarnished Joe Campisano? Within months after the union hailed his lack of criminal record, he, too, was shopping for a good defense attorney. Along with his rogues' gallery of fellow Local 945 officialdom—Vito Cariello, Ernest Palmeri, Flen Chestnut, and another business agent, Frank Smith—a federal grand jury in October 1978 indicted the forty-seven-year-old Campisano in a multi-million-dollar scheme to loot banks by the misuse of union funds. The indictment charged all five officers with racketeering, soliciting and receiving kickbacks and loans to influence the investment of the local's funds, and submitting false statements to banks. The scheme involved large deposits of Local 945 money in various banks in exchange for loans and kickbacks from the banks for the defendants themselves, family members, friends, other union officials, and a long list of mobsters, loan sharks, and alleged murderers. Tens

---

*In April 1976, Lardiere was released from prison. Twenty-four hours later he was dead, murdered "gangland-execution style."

of millions of dollars in such loans were defaulted on. Nine New Jersey banks were named in the indictment, three of which folded because of the looting.

The case came to trial in April 1979. All five defendants were convicted. One, Flen Chestnut, won acquittal on appeal; by default he became the next president of Local 945. The others would be sentenced to prison for terms ranging from three years to seven years. The government's case relied largely on an informant named George A. Franconero, a thirty-eight-year-old well-connected attorney—he was a former law partner of New Jersey governor Brendan Byrne and co-owner of a Bergen County restaurant and bar with Ernest Palmeri. (He was best known for being the brother of singer Connie Francis.) Franconero was the middleman between the banks and the union and arranged for the loans and payoffs. He avoided jail in return for his cooperation, but the plea bargain cost him his life. "There have been suggestions the world found out he was cooperating with me," recalls Michael Himmel, the assistant U.S. attorney who prosecuted the case. Those suggestions were grounded in the fact that within a week after the Supreme Court upheld the four Teamsters' convictions, George Franconero was, in Himmel's words, "blown away."

On October 4, 1980, while Joe Campisano and his co-conspirators were out on bail and awaiting word of their final appeals, the local's three-year contract with Universal expired. It was barely a month after Paul Einhorn's farewell party, and for Otto Payonzeck, in his first weeks on the job as Universal's lone chief executive, it was a baptism by fire. No pact had yet been reached, but Campisano and Payonzeck had signed a "letter of agreement" extending the prior contract until a new contract was ratified.

That was fine with everyone but the workers. "Nobody asked us about a letter of agreement," recalls Carmelo Colon, a shop steward at the time. "That was strictly between the company and Lyons." Lyons was William J. Lyons, Local 945's business agent for Universal. Although Lyons had no criminal record or known mob associations, many workers trusted him no more than they did the local's jailbirds. Their reasoning was simple and compelling: Joe Campisano hired him away from Universal, where he had worked for six years as personnel director. In her mind's eye, Mollie James, for one, could not erase her run-in with Lyons back in 1972. She had just wrapped up her day shift at her other full-time job, in the shipping department at Popular Merchandise, and was driving to her second-shift job at Universal when she felt dizzy and decided she'd better detour to the doctor's office. "My blood pressure was sky-high. The doctor told me, 'You're not going to Universal today, you're not going anywhere for two or three days.'"

When she returned to Universal after the prescribed rest period, she says Bill Lyons fired her.

"What for?"

"You worked at Popular, but you didn't come in here."

Mollie says Joe Campisano not only refused to file a grievance in her behalf but likely supported her termination. "I had been there seventeen years. I wasn't afraid to speak my mind, and Joe and all those crooks in 945 kind of considered me a loose cannon. I think he wanted me out of there as much as Lyons." (She reclaimed her job only when her old boss Sig Steinberger interceded from his posting in Mississippi.)

Lyons says he does not remember the incident. He characterizes the union-company relationship as "very professional. It was truly a working relationship, nonadversarial." As Carmelo Colon sees it, that attitude was precisely what so frustrated the rank-and-file. "We needed the guy to go in there punching, and all Bill Lyons ever did was sit on his hands."

The employees continued to work under the terms of the old contract for two weeks after it lapsed. During that period, Colon recalls, Bill Lyons continually pressed them to modify their wage demands. "He kept telling us we were asking for too much, when most of us were hardly making enough to feed our families."*

On a Wednesday morning in mid-October, the workers forcefully and formally declared their dissatisfaction with their union representation. They called a wildcat strike, shutting down their machinery and walking out of the plant. Joe Campisano defended his business agent, blaming the workers' woes on the company's decision to reduce its workforce in Paterson while expanding operations in Mississippi and

---

*Lyons has since returned to the management side of labor relations. In a 1996 interview, he pointed out proudly that his present employer, a precious-metals firm, has been union-free since he began there in 1983, the year he left Local 945.

in Arkansas, where the Blytheville plant was just reaching full capacity. "But they don't want to hear that," Campisano told a reporter. "They only know that their landlords want the rent. Or their grocers want their money."

The walkout lasted two days, until Friday. On the following Tuesday, the union presented its members with the proposed contract. It called for an hourly wage increase of $1.10 over three years—a 25 percent raise over the average wage of $4.33. But the rank-and-file called on their union to seek a raise of $2.10 an hour over three years, an increase of about 48 percent over the course of the contract, which, they argued, was more in line with the nation's double-digit annual rate of inflation. The workers were also calling for an improved health plan, additional holidays and vacation days, and paid sick days.

The contract proposal Bill Lyons presented them was overwhelmingly defeated, and once again the workers walked off the job. "I got two kids," explained a twenty-three-year-old shipping-department employee, Louis Arcelay, as he stood on the picket line. "How am I supposed to tell them I can't afford to buy them a glass of milk or some corn flakes?"

On the first day of the latest walkout the buzz on the picket line was about a front-page story in the morning paper that administered yet another public relations black eye to Local 945. A few days earlier, during the wildcat strike, a New Jersey grand jury handed down a massive indictment charging bid rigging and mob involvement in the state's garbage industry. Among the fifty-seven alleged co-conspirators was Anthony Rizzo, a former garbage collector who was the local's new business agent in charge of the sanitation department. He replaced the recently incarcerated Ernest Palmeri. Rizzo was a nephew and associate of Joseph Sciapani, a member of the Genovese family, according to state-police intelligence.

The article (AUTHORITIES FEAR FOR WITNESSES' LIVES IN GARBAGE CASE) briefly recited the current allegations and then recounted earlier investigations of the garbage industry, dating to Local 945 president John Serratelli's "reign of terror" during the late 1950s. "Using the union to keep the contractors in line," the article quoted a state attorney general's report of 1958, "[Serratelli] . . . used threats, violence and bribery. Dumps were set on fire, sugar was put in gas tanks, brake hoses were cut."

After citing a similar 1969 investigation, the story pointed out that

"Local 945 . . . is often involved in probes of the industry, and law enforcement officials say the latest ongoing probe will be no different."

While union and management negotiators met inside the plant with a federal mediator, picketers outside Universal clucked and hooted while one man read aloud choice excerpts from the article, including these sentences about their local: "Besides the propensity of its leaders to vanish, the union has a history of organized crime connections. According to a Teamsters dissident group, 'There is no doubt that the local is one of the crown jewels of the old Genovese crime family.' "

Following a six-hour mediation session on the third day of the walkout, the membership ratified a new contract. The wage increase, $1.50 an hour over three years, basically split the difference between the two sides' proposals. The contract also provided for a 32¢ increase for fringe benefits and an improved dental plan to take effect during the third year. "We're glad the strike is over," said Universal's William Donigan, the personnel director who succeeded William Lyons. "Everyone will be back to work Monday."

Even as the Paterson workers were streaming back to work, Otto Payonzeck had a foot in Mississippi, trying, unsuccessfully, to stamp out another flickering hot spot before it burst into flames. The company's contract with IBEW Local 2198 in Simpson County was due to expire three months later, on January 31, 1981, and although negotiations had already begun, progress was nil. The issue was as much about Payonzeck and his new management style as it was about wages and benefits, a point Payonzeck concedes.

"The union slowly but surely had gotten to the point where they drew the line at the number of ballasts their people would make a day," he says. "It was something like two thousand ballasts per line per day. And I remember the first time I sat down there in the industrial engineer's office overlooking the plant at like two P.M. and the shift broke at three. And I watched the guy at the head of the line stop working, and slowly but surely as the line worked towards quarter till three, which was their washup time, there wasn't a ballast on the line. And the next shift came in and the first guy went to work and then the next and the one after, and about a half hour later the last guy finally was taking something off the line. And right then and there, I made an executive decision that that wasn't gonna fucking work. We tried to push the union not to shut the lines down the way they were doing at the end of each shift. And that's when the IBEW got on our back about changing work methods, and forcing them to work harder."

To the union, though, Payonzeck's "executive decision" demonstrated a lack of respect for the membership and for the collective-bargaining process. "They wanted us to work harder, but they didn't want to pay us any more," Louis Carter says. "That right there was the problem with the new management. They had an attitude that they could run right over you, talk to you in a condescending way." A worker quoted anonymously in the *Simpson County News*: "The people who stand in the assembly lines are treated by management like they don't matter. . . . It's just a job and someone else can be found to fill it."

On Sunday, February 1, the fourteen hundred union members authorized a walkout, the first in the plant's seventeen-year existence. The vote was extremely close, only a six-vote margin, and management countered with a sweetened proposal it believed would topple the fence-sitters. But when members voted down the new offer, Payonzeck decided it was time to play hardball. Over the signatures of Sig Steinberger and the assistant plant manager, Universal sent a letter to every union member.

"To My Fellow Employees," it began, "The Company has made its best offer. It cannot be increased. . . . Let us assure you that no matter how long the strike lasts, the Company will not be pressured into changing its mind. *Moreover, we now must study whether it is good business to remain in Simpson County with an unreasonable labor force. . . .*" (Emphasis added.)

The labor force quickly came to its senses. On February 12, the membership ratified the new proposal by better than two to one; a day later they were back at work.

There was one other strike in Mississippi that year, a nine-day walkout at the company's wire mill in Gallman. The company had installed new machinery designed to significantly improve productivity. The workers believed their rate of pay should also have been improved to reflect the increased output. "If you want to say there was a strike we lost, it was Gallman," Payonzeck says. "They picked up a little more money than we'd planned on giving them. But they got new equipment and their productivity went up, so it didn't really matter, and after that we had nothing but good labor relations."

The same could not be said of Paterson. In October 1983, when the latest three-year pact there was due to expire, Local 945's battered negotiator Bill Lyons was gone, replaced by Anthony Rizzo, the alleged mob associate who had recently served six months in jail after pleading guilty a year earlier to restraint-of-trade conspiracy charges in the garbage-industry case. This time around, despite stalled contract negotiations, there was no need for a wildcat strike. When the expiration date passed without an agreement, Rizzo ordered a plant-wide walkout.

Three weeks into the strike, the two sides had yet to meet for a bargaining session. Prior to the strike, Mollie James was working double shifts—she had quit her other full-time job, at Popular Merchandise, a few years earlier. The eighty-hour weeks in the Universal stamping department left her in better financial shape than many, especially since the union chose not to pay strike benefits. "They told us we weren't out long enough to qualify," Mollie says, "but the real reason [they wouldn't pay us] was because the company and the union were still just like interlocking fingers."

Nor were the strikers eligible for unemployment. After three missed paychecks, they saw no option but to return to work. "We went back too quickly, but most of the people had no savings and nothing coming in," Mollie says. The company's two Southern plants clearly gave management the upper hand, a reality Payonzeck exploited well. He ordered increased production in Mississippi and Arkansas, and, as he had two years earlier in Mississippi, sent a letter to every union member underscoring that fact and warning that the strike jeopardized the very survival of their plant.

As it had in Simpson County, the mailed threat snapped heads, working every bit as well in Paterson as it had in Simpson County. Even Tony Rizzo seemed a bit taken aback—saying the union was "certainly concerned about the plant moving"—before recovering his footing: "But we'll not be intimidated by it." And Paterson Mayor Frank X. Graves Jr., who was in the latter stages of a run for the New Jersey state senate, declared he would personally do whatever was necessary to help settle the standoff and keep Universal in the city. "We're going to break our backs to keep them. I'll quit the campaign and I'll sit there for two weeks if I have to," Graves said.

He didn't have to. A settlement was reached within a couple of days of the persuasive mailing. As further evidence of the company's winning hand, the agreement (which centered on a 20.5 percent wage increase over three years) was nearly identical to management's original, pre-strike proposal. Payonzeck was conciliatory in victory but in no mood to disavow his successful gambit. He described the contract as "very fair," one that "will maintain us in a competitive position." He added: "We do not intend to move anything out of Paterson. On the other hand, we can't go through this every three years. This was not the first strike here, and any time you have difficulty communicating, you have to look at the alternatives and keep your options open."

PAYONZECK WAS also looking at his own alternatives. Approaching fifty years old, he had been a quintessential organization man for more than two decades. He had moved himself and his family all over North America, wherever and whenever ITT had asked him. And now, after three years in service to Universal and its parent, Northwest Industries, a far smaller conglomerate than his previous employer but nevertheless one in which all the major decisions and profits were made by other people in distant offices, Payonzeck was considering his future. "I was ready to run my own show, I thought I could do something with the company, and I could see that Northwest was experiencing some growing pains."

What he saw in Northwest was a company in the throes of restructuring. Its largest operating company, Lone Star Steel, was in trouble, its markets eroded by imports and slumping demand, and it was known that Ben Heineman had on the block it and at least one of Northwest's other businesses, Velsicol Chemical. What about Universal, Payonzeck wondered. Might it, too, be for sale, and could he pull together a financing package to bid for it?

With these questions in mind as the new year turned, Payonzeck teamed with a capital-investment group at Donaldson, Lufkin & Jenrette, a New York brokerage house. Payonzeck and his partners approached Northwest with an offer of seventy million dollars to buy

Universal. By the end of June 1984, it looked as if they had a deal; the major snag was which party would be liable for an ongoing lawsuit against Universal. (The company was sued in 1984 by two inventors who claimed Universal defrauded them by buying the rights to their new energy-saving ballast only to keep it from coming to market.) Negotiations had proceeded so well, in fact, that a wire-service story published in the *New York Times* reported that Northwest had "agreed in principle" to sell Universal for seventy million dollars to Payonzeck's group.

Before the deal could close, however, a tidal wave of takeover activity washed over Northwest, drowning the Universal sale and all other restructuring plans Ben Heineman had been floating to rescue the company from its two-year sales slump, poor earnings performance, and sharp dip in stock price. (In 1983, the company had revenues of $1.6 billion, a steep decline from the previous year's sales of $2.3 billion. It reported a loss of $59 million in 1983 against net income of $185 million in 1982. And the 1982 performance was itself considerably below that of 1981, when Northwest had net income of $253 million on revenues of $3.1 billion.)

Northwest's poor performance mirrored that of many other conglomerates, which as a group by the early 1980s were considered stock-market laggards—"corporate dinosaurs," wrote one financial paleontologist, "that are not long for this world, at least not in their current form."

Northwest certainly felt the sea change on Wall Street, where investors were far more interested in "break-up values"—the price a company could be sold for in pieces—than they were in its whole. "They've come full circle now," one prominent investor said in early 1985. "They were worth a premium when they were buying companies. Now they're worth more split up than when they were together."

Ben Heineman had had a long, varied, and successful career—as a lawyer, railroad magnate, company builder, and politico. (He was a liberal Democrat who chaired presidential commissions on race and welfare during the Johnson administration.) At the age of seventy, he had not the heart nor the energy to dismantle the company he had begun assembling fifteen years earlier. He was "tired and bored," he recalled years later, and he was looking for an out.

He thought he had found it when an old and close friend, Donald

P. Kelly, came calling in the late spring of 1984 to say he was interested in buying Northwest. Kelly could certainly afford to do so, or so it seemed. He had been chairman and chief executive of Esmark, a Chicago-based company he grew out of the old Swift meatpacking business into a conglomerate that sold everything from Swift bacon to Playtex bras to Avis rental cars (Avis had since been passed from ITT) to Max Factor cosmetics. In May, another Chicago conglomerate, Beatrice Foods, the nation's largest food company, had acquired Esmark for $60 a share, a total value of about $2,000,800,000. (Esmark itself had only the previous September cannibalized its fellow conglomerate Norton Simon, Inc., for slightly more than $1 billion.)

"It's a wonderful thing for the shareholders," Kelly said at the time of the Beatrice sale. For none was it more wonderful than for him. He and his family owned 220,000 shares in Esmark, worth more than $13 million. (All together his "golden parachute," or compensation package on leaving the company, totaled nearly $18 million.)

Kelly took his healthy slice of the Esmark pie and along with Roger T. Briggs, the company's departing vice chairman, established a management-buyout boutique, Kelly, Briggs & Associates. By late June, when Otto Payonzeck thought he had a letter of intent to buy Universal from Northwest, Donald Kelly was in superseding talks with Ben Heineman about acquiring Northwest for himself.

The Universal deal fell into limbo pending the summer's negotiations with Kelly, Briggs. On September 20, Northwest agreed to the firm's billion-dollar leveraged-buyout offer. (In a leveraged buyout, one buys a company by borrowing against the assets of the company.) The deal called for Kelly, Briggs to pay Northwest stockholders fifty dollars a share in cash as well as one share of its Lone Star Steel subsidiary for each share of Northwest common stock. (Lone Star was to be spun off as an independent, publicly owned subsidiary.) The transaction was contingent, of course, on approval by Northwest shareholders and on Kelly, Briggs securing the required financing. No one doubted the financing would fall into place. Recalls Heineman: "Don was extraordinarily confident he could raise the money." With the nearly consummated deal on the table, Northwest announced a week later that it had "terminated" the sale of Universal to Otto Payonzeck and his investor group. Universal's fate, apparently, would be in the hands of Northwest's imminent new owners.

The Northwest board gave Kelly, Briggs a deadline of December 31 to arrange financing. During the period the investor group was busy soliciting backers, the principals took time out to meet with Payonzeck regarding the future of Universal. Over breakfast with Kelly and Briggs early one morning in New York, Payonzeck recounted the terms of the letter of agreement he had reached with Northwest. "They told me that if they got the damn thing through, we'd still have a deal," Payonzeck recalls.

But Kelly and Briggs never could get the damn thing through. Even as Don Kelly was reassuring his old friend Ben Heineman that he was "going to get the money," Heineman's investment bankers at Goldman, Sachs & Company were whispering that Kelly, Briggs was in trouble, that it was facing insurmountable problems with "equity financing sources." (The debt financing was in place.) And even after Northwest exercised its option to extend the deadline a month, until the end of January 1985, the $175 million in equity financing never materialized. On January 28, Don Kelly made his concession speech. "We just got to the point where there were divergent views about what to do long-term and what to do short-term, so at ten this morning I said the hell with it."

So did Wall Street. Reports that the deal was dead sent Northwest's stock plunging. The low price—one day it dropped 7.5 percent, the third-largest percentage loser on the New York Stock Exchange—attracted some of the financial world's most renowned scavengers. Among those smelling blood was Warren Buffett, the Omaha-based investor who controlled Berkshire Hathaway Inc. Between mid-December and mid-January, when it appeared likely to all but Don Kelly that Kelly, Briggs's bid would fail, Buffett bought a 6.1 percent stake in Northwest. Others who swooped in for a quick look included the Bass Brothers of Texas, the British financier Sir James Goldsmith, and the Pritzker family of Chicago.

Even as those celebrated foragers popped up in bold type in the financial gossip columns, Heineman was quietly weighing an offer from an obscure investor named William F. Farley. In early January, Farley's investment banker, Leon Black, a thirty-two-year-old whiz kid who headed the leveraged-buyout group of the New York firm of Drexel Burnham Lambert, approached Heineman through Heineman's banker, J. Ira Harris, the managing partner of Salomon Brothers in Chicago. Harris was one of the leading lights of the mergers-and-acquistions world; it was he who brought together the principals in the nearly three-billion-dollar Beatrice buyout of Esmark.

Salomon's Chicago offices were in the city's Tower of Power, the Sears Tower, as were both Farley's and Northwest's. And when Harris rode the elevator up to the eighty-seventh floor from his office on sixty-three, he told Heineman that Leon Black of Drexel Burnham was representing Bill Farley.

"Who is Bill Farley?" Heineman replied.

Bill Farley, if Farley himself and the adoring splash of forthcoming business-press ink were to be believed, was none other than the second coming of Horatio Alger. As Farley spun his story in one admiring profile after another, his life fairly leapt out of the pages of an inspirational dime-store novel for young readers. Irish Catholic son of a postal worker in a working-class town in Rhode Island rises before dawn to deliver newspapers and work other odd jobs around town. Earns scholarship to fine private college in Maine. Heads out west. Peddles encyclopedias door to door in Los Angeles. Attends law school. Chooses a business career instead. Joins New York investment company. Works in mergers and acquisitions by day, attends business school at night. Transfers to company's Chicago office, and then to Chicago office of Lehman Brothers, one of Wall Street's eminent investment-banking houses. Working on other people's deals soon grows tiresome for our restless hero. In 1976, at the tender age of thirty-three, he buys his first company, a small citrus-processing firm. He pays $1.7 million, all but $25,000 of which he borrows. The deal sets the pattern for nearly all his subsequent buys: He borrows heavily against the company's assets.

Debt became Bill Farley's way of life. While remaining at Lehman, he paid $8 million for another small company, a manufacturer of paper-folding machines, borrowing all but $800,000. He quit Lehman in 1978, and by 1984 had borrowed ever more heavily to add two more low-profile companies to Farley Industries, the umbrella organization for his holdings.

Although Bill Farley by then had moved up in the clubby world of Chicago business, to the eightieth floor of the Sears Tower, just seven floors below Ben Heineman's offices, he had yet to register on the radar screen of the Northwest chairman. By the beginning of 1985, when Heineman is wondering who Bill Farley is, when Don Kelly is muttering about what this brash upstart has to offer that he doesn't, the answer is two words: Michael Milken.

Ben Heineman may not have known Bill Farley. And he may not have known Leon Black. But he knew of Michael Milken. *Everyone* knew of Michael Milken, the resident evil genius of Drexel Burnham Lambert.

It wasn't always so. As recently as a half-dozen years earlier, Michael Milken was a successful but little-known bond trader in the new Beverly Hills office of the firm *Forbes* tagged "distinctly minor league, an also-ran in the race for survival in a fast-changing Wall Street." But the also-ran became the pacesetter. It did so by out-hustling the other guy ("We get up at four A.M.," a Drexel bond salesman told the *Los Angeles Times* in 1984, "and we don't go out to lunch, we don't take personal phone calls, we don't tell jokes, don't talk about the ball game") and because Michael Milken began sermonizing nonstop about the higher power of high-yield bonds, or "junk" bonds—securities that were rated below investment grade by the rating agencies. Using a junk bond, *Forbes* explained, "an acquisitor can almost literally buy a company with its own money." Milken was not the first to recognize the power of junk—academic studies had reached the same conclusion years earlier—but he was the first to popularize it. For small companies, or companies without credit histories, most of which were typically not rated investment grade by either of the two rating agencies, Moody's or Standard & Poor's, Milken's creative financing was a godsend, "the right product at the right time." For those companies, which had been unable to raise funds by issuing bonds in the public market, borrowing money usually meant short-term loans from banks.

Then, beginning in the late 1970s, Michael Milken and Drexel Burnham started rewriting all the rules of Wall Street. Drexel volunteered to underwrite for the public market the low-rated bonds of those companies ignored by Wall Street's heavy hitters. The only requirement, writes Connie Bruck in her seminal history of Drexel, "was to pay the price: a high yield to the investors, and an enormous fee to Drexel."

Bill Farley willingly paid the price.

In return the wizardly Milken provided much more than mere access to fathomless pools of capital and an instant credibility among the big-cat finance capitalists who roamed the corporate landscape; he essentially waved his wand over Bill Farley, transforming him from another two-bit entrepreneur with a dream into a powerhouse takeover artist. In eight years, from the day he bought the citrus business, his Farley Industries went from a company with $4 million in sales to one with $700 million in annual revenues and $90 million in operating profits. And that was before he would gulp Northwest Industries, a company three times the size (1984 sales: $1.4 billion) of his own. "At only forty-two," gushed a *Fortune* writer in 1985, "he owns one of the nation's largest privately held industrial corporations. There's talk of a glittering future in politics, perhaps a run at the U.S. Senate. The American dream is alive and well, residing on the North Side of Chicago." It was Mike Milken who catapulted Bill Farley into the rarefied air of high finance, who orchestrated Bill Farley's early feats of leveraged acrobatics, and it was Milken who would enable him to perform his greatest high-wire act yet. "Yeah, it's all pretty amazing," Farley allowed in a 1985 interview. "I still pinch myself sometimes."

Ben Heineman was feeling pinched. He could ill-afford another public relations and stock-price debacle. "We were not going to do another Don Kelly," Heineman said at the time Farley's name surfaced. "I have great respect and affection for Don, but he did not have the means." But unlike Kelly, who had arrogantly failed to arrange financing *before* declaring he was ready to acquire Northwest, in Bill Farley Heineman had a credible buyer. "I understand why he [Heineman] was initially skeptical," Farley recalls. "Because, after all, if his old friend Don Kelly could not complete the deal, why would a young kid who he didn't know be able to do it?"

Farley could do it not because he actually had the money in hand, but because in the new coin of the corporate-takeover realm he possessed solid gold: a "highly confident" letter from Drexel Burnham Lambert. Drexel had devised the letter as a means of enabling its clients to make offers without actually having raised the money for the takeover; the letter staked the word of the firm on the claim that it was "highly confident" it could raise the amount necessary. Recalls Ira Harris: "I remember the Northwest board asked me what was going on, and I made the comment that a Drexel Burnham 'highly confident' letter in those days was considered the equivalent of a bank commitment." Any queasiness Ben Heineman felt about entering into an agreement with the unfamiliar Farley was allayed; the deal was done.

On April 10, 1985, Heineman handed the corporate keys to Farley. The terms were substantially equivalent to what Kelly, Briggs had offered, fifty dollars a share. Heineman got what he wanted, a cash transaction and assurances that his headquarters staff of two hundred would be provided a generous severance package. He had been on vacation in Austria and flew home to Chicago for the announcement. A day later, he rejoined his family in Europe. "There really wasn't anything else to be concerned about," Heineman says.

Not so for Farley. Not only was the $1,000,400,000 sale one of the biggest leveraged buyouts ever, but it was one of the most highly leveraged. For each share up to 79 percent of the company, Farley offered $50 of mostly borrowed cash, half of which, roughly $570 million, was advanced from banks and half from a Milken-raised issue of junk bonds placed with institutional investors. (In addition to the $50 million in fees Farley paid to his investment advisors and banks, he gave Drexel a 10 percent equity stake.) Farley himself put $70 million in cash equity into the company, but that he borrowed as well. To do so, he leveraged up Farley Metals, a group of four companies that made automotive components.

The new Farley/Northwest Industries, Inc., took on a boggling level of debt. Where Northwest carried $410 million in debt under Heineman, it would now carry debt of $1,000,200,000. Half of that debt, the bank loans, was on a floating interest rate, and so any upturn in rate would be potentially devastating. If Farley felt the pressures of such a crushing debt burden, he didn't show it. "This is an exciting time for corporate America," he said at the news conference announcing the deal. "There are tremendous values in the marketplace."

To Farley the primary value of Northwest Industries was its Union Underwear subsidiary, maker of Fruit of the Loom and BVD underwear. Union was the industry leader and the heart of Northwest. Union and Acme Boot, both of which Northwest had acquired in the 1968 merger with Philadelphia & Reading, contributed the lion's share—84 percent—of Northwest's nearly $200 million in operating earnings in 1984.

Farley would hold tight to those companies; he was dependent on their generating enough cash to meet his loan obligations. (He would also retain, for the time being, Northwest's General Battery Corporation.) For Northwest's three other, smaller operating companies, including Universal (Northwest had already moved to divest itself of Lone Star Steel), Farley had other plans. Their utility to Farley was not as manufacturing enterprises. What mattered to Farley about Universal was not its product line or its commitment to customer service or its employees or the communities in which it operated. What mattered was its sale value. "I never planned on owning it long-term," he says. In the parlance of the high-flying financial universe Bill Farley and Mike Milken lived in, Universal Manufacturing Company existed only on paper, as an "asset" to "spin off" to raise cash to pay down debt.

OTTO PAYONZECK lived in another universe. He lived in the messy world of cantankerous machinery and improvised production schedules and wildcat strikes; of innumerable sales and distribution meetings, roller-coaster metals prices, product research and development. In Universal he saw a proud, old manufacturing firm that embodied America's industrial prowess. By the middle 1980s, however, the face of industrial America had changed almost beyond recognition. No longer was bigger better. No longer was patience or loyalty rewarded; the fast, speculative buck replaced long-term growth. "Greed is all right," the famous Wall Street arbitrageur Ivan Boesky infamously assured the 1986 graduating class of the business school at the University of California at Berkeley. "I want you to know that. I think greed is healthy. You can be greedy and still feel good about yourself."* Guilt was out, wealth was in; the crowd applauded wildly.

The best and brightest business school recruits were shunning the relatively low salaries, long apprenticeships, and drowsy pace of corporate life. The top schools were lousy with budding aspirants to careers in investment banking—fresh-faced twenty-five-year-olds who followed Boesky's every exploit, salivated over Milken's thirty-million-dollar

*In November 1986, six months after his speech, Boesky would agree to settle Securities and Exchange Commission (SEC) charges of insider trading by paying a $100 million fine and serving three years in prison.

income, yearned for an invitation to the "Predators' Ball," the annual Drexel Burnham Lambert junk-bond conference and corporate-raider love-in in Beverly Hills.

Otto Payonzeck lived in a different world. As Universal's chairman and chief executive officer, he led a ballast-manufacturing company whose earnings, reliable if unspectacular, were precisely like its product. And he led a company of experienced managers and a stable, productive workforce. It was not unusual for Payonzeck to preside over retirement parties for both salaried and hourly employees alike with twenty-five years or more of service to Universal. But that world was coming to an end, obliterated by a business culture that venerated the Bill Farleys, the latter-day robber barons who acquired the Universals through asset-shuffling and debt-financing and stock-buybacks—acquired them as if they were used cars to be stripped of their parts and sold for salvage, or, if they were in good operating condition, to be kept only long enough to spiff up and slap on a "For Sale" sign.

Universal was a cream puff, a sturdy, well-maintained classic. No one knew better than Otto Payonzeck what was under its hood, and no one kicking the tires on Farley's lot wanted it more. This Payonzeck made clear to the new proprietor. "I told him I had a promise from the people who were in his shoes before, the two LBO guys [Donald Kelly and Roger Briggs]," Payonzeck says. "So I got a promise from Farley. He promised me 'last look.' "

Farley officially completed the tender offer for control of Northwest on May 31, 1985. Invariably described as affable and athletic—he lettered in three sports in high school and still adhered to a fitness regimen—Farley proved it to the senior managers of his new operating companies by inviting them to bond with nature and him on a rafting trip down the Colorado River that Memorial Day weekend. For Payonzeck the timing was inconvenient. His daughter was graduating from high school in New Jersey, and he and his wife had agreed to host the class graduation party—an all-night affair. But Payonzeck wanted to meet personally with Farley, establish a rapport. What better time than while floating the mighty Colorado?

To demonstrate he was a player, Payonzeck needed nothing so much as a competent travel agent. He bid the graduating revelers good-bye at one A.M., sped to the Newark airport, caught a red-eye bound for Los Angeles. From there he hopped a flight to Las Vegas, where he successfully rendezvoused at nine that morning with the Farley contingent—some two dozen corporate managers—for what their boss, who styled himself as a bit of a New Ager, called his Togetherness Group. From there, they drove into Utah to begin their commune with the great outdoors. "We had a ball," says Payonzeck, who returned from the river trip convinced he and Farley saw eye to eye on Universal.

Farley was indeed affable, but it could not be said he was candid with Payonzeck. What could be said, in a proper blend of metaphor and reality, was that Bill Farley sold Otto Payonzeck down the river. There would be no "last look" for Payonzeck; Farley had already promised Universal to another bidder. Payonzeck would not realize this until he returned to his desk the following week, when he took a phone call from his investment banker, who told him Farley had sold Universal to MagneTek, Inc., a Los Angeles–based company headed by one Andrew G. Galef.

Bill Farley knew Andy Galef only in passing—their paths had crossed socially at a Predators' Ball or two—but the two men shared membership in an elite brotherhood: They were fellow clients of Michael Milken. Beyond what the brotherhood provided them—the deep pools of capital, the invaluable "highly confident" letters—it had a larger purpose: to unite Milken's clients as spokes in a giant wheel, at the hub of which sat Milken himself. From that central, indispensable perch, he alone could see how to extract ever more "advisory" fees and equity stakes from his grateful brethren, whether by originating new transactions or by generating spin-off deals between two of his spokes, thus enabling him and Drexel to earn fees from both buyer and seller.

It was against this vast and powerful wheel that Otto Payonzeck collided. Vast and powerful, and yet stealthy—Payonzeck never saw it coming. He knew, of course, that Farley owned Universal; he did not know Milken owned Farley and Galef. Nor did he know at the time that the bidding process was about as genuine as Milken's hairpiece. Andy Galef won Universal not because the terms of his financing were superior to those of Payonzeck's group. And he certainly didn't win it because he was a better fit for the company than Payonzeck. Bill Farley sold Universal to Andy Galef because both were Milken men—period.

"I knew Andy through the Drexel connection," Farley recalls, "and he was probably a little more sophisticated on the deal side than Otto."

Payonzeck is a large, excitable fellow. He did not take the news well. "I went absolutely bananas," he says. "There is no way Farley hadn't already made the deal with Galef by the time he was promising me last look. I'm a hundred percent sure after the fact." When Galef called Payonzeck to say he wanted to meet and tour the Paterson plant, Payonzeck demurred. "Not now," he said, the wound still fresh. "I'm going on vacation for a week."

MagneTek was a privately held joint venture Galef organized with Milken. Galef and Milken did their first deal together, a leveraged buy-out, in 1981. LBOs were nothing new; a number of firms had been specializing in the investment technique for many years. But those deals mostly consisted of buying a *private* company by borrowing against the company's assets. It was not until about 1980 that the LBO market began for taking large public companies private. Although Milken did not originate the LBO, he was the first to utilize junk bonds to finance such a buyout.

Milken's LBO breakthrough came with Andy Galef, himself a devotee of maximum leverage. Galef was a native Easterner. The son of a corporate attorney, he grew up in suburban White Plains, New York. After receiving an MBA from Harvard, he moved to Los Angeles. His business career there began ingloriously: A sink-manufacturing company he ran went bust in the middle 1960s. Then his wife, to whom he had been married ten years, left with their three children. "She didn't want to be married to someone who was a failure," Galef reportedly told a friend.

Galef rebounded nicely, however, plumbing the sink failure for lessons learned. In 1968, he and Frank A. Grisanti, a veteran "turnaround specialist," formed Grisanti & Galef, Inc., to overhaul sick companies and help them avert bankruptcy. After a decade of performing corporate rescues for others, the pair decided to test their fix-it skills on their own companies. In 1978, Grisanti, Galef, and a third partner formed Spectrum Group, Inc., to acquire underperforming companies. A year later Spectrum embarked on a highly leveraged buying spree with the purchase of an aircraft-engine repair business for $20 million, most of which was borrowed from banks. And in late 1981,

Spectrum added a complementary business, an aircraft-parts concern purchased from Cooper Industries, of Houston. The $150 million transaction was a milestone in corporate finance: the first LBO underwritten by Drexel.

For Galef the deal tapped an enormously lucrative pipeline to Milken, and in turn led to big equity stakes for Drexel in Galef's crowning achievement, MagneTek.

Galef and his Spectrum partners concocted MagneTek in 1984 to acquire four spin-off companies from Litton Industries. Litton was a classic King Konglomerate of the go-go sixties. In 1967 alone, the year it acquired two of the businesses it would sell to MagneTek, Litton devoured a new company every three weeks. Wall Street had lately deemed that Litton's "break-up value," like that of most other eat-or-be-eaten corporate behemoths, was of more interest than the sum of its parts, and so the company was paring to its core businesses. Among the Litton divisions up for grabs was its "Magnetics Group" of four electrical-component companies: Liberty Wire; Triad-Utrad, a maker of ballasts and power supplies; Louis Allis, a motor manufacturer; and Jefferson Electric, a maker of ballasts and transformers.

Galef's idea in buying the Litton group was to start a sort of restricted-diet conglomerate. MagneTek's appetite would be hearty and healthy, selective rather than gluttonous. It would consume only well-established, market-leading companies in electrical-equipment manufacturing.

Universal fit those dietary guidelines well—too well, in the eyes of MagneTek's competitors. Both Jefferson Electric and Triad-Utrad were former competitors of Universal, and the proposed acquisition raised federal antitrust eyebrows. "Triad-Utrad had invented the electronic ballast," Galef said during a brief interview, "and the marketplace demanded that you have entries on both sides [magnetic and electronic] of the market. So we approached Farley/Northwest to purchase Universal. That was the sole motivation."

Only after a lengthy review of the competitive impact did the Federal Trade Commission grant approval. The transaction closed in February 1986, after some eight months of regulatory scrutiny. Universal fetched Farley a cash purchase price of $68.7 million. It would register barely a fender-bender of a dent in Farley's total debt of $1.5 billion, but it would spare him nearly $9 million in interest expenses on the debt. MagneTek financed the deal with $54 million in bank loans and $12.5 million from the junk-financed issuance of 15¼ percent senior preferred stock.

Under the terms of the financing Galef and Milken arranged, the Spectrum partners controlled 21 percent of MagneTek. The largest block of common stock, 50 percent, was held by three Drexel-employee partnerships; the other large holder was Executive Life Insurance Company, which owned a 10 percent stake.* (Executive's head was one Fred Carr, a fellow Drexel client who "generally did what Milken told him to," as one close observer of Drexel wrote.)

Aside from the ownership positions for Drexel, the firm received advisory fees for each of MagneTek's acquisitions, including $1,320,000 for the Universal deal. MagneTek also paid Drexel an annual million-dollar fee for "financial advisory" services.

For Galef the initial payoff came not from his stock in MagneTek or from direct compensation from the company; although he was chairman and chief executive officer of MagneTek, Galef received no salary as an employee of the company. (In 1986, he accepted an $85,000 "bonus for services rendered.") Instead, he arranged for his left hand, MagneTek, to pay his right hand, Spectrum Group, to provide "management services" to the company. The fees for those services nicely compensated Galef for his lack of salary. Spectrum hauled in $1.6 million for services related to the acquisition of the four Litton companies in 1984 and thereafter extracted $25,000 a month, plus expenses, until the purchase of Universal in February 1986. Then Galef shook the piggy bank again for a $500,000 fee to Spectrum for the Universal transaction and a revised monthly consulting tab of $50,000, plus expenses.

MagneTek's board of directors determined that the lucrative fees

---

*MagneTek also transferred about twenty-three million dollars in pension plan assets it received from Litton to Executive Life to purchase annuities. In April 1991, Executive Life collapsed under the weight of its junk-bond holdings and was seized by California regulators. The company's failure threatened the pensions of some six hundred MagneTek retirees in Wisconsin, whose union, the IUE, filed a class-action suit to recover their benefits. The case settled in May 1992. "I committed the union to this case because someone had to stand up to those greedy SOBs on Wall Street," IUE president William Bywater said. "They learned they can't take advantage of working people."

paid Spectrum were "as fair to the company as those which could have been obtained from unaffiliated parties." An unstartling appraisal, considering that the five-person board consisted of Galef; the vice president of Spectrum; two Drexel employees; and a director Spectrum and Drexel chose jointly.

The fruitful arrangement—exploiting an operating company's assets for a shell company—begged for replication, and within a month of the Universal acquisition, Galef and Drexel were already plotting to milk another cash cow. In March, Galef hatched W Acquisition Corporation, a shell of his Spectrum shell, to launch a hostile-takeover bid for Warnaco, Inc., a leading apparel manufacturer. (Among its labels were Hathaway shirts, Olga bras, WhiteStag sportswear.) His partners were his two Spectrum associates and Linda J. Wachner, a former cosmetics company president. In late April, W Acquisition announced it was buying Warnaco for about $488 million, of which the individual bidders would provide barely more than 1 percent of the needed financing; the rest Milken would raise by issuing junk bonds.

Galef became chairman of the Warnaco board but drew no salary; instead he cashed in with big equity stakes for himself and a monthly consulting-fee arrangement for Spectrum similar to that which Spectrum enjoyed with MagneTek (and with Exide Corporation, a maker of automobile batteries Spectrum acquired in 1983). Between 1986 and 1989 alone, Galef would pay himself nine million dollars in fees, a sum that made him one of the highest-paid executives in the country, according to *Forbes*. (The consulting arrangement also shielded him from the onerous income-disclosure reporting the Securities and Exchange Commission required of senior management of publicly held companies.)

Galef celebrated the new acquisitions in a style befitting a mid-eighties titan of finance. He bought a house valued at nearly $2.5 million in 1986 above Sunset Boulevard on Copa de Oro (Cup of Gold) Road in the tony Los Angeles enclave of Bel Air. Clark Gable and Carole Lombard once had a tennis court on the property; Alfred Hitchcock once lived next door. Among Galef's contemporary neighbors were Jean Stapleton, the actress, and Joanna Carson, Johnny's ex. He filled the walls of his trophy house with trophy art: French Impressionist paintings, including a Renoir valued at $80,000 and a Pissarro worth $700,000 in 1989.

When not at home, Galef and his second wife were often tooling around town, perhaps to the Bel Air Country Club, or to their Palm Springs or San Francisco condominium, in their Mercedes or Jaguar or Rolls-Royce. Or they were cruising in the private jet Spectrum and his other companies co-owned. Shortly after the Warnaco deal closed, in July of 1986 the Galefs treated themselves to a whirlwind tour of the Pacific Rim. In three weeks they covered Australia, Hong Kong, China, and Japan. "We stayed, as we always do, in first-class hotels, ate at the best restaurants, and generally traveled by limousine," Billie Galef subsequently noted. A month later they were off again, to Europe. "In September," Mrs. Galef wrote, "we took the Concorde to Paris and London, where we spent a week, again staying at the best hotels and eating in the best restaurants."

FOR THE MORE than two decades since Archie Sergy sold out in 1963, outsiders controlled the economic destiny of the women and men who toiled at Universal. Whether those who held the purse strings were faceless financiers from New York or Chicago or Los Angeles didn't matter much to Mollie James and her co-workers in Paterson. Owners came and went, and the principal visible sign of each transition was a new company name on the payroll checks.

So when word spread in early 1986 that an outfit called MagneTek, of Los Angeles, was the new owner, Mollie took the news calmly. For one thing her boss would not change: Otto Payonzeck had agreed to stay on—with the added title of executive vice president of the ballast division and a salary of $215,000, a raise of $71,000. Surely some things would change—managers in, managers out, maybe—but she had no reason to question her job security. She'd recently marked her thirtieth year with the company, and although the Mississippi plant had surpassed Paterson in employment and production, and even the new plant in Blytheville, Arkansas, was approaching the personnel level of Paterson, Paterson was still the flagship, still the headquarters. "We were the ones who made the specialty ballasts," Mollie says. "The bread and butter they sent down South."

But right away Mollie could tell big changes were in store. As were the earlier owners, MagneTek was a faraway, far-flung holding company, but the previous stewards' hands-off, don't-fix-it-if-it-ain't-broke page was missing from its corporate manual. "You could see it right away," she says. "It started the day our name disappeared from the building—poof, no more Universal."

A principal tenet of MagneTek's business plan was the centralization of all aspects of its businesses under one big umbrella. "Synergy"—that is, the harmony that the combined whole would create—was the mantra. Marketing, accounting, distribution, and shipping, all would be coordinated from the home office. As part and parcel of this philosophy, all the established businesses and brand names the company acquired would be subsumed under MagneTek.

As its name faded, so, too, did most of the vestiges of the Universal the old-timers knew. Like Mollie, Harold Harris spent his working life, forty-one years, with the company. He was in management, accustomed to rolling with the punches of a new owner. "It didn't mean a hell of a lot to anybody," Harris says of the MagneTek acquisition. "Because we'd been sold a few times before, and nothing seemed to change much."

Harris had worked in a variety of capacities for Universal—purchasing, sales, service—before taking over as chief scheduler. (His title was director of sales order, service.) His varied and deep knowledge of the entire operation—from each of the manufacturing plants to the distribution sites to the customer base—served him and the company well. "I coordinated all the plants' output, making sure supply met demand. But I knew exactly how to work miracles for certain customers. I knew when to rob Peter to pay Paul. That was the way we retained our business. You knew which guys you could screw and which guys you had to live up to a promise and commitment.

"And I'd get calls in the middle of the night, because the plants were operating sometimes around the clock. Mendenhall might call and say, 'We ran out of this or that on the assembly line,' and I'd have to yell and scream to gear up, or 'A truck from Lithonia Lighting is waiting for a pickup, but the stuff isn't ready yet. What should we do?' I knew there were other units in stock that I could substitute on that truck and make it up that way. And I knew I could straighten it out the following day with the next truck coming in."

But no one without the accumulated wisdom of a Harold Harris would have known that. No software magician at MagneTek, which was hell-bent on implementing a centralized traffic system for all its businesses, would have understood the delicacy of such situations, when to employ the light touch, when the heavy hand. And so after attending a conference in St. Louis of sales managers from all of MagneTek's companies, Harris realized it was time to retire. "Old-school guys like me had nothing to teach those young go-getters." He says MagneTek was "trying to become an overnight GE, only GE had a hundred-year head start. They thought all they had to do was 'trim this department, cut that one, combine those,' and most of all, 'centralize, centralize, centralize.' But all that central distribution network did was handcuff us. You couldn't satisfy customers that way, couldn't treat them the way they'd been accustomed to."

MagneTek's cavalier attitude infected all aspects of Universal; from senior management to the local unions, few would survive unbowed, and many would be bloodied. In mid-September of 1986, the company's human-resources director told Otto Payonzeck to hop a plane to Mississippi to deliver the news to Sig Steinberger that his services were no longer required. Steinberger was in his thirty-sixth year with the company (of which twenty-three were spent in Mississippi). That much the human-resources director knew from the personnel file. He likely also knew Steinberger had overseen construction of the Simpson County plant in 1963, and had managed it all the years since. But he did not likely know—any more than MagneTek's vice president of distribution knew about Harold Harris's incalculable value to the company—about Steinberger's critical role in the life and times of his community. About his courage in standing up to the state's frothing racial and antilabor extremists; about his efforts to peaceably integrate both the plant and, as a ten-year member of the Mendenhall School Board, the public schools. To the local citizenry Sig Steinberger was "Mr. Universal," an honorific that bespoke his powerful position as head of the county's largest employer. But it spoke to something more, too. Steinberger was no preacher, but he used his position as a pulpit from which to quietly and resolutely spread the gospel of respect for one another and equality for all. He was no less than a moral force for change, a shining exemplar of leadership, of heart and soul and wisdom.

Nowhere was this a part of the job description. Sig Steinberger was three weeks shy of his sixty-fourth birthday, a year and three weeks shy of his intended retirement date, when, as Steinberger recounts it, Payonzeck strode unannounced into the plant. It was noon on a Tuesday. "Sig, I need to see you in your office."

They walked in; Payonzeck shut the door.

"Sig, I need you to retire."

Payonzeck paused, waiting for a response from the speechless Steinberger.

"One other thing, Sig," Payonzeck continued, "I need you out of here by four o'clock this afternoon."

More silence until Steinberger found a few words.

"Otto, I don't understand this. I've been here thirty-six years and you're firing me on four hours' notice? What the hell have I ever done to this company to deserve this?"

"I can't explain it," Payonzeck replied. "Just take my word for it, it's best for you this way." (Steinberger asked for and was granted a reprieve of three weeks, until October 8, his birthday.)

Years later Payonzeck was asked why he gave Steinberger one afternoon to clear out the office he'd occupied for twenty-three years. "That's how much time I was given to get him out of there. Sure it was a heartless thing to do, but that's the way Galef and Perna worked. [Perna was a Spectrum Group partner as well as president of Magne-Tek.] They always wanted it done quick and bloodless, before the rumors got into the mill."

Payonzeck explained that Perna was an electrical engineer "whose people skills left something to be desired," adding that Galef's financial background allowed him to dwell on the bottom line "with no room for commiseration." He continued: "It was always a dollars-and-cents calculation with them. This is what the numbers say you've got to get done. It didn't matter if somebody had been there fifty years or somebody's mother was dying. You still kissed 'em good-bye."

Eight months after Payonzeck had played the hatchet man, the ax would fall on him, too. He had cleared so much of the old growth from the Universal forest, including the company's operations director, Sidney Cohen, that he was one of the few pre-MagneTek managers still standing. In May of 1987, Perna and Galef rectified that oversight. Following a sales meeting he attended in San Francisco, Payonzeck was asked to drop by "corporate" in Los Angeles. He was ushered into Perna's office, where Perna and the house counsel greeted him. Perna told Payonzeck they were doing some "housecleaning" and that he was asking for Payonzeck's "resignation." (Four other senior corporate officials were also "wiped out" concurrently, Payonzeck says.) Payonzeck was escorted home to New Jersey by a corporate vice president. "They sent the guy to watch me clean out my desk, make sure I didn't steal anything."

Nearly a decade later, Payonzeck met a guest for breakfast one cold, drizzly November morning at a country club not far from his former Universal offices. Asked what mistakes MagneTek made during that first tumultuous year it owned Universal, he raised the issue of entombing the company's good and venerable name. "We went from 'Universal' to 'Universal, a division of MagneTek,' with MagneTek in small letters, to 'Universal, a MagneTek company,' with MagneTek in bigger type. And then we just became the MagneTek brand." Payonzeck paused for a few moments, seeming to study the hardy golfers on the distant, soggy putting green. "Universal," he said softly, his normal robust voice lowered nearly to a whisper, "Universal, to the best of my knowledge, doesn't exist anymore."

THIRTEEN

"On the Border, By the Sea"

N OT ONLY HAD Universal's name vanished from the plant, by early 1988 its equipment was disappearing, torn from the floor like trees from their roots. "The movers came at night, like thieves," Mollie James had recalled, "sometimes just taking one piece at a time. We'd come in in the mornings and there'd be another hole in the floor." The machinery had been used to make a large, fifty-pound specialty ballast known as the HID, or high-intensity discharge, the kind used in thousand-watt fixtures installed in outdoor stadiums. Paterson was the lone Universal plant making the HID; its precision-wound coils required training and equipment different from that of the garden-variety, one-pound, forty-watt fluorescent ballast the two Southern plants pumped out by the tens of thousands daily.

If Paterson's workers were more sophisticated, they were also more costly; their labor averaged about eight dollars an hour, seventy-five cents more than the company paid its workforce in Mississippi and almost a dollar more than in Arkansas. But if the wages down South were low, they were not low enough. They were not the cheapest possible wages. They weren't, say, as low as workers earned in Mexico, where the prevailing wage in the *maquiladoras* was less than four dollars a *day*. How could MagneTek compete in a global marketplace if its competitors were paying many times less than what American workers earned?

The long-term answer for MagneTek was to go global itself; the short-term answer was to lower its costs of doing business domestically. Andy Galef had trimmed overhead by pruning Universal's senior management; it was time to clear-cut its union workforce. The slashing would begin in Paterson—in the grimy old town's obsolete plant filled with obsolete, strike-prone workers who belonged to a corrupt and bloated local union. And so, in the early months of 1988 the machines began disappearing—where to, they weren't told. "All we kept hearing was how good a job we were doing," Mollie says, "that we had nothing to worry about, that we'd always have work in Paterson."

They soon learned the fate of the machines; as for their jobs, still no one was saying. The equipment was routed to the plant in Blytheville, Arkansas, as a dubious reward to the workers there for surviving their own close brush with occupational death. Some months earlier, in November 1987, MagneTek had dispatched a lawyer to Blytheville to engage in what the company bloodlessly termed "concessionary bargaining" but what in reality was a mob-like proposal to local union leaders—an offer they could hardly refuse: Take a pay cut, and we'll send down the HID-ballast production from Paterson; decline, and lose your jobs. "He told us if we didn't take the cut, we could go on unemployment for six months and then we could go on welfare," recalls Deanna McComb, who was forty-two at the time and who worked in customer returns and served as the union's chief steward.

The lawyer backed up his straight talk with a loaded gun: Only last month, he told the local's negotiating committee, MagneTek broke ground on a ballast-manufacturing plant—in Mexico.

With the gun to their heads, the Blytheville membership voted to accept the concessions. The wage decrease ranged from $1.25 an hour to $2.05 an hour. Deanna McComb's check shriveled from nearly $7.00 an hour to less than $5.00—a loss of $80.00 a week. And she was one of the more fortunate employees. Her house and car were paid for, her husband worked, and they had no young children to support. For Sally Miller, a forty-two-year-old who made repairs in the winding and finishing departments, the pay cut was nothing short of ruinous. Her husband, a construction worker, had recently been seriously injured on the job. He was laid up at home, recovering from back surgery, and drawing only $100 weekly in workers' compensation. He also suffered a heart attack; the twin maladies permanently disabled him. Sally's earnings, meanwhile, dwindled to $4.75 an hour—not nearly enough to make mortgage payments *and* put food on the table. The Millers chose food, giving up their three-bedroom brick home for a mobile home. Nor were they as bad off as others. "People lost cars, homes, their marriages broke up," Sally says. "People's bills piled up so high, they had to declare bankruptcy. We gave this company everything, and you know what for? So they could take our pride away."

As MagneTek methodically stripped Paterson of its machinery and Blytheville of its dignity, the company was steaming toward Mexico. The new plant was under construction in an industrial park in Matamoros, the border city across the Rio Grande from Brownsville, Texas. The company had neatly pitted one facility against another, had brandished the Mexico plant to force the Blytheville workers effectively to sign the death warrant for Paterson. On the first Tuesday in June of 1988, MagneTek's director of industrial relations, Jim Kaja, met with representatives of Teamsters Local 945 to discuss the fate of the Paterson plant. Kaja spoke fluent corporate blather; he cited the "concepts" of "synergies" and "lowest cost producer." He explained that the company was "consolidating" some divisions, transferring others within the "MagneTek family of plants," and closing still others. He warned the union that in addition to the 135 Paterson workers already laid off or soon to lose their jobs in the wake of the HID-product-line transfer to Blytheville, there was "a significant probability" that the fluorescent ballast lines would be relocated to Mississippi. "Should this occur," Kaja wrote in a follow-up letter, "an additional three hundred–plus employees will be affected."

Three days later, MagneTek celebrated its grand opening in Matamoros. After the innumerable toasts and speeches, after the ribbon was sheared and the plant inspected, the entourage of revelers—the corporate honchos in from Los Angeles, the Mexican union officials, the economic developers and power brokers from both sides of the border—shuttled over to American soil for a cocktail party at Rancho Viejo, a country club and condominium development a few miles north of Brownsville. There in the Casa Grande room, the proud MagneTek execs rubbed elbows with fellow American and Japanese manufacturers along the border, members of the Matamoros Maquiladora Association. Drinks flowed from the open bar, tuxedo-clad waiters served fresh shrimp, taquitos, cheeses, and fresh fruit. Hector Romeu of the Finsa Group, who had worked so feverishly to put together the day's program, moved serenely among the guests, nodding, touching an elbow here, slapping a back there, introducing MagneTek officials to their counterparts at General Motors, ITT, and Mitsubishi and to others of his fifteen American and Japanese corporate clients in the industrial park.

MATAMOROS HAD only recently become a mecca for industrial capitalism. Even after Mexico founded the Border Industrialization Program in the middle 1960s, the early American investments centered on the more prosperous and populous northern borderlands to the west: in Tijuana, under San Diego, California; and Ciudad Juárez, south of El Paso, Texas. Matamoros was the commercial center of a lush agricultural region of broad, alluvial bottomland. Like the Mississippi Delta, a landscape it somewhat resembled, Matamoros was cotton country. Unlike the Delta, the climate of the Lower Rio Grande Valley—the southernmost stretch of the United States—was subtropical, and there palm trees flourished, sugarcane grew twelve feet high, and citrus groves yielded the finest oranges and ruby red grapefruits.

In the mid-sixties, not quite 150,000 persons lived in Matamoros. Many were either farmers or ranchers, or people who sold them goods or services or labor. Some were farmworkers returned to the border after the U.S. Congress ended the bracero program in 1964. These were the people for whom the Border Industrialization Program intended to create jobs. (Commercial fishing, tourism, and international governmental functions—customs and immigration—were the other notable contributors to the local economy.) By 1967, the BIP was operational, most visibly in Tijuana and Juárez, where were located the majority of the seventy-two American-owned plants on the border. Juárez, especially, initially prospered from the program; its success in attracting corporate interest stemmed from the outsize influence of

Antonio J. Bermudez, a Juárez resident whom Mexican president Adolfo López Mateos had appointed in 1961 to head PRONAF, the national border reformation project that led to the creation of the BIP. Along with his brother, Jaime, Bermudez parlayed the family's governmental ties—Antonio was also the founding director of PEMEX, the nationalized oil industry—into building Mexico's first industrial park: the Antonio J. Bermudez Industrial Park.

No Matamoren had such connections, and the city was consequently denied the choicest political plums. By 1967, Matamoros had yet to attract a single American manufacturer, and would not until officials on the Texas side of the Rio Grande took the initiative. In May of the previous year, the chamber of commerce in Matamoros's twin city, Brownsville, recruited a man named Lindsey Rhodes to establish and direct an economic development office. Until that time the Valley had promoted itself primarily as a playground for "winter Texans"—the snowbirds who flocked annually from the Midwest and Canada to encamp in one of the innumerable motor-home parks. In "On the Border, By the Sea," a soothing breeze of a story welcoming the winter tourist crop, *The Brownsville Herald* sketched the region's bounteous hunting, fishing, and sightseeing offerings. "If all this weren't enough," the story continued,

> Mexico is just a stone's throw from Brownsville. The door to our sister republic is always open and once you pass through it a world of beauty and tranquility, reeking of lost civilizations and the dead age of Spanish conquest, lies before you. Life in South Texas and Northern Mexico is not at all like the hectic, ulcerous pace found in many metropolitan areas of the United States. You could not say this is the land of mañana because mañana does come, but it seems to take just a little longer to get here.

Lindsey Rhodes arrived from Los Angeles, where he had worked as a technical writer for a company active in the budding *maquila* industry in Tijuana. Prior to that job, Rhodes, a native Louisianan, had worked for chambers of commerce in his home state and in west Texas. Each summer during those years, he attended a weeklong training institute in Houston for chamber of commerce staff members throughout the

Southwest. It was there Rhodes became acquainted with the chamber director from Brownsville, with whom he remained in touch after moving on to his new job in Los Angeles. When Rhodes and his wife, an Arkansas native, determined Los Angeles was not the place to raise their children, they investigated the possibilities in Brownsville.

"When I got here in sixty-six," Rhodes recalls, "Brownsville had no development strategy to speak of. It was dirt poor"—here, like any good chamber official, Rhodes breaks from his narrative to spew a statistic—"in the lowest twenty out of three hundred SMSAs [Standard Metropolitan Statistical Areas]" in the country in terms of economic growth. Rhodes spent six months studying the "whys and wherefores" of the Border Industry Program. Then he had an epiphany. "It just dawned on me that what we had was Taiwan right at our back door, only U.S. corporations wouldn't have to cross the Pacific Ocean to get there. I could sell Matamoros to U.S. businessmen by telling them, 'You come to Brownsville, you live in the U.S., you keep your children in U.S. schools, you cross the river to work during the day, you get paid in dollars, you come home to the U.S. at night.' " For Brownsville the payoff would be new shipping and warehousing facilities—"twin plants"—on its side of the border and a wealth of industrial support services, such as parts suppliers, machine-tool repair shops, and so on, to feed the manufacturers across the river.

The first to take Rhodes's bait was Electronic Control Corporation, a Dallas-based maker of light dimmers. The company opened in 1967 and was quickly followed by two electronics-components businesses from the Midwest. But for his early successes, by 1969 only those three manufacturing *maquilas* and a couple of shrimp-processing plants had relocated to Matamoros. It wasn't for lack of a line in the water. "We were really trying," he says. "I was one of those seven-day-a-week guys in the office on Sundays putting proposals together." And at the end of that year, he reeled in his biggest catch: Zenith.

The big Chicago-based television manufacturer opened its tuner-assembly plant in a new industrial park on the east side of Matamoros. The Zenith plant would eventually employ as many as five thousand Mexicans, but at the beginning its greatest value, as Rhodes saw it, was its endorsement. "Zenith gave us a name-brand Fortune 500 company. And people started saying, 'Maybe we should take a look at the Valley, too.' "

Sure enough, soon after Zenith committed, one of its primary competitors, RCA, came calling. Rhodes found the RCA scout an old cotton-compress building owned by a banking family in Matamoros— "just what he was looking for." The family sought twice as much as RCA was willing to pay, however, and after three or four unsuccessful negotiating sessions over the course of a year, the company decided to look elsewhere, eventually accepting an offer from the Bermudez family in Juárez to move into their industrial park. "When that one got away," Rhodes says, "it was like pulling my jaw-teeth out."

Rhodes recovered quickly enough; in the early 1970s he helped lure another seventeen American companies to Matamoros, all of which were electronics-related manufacturers and four of which were also members (or subsidiaries of members) of the Fortune 500 club. More big names (Du Pont; a wire-harness division of ITT; the Fisher-Price division of Quaker Oats) followed, and in the late seventies, Matamoros landed the biggest fish of all: General Motors, the world's largest, richest corporation.

Rhodes served as tour guide for GM officials, but the company's most ardent pursuer was Sergio Arguelles Gutierrez, patriarch of one of Matamoros's prominent families. Arguelles had large agribusiness holdings in the region and throughout the country; at one time he was Mexico's largest popcorn-seed supplier. Arguelles had watched idly in 1970 as another group of local entrepreneurs acquired a thousand acres to build the city's first industrial park, in the northeast corner of the city near the International Bridge to Brownsville, the site to which Zenith migrated. The success of that park and another built in 1975 in southeast Matamoros prompted Arguelles to buy up five hundred acres of farmland some eight miles southwest of the bridge.

With no track record as a *maquila* facilitator, and nothing to show but the real estate—"nothing," as Lindsey Rhodes recalls, "but barren land with a big Caterpillar tractor sitting out there in the middle of one sweep"—Arguelles boldly went after GM. "He took them out there in a pickup truck on a muddy day and said, 'Here is a good site for you,'" says Hector Romeu.

The sixteen months it took to negotiate the deal was time well spent: In 1979 Arguelles opened his Finsa park with a bumper-making division of GM as his anchor tenant. Soon another GM unit, Delco, the car-radio manufacturer, followed, and then another, and within a decade Finsa would become the second-largest *maquila* park in Mexico and among the largest on the entire border. As Rhodes explains it, the same herding instinct that caused companies to follow the high-profile Zenith a decade earlier was in full force from the late seventies on. "The thinking went, If doing business with Sergio Arguelles was good for GM, it must be good for us."

And what was good for GM was good for the country, at least as the Reagan administration saw it. In the March-April 1986 edition of *Boletín Comercial,* the newsletter of the U.S. Commerce Department's outpost in Mexico City, the department announced its sponsorship of a Mexican business exposition called "Expo Maquila '86." The expo was to be held during the first week of December at the Hyatt Regency hotel in the resort town of Acapulco and would feature Commerce Department representatives and others advising U.S. companies about the "extraordinary business opportunities" and "benefits" of the *maquiladora* program. In a brochure sent to thirty-nine thousand firms across America, the Commerce Department touted Expo Maquila for "the entrepreneur. The financial visionary. The forward-thinking businessman. In short, anyone who has a need for more cost-effective, more lucrative manufacturing arrangements."

But what about Americans who had a need for a paycheck—the people who punched the clock for those thirty-nine thousand firms their government was inviting to export their jobs? WHY ARE YOU MOVING OUR JOBS TO MEXICO? the United Auto Workers asked President Reagan in full-page ads placed in midwestern newspapers in late October. It was a question to which outraged members of Congress from Rust Belt states and from both sides of the aisle demanded an answer. At the end of November, one week before the scheduled expo in Acapulco, a subcommittee of the House Banking, Finance and Urban Affairs Committee summoned a Commerce Department official to provide one.

Alexander Good, director general of the United States Foreign and Commercial Service, told members of Congress the administration supported the *maquila* industry because it "certainly improves U.S. competitiveness in world markets. It certainly improves profitability in U.S. firms. It maintains employment that would go to other parts of the world, primarily into the Pacific Rim, and therefore encourages maintaining employment levels in the United States."

Representative John LaFalce, the western New York Democrat who chaired the Subcommittee on Economic Stabilization, was unimpressed. LaFalce's Buffalo-area district was crippled by plant closings and corporate defections to Mexico; its largest manufacturing employer, Trico Products Corporation, which had made windshield wipers in Buffalo since 1917, had announced only months prior to the hearing that it was relocating most of its operations to the Finsa park in Matamoros.

"The fact of the matter is if we left U.S. interests to so-called U.S. companies, we would be in terrible shape, because their primary concern is their bottom line; and if their bottom line is going to be enhanced by going offshore, by producing products and services out of the United States, they could care less about jobs in the United States.

"They simply want a better bottom line," LaFalce continued. "It is time that we woke up to that fact. If we are going to help so-called U.S. companies—and that is what I want to do, if we want to enhance their competitiveness, if you want to avoid protectionism, that *quid pro quo* must be the retention and expansion of jobs in the United States."

LaFalce told Alexander Good that he read the Expo Maquila brochure and found nothing "that said if you are having difficulty we will help you become more competitive. . . . Instead what I saw was Expo Maquila 1986, designed 'to unlock the riches of the Mexican *[maquila]* industry for you to help maintain high quality, high efficiency production with an even higher potential for profit.' " (The brochure also emphasized "low-cost foreign labor.") "It is not that these companies are unprofitable," LaFalce added, "it is just that with these unbelievably low wages—ninety cents an hour—these multinational companies can make even higher profits."

It was open season on the Commerce Department, and Alexander Good was a sitting duck. "We collect taxes here . . . from the people [who] are working in this country, then you use these workers' dollars . . . to help facilitate moving their jobs to Mexico?" Bruce Vento, Democrat of Minnesota, inquired. Good: "Our position is we are making a job base, hopefully increasing jobs in the United States."

That was one disingenuous retort too many for one member, Bob Carr, a Michigan Democrat. "Frankly, I have to say what I have heard here today is a bunch of crap." Carr was not a member of the subcommittee; he spoke as a member of the Appropriations Committee and as a representative of a state that had suffered as much job loss as any in the early and middle eighties. In Detroit, home of the United Auto Workers and where Henry Ford had invented the assembly line, the Big Three auto companies had closed virtually all their assembly operations, moving them to the suburbs, or to the American South, or to the Mexican border and beyond. Jobless levels in Detroit were so high that Mayor Coleman Young had declared "a state of human emergency"; he called the city's economic situation "a crisis unparalleled since the nineteen thirties."

Bob Carr and Ralph Regula, an Ohio Republican and fellow Appropriations member, had added language two weeks earlier to a Commerce Department appropriations resolution forbidding the department from using 1987 funds for any conference that "conveys the advantages" of U.S. companies moving outside the country.

"On the Appropriations Committee," Carr lectured Good, "we are in charge of U.S. taxpayer dollars. What is so offensive about what you have done is you are taking U.S. taxpayer dollars to promote the relocation of jobs from the United States to Mexico. And you can dress it up all you want with good intentions about how you are really bombing the village to save it, but the Appropriations Committee, on a bipartisan basis, didn't buy it."*

While the hearing was surely useful to lawmakers for cultivating friendships with organized labor and for expressing frustration with an administration that was deaf to the concerns of working Americans, there was also about the committee room a pervasive sense of resignation, of damage done, and that the many voices raised in protest were no match for the swirling global economic forces that had no regard for national borders or the greater good. Chairman LaFalce implied so in his closing remarks. "What I am saying is basically most of these corporations don't give one damn about whether the job is in the United States or abroad, and basically, the ones who are making the decisions

---

*In a subsequent congressional hearing, held the week after Expo Maquila, Carr reminded his colleagues that in spite of the limitation in the Appropriations Committee's resolution, taxpayers were still footing the bill for the expo. "The firms that traveled to Acapulco for this event no doubt made those trips as a tax-deductible expense," Carr said.

feel no personal pain whatsoever. For that matter," he added, "they don't care that much about the pain they are causing to the individuals that are unemployed or to the communities that are adversely affected. Maybe they should have the right to make those painful decisions not painful to them, but painful to their former employees, painful to the communities where they used to live for twenty years, thirty years, fifty years, but it ought not to be the policy of the U.S. Government to promote that."

Resignation filled the confines of the committee room, and so, too, did inevitability; whether or not the Commerce Department ever spent another penny on *maquila* promotion, the rush to the border was on.

Though the number of American companies migrating to Matamoros had grown steadily since General Motors in 1979 bestowed on the city its seal of approval, the real boom came after 1982, when the Mexican government devalued its currency. American firms paid their workers in pesos, earned their profits in dollars. And when the peso plummeted in 1982—it began the year at less than twenty-seven to the dollar and ended the year at around one hundred—Mexican workers' wages were cut nearly in half, to a rock-bottom rate comparable to the world's established low-wage havens in the Caribbean basin and the Far East. When MagneTek broke ground in Matamoros in late 1987, the value of the dollar against the peso had soared by an unfathomable 5,000 percent since 1982. The city teemed with global bottom-fishers: Sixty-eight *maquilas* employed twenty-nine thousand workers—a doubling of the workforce since the devaluation.

Most of those *maquilas* produced electronics components, and many of them assembled products similar to MagneTek's: transformers, motors, and other parts that utilized coil-winding machinery. That such businesses were already in place in Matamoros the company considered a plus; there were established support services, and a workforce accustomed to the demands of coil-winding production. And the city was also closer than the other *maquila* centers to the company's supply line—the steel-stamping would still be done at the Simpson County plant. But there was one negative: Matamoros was home to a powerful union leader reputedly responsible for driving wages higher than those in other border cities. So MagneTek looked elsewhere, most earnestly at Ciudad Juárez. "But Juárez was more of a TV [manu-facturing] town, and when we interviewed a lot of the *maquila* managers in Matamoros, we found the wage differential wasn't a big deal," says William J. Landry, the company's chief site selector. Landry, a native Bostonian, had gone to work for Universal in 1978 as its industrial engineer. He was one of the few in upper management (he was also vice president of operations) to have been spared the layoff ax after MagneTek bought the company. Landry's study of the availability of labor and the wage rates determined that Juárez was "a more competitive market where you had a lot of the *maquilas* offering free bus rides to work or free food. We didn't find they had those benefits in Matamoros, where the unemployment rate was something like thirty-five percent." (The company had also recently acquired a small coil-manufacturing business with twin plants in Matamoros and Brownsville.)

Landry negotiated directly with Sergio Arguelles of the Finsa Group, and in the late summer of 1987, they came to terms on an agreement that called for Finsa to build the five interconnected plants to MagneTek's specifications. Ground was broken on the 250,000-square-foot complex in October. It was an expeditious job; only six months later, in early April, the first ballasts were coming off the line. By then the Blytheville workers were poorer by as much as two dollars an hour and learning how to make high-intensity discharge ballasts. The Mississippi plant was not yet affected, and the Paterson plant was breathing but skeletal—135 workers had already been laid off, with the promise of more to go soon. By virtue of her seniority, Mollie James was still on the payroll, but just then she was out of town; the company had sent her to Blytheville for a week. Like a death-row inmate building her own casket, Mollie was training the workers there to do her job.

While MagneTek celebrated its cost savings and feasted on the advantageous exchange rate, the company's Mexican workers subsisted on the equivalent of $3.90 a day—49¢ an hour—not enough to feed, clothe, and shelter themselves, let alone any children. Even *Twin Plant News,* the cheerleading trade-magazine for *maquila* executives, acknowledged the impoverished state of the industry's workforce. But rather than raise wages, the magazine counseled, "there are some things you can do to help, such as setting up a clothing exchange in the plant. . . . Buy some bulk food items such as flour, beans, potatoes, etc., and distribute these among your employees." (The magazine's advice columns and how-to stories typically ranged from "union avoidance" ["we already know the heartaches that come from unionization"], to vacation tips ["*Maquila* managers with a love of nature can take advantage of Yucatan's bird refuges"], to suggestions on how to meet and greet Mexican executives ["First shake hands warmly—NOT a bone crusher"], to commiserating with "maquila wives" whose husbands had dragged them to the outer limits of American civilization ["They are homebound . . . and have to put up with repairmen that show up late or not at all"].)

If one was struck by the vacuousness of *Twin Plant News*, one could also appreciate that its editor understood that no matter how low *maquila* wages dipped, the border plants were an absolute magnet for those with *no* wages, those from Mexico's jobless interior. And to the border they came—single women mainly, single young women, for it was they whom the *maquila* managers wanted. Their fingers were nimble, their minds pliable. When they arrived in the late eighties and early nineties, they found a city that had split its seams: Built to accommodate 50,000 people, Matamoros was bursting with upwards of ten times that. (No one knew how many people lived there, but estimates ranged from 500,000 to 600,000.) It is difficult to overstate the city's miseries. Adequate roads, affordable housing, public transit, were nil. City services—electricity, water, sewage, drainage, pavement, garbage collection, law enforcement, firefighting—were nonexistent in a third of the city's 180 registered *colonias*—neighborhoods. But many of the newcomers lived not in city-recognized *colonias*, but in the city dump, where they competed with animals for food, or in remote squatters' camps—in open-air shacks constructed from scrounged plywood or warehouse pallets or cardboard and chicken wire and tar paper, or in tents fashioned from opaque plastic. These souls were the *paracaidistas*—the parachutists who seemingly fell from the sky. From their shantytowns they would find their way downtown on foot or by private, costly "maxi-taxi"—a small school bus—to the central hiring hall, at Ninth and Iturbide streets, and, if fortune smiled, to a job at a *maquila* in one of the city's sprawling industrial parks. No sooner would word of the good news spread back home than a younger sister or a cousin would be on the next bus north. "You've got to realize," MagneTek plant manager Chuck Peeples says, "that when one person goes to work here, two more come up from the interior."

On a brisk January morning in 1997, Peeples shook hands warmly (not a bone crusher) with a visitor in the plant's reception area, a wood-paneled anteroom amply stocked with plastic flowers and the latest issue of *Magnevision,* the in-house Spanish-language newsletter brimming with employee-of-the-month mug shots, health-and-safety tips, perfect-attendance logs.

Peeples was sixty years old. He wore a short-sleeved shirt with no tie ("We're business casual around here"), aviator glasses, and flyaway hair. A Blytheville native, he enlisted in the Navy after graduating from high school in 1953. He was discharged in 1960 and bounced around the country for a half-dozen years before settling in Cheyenne, Wyoming, where he spent thirteen years working for a refrigeration company, rising to head of manufacturing. In 1979, he went home to Blytheville to manage Universal's new plant, a job he would keep until late 1987, when MagneTek transferred him to oversee construction in Matamoros.

After conducting a lengthy and thorough tour of his domain—the clean, noisy shop floor and the utilitarian executive offices—Peeples escorted the visitor into his office, a similarly modest space with a three-chair conference area, a vinyl marker-board, and a bookcase housing numerous but indeterminate works—the spines of most faced the wall, the exception being the four-volume *Tax Laws of the World* and the companion *Commercial Laws of the World.* Above the bookcase was a small wooden plaque: "Leaders are like eagles. They don't flock. You find them one at a time."

The visitor told Peeples he had been in Matamoros for some weeks, and that he had spent much of his time in a *colonia* in the literal and figurative shadow of the MagneTek plant—the *colonia* was separated only by chain-link fence from the rear of the plant. The visitor added that the *colonia* reminded him in many ways of the old cotton mill villages he had seen in isolated towns of the American South. Though the *colonia* was neither built nor owned by MagneTek, most of its households included at least one family member who worked for the company or for another of the foreign-owned firms in the industrial park. And all lived from paycheck to paycheck to keep their woeful roofs over their heads.

The visitor was curious about Peeples's awareness of his employees' living conditions. "Well, I know the associates"—MagneSpeak for employees—"don't make enough money to buy homes," Peeples replied, "they live in federal housing or whatever." (He added that in the wake of the most recent peso devaluation, in 1994, the company had made one-time emergency loans to some of its "professional managers," supervisors, who were buying homes.) Asked if the hourly wage the company paid (about $1.40 at the time) was enough to live on, Peeples said, "Yeah, I think so. But nobody's getting rich." His tone was not so flip as it might suggest, but neither was Peeples ashamed for his workers—his "associates"—to live in penury.

The phone rang—"Whatcha need, Sugar Jam?" Peeples asked—and then he told the visitor he had to run. One last question: Is it sensible for a young person to leave her hometown for a job with MagneTek, and for the hardships of life on the border? "That's a tough one," Peeples answered. "I guess it depends on what they were leaving."

FOURTEEN

The Lucky Ones

Balbina Duque

CIUDAD DEL MAÍZ, APRIL 1991. The nightly bus to Matamoros from San Luis Potosí, the capital city of the central
Mexican state of the same name, would not roll through
here until nine-fifteen. It was only midmorning, just a couple of hours
since she'd said her good-byes to the family, since she'd pressed her
lips for the last time to her baby son's cheek and handed him to her
mother. It was only midmorning, and already she could feel the tropi-
cal sun on her face, could feel her funds dwindling fast.

She'd had two hundred pesos, the equivalent of about sixty-six
dollars, to begin with, and now that she'd paid a man nearly twenty
dollars to taxi her from Monte Bello, her mountain village—a place of

clean and clear air, brilliant high-desert flowers, and almost surrealisti-
cally bright light—to the bus station in town, and now that she'd
bought a couple of tamales from a sidewalk vendor and a one-way
ticket to the border for thirty dollars, Balbina Duque Granados was
down to less than fifteen dollars. It was only midmorning, and though
the bus would not depart for another eleven or so hours, Balbina's
driver had needed to make the trip early. It took an hour of precision
steering around outcrops and ruts and loose rocks to negotiate the
seven unrelievedly bumpy miles from Monte Bello to the Maíz highway. The only spot he could offer Balbina was in the bed of the pickup.
By the time she hopped out at the bus station, she and her three bags
were coated with the grit and dust of the open rocky road. She would
spend the day keeping vigil over her belongings in the bus station, a
green-and-white cement building spared from full-onset drab by the
presence on the walls of numerous framed color photographs of luxury coaches.

Balbina turned twenty only weeks earlier. She is five foot three,
with an open, copper-colored face, an easy, dimpled smile, and long
black hair worn in a ponytail. She is leaving for Matamoros, four hundred miles northward, to work as a caretaker for an elderly couple with
ties to her village. She is torn about going, especially about having to
leave behind her eighteen-month-old son, Iban. "If there were work
here," Balbina said in Spanish during a visit home some years later,
"everyone would stay." As a grocer in town amplified: "You really don't
have a choice. One girl will come home in new clothes, and three or
four girls will be impressed enough to follow her—to Matamoros or
wherever."

There is nothing to keep them at home, in Ciudad del Maíz,
a scenic but scrawny farm town of eight thousand persons, or in
Monte Bello, in the high valley above Maíz where Balbina's family lives.
The village is comprised of maybe a thousand people who live in a couple hundred pastel-colored cement-block and thatched-roof homes.
Most everyone attends the fine, whitewashed church and sends their
young children to the primary school. (The older ones have to find
their way to school in Maíz.) There is a tiny in-home general store, and
a fruit and vegetable truck comes weekly.

Monte Bello lies near the easternmost portion of San Luis Potosí,
in the Huasteca region, so named for a one-million-strong indigenous

civilization that was largely wiped out by the Aztecs in the fifteenth century and finished off by the Spanish in the following century. By the late nineteenth century, Monte Bello was a single hacienda, a ranch, on which Balbina's paternal great-great-grandparents worked. During the Revolution, in the second decade of the twentieth century, followers of the insurgent Zapata fled to the mountains, some taking refuge in Monte Bello. The Zapatistas' cry of *"Tierra y Libertad"* (Land and Liberty) ultimately became the law of the land, and after the Revolution the peasants of Monte Bello formed an *ejido*—a cooperative farm.

Balbina's grandmother was born on the *ejido* in 1922. She is a diminutive woman with white hair, blue eyes, a face as creased as cracked earth, and strong, tough hands with bulging knuckles that belie her tiny frame. (When a visitor made her acquaintance from the opposite side of a split-rail fence, she scampered under it for a proper handshake—a bone crusher.) People in Monte Bello have always been poor, she said. "When I was young, only the men who worked in the fields had shoes, and those were only huaraches"—sandals. Hardly anyone of her generation learned to read, she said, because there was no school in the village until 1953. At that time, she enrolled some of her twelve children, among them her five-year-old, Angelo—Balbina's father—in the new school, but after three years the lone teacher departed and the school closed, ending Angelo's formal education.

Even before he was finished with school, Angelo worked in the fields alongside his siblings and parents, picking corn and squash, alfalfa, cotton, lettuce, wherever and whenever they could find work. In 1963, when he was fifteen years old, he and some of his brothers and sisters were picking cotton northeast of their village, near Ciudad Mante. There in the field he met a girl named Juana. She, too, was fifteen, with high cheekbones and long, braided hair. She had never been to school. "My mother wouldn't let me go," she says. "She thought the girls should work at home with her." Juana's family—she was one of eighteen children—lived in Guanajuato, some three hours southwest of Monte Bello. Juana and Angelo began dating, furtively at first, and married a year later.

By the time the first of their nine children, Francisco, was born in 1967, the couple was living in Mexico City, where they both worked in a textile factory, a cut-and-sew plant that made women's underwear.

(Juana learned to write her name only after a co-worker there noticed that she used her thumbprint for her signature.) Two years later another son was born, and on March 31, 1971, Saint Balbina's Day, the first of their five daughters was born. Juana worked alongside Angelo in the plant; their workday began at five A.M. and often lasted until nine P.M. As far back as she can remember, Balbina was a "daughter-mother," responsible for her sisters and her two younger brothers.

The long hours enabled Angelo and Juana to buy a small house in Ecatepec, a sprawling working-class suburb. When Balbina turned sixteen, she went to work for the same company, but in a different plant, where she sewed raincoats. There she met a young man, a year older than she, and in time they became a couple. In October of 1989, their son, Iban, was born.

By then Angelo was thinking about moving the family back home. Their Mexico City neighborhood was overrun with drugs and gangs, and Balbina recalls that her older brothers, Francisco, then twenty-two, and Rogelio, twenty, were drawn to the *"mala vida"*—the evil life. At home in Monte Bello, meanwhile, Angelo's father was dying and his mother needed help caring for him. Toward the end of 1990, Angelo and Juana sold their house and returned to Monte Bello.

It was a difficult move for Balbina, a self-described "city girl." She had visited her grandparents at the *"rancho"* countless times, but had never contemplated actually living there. Yet she needed the help of her family with the baby—his father had vanished—and it was far less expensive to live with them in the country than alone with her new-born in the city. And while Monte Bello was unsurpassed in serenity— "Walk up in the hills," Balbina's mother says, "and you're walking in the clouds"—and safety (the only crime was the cultivation of marijuana plants), the village was wholly lacking in modern conveniences. There was neither running water nor electricity, amenities Balbina had taken for granted. Much of her day was consumed with the arduous task of filling and refilling a water bucket from a central well down a hill and carrying it on her head from the well to the kitchen or the yard, depending on the task at hand—bathing, washing dishes or clothes, boiling for food preparation or to drink. A typical day might require twenty-four trips to the well, a chore that claimed three to four hours and that would begin at first light.

While the women tended to those chores, Angelo and his sons set about building a house next door to his mother's house, where he was born. They ended up building two unattached concrete-block structures separated by the sandy yard. The smaller one was the kitchen; the other, the bedrooms. The kitchen housed two stoves. One, the wood-burning *pretil,* was built into the adobe wall and used primarily to heat the handmade tortillas and to boil beans and water; above it on a row of pegs hung pans and cooking utensils. The baking was done in a propane-heated oven, over which was a framed poster of *The Last Supper.* Without electricity there was no use or space for a refrigerator. A kitchen table tripled as dining room, counter space, and meeting place.

The other building, across the small yard and beyond the clothesline, was a work in progress. Built into a hill for insulation purposes, it housed three bedrooms, in various states of completion. Night lighting came from kerosene lamps and candles. The floors were rough cement and the walls adorned with numerous portraits of the Virgin of Guadalupe, Mexico's patron saint, and framed photographs of family— an eight-by-ten wedding-day picture of Juana and Angelo, a shot of an eight-year-old Balbina in pigtails, several collages of family members.

Job opportunities were as scarce as potable water. Work meant field work, and field work meant leaving town. "We traveled like gypsies," Juana says. At forty-eight, Balbina's mother is short, lean, and muscular, her skin baked to a deep brown, her hair in two long braids, as it was as a child. "We were always working, dawn to dark, picking chilies, onions, melons, peppers—whatever."

The interminable, grueling days of hauling water and picking fruit and vegetables, the very life her grandparents and their parents had led, was not for Balbina. Born and raised in Mexico City, to Balbina moving "home" to Monte Bello felt like a sentence from which she needed to escape. It was a place for "people too old to work or too young to work," she says. "For me there was nothing. If you do not work in the fields, there is nothing else to do."

She decided she would celebrate her twentieth birthday with her family, and then, as soon as she had saved enough for the bus fare, would take off for the border. "I'd heard there were a lot of factories and that they paid well and hired young women. But I was scared because I also heard there was a satanic cult [in Matamoros] who robbed, killed, took out hearts." Her parents told her not to believe everything she heard. Juana volunteered to care for Iban until Balbina could establish herself, and Angelo even encouraged her to cross to *"el otro lado"*—the other side, the United States—to look for work. But that idea felt even more dangerous: wading across the river, eluding the American authorities. "I was afraid of being captured by *la migra*"—the U.S. Border Patrol—"and never again seeing my baby." (Angelo himself would soon depart for the United States, where he would join the migrant farmworker stream along the eastern seaboard.)

Then a woman in the village told Angelo she knew an elderly couple in Matamoros who needed an attendant. "Would your Balbina be interested?"

"Creo que sí"—I believe so.

It was dark when she boarded the bus, and though she had spent the entire day since her early morning trip to Maíz sitting in and around the bus depot, Balbina was exhausted. She missed her baby, and as many times as she told herself it was best to leave him behind, she couldn't help her second thoughts. Sleep, she told herself, you'll feel better in the morning.

Heading north out of Maíz, through the vast valley of corn (from which, of course, the town derives its name), Highway 85 is flat as a tortilla. With two seats to herself, Balbina was able to curl into a comfortable enough position, and sleep came at once. But she awoke during the stop in Mante, only fifty miles away (and the town where her parents had met in a cotton field), and would sleep no more the entire night. From there, at least for the next hundred or so miles until Ciudad Victoria, the steep, sharply winding two-lane road climbs and descends northeast across the Sierra Madre Oriental. The region is known as Ixtlera, for the aloe plant widely cultivated there. But there are also houses dressed from head to toe in deep-purple bougainvillea; flourishing groves of oranges and mangoes (roadside stands specialize in things mango: juice, jelly, ice cream, pie); and at the higher elevations, up around seventy-five hundred feet, tall, lush canopies of pine and oak. Thirty miles south of Victoria, the bus passed the turnoff for the spectacular El Cielo Reserve, North America's northernmost cloud forest. On this night, Balbina wishes the terrain wasn't quite so dramatic. She is prone to motion sickness, and the highway's many dangerous curves (and the driver's penchant for making them seem all the more so) lend themselves more to nausea than to slumber.

Ciudad Victoria marks roughly the halfway point of the trip—

there are four and a half hours to go—and affords Balbina her first opportunity to hop off the bus for a few minutes to gather herself. Although Matamoros is three times bigger, Victoria is the capital of the state of Tamaulipas (pronounced Tom-ah-LEEP-us). (Tamaulipas is a difficult word for Anglo tongues, as illustrated by a former governor of Texas, Bill Clements, who during a radio interview in the early 1980s referred to his border-state counterpart as the governor of "Tamale-puss."*

From Victoria the road flattens, hews closer to the coast. By the time the bus pulls into Matamoros at dawn, Balbina has to rouse herself from a dream about her son. Meeting her at the central station on Canales Avenue is a distant aunt, who escorts her to the home of her new employers, an infirmed couple who live in the liltingly named *colonia* of Vista Hermosa—Beautiful View. But there is little beauty in the *colonia*; it is wedged between a pungent milky-white irrigation canal and the Finsa, the massive industrial park whose foreign-owned *maquiladoras* employ most of the working-age residents of Vista Hermosa.

Balbina worked as a live-in caretaker for seven months. In addition to providing room and board, the couple paid her 120 pesos a week—about $40. Shortly after she moved in, Balbina was invited to play in the neighborhood's informal weekly volleyball game. (She had played the sport in school in Mexico City.) There she met Guillermo DeLeon Moreno, a handsome twenty-eight-year-old and scion of one of the *colonia*'s founding families. Later that afternoon Balbina mentioned her new friend to her aunt. "Yes," she replied, "he's a good boy from a good family."

Balbina showed up at the volleyball court again the following weekend—this was late May or early June—and at the end of the game Guillermo asked her out on a date. "He was a charmer, no doubt, and I fell hard," Balbina says. "I remember telling him, maybe not on the

---

* Clements, as may be gathered, was not known during his two (nonconsecutive) terms in the Governor's Mansion in Austin for being overly sensitive to his southern neighbors or his many Mexican-American constituents. He once described Mexico's preeminent demographer, Jorge Bustamante, as "just another Mexican with an opinion"—one of many gaffes that occasioned former Texas agriculture commissioner Jim Hightower to famously label Clements "bi-ignorant."

first date, maybe the second time we went out, that I wanted to be with him always." And soon after that, sometime in late August, she took him aside during a picnic with his family to tell him something else: *"Estoy embarazada"*—I'm pregnant.

In November, Balbina quit her caretaker's job and moved in with her aunt; the new accommodations provided the young couple a shred of privacy, but no more: Guillermo lived with his mother, his sisters, and assorted nieces and nephews in a cramped house. Balbina went to work in a nearby hot-sheet motel as a desk clerk. The fifty dollars weekly enabled her to send money home to her mother, and the work involved lighter lifting than her former job. It was a rent-by-the-hour joint, that much she knew. But the place proved even seedier than she'd imagined. What she didn't know was that the owner expected her (and all his clerks) to sleep with him on demand. She quit after less than two months and found a job as a secretary in a glass shop.

In March of 1992, two months before her due date, Guillermo told Balbina he had scraped together enough money to rent a house. He was a carpenter, and he had lately found higher-paying work, he told her, on *"el otro lado,"* in Brownsville.* They found a place in another *colonia* and stayed there until their baby, Mariana, was born in May. By then Balbina had stopped working, and Guillermo said his contractor could offer no more work for the time being. Within weeks of Mariana's birth, the couple married in a civil ceremony at Matamoros City Hall and moved in with Guillermo's family.

Right from the start it seemed to Balbina that her mother-in-law resented her. Whether it was because she believed Balbina lured her son into fatherhood against his wishes, or because she was a woman of little means, or because Balbina had had a child with another man, or for some other reason she could not fathom, Balbina never understood. But Guillermo's mother made it plain that his new bride and their daughter were living there against her wishes.

The arrangement did not last long. Guillermo said he had been

---

*It was not uncommon for Texas contractors to hire Mexican day laborers and pay them subminimum wages, which were a vast improvement over the prevailing carpenter wage in Mexico, but which also served to drive down the cost of American labor.

called back to work on the other side and that it would be easier if he stayed over in Brownsville most nights. He came home on the weekends and sometimes stopped in for a while during the week as well. But by early October, Balbina was seeing less and less of him. Then one day Guillermo's mother told Balbina she was at the grocery store and had overheard a conversation about Guillermo to the effect that a television news program had reported that he had been arrested on the other side. Then someone else heard that he had been arrested for possession of drugs in Harlingen, Texas, a town twenty-five miles northwest of Brownsville, and that he was being held in the Brownsville jail.

The reports were accurate, if incomplete. It turned out the U.S. Border Patrol in Harlingen had arrested Guillermo on two felony charges: possession of and intent to distribute 318 pounds of marijuana; and carrying a .22-caliber semiautomatic pistol during the course of the crime. In late October, a federal grand jury in Brownsville returned a five-count indictment against Guillermo. In addition to the charges made at the scene, prosecutors alleged that Guillermo was part of a conspiracy "to import into the United States from the country of Mexico a quantity exceeding 100 kilograms" of marijuana.

The news astounded Balbina and her mother-in-law, neither of whom apparently had "a single clue," in Balbina's words, of what Guillermo was up to. "If he *was* making any money on the other side, he sure wasn't sharing it with the family."

In early December, Guillermo's court-appointed attorney arranged for him to plead guilty to two of the counts: possession with intent to sell, and carrying the firearm. In return for the guilty plea, the government agreed to dismiss the conspiracy charges, each of which carried a mandatory sentence of up to forty years in federal prison and/or a two-million-dollar fine. The plea bargain resulted in two five-year sentences, to run consecutively, and to be served in the custody of the U.S. Bureau of Prisons. (In 1994, however, the overburdened Bureau of Prisons released him to serve out his sentence in the custody of Mexican authorities.)

Guillermo's incarceration broke the fragile peace between Balbina and her mother-in-law, and in November Balbina moved out. She went home to Monte Bello and stayed through Christmas. When she returned to Matamoros at the turn of the year, she had her hands full.

In addition to her two children—Mariana was eight months and Iban, whom she had to "kidnap" from her mother, was three—accompanying Balbina were two of her sisters, the seventeen-year-old Elsa, and Faviola, who had just turned fifteen. They all piled into a two-room flat in Vista Hermosa, a short block away from Guillermo's family. The flat was on the southern edge of the *colonia,* in a section known as the *Ampliación*—the Extension. It was no more than seventy-five yards from the chain-link fence demarcating the northern property line of the Finsa park. Indeed, the flat was so close to the nearest plant that if the wind was blowing north she could hear the loud hum of the massive twin air conditioners mounted on its rooftop and she could smell the foul air emitted by its extractors.

The name of the plant was MagneTek, and she had heard much about it from one of her sisters-in-law, Teresa, who started there a few months after the plant opened in 1988 and left the following year. "Back then," she told Balbina, "the conditions were horrible. Bathrooms were in bad shape, and even though there was air-conditioning, it was so hot, it did us no good. And the air was so filthy they gave us masks. But because they were so uncomfortable and made us even hotter, nobody wore them."

Nevertheless, Teresa counseled Balbina, "the money was good, and you would be lucky to get a job there." At the time she quit, Teresa was earning thirty-nine dollars a week.

On the first Friday of 1993, Balbina and Elsa caught a ride downtown to the headquarters of the big *maquila* workers' union, the SJOI, the Spanish acronym for the Union of Industrial Workers and Day Laborers. The SJOI claimed forty thousand members, virtually the entire nonsupervisory *maquila* workforce in Matamoros. With such leverage it might seem that the union could impose its will on the industry, could fairly dictate wages and working conditions. But the union's power came not from its rank-and-file, those most concerned with wages and working conditions, but from on high: from the nationwide Confederation of Mexican Workers—an arm of the government's long-ruling party. The Confederation, or CTM, was the most efficient cog in the party machine. Under CTM bylaws, all union members—and there were some five million in 1993—were also automatically registered members of the PRI, the Institutional Revolutionary Party;

a portion of their monthly dues, paid by payroll deduction, went directly to PRI coffers. And during political campaigns, CTM members were required to participate in party rallies or face fines or suspensions from their jobs. In exchange for the labor federation's collaboration with the government, its lockstep support of the PRI's economic and political goals, the CTM's leaders were rewarded with lifetime jobs, lavish perquisites, and boundless power.

The labor federation's patriarch was ninety-three-year-old Fidel Velázquez Sánchez, whose sovereignty over the CTM and its fourteen thousand affiliated unions stretched back to his first election in 1941. Velázquez during his first few decades in office was known as a fighter for his people. He won substantial raises for workers during the 1950s and early 1960s and pressed for and obtained legal recognition of the right to strike. In the mid-sixties, however, when the government announced its Border Industry Program, Velázquez fell in line, vowing that the CTM "would not pressure without cause the industrialists who come to [the border]. . . . On the contrary, in every occasion, it would support those investments, avoiding unjustified labor-management conflicts."

Velázquez and most of the CTM's regional leaders never budged from their accommodationist stance. From time to time in the *maquilas* an unofficial union or ad hoc employee group would call a strike, only to be routed by the allied effort of the CTM affiliate, the government, and the local *maquila* association. In a notorious instance at the gargantuan seven-thousand-employee Zenith plant in Reynosa—another Tamaulipas boomtown, sixty miles west of Matamoros and south of McAllen, Texas, along the Rio Grande—Velázquez himself intervened. It was the fall of 1983, and the government's devaluation of the peso, begun the previous year, was having a calamitous effect. "The workers, battered between the hammer of Mexican inflation and the anvil of their reduced purchasing power in the U.S., put pressure on the union to ask for an emergency wage increase," writes Leslie Sklair in *Assembling for Development,* his landmark history of the *maquila* industry. When the union offered no support, a group of employees blockaded the plant and detained the personnel manager, a U.S. citizen, for a full day. The standoff ended only when diplomats from both nations' capitals interceded to negotiate the manager's release.

As for the striking workers, their leader, predictably, was jailed, and the others began laying plans to withdraw from the CTM and form their own independent union. At that point Velázquez arrived in Reynosa on a damage-control mission. He promised to hold new elections for local CTM officers and to spring the dissident leader from jail. The leader subsequently led a reform slate (including, for the first time, four women) to an "overwhelming" victory over the Velázquez loyalists—a result that so disappointed Velázquez he nullified the elections and ordered a new round. When again the reformists prevailed, it was determined that democracy in Reynosa would rear its ugly head no longer. This time Velázquez and Zenith forced the "resignation" of ten members of the winning slate, sparking a hunger strike in the town's central plaza—a protest the police viciously doused.

Six years later, in 1989, the ashes of discontent with the official union in Reynosa were rekindled, and again the CTM prevailed, defeating a decertification campaign. Afterward, Velázquez assured a visiting U.S. congressional delegation that "there would be no further labor problems."

But Velázquez had not reckoned with his chief deputy in Matamoros. Agapito Gonzalez Cavazos was the top-ranking officer of both the regional CTM and the SJOI, the *maquila* workers' union, but his title, secretary general, barely hinted at Gonzalez's power. Gonzalez, or Don Agapito, as he was universally called, was every bit as irascible and wily as Velázquez, and his grip on the reins of labor locally was as firm as was Velázquez's nationally. He was the strongman of Matamoros, feared and respected by workers and *maquila* owners alike.

Gonzalez, too, was a member of the Mexican labor gerontocracy. Born in 1916, he joined the local, then a union of agricultural workers, mainly cotton pickers, in the middle 1930s, and was first elected to the executive committee in 1941 and as secretary-general in 1948. When the *maquilas* came knocking in the late sixties, Don Agapito's union welcomed them—and immediately organized the plants. Over the ensuing years until the peso devaluations of 1982, there was the occasional skirmish with the few recalcitrant U.S. companies that failed to accept Gonzalez's authority. But most recognized his power, and in 1983 they formalized it with a negotiated agreement: a guarantee of labor peace in return for a shorter work week. For the *maquilas,* the agreement promised less endemic turnover, their major headache; for the workers of Matamoros it meant a forty-hour week for no less pay than workers in other border cities earned for a forty-eight-hour week;* and for Don Agapito, the pact bolstered his unchallenged reign.

For the most part, although Gonzalez's local was reputedly the most militant in all the border cities, the SJOI and the *maquilas* in Matamoros peacefully coexisted through the remainder of the eighties. By the turn of the decade, however, Gonzalez had grown disenchanted enough to declare war. The *maquilas* were thriving, he argued, yet his members were earning only forty dollars a week. In early January of 1990, with contract talks stalled between the union and the Matamoros Maquiladora Association (which negotiated a broad master contract supplemented by individual company side agreements), Gonzalez threatened to empty the city's plants if the Association did not accede to a 25 percent pay raise. The Association delayed the proceedings long enough to appeal to a higher power, and ultimately the walkout was averted, most likely, says a close observer of the internecine politics of Mexican labor, because Fidel Velázquez threatened Agapito with removal from office if he carried out the strike plan.

By September, with another round of contract negotiations under way, Don Agapito again was tormenting the *maquila* operators with the specter of a work stoppage. This was one too many times for Velázquez, who swiftly ousted Gonzalez from his position as secretary-general of the regional CTM. "Agapito was making things real bad for the old man"—Velázquez—"and the old man didn't have any choice but to get rid of him," says Fred J. Quintana, who at the time served as executive director of the Maquiladora Association.

His replacement promised a more conciliatory approach to negotiations, but Don Agapito remained as secretary-general of the local union, an elected position, and he would soon prove to any doubters that it was with him the power in Matamoros still resided. On Wednesday, November 7, he pulled four hundred workers at four *maquilas* off the job. "We can't afford to send our children to school," a worker at a struck floral-supply manufacturer told a local reporter. "We agree that American companies should grow here, but they must pay us accord-

*New *maquilas* were granted "honeymoon contracts" permitting them to operate on a forty-eight-hour week during their first five years.

ingly. We make in a week what [an American worker] makes in a day."
Gonzalez announced that if the Maquiladora Association did not
agree to his renewed call for a 25 percent raise, the remainder of the
union's forty thousand members would join the strike.

Maquila operators were panicked. Gonzalez, said one industrialist,
"is not practical, not legal, not reasonable." Fred Quintana declared
"the wage rates and fringe benefits [to be] totally out of control,
mainly due to Agapito." And the Association's president rang the
death knell. "It will cause an inflationary situation where the plants
would not be able to compete with the plants at our other border
towns," he said.

Indeed, the competition seemed almost to gloat in the face of Matamoros's trials. Said an economic developer from McAllen, sister city to
Reynosa: "The last round of contract negotiations with Agapito has
taken Matamoros out of competition for new *maquila* construction."

But even as the *maquila* operators publicly lamented Gonzalez's
intransigence, moaned that he was stunting growth, the Association
provided no evidence that a single business picked up and left town, or
that potential recruits selected other border sites for fear of Gonzalez.
(Close to a decade later, Fred Quintana continued to maintain that
Gonzalez "forced a lot of companies out of Matamoros." Asked to cite
a few examples, he could provide none "off the top of my head.") Don
Agapito may have made for a convenient bête noire, but as even Quintana acknowledges, the higher wages and shorter work week Gonzalez
won for his members also ensured a more stable workforce. And one
other central truth was that overall labor costs in Matamoros were no
higher than elsewhere along the border. Due to lower unemployment
rates in other cities, operators there were forced to offer fringe benefits—day care, transportation to and from work, subsidized cafeteria
meals—to attract workers in those competitive markets.

But the tight labor market in those cities did not stop local *maquila*
associations from lobbying the federal government to reduce annual
cost-of-living increases, a request the administration of President Carlos Salinas de Gortari was pleased to consider. Salinas, a business-
friendly technocrat, won office in 1988 in what many believe was a
rigged election. (Salinas was declared the winner over the center-left
candidate—a PRI defector—after a mysterious three-day breakdown
of the PRI-controlled vote-counting computers.) Salinas was deter-

mined, at any cost to his people, to sell off state-owned industry, to open Mexico's protectionist economy to all comers, and to crush any institutions, organized labor included, in his way. Although some dissident border-town unionists recognized that the worker shortage in many of those towns should have given the upper hand to the unions, they were routed by CTM officials who made sure their affiliates from Reynosa westward to Tijuana fell into lockstep obedience. They were, after all, laboring under "protection contracts"—the notorious sweetheart deals that Fidel Velázquez (who in 1990 celebrated his ninetieth birthday and fiftieth year as chief of the confederation) had pioneered and that allowed the *maquila* associations to dictate the terms of the contracts without the muss and fuss of rank-and-file consent.

Only in Matamoros were circumstances different. In December of 1991, Don Agapito had turned seventy-five, and while some thought his health problems—cataracts on both eyes, a persistent cough, high blood pressure—would conspire to silence him, none doubted his heart, particularly come contract time. (And in truth, Gonzalez did look frail. His eyes were puffy and half shut, the corners of his mouth moist with saliva, his chin a field of stubble.) In late January of 1992, Gonzalez once again was grumbling that the latest proposal by the employers—he had taken to calling them "the foreign exploiters"—would mean further suffering for the workers.

The Maquiladora Association had offered wage increases ranging from 10 to 15 percent; Gonzalez demanded 30 percent. But this year the employers were steadfast. "Our offer was deliberately low," recalls Chuck Peeples of MagneTek. "We wanted to send a message to Agapito, and to Salinas, too."

After talks broke down on the last Monday of the month, some seven thousand workers struck MagneTek and two of the three GM plants in the Finsa park. Those plants settled quickly, for a wage increase of 25 percent, but officials of a fourth plant whose workers had also walked out had refused to settle with the union, and twenty more plants, with a total of fifteen thousand workers, were facing a strike deadline of midnight Tuesday, the following day.

Negotiations continued throughout Tuesday. In addition to the proposed trifling pay increase, the companies were asking for a seven-day workweek. Employees would continue to work forty hours, but some would be required to work Saturdays or Sundays. *"Imposible,"* Gonzalez replied. The lieutenant governor of Tamaulipas stepped in, as did Fidel Velázquez, but Gonzalez was resolute. With no settlement in sight and the sun setting on the deadline, President Salinas apparently heard the message: The long arm of the Mexican government reached out and snatched Agapito Gonzalez—literally. In a surprise onslaught, coordinated, in all probability, among the employers, President Salinas's office, and Fidel Velázquez, federal police stormed the bargaining session to pick up Don Agapito on a charge of . . . *income tax evasion.* The feeble labor leader was whisked away to Mexico City by plane and placed under house arrest in the Hospital Los Angeles.

The blatant pretense drew wails of protest from American labor leaders. "The real crime of Gonzalez and his members was to win improved wages and working conditions," said Thomas R. Donahue, secretary-treasurer of the AFL-CIO. And in a letter to the Mexican ambassador in Washington, United Auto Workers president Owen Bieber said the arrest smacked of "South Africa, or Korea—countries known for their repression of workers and unions."

Fred Quintana, of the Maquiladora Association, expressed no qualms about the detention of his foe. "They nabbed his butt because the *maquila* companies were just raising merry hell about him." Did Quintana consider the timing of the arrest motivated by anything beyond the government's zealous pursuit of an alleged tax cheat? "Look, he [Gonzalez] went too far. He felt like he was totally independent, that he could do anything he wanted—to hell with the government, to hell with the CTM, to hell with the old man [Fidel Velázquez]. But he had done a lot over the years for the PRI and the CTM. He had delivered a lot of votes, so for the longest time they put up with his shit. If he had been a younger man, they would have gotten rid of him in a New York minute. Finally they just put their foot down and said that's enough of this crap. And they went after him. Sure, it was a wild situation, but we [the Maquiladora Association] had nothing to do with it. It was strictly a Mexican thing."

With Gonzalez silenced, the Association set about getting "something better for our companies," as Quintana said at the time. The Association began by dropping its wage offer below the 20 percent increase to

which some companies had already agreed, and demanded negotiations be reopened on a host of other issues. "[We're] trying to help the
companies that signed under duress," Quintana explained. "It's unfair
that they signed under strike pressure." (The new contract, which
would be signed in mid-February, called for increases ranging between
18¾ percent and 20 percent, and required, for the first time, that
workers would have to make their own federal income tax and Social
Security payments.)

As for the union, its dumbfounded new chief negotiator said that
company representatives were "not acting like gentlemen." He dis-
puted their claim that workers in Matamoros were overpaid, adding
that the union would carry on in Don Agapito's name. "This is still the
struggle of the labor movement," he said. "The need is still there to
improve. You can't support a family on a worker's salary."*

That self-evident truth failed to quell the rising tide of job seekers.
Four times weekly, waves of several thousand applicants washed up at
dawn at the offices of the Union of Industrial Workers and Day Laborers. The SJOI was the de facto employment agency for the *maquilas,*
and all nonsalaried workers applied through its central hiring hall. On
Mondays and Fridays the women poured in; on Tuesdays and Thursdays, the men. (Wednesday was sign-up day—all were free to drop in
and fill out an application form noting one's age, sex, work experience, years of schooling, marital and parental status, hometown.)

On this morning, the first Friday of 1993, it is not yet seven o'clock
and Balbina and Elsa Duque have been in line for an hour, a line that
snakes through the three-story building, past the armed guard at the
door, and stretches outside for more than a block. By eight, they will
have squeezed and elbowed and prodded their way inside the assembly
hall, a room of roughly the size and ambience of a drafty, old high
school gymnasium. Mounted fans whir overhead, efficiently distribut-
ing the rank air and grime into all corners. In the rear of the hall, near

---

* Gonzalez was held in Mexico City for nearly nine months. He was released in
October, weeks before the November 1992 municipal elections. "The PRI
needed our votes and this was their way of pacifying us," recalls a union delegate
in Matamoros. The PRI won, in the usual manner. "With the exception of a ballot box stolen from voting precinct 50B and a few fist fights here and there,
today's elections were held in relative tranquility," the city's chief elections officer
reported.

the entrance, is a snack bar from which union employees dispense soft drinks— *"Siempre Coca-Cola"*—to be sipped through straws in small plastic Baggies. (The returnable bottles are dear.) There are two permanent murals. On the wall above the stage is a colorful work depicting the first hundred years of the CTM. Scenes range from the bullwhipping of a cotton-field worker in the 1880s to a triumphant Fidel Velázquez in the 1980s wrapped in the Mexican flag with the CTM logo hovering overhead like a halo. At the far side of the room, suspended between the tall ceiling and a low anteroom, towers a huge, three-panel mural: a head shot of a jowly and white-mustached Agapito Gonzalez flanked by the logos of the CTM and SJOI. Under the beatific portrait is inscribed: *"Todo Una Vida Dedicada al Progreso y Bienestar del Trabajador Matamorense"*—A Whole Life Dedicated to the Progress and Well-Being of the Matamoren Worker.

By eight-thirty, with no conspicuous signal that the cattle call is on the verge of starting, there is a near stampede toward the makeshift elevated stage at the front quadrant of the room. For the uninitiated, it seems as if the room has somehow morphed into an aquarium, one rear corner of which has suddenly been tipped, causing its entire contents to flow into its diagonal. For the next few hours, Balbina, Elsa, and sixteen hundred other hopefuls will be crammed, nose to shoulder, as close to the stage as possible, like groupies at a rock concert.

At eight-forty, three union officials emerge from the anteroom beside the stage. Through a two-way mirror, they have been keeping an eye on the surging crowd while their clerks match the day's *maquila* employment needs with the application forms on file. All morning long, the fax machines and phones in the union headquarters have been ringing with the day's specifications from the companies. One *maquila,* for instance, asks for ninety-one applicants, all of whom should be seventeen (the legal minimum age) or older, with a secondary school education and without "scheduling problems"—code for childless. All the *maquilas* favor youth, and some, MagneTek for one, insist on it. *"No mayores de 27 años"*—None older than 27—the company's director of industrial relations instructed in a faxed letter to the union. Women in their late teens and early twenties are considered in the prime of their working lives, a thirty-year-old is unlikely to be hired, and a thirty-five-year-old is considered a relic.

•   •   •

When the tally of the day's employment needs is deemed complete, the officials step onto the stage, and into the bedlam. Between them and the spirited throng are three steps cordoned by a thin chain, a flimsy plywood railing, and an offensive-lineman-sized bouncer whose sartorial taste runs to late Elvis: a white shirt unbuttoned nearly the length of his heroic torso, a gold medallion dangling to mid-midsection, and a formidable, gleaming pompadour crowning a Frigidaire face and muttonchop sideburns.

Following a call to order on a tinny public-address system, a woman unceremoniously announces the day's hiring needs: "We're calling workers for Deltronicos"—the GM car-radio subsidiary—and then reads a list of maybe fifty names. Afterward, in the hope there are unfilled spots, there is a renewed surge toward the stage, and an accompanying cacophony of shrieking, laughing, pointing, waving, winking, smiling, nodding—anything to win the attention of the bouncer or one of the male functionaries onstage in the hope they might claim one of the few vacancies. Once the Deltronicos roster is filled, those whose names are called make their way to the exit on the far side of the room. Outside a pair of swinging doors, a fleet of old Loadstar school buses await their cargo—the "lucky ones," as one disappointed applicant put it—who will be transported to the Finsa park for a job interview and medical screening with their prospective employer. If their luck holds, they are then hired for a thirty-day probationary period (for lower, "training" wages) before attaining full-employee status.

The drill is repeated for each *maquila* until the day's hiring needs are met. Neither Balbina nor Elsa is among the lucky ones today, but they are aware that few are chosen on the first go-round; some they meet have endured several months of twice-weekly trips to the hall. Each Monday and Friday over the next few weeks, the Duques return faithfully. In February, finally, Elsa is called to Componentes Mecánicos, another GM subsidiary, and in early March Balbina's prayers are answered. She is assigned to a third-shift coil-winding job at Magne-Tek. All she knows about the job is that it is in the same plant where her sister-in-law, Teresa, used to work, inside the low-slung white building practically in her backyard. What she does not know is that both Mollie James and Dorothy Carter once held that very job.

FIFTEEN

Sleeping with the Elephant

THE PRESIDENT OF MEXICO, Carlos Salinas de Gortari, is basking in the warmth and admiration of his people. It is New Year's Eve 1993, and the forty-three-year-old Salinas is standing on the balcony of the National Palace, surrounded by functionaries, family, and military police. He is resplendent in his crisply tailored black business suit; white shirt, extravagantly cuffed; and presidential sash of red, white, and green, the colors of the Mexican flag. He overlooks the crowded *Zócalo*, the central plaza, waving the wave, flashing the broad smile of the self-satisfied autocrat. And why not? Salinas is capping a remarkable year of progress and hope. He has transformed the moribund state-run economy into a sleek, globally integrated dynamo—at least it appears he has. If Mexico is not yet roaring like an Asian tiger, it is poised tonight to leap the precipice between First and Third Worlds, from developing country to twenty-first-century juggernaut.

In the spring of the year, it looked as if his grandiose plan—indeed, the issue on which he had staked both his presidency and his country's economic future—was dead in the Rio Grande. The U.S. Congress was considering passage of the North American Free Trade

Agreement (NAFTA), which would bring the continent—"from the Yukon to the Yucatán"—into a single market free of trade barriers. The Salinas administration had negotiated the pact in 1992 with the Bush administration, but by the spring of 1993, it seemed to lack the political muscle to push it through the U.S. House. George Bush no longer resided in the White House, and it was thought that Bill Clinton, for whom organized labor had campaigned vigorously, and who at the very least appeared to be receptive to labor's concerns—a marked change after twelve years of knee-jerk Reagan-Bush hostilities—might be disinclined to support the Republican initiative.

The U.S. labor movement, naturally, despised the prospect of NAFTA, which union economists predicted would hasten the already steady flow of manufacturing jobs to Mexico, while depressing domestic wages and failing to lift living standards in Mexico. Other critics argued that even if NAFTA proponents *were* correct about the economic windfall portended for both countries, the core question came down to whether the modestly democratic United States ought to enter into economic matrimony with the repressive ruling party of Mexico—a government intolerant of civil rights, civil liberties, and free speech, and a government indifferent to its own environmental, labor, and workplace health and safety laws.

But if the U.S. labor movement thought it had a friend in Bill Clinton, at least in the realm of trade policy, it was mistaken. In a speech delivered in February 1993, one month after his inaugural address, Clinton telegraphed his intent to jump aboard the Republicans' NAFTA bandwagon. America is still "the engine of global growth," he told students at American University in Washington. "The truth of our age is this and must be this: Open and competitive commerce will enrich us as a nation. It spurs us to innovate. It forces us to compete, it connects us with new customers. It promotes global growth without which no rich country can hope to grow wealthy. It enables our producers, who are themselves consumers of services and raw materials, to prosper. And so I say to you in the face of all the pressures to do the reverse, we must compete, not retreat."

In Mexico City, meanwhile, Carlos Salinas, a Harvard-trained economist, was following the footsteps of his PRI predecessors, who had begun dismantling the country's nationalistic economy in favor of free markets and a cozier economic relationship with the United

States. "They say that living next to the United States is like being in bed with an elephant," a Salinas aide said. "Well, we have decided to sleep with the elephant."

In 1991, Salinas had lifted the restrictions that had blocked U.S. companies from opening franchises in Mexico. Practically before one could utter "Two all-beef patties special sauce lettuce cheese . . . ," McDonald's and its deep-fry brethren, Taco Bell included, were sprouting like, well, fast-food outlets at an interstate highway off-ramp. Soon the "big box" retailers from the United States invaded, all of which helped Salinas forge closer ties to American financiers, but which also imported the "Wal-Mart effect"—driven out were hundreds of small businesses in the orbit of the new superstores.

Salinas also embraced the previous administration's privatization program, selling off or closing more than nine hundred of the eleven hundred businesses the government once operated. The deals generated more than twenty-one billion dollars for the government, but at a steep price to the Mexican people: Four hundred thousand jobs were lost. Critics charged that the program amounted to little more than handouts for Salinas's wealthy patrons. "The booty of privatization has made multimillionaires of thirteen families, while the rest of the population—some eighty million Mexicans—has been subjected to the same gradual impoverishment as though they had suffered through a war," a columnist wrote in *La Jornada,* an opposition paper in Mexico City.

Sleep with an elephant and inevitably something will be squashed. In Mexico, where the PRI continued to hold captive the union movement, there would be no real debate as to who would bear the disproportionate weight of the mammoth burden. President Salinas enjoyed the unconditional support of the Confederation of Mexican Workers, the CTM, and its fossilized leader, Fidel Velázquez. He used the party-controlled mass media to sell his own people on the benefits of free trade, and he used the CTM to squelch dissenting voices. It would be as always: The workers would pay a lopsided share for the costs of economic revolution—through lower real wages and steep cuts in social services, education, health care.

In Washington, Salinas hired a flotilla of lobbyists and flacks, spending at least ten million dollars on his pro-NAFTA campaign in the United States. Mexico's chief hired gun was the public-relations colossus Burson-Marsteller, to which the Mexican Ministry of Commerce and Industrial Development paid more than $7.5 million to "basically help get their [the Mexican government's] message out," as the firm's senior vice president told the Washington-based magazine *Multinational Monitor.* To pass the word, Burson-Marsteller issued reams of press releases and video "news" clips, created and funded a fifty-state campaign of supposed "grassroots" support for NAFTA, and worked closely with a network of regional PR firms and former elected officials the Mexican government hired in key border states. One California firm earned at least $600,000 to "contact business re: voicing NAFTA support to Congressional representatives," "position NAFTA with media," "coordinate speaking opportunities for supporters of NAFTA," etc.

This sort of corporate grassroots politics—or AstroTurf politics, as it has been dubbed—is perfectly legal and perfectly perverse. It is democracy for hire, and it has come to dominate political discourse. "Democracy is held captive," William Greider has written, "not just by money, but by ideas—the ideas that money buys." During the NAFTA debate, for example, authentic citizens' groups raised concerns about ways in which the trade agreement might further environmental degradation in Mexico. The Mexican government responded by staging a conference on NAFTA at prestigious Brown University and commissioning two prominent scholars to refute the environmentalists' concerns. Mexico gave the academics stipends and covered their travel expenses. The two economists concluded that NAFTA "would heighten [Mexico's] sensitivity to the environment and give it the resources to manage critical pollution problems." The study was included in an offensively fanciful Burson-Marsteller press kit—"A Better Mexico; a Better Environment"—and cited in major American newspapers, none of which mentioned the conditions under which the study was funded and presented.

Even with the hardest of sales tactics, by early October of 1993, with six weeks to go before the scheduled vote in the House, polls showed NAFTA was headed for the political graveyard. President Clinton was distracted with the details of his ill-fated health-care reform plan, and most members of his own party were on record against NAFTA since the Bush administration had completed negotiations in August 1992. For Clinton to win would mean taking on his natural allies, the House Democratic leadership.

On the verge of losing another major legislative battle, Clinton shifted into high gear. He recruited three former presidents to speak out in favor of NAFTA. He attended one pro-NAFTA public event after another, eighteen in all. He and Al Gore made the rounds of the Sunday morning chat shows. In October alone, Clinton met personally with 150 "undecideds"—wavering House members—dishing out presidential pork: a public works project for this district, a farm subsidy for that one.

On November 17, 1993, NAFTA passed by a thirty-four-vote margin. U.S. HOUSE SAYS SÍ TO NAFTA, the *Brownsville Herald* rejoiced. (The *Herald* and its journalistic siblings throughout the border states spoke as one in support of the agreement.) The White House, too, exulted, but at the expense of alienating organized labor, whose leader, Lane Kirkland, said Clinton had "stiffed" working people, and accused the president of outright bribery. "Amid all the planes, trains and bridges and all the protections for citrus, peanuts, sugar and wheat," Kirkland, the president of the AFL-CIO, said, "there was not one word about the rights of workers on both sides of the border to obtain decent wages and safe working conditions or to defend themselves from gross exploitation."

If President Clinton emerged from the ring with a political shiner, President Salinas walked away the unscathed winner. Within a news cycle or two, Salinas was anointed one of the world's visionary leaders. "Salinas has really clinched his whole economic revolution," the Mexican novelist Carlos Fuentes said on the front page of the *New York Times*. "Mexico's economic position in the world is assured." In saluting him as a runner-up for its Man of the Year, *Time* magazine wrote that Salinas "almost single-handedly energized a nation that used to be jealous and resentful of the dynamism exhibited north of the border." *The Economist* went a step further, all but carving his likeness into the Mount Rushmore of contemporary statesmen, alongside Mandela, Havel, Rabin. "Mr. Salinas," the London-based magazine gushed, "has a claim to be hailed as one of the great men of the twentieth century."

• • •

As the clock nears twelve on New Year's Eve 1993, President Salinas has a champagne bottle and the world in his hands. From his perch atop the ornate colonial-era palace, he offers a toast to his political legacy and his country's good fortune. *"¡Viva Mexico!"* he shouts to the party faithful in the *Zócalo*. *"¡Viva Mexico! ¡Viva Mexico! ¡Viva Mexico!"* All eyes in the main plaza of the world's second-most-populous city are on Salinas. As he pops the cork, fireworks explode in the midnight sky.

The real fireworks, an explosion that would shake the very foundations of the country, would come hours later. Even before the sun rose on the new year, squadrons of ragtag guerrilla soldiers were marching out of the highland jungles and into the streets of San Cristóbal de las Casas, a tourist city of nearly a hundred thousand persons eight hundred miles south of Mexico City. In Canada and the United States, the citizenry had debated the North American Free Trade Agreement; in the state of Chiapas, the indigenous, quixotic Zapatista Army of National Liberation, on behalf of the "miserable and dispossessed," declared war over it. "The well-being of a few cannot be based on the suffering of the masses," their leader wrote, by way of explanation, to two leading Mexico City newspapers. He termed NAFTA "a death sentence" for Mexico's Indians.

The rebellion in Chiapas was timed to coincide with NAFTA, but the movement had been gaining force for at least a dozen years, since the 1982 peso devaluation. Prices had been rising and wages stagnating; working Mexicans since then had lost 60 percent of their purchasing power. And though Salinas's Mexico presented to the outside world a pretty face of economic modernization, beneath the heavy makeup was a peasantry seething with anger over the lack of real democracy. Says one longtime opponent of the PRI: "Those who applauded our growing economy, what they ignored, what they olympically ignored, is that while the rich got richer, the nation got even poorer."

In the cold light of New Year's Day, Carlos Salinas could no longer ignore the class war in Mexico. The first political casualty would be Salinas himself, whose "Mexican Miracle" would be exposed by year's end as a sham—a house of cards built on borrowed money and a currency grossly inflated to attract foreign investment. On December 20, three weeks after Salinas's term of office expired (he was ineligible for reelection), the peso collapsed, unable to withstand any longer the inconvenient fact that the country was insolvent. Wall Street investors, who had giddily been pouring money into the overvalued Mexican stock market, fled the country, dumping assets and withdrawing some twenty-five billion dollars. During the next few days—dubbed "The Nightmare before Christmas"—the peso lost 30 percent of its purchasing power. By the end of the first week of January, the value of the national currency had tumbled 40 percent.

The consequent recession—some economists termed it a full-blown depression—would be the country's worst in fifty years. Salinas, however, was not around to accept responsibility. He had slipped out of the country, whereabouts unknown. Later it was revealed he was living in Ireland, in self-imposed exile. The president was charged with no crimes (though his brother, Raul, was jailed for ordering the murder of a PRI official—and former brother-in-law—and was under investigation by Swiss authorities for money laundering).* But neither did Carlos Salinas escape scot-free; he was swiftly convicted in the court of popular opinion. Street vendors did a brisk business in Salinas piñatas, and the cover of the Christmas Day edition of *Proceso,* the country's leading news magazine, depicted a Salinas doll clad in jail-house stripes and clutching a big bag of cash. The cover line: "Popular Vengeance."

Carlos Salinas would forever be the disgraced ex-president, but neither he nor his fellow members of the ruling elite would suffer unduly. "I'm quite calm," the director-general of Banco Mexicano said three days before Christmas, the day the peso fell 30 percent. "I plan to have a great game of golf on Saturday and then a magnificent Christmas dinner with my family on Sunday."

In the aftermath of the crash, the Clinton administration arranged fifty billion dollars in loan guarantees (a bailout figure without precedent) to break the free fall of the peso, to stabilize the Mexican stock market—and to cushion the blow to U.S. financial institutions: prominent banks, mutual funds, and pension funds suckered into the Mexican bubble. So much for free markets.

The country would need to swallow some harsh medicine, the new president, Ernesto Zedillo Ponce de León, announced in his televised

---

*The Salinas family allegedly raked in $100 million during the six years Carlos held office, at least some of which was reportedly payoffs from a drug kingpin who rose to prominence during the Salinas presidency.

"Economic Emergency Plan." "Mexico's development demands that we recognize realistically that we are not a rich country, but a nation with serious needs and shortages," Zedillo told his countrymen. He called for "sacrifice," for "austerity," and pledged to slice government spending by \$1.7 billion, a cut that would radically curtail antipoverty public works programs. Two days later, thirty thousand workers, enraged over the plunging value of their money and the paralysis of their labor confederation, took to the streets of Mexico City to protest the drop in the real minimum wage from \$4.00 a day to \$2.82 a day. *"¡Basta Ya!"* they chanted—Enough!

Within days the American press trotted out a stable of economists to reassure investors that the bitter bailout pill would produce the desired effect. "This crisis is just a pothole along the road," professed a Morgan Stanley analyst in New York. "Most people still think Mexico's future looks pretty good," seconded an international economist for a Boston-based forecasting firm.

MEXICO'S FUTURE may have looked bright enough from a skyscraper in New York or Boston, but the horizon darkened considerably the closer one was to the ground, and to the border. For Balbina Duque, Salinas's plundering, the crash of the peso, and the ensuing bailout had truly grave consequences. Balbina had neither speculated in the Mexican stock market nor borrowed any money from foreign banks or the U.S. Treasury or the International Monetary Fund, and yet it was she to whom President Zedillo turned to bail out the binational cigar-and-suspenders class. It was Balbina and her campesino family in Monte Bello and her neighbors in *Colonia Vista Hermosa* and her co-workers at MagneTek and her 800,000 fellow *maquila* employees up and down the border on whose backs the government intended to repay the \$50 billion in loan guarantees.

By early 1997, when an inquisitive visitor insinuated himself into her life, Balbina was earning 391 pesos a week—about \$49.36 at the current exchange rate. She brought home twice as many pesos as she did when she started in March of 1993, but they were worth 40 percent less. And with inflation having soared above 100 percent in that period, her real wages in 1997 were less than she had earned in her first days as a full-fledged employee four years earlier—before NAFTA. Here is a weekly budget for her and her three children, ages seven, four, and two. (Her youngest, Guillermo, was conceived during a conjugal prison visit with her husband.)

Income: **391 pesos**

Expenses: rent: 50 pesos
                                 groceries: 350 pesos
                                 day care: 60 pesos
                                 electricity: 12 pesos
                                 propane gas: 9 pesos
                                 total expenses: 481 pesos

Even when she worked an eight-hour overtime shift, as she did at least once weekly, and usually two or three times, Balbina found it impossible to make ends meet on a MagneTek salary. *"No alcance,"* she would say. It doesn't reach. The 90-peso ($11.39) shortfall fails to take into account other necessities, including clothes, shoes, school uniforms and books, bus fare to the grocery store. Then there are the less predictable but inescapable expenses, such as doctor visits and medicine.

She surmounts her weekly shortfall by pooling her income and expenses with her sister Elsa, the GM employee. They live, like nearly all of their co-workers, *"en montón"*—in a heap: two adults and five children in two small rooms. Their shared three-family flat in *Colonia Vista Hermosa* is a one-story cement structure that measures roughly forty-five feet long by fifteen feet wide by ten feet high. It is topped by a corrugated metal roof that doubles as the ceiling. There are cement-block walls between the three units, but they stop about a foot short of the ceiling/roof, which makes for a pungent stew of sound and aroma when all three families are home.

A cement wall with an open doorway divides the flat in two: kitchen in front, bedroom in the rear. In the kitchen is the propane stove, a card table with plastic tablecloth and a couple of folding chairs, a wood-and-glass display cabinet over a chest of drawers, and a small refrigerator. In the bedroom is a single chest of drawers and two full-size mattresses, separated by eighteen inches. One is elevated in a metal frame but with no box springs, and with a pronounced sag in the middle. The other has both box springs and mattress, but no frame. This makes a difference in winter, because there is no buffer between the bed and the cold cement floor, and in hot weather, when crawling insects are more likely to find their way into the lower berth. In one bed sleeps Balbina and her three children; in the other, Elsa, her two-year-old, and her three-year-old. (The house is unheated, save for the stove, and on the coldest days, Balbina must choose between working and staying home with the children, who need her body's warmth. "The kids pee in bed when it's cold and so Elsa doesn't want them in her bed.")

There is a kitchen window facing the street, and two windows in the bedroom. The side window faces the plywood wall of another flat; through the rear window, if not for the colorful covering, a bedsheet of circus characters, and if not for a few neighboring houses, one could view the rear of the MagneTek plant, about seventy-five yards distant. All three windows are screened, and all three screens are broken, offering little deterrent to the swarming fly population. Between the two rooms is a single naked lightbulb dangling from the ceiling. There is no switch; to turn the light on or off one must perch precariously on the flimsy kitchen cabinet.

The shadeless yard, of mud or dust, depending on the season, is fenced by chicken wire and a rickety gate, and serves as an extension of the kitchen. It houses a shared clothesline, a shared outhouse, and a shared spigot—the lone source of water. Balbina believes the water flows from an open canal running near plants in the Finsa park that manufacture pesticides or use toxic solvents. The water must be boiled, of course; sometimes there is propane to do so, sometimes not. (For those who can afford it, purified water is sold from a boxy, fire-engine-red truck with wide, oversize tires, its hundred-odd five-gallon plastic jugs stacked along both sides and sloshing madly as the driver bumps slowly along the deeply rutted roads. At $1.25 for a jug, potable water is a luxury for which the Duques can seldom spare the money.)

Just outside the door, a wooden table made from a pallet holds a collection of deep wash pots. To wash clothes and dishes (and their children), the sisters heat water inside (again, provided there is propane in the tank), haul it outside, and scrub and rinse on the makeshift table. The table is perhaps two and a half feet high, and so washing, like field work, is stooped labor—hard on the spirit, hard on the back. The outhouse is a wooden shack in the front corner of the yard. The three households split the cost of a lime-like chemical used to decompose the waste. When there is no money for the chemical, the raw sewage is dumped into a nearby stream.

Vista Hermosa exists in a commercial and municipal twilight zone. There are several high-priced convenience stores in the neighborhood but no full-fledged grocers, no place to buy meat. Nor is there a pharmacy or medical clinic. There is no police presence, and vandalism and petty theft are rampant. There is one school, an overcrowded kindergarten. Older students catch the same bus to school that drops off the first-shift workers at the Finsa park. "You have to adapt to the *maquilas*' routine," says a neighbor with high-school-age children, "because they're not going to adapt to ours."

The city mostly shuns the neighborhood because of the high cost and low return of providing services. "They [residents of poor *colonias*] have no money," says Andres Cuellar, the Matamoros city historian, "so no city official accepts responsibility." But a former mayor complains that federal tax policy prevents the city from collecting municipal taxes from the *maquilas* to finance improvements in the *colonias*' infrastructure. "We insisted before the federal government that we don't have the financial means to support the *maquilas*' growth," says Fernando Montemayor Lozano, who served as mayor from 1987 to 1989. "Besides the salaries paid to Mexican workers, the *maquiladora* contribution is practically zero here," he added.

It was not until 1991 that running water was piped into the neighborhood (but not as yet into houses), and only in 1993 were the first houses wired for electricity. The roads remain unpaved and deeply rutted, which makes for a muddy, often impassable mess during the rainy season and for unsparing dust and filth the rest of the year. Nor does the city provide trash pickup; the Duques and their neighbors burn their garbage in a nearby ditch.

Vista Hermosa breeds disease like it does mosquitoes. The lack of septic and sewage lines, of potable water and sanitation services, puts the neighborhood at great risk for all manner of environmentally related illnesses: intestinal parasites, dysentery, hepatitis, cholera, skin rashes, respiratory infections, tuberculosis. But the gravest, most frightening environmental threat comes not from the neighborhood but from beyond the chain-link fence around the Finsa park. The fence, less than a football field away from Balbina's house, may divide the First and Third Worlds, but it also unites them under a single toxic cloud. When the *maquilas* illegally dump toxic waste into irrigation canals,* when a hot north wind blows the acrid smell of *chapapote*—pitch—from the MagneTek plant over its workers' homes, when runoff from a pesticide plant spills into a ditch, when chemical spills or leaks or explosions or fires erupt in the air, it doesn't take a Sierra Club member to understand the environmental wasteland the *maquilas* have created.

Nor does it take an epidemiologist to fathom the cause of an outbreak on both sides of the border of anencephaly—babies born with either incomplete or missing brains and skulls. In one thirty-six-hour period in the spring of 1991, three babies were born without brains at a single hospital in Brownsville. Two of them were stillborn; the third lived for three days with an open skull and a partial brain. Doctors soon learned of at least ten more cases in Brownsville and surrounding Cameron County, all within a two-and-a-half-mile radius of the Rio Grande, and ten more anencephalic births in 1991 across the river at the general hospital in Matamoros. The rate of occurrence for Brownsville from 1989 through 1991 was ten times the U.S. average, or about thirty anencephalic cases per ten thousand births.† During the same years, there were sixty-eight anencephalic births in Matamoros and eighty-one in Reynosa, the upriver *maquila* site. "We think something terrible happened to cause this, but we don't know what it is," said William Lipps, a Brownsville chemist who assisted an investigation by the U.S. Centers for Disease Control.

If the government was at a loss for an explanation, many others suspected the epidemic was due to industrial pollution—pollution that went unchecked by regulatory agencies in both countries. "These were atrocities committed by two uncaring governments," said Dr. Margaret Diaz, an occupational-health specialist in Brownsville who

---

* The *maquilas* are required to ship all waste back to the country of origin for proper disposal, but the law, like most Mexican environmental regulations, is routinely ignored.

† Public health officials say the true rate was surely higher, but that unlicensed midwives, who deliver 40 percent of the babies in Cameron County, were unlikely to report birth defects for fear of exposure.

detected the anencephaly cluster. "They are the product of years of neglect."

In a class-action lawsuit filed in March 1993, families of twenty-eight children born with anencephaly or spina bifida—an incomplete closure of the spinal cord—blamed the outbreak on contamination from the Matamoros *maquilas*. The families sued eighty-eight *maquilas*, including MagneTek, charging that the companies negligently handled "toxic compounds" and that the birth defects occurred after "exposure to toxins present in the local environment." The companies steadfastly denied wrongdoing, but internal memoranda gathered during discovery for the lawsuit documented that some plants released toxic emissions into the air in quantities impermissible in the United States. And plastic bags full of dashboard and bumper parts and electrical components obtained from the Matamoros city dump established that the *maquilas* were burning their industrial waste there, rather than returning it for disposal in the United States, as required by law. (One videotape made by an investigator for the plaintiffs' lawyers portrays the charred but clearly visible remains of a MagneTek rapid-start ballast.) In 1994 and 1995, the companies paid a total of seventeen million dollars to the stricken families, the Mexican government began to enforce its own environmental protection laws, and the plants themselves cleaned up their worst excesses. By 1997, Domingo Gonzalez of Brownsville, a tenacious environmental watchdog with the nonprofit Texas Center for Policy Studies, could say that "the rates of birth defects have dropped, an indication that there was an environmental relationship. Though we can't say with any precision which chemicals cause birth defects, we can't ignore the obvious."

Inside the plants, too, the American companies cleaned up their abusive behavior. Just as the *maquilas* used Matamoros as a private dumping ground, their managers routinely tormented the local workforce in ways that would not have been tolerated in the United States. "American managers used to consider it some kind of punishment to be stuck on the border," says Rolando González Barrón, a *maquila* owner and president of the Matamoros Maquiladora Association. González himself is a creature of the border, born in Matamoros in 1952 to U.S.-born parents. "I think some of the Americans used to take it out on the workers," he says. "Back in the mid-seventies, a Houston man would throw hot coffee on the workers if he didn't like the way they were doing things on the line. I saw this with my own eyes."

González says those days are long past. "We're doing everything we can in the *maquila* industry to improve. The sweatshop era is over."

At MagneTek, for one, working conditions have improved over the early years. Ines Barrajas Cruz hired on before the first assembly lines were even completed, in April 1988. She was eighteen years old and assigned to inspect the ballasts as they came off the line. She worked a six-day, forty-eight-hour week. "At the beginning there was so much pressure to make production goals that they would not let us go to the bathroom," Barrajas recalls. "They said that if one of us goes, they would have to stop the line, and they could not do that and meet their goals. Some of us complained, and they said that if someone *really* had to go, they would stop the line and let the person go, but that she would be written up and taken to the personnel office. Repeat offenders were suspended for three to six days." (And even though the original bathrooms were in "bad shape, with the doors falling off," as Balbina's sister-in-law, Teresa, recalls, they were still an improvement: "I had never used a flush-toilet before.")

Barrajas lived in a *colonia* on the south side of the city, near the airport. She shared her small house with her mother, six of her eight brothers and sisters, and two toddlers. The family built the house themselves, out of scrap wood. When they first moved in, in the late 1980s, the house had no floor, no electricity, no water. Then a neighbor passed them a *diablito*—a pirated power line—and they scraped together money enough to pour a cement floor. A year or so after they arrived, the city laid water pipes. As in *Vista Hermosa,* there is still no sewage system. "The president of our *colonia* is PRI, but the municipal government is PAN"—the opposition National Action Party—"so we don't get much help."

To reach the plant in time for first shift, Barrajas awoke at four-thirty A.M. She was out the door and on the first of two buses by five. The bus dropped her at Soriana Shopping Center, and from there she caught another to the Finsa. The half-hour commute allowed her to arrive by five-thirty—an hour and fifteen minutes before her shift began. "There were not enough chairs to go around and people would go early and fight the world to get one," she says.

Seated or standing, Barrajas and her co-workers were hardly comfortable. "It was always very hot and very poorly ventilated," she says. "The fumes from the *chapapote* made it difficult to breathe. Some wore masks, but that made it harder to breathe." Was the plant air-conditioned? The question elicits a belly laugh. "Only when the *gringos* came in [for a tour]. Then they cleaned everything up and turned up the air-conditioning." The original plant had no cafeteria, a signal to the workers that time was not to be wasted on eating. (Or speaking: Line workers were not permitted to talk to one another for fear of distraction.) "If the weather was OK, we would eat outside," Barrajas says, "on the bank of the drainage ditch. Otherwise we would eat on the line." They had a twenty-minute lunch break at noon, and two ten-minute breaks, at nine A.M. and one forty-five P.M. The shift lasted until three, when rush hour ensued. Dozens and dozens of old school buses and "maxi-taxis" lined up at the gates of the Finsa park's plants—the work hours were synchronized—to ferry the predominantly female workforce back to their far-flung *colonias*. Few of the women appeared to be over thirty, and many, if not most, were *dressed*—lipstick, makeup, miniskirts, pumps.

The glamorous getups—"like they're going to a cocktail party," Domingo Gonzalez puts it—are fundamental to *maquila* life, where male supervisors and managers hold in their hands the economic destiny of the *muchachas,* as the line workers are called. "It's an accepted part of the culture of the plants," Gonzalez says. Indeed, the companies used to sponsor an annual "Señorita Maquiladora" contest, ostensibly for charity, and replete with swimsuit and evening gown competitions.

Years after MagneTek upgraded the bathrooms, built a lunch room, added more chairs on the shop floor, and improved the ventilation, sexual harassment and discrimination remained a constant of factory life. Every female MagneTek employee asked about sexism on the job had a firsthand story to tell. "When new girls come in," says a thirty-one-year-old MagneTek retiree who asked that her name not be used, "a supervisor gives them the eye and asks them to go for a walk." She says her supervisor "brought me gifts to see if I would fall into his arms, go with him to the hotel." Balbina says that is precisely what happened to her when she started at Plant 1. "My supervisor asked if I wanted to work more overtime. I told him I did, but that I wouldn't go to a hotel with him to get it." Another employee, who also requested anonymity, recalls a particularly egregious American mechanic. "He used to bother the *very* young girls. He could not speak Spanish, so in English we called him 'Ladies' Man.' "

The other constant of factory life was the low wages. When Rolando González Barrón, of the Maquiladora Association, was asked about the desperate economic straits of the Matamoros workforce, he pulled out an advertising supplement to the *Brownsville Herald* touting the Association's voluntary contributions to the community. "Take 'Adopt-a-School,' " he says, pointing to the page lauding the companies for their financial contributions to schools in Matamoros. "We put sewage and bathrooms in schools where little girls had to do their necessities outside."

What about paying a living wage, his visitor persisted, so that the parents of those little girls could afford indoor plumbing themselves? "Yes," González replied, "housing needs to be developed, but our main goal is to create value for our customers."

What about your employees? What is your obligation to them?

"If a worker is not eating," González said, sounding every bit the farmer discussing a plow horse, "he's not going to work for you. We need to meet at least the basic needs."

But the basic needs—"eating, housing, clothing," as González put it— went unmet, and the evidence was as obvious and irrefutable as the *colonia* of the damned in MagneTek's backyard, where Balbina and her neighbors wrestled every single day with ferociously difficult decisions: Should I work overtime or huddle with my children to keep them warm? Buy meat or medicine? Pay the light bill or the gas bill? She made those decisions based on a daily salary, in early 1997, of 58 pesos, the equivalent of $7.34—or an hourly wage of 92¢. And she often made those decisions after working a grueling double shift: from three-thirty in the afternoon until six the following morning, after which she would arrive home in time to fix breakfast for her children, accompany her oldest to school, and hope to squeeze in a few hours of sleep before heading back to the plant in the afternoon.

No alcance. It doesn't reach. Over and over one heard this. *No alcance,* but we make it reach. From a family of three MagneTek employees in

Colonia Santa Lucia: "We drink a lot of water, eat beans, soup, work overtime. We used to buy meat three times a week. We buy meat every eight days now."

And they made it reach by taking odd jobs, or peddling wares in the plant during breaks and shift changes. "It's prohibited," Balbina says, "but the company looks the other way and almost everybody does it." There were the ubiquitous Avon ladies, as well as sellers of home-made candy, tamales and gorditas, shoes and clothes, marijuana.

And some sold their bodies, living *la doble vida*—the double life of coil-winder by day and prostitute by night. One scantily clad woman encountered in the red-light district of Brownsville, a dingy downtown strip of failed retail outlets and deserted sidewalks, said she worked her regular first-shift job at the plant and then waded the river three or four nights a week, always on Saturdays and Sundays, and usually on Tuesdays and Wednesdays, to ply her trade on the American side. "The money's so much better over here," she said between engagements one brisk Saturday night. "I can make a hundred and twenty a night, and we're paid in dollars. Over there [in Matamoros] I might make a hundred pesos"—about $12.65.

A more common moonlighting alternative was scavenging for recyclables at the Matamoros city dump, an otherworldly and self-contained fifty-acre metropolis of its own, six miles south of town off the highway to the airport, where experienced pickers could earn more in a day than a *maquila* employee. But the work was hard and the occupational hazards considerable: Here one poked and shoveled and dug amid valleys and peaks of burning rubber and plastic and hospital waste and roadkill and hypodermic needles and livestock carcasses and rotting fruit under a smoldering, apocalyptic sky darkened by smoke and thousands upon thousands of gulls that could have been Hitch-cock extras, all the while fending off endless swarms of insects and gusts of plastic bags and competitors human and otherwise—the birds, of course, and packs of wild dogs and Roadmaster-size hogs snorting and rooting around the decomposing organic matter.

To spend even a few hours in the dump is searing; it is a throat-stinging, eye-watering, chest-tightening experience. To live in the dump, as dozens of families do, is to sacrifice one's health for one's livelihood. It is not a choice. It is where people go when there is nowhere else. It is the end of the line. One couple lived there in a chicken house, a fifty-one-year-old carpenter and his forty-two-year-old wife, who two months earlier had become parents of their third child. Their shanty backed up to the bank of the ravine that bounds the dump on one side. The ravine held a stagnant pool of bluish-gray liquid, a color not found in nature, and it discharged a sharp, chemical smell. The couple's second child, a two-year-old daughter, was born with spina bifida. Their newborn was born in the dump, when the hospital turned them away for lack of money.

Balbina had yet to resort to a second job. Instead, she and Elsa worked overtime as often as possible, and the sisters always tried to stagger their shifts so that one could provide child care if the other was working.

The last time Balbina and her inquisitive visitor lunched together, the visitor broke a journalistic canon and asked if there was anything he could do for her.

"I need a lock," she said, "for the door. I don't need it now, but soon I will."

Why not now?

"You know there is nothing worth locking now. But tomorrow maybe. Come back and see, will you?"

EPILOGUE

"Thank God for NAFTA"

MagneTek closed the last of the old Universal ballast plants, in Blytheville, Arkansas, and Simpson County, Mississippi, in 1997 and 1998, respectively. On the final day at the Blytheville plant, the company treated the four hundred remaining workers (an equal number had already been laid off) to a "last supper" of fried fish, potato salad, and pickles in the employee cafeteria. For dessert there was a large chocolate sheet cake with white frosting and in blue trim, a farewell message: "MagneTek . . . So Long . . ."

After lunch, the plant's personnel director, Frank Waters, addressed the workers. "The day has arrived for all of us," Waters began, his voice cracking slightly. A large man, dressed in a long-sleeved black polo shirt, blue jeans, and tennis shoes, he took a moment to steady himself by lifting a leg on a cafeteria seat. "After tonight at midnight, you will be out of insurance from the company. You will be eligible for COBRA [the federal program that allows workers to retain their health coverage—if they pay for it]. You have sixty days to make up your mind."

Following a few questions and answers about insurance and taxes, Waters asked if there were any more questions. One woman put up her hand.

"I grew old with you in this plant," she said.

"I know," Waters replied. "Seems like we all did."

At the stroke of three-thirty the assembly-line workers punched out, sliding their photo ID cards across the electronic time clock for the last time. As I watched, an office employee motioned me aside.

"Come upstairs," she said. "I want to show you something." Her name was Leila Kackley, and she had written a six-verse poem, "Plant Closure," from the perspective of the board of directors, "sixteen men in coat and tie," who decide to "move our only money-maker/and spread it over Hell's half acre." An excerpt:

> *Some of it will go south of the border*
> *where the hourly wage is only a quarter. . . .*
> *All that's left is figuring out a way*
> *to stamp it "Made in the USA."*

I asked her for a signed copy, which she cheerfully inscribed with the day's gallows humor: "Thank God for NAFTA!"

Because MagneTek was moving the plant's operations to Mexico, the U.S. Department of Labor certified that the Blytheville workers were eligible for an aid program under NAFTA. The program, called NAFTA–TAA (Transitional Adjustment Assistance), extended unemployment insurance for up to a year beyond the standard twenty-six-week limit and was supposed to pay for up to two years of retraining for a new career. But according to Deanna McComb, the former chief steward of IBEW Local 1516, the program failed markedly. "It was supposed to last you up to two years depending on the type of schooling, but it didn't always happen that way. Some of them had to finish [paying tuition] on their own and nobody got a good job anyway. Most of them ended up in fast food, or part-time at Wal-Mart."

Two years after the plant closed, McComb, at the age of fifty-four, was working nights, eleven P.M. to seven A.M., as a certified nursing assistant in a nursing home. She was earning $5.80 an hour—$3.05 an hour less than she made at MagneTek. Neither she nor her husband, who was self-employed, had health insurance. "If we go somewhere for insurance, it's, well, you've got a preexisting condition and we're not going to touch you. And these hospitals around here won't take you without insurance. So where does that leave us? What are we supposed to do?"

The Mississippi plant held on a while longer, principally because it continued to supply steel laminations for the Matamoros facility. But in June 1998, thirty-five years to the month after Sig Steinberger trained the plant's first coil-winding operators, it, too, was closed. Eight hundred and fifty-seven people, many of whom had spent their entire working lives at the plant, were out of work. The county's unemployment rate soared to 12½ percent from 4½ percent.

By then Dorothy Carter had long since moved on. After twenty years at the company, during which she was promoted to management, she retired in 1985 to start a bakery. The bakery closed, and Dorothy works as a pharmacy clerk in Mendenhall. She and Louis Carter are divorced. Louis served as the local union's president from 1973 to 1998. Louis: "I don't blame [MagneTek chairman and CEO] Andy Galef for trying to cut costs and operate as efficiently and proficiently as possible. But the people here in Simpson County gave the company all those tax breaks and the employees here really made this company what it is. And it's not like the wages have ever been all that extreme—about eight-fifty [an hour].

"Now are we supposed to go back to work in Mr. Charlie's chicken house, on his farm, fixing his fence? Or should I stick some sumbitch up to get me some money? If we don't get some jobs in here, just watch the crime rate. But Andy Galef doesn't care about the crime rate in Simpson County. He cares about the crime rate in Bel Air [California], where he lives."

Sig Steinberger, the founding plant manager, cares about the quality of life in Simpson County. Simpson County is his home. He raised his three sons there, sent them to public school in Mendenhall, and he served on the town's school board. Steinberger put in thirty-six years with the company, all but the first thirteen in Simpson County. His career began with Archie Sergy at the Westwood, New Jersey, plant in 1950, and ended in 1986 when Andy Galef gave him four hours' notice to clear out his desk. Steinberger went on to serve as manager of the Mendenhall Area Chamber of Commerce, a volunteer position. In 1989, he and his wife, June, were jointly given the town's Outstanding

Citizen Award. Steinberger recently retired from the chamber. He remains active in his church.

Not long after the company announced the closing, it established, in conjunction with the local union and state and federal job-training programs, the "MagneTek Career Transition Center." The facility provided guidance counselors, high-school-equivalency classes, truck-driving seminars, computer-literacy and resume-writing workshops. The center started out in a trailer on company property and later moved to a storefront office on South Main Avenue in Magee, the southern pillar of Simpson County. On the day I visited, in April 1998, its bulletin board of "Hot Job Leads" was not exactly smoking; no leads were posted. There were, however, stacks of how-to pamphlets: "Your Resume—Key to a Successful Job Search"; "How to Get Out of Debt"; and the sequel, "Steps to Successful Money Management." And there were piles of recruiting brochures: "What's the Best You Can Be?" asked the U.S. Army, which also touted "Army Opportunities for Women"; the Coast Guard declared itself "Ready for Action."

To many laid-off employees it seemed awfully late in the day to contemplate a new career in a big rig or a foxhole or on the high seas. "At my age, nobody will want to hire me," fifty-five-year-old Bobbie Ainsworth told the *Clarion-Ledger* in 1997, when the first wave of layoffs swept the plant. "I've given MagneTek the best twenty-five years of my life. I'm going to have to try something, but I don't know how much I can learn."

Two years later, I looked up Ainsworth to see how she was faring. "It's been rough," she reported. She said she was disabled due to chronic shoulder pain and numbness in one thumb "from all those years on the line. . . . I never did get another job. I took that little computer class, but when we finished there wasn't anybody hiring. We all of us looked, but nobody got anything but minimum [-wage] jobs, and I couldn't even get one of those. I couldn't lift anything, so who in their right mind was gonna hire me?"

At the time the Mississippi plant closed, it had been nearly a decade since Mollie James lost her job in Paterson. She had received a sever-ance payment, after taxes, of $3,171.60—about $93 for each of the thirty-four years she worked. She collected unemployment benefits for six months and then enrolled in a six-month-long computer-repair school, receiving a certificate of completion and numerous don't-call-us responses to job inquiries. Mollie never again found work. She lives on Social Security and rental income from the three-family house she owns, as well as a monthly pension of $71.23 from her union, Teamsters Local 945. "That's nothing," she says. "That doesn't even pay your telephone bill. It's gone before you know it."*

Paterson itself seems defined by what is gone. It is a city justly conscious of its rich history, from its founding in 1791 as the cradle of American industry to the landmark immigrant silk workers' strike of 1913 to its last heyday, during and after World War II, when entrepreneurs like Archie Sergy and migrants like Mollie James helped sustain Paterson as a proud symbol of industrial might. But the old factory district near the Great Falls has been in ruins for decades, and although a number of the ancient brick mills have been splendidly restored—as a museum, a hospital clinic, and artists' housing—Paterson today is thought of as one of those discarded American places, a city so crime- and grime-ridden, so defeated, that few people who do not live or work in Paterson venture there. They are missing something. They are missing the rebirth of a tenacious city, a city shaped and reshaped by succeeding waves of immigrants: from Europe in the nineteenth and early twentieth centuries, from the American South during and between the world wars, and most recently from Latin America. Paterson today is 41 percent Hispanic, 33 percent black, 24 percent white. "No city boasts a more encompassing mosaic of what America meant and still means than Paterson," U.S. representative William J. Pascrell Jr., a former mayor of Paterson, said at a Fourth of July celebration not long ago. "The true story of America is right here."

To be sure, Paterson is a poor, ravaged city. Nearly 1 in 5 of its 140,000 residents lives in poverty and about 15 percent of Patersonians receive public assistance; the city's per capita income is under $11,000. Unemployment is high, more than twice the state's average. Affordable, adequate housing is in short supply; with the exception of

---

*The local's richly deserved reputation for corruption endured well beyond Universal's passing. In 1995, the international union placed Local 945 in trusteeship, citing "pervasive financial malpractice."

public projects, most of the housing stock is a century old. Schools are overcrowded and dilapidated; at one elementary school the author Jonathan Kozol toured, he found children eating lunch in a boiler room, taking reading class in a bathroom. The school system is so troubled that the state seized control in 1991 and has yet to relinquish it.

Another of Paterson's educational pillars is also crumbling. In the middle 1990s, the city was so desperate for cash it not only closed three branches of the public library, it sought to auction off the three buildings. "We have seen businesses leave Paterson," the local newspaper editorialized. "We have seen institutions close their doors. We have seen historic buildings burn and sinew melt away from the once-mighty city by the Great Falls. But this quiet moment in the city's history is one of the bleakest in recent memory."

Downtown still pulsates, but to a different beat. The luxe department stores are long gone (although an incongruously high-end furniture dealer hangs on), replaced by what the city's economic developers call "value-conscious retailing," much of it, naturally, catering to the influx of immigrants. At the busy corner of Main and Ward streets is Las Americas Super Market. Next door is El Mundo, a discount store, which adjoins Dresses for Less. A consignment store advertises its prepaid phone cards—LLAMADOS INTERNACIONALES 5¢ EL MINUTO—and Spanish-language billboards hawk cigarettes and malt liquor; on a Wednesday afternoon Mi Ranchito bar bustles as if it were Saturday night. Nearby is a jumble of storefront churches, an all-day bingo hall, a soup kitchen, a women's shelter, nail- and hair-care emporiums, check-cashing outlets, and the employer of last resort, the U.S. Army, whose recruiting-office sign reminds residents: WE'RE STILL HIRING.

What was once the cultural district teems with mangled people and mangled buildings. The Fabian, the city's last surviving movie theater, was boarded up years ago. Next door, the Alexander Hamilton, the once-glorious hotel that hosted all-night dinner-dances and the country's biggest stars and starlets, is a flophouse; another downtown hotel is running a special: $37 ALL NIGHT. With poverty and unemployment comes crime. There have been so many car thefts that the police department itself took to selling The Club—the steering-wheel lock. A sticker seen on not a few bumpers: FIGHT CRIME, SHOOT BACK.

Paterson is fighting back—through community development. Just as the massive old Universal plant was sold to a chemical manufacturer; just as the magnificent Art Deco Temple Emanuel, at Broadway and Thirty-third Street, became a mosque; just as the Van Dyk Furniture Company building mutated into El Mundo; so Paterson is transforming, reinventing itself. TAKE PRIDE IN PATERSON, exhort green-and-white banners on Main Street lampposts. And people do. Ethnic parades down Broadway are spirited, flag-waving affairs; the Labor Day festival at the Falls attracts large crowds for the live music, politicking, and Hot Texas Wieners—a Paterson specialty. The city planning board recently approved a private developer's blueprint to convert the heart of the burned-out, albeit historic, mill district into 190 units of "affordable and market-priced" two-family housing. Plans call for a nearby café and river walk as well.

These hopeful signs notwithstanding, a Paterson renaissance, economic and cultural, is not imminent. Mollie James has spent a half century there. She married (and divorced) in Paterson, raised four children, bought a house. She sunk deep roots and would like nothing better than to see the seeds of renewal take sprout, but she is fed up with high taxes, crime, the unstable economy. Like many "Up-South" blacks of retirement age, she thinks often about going home, to Cartersville, Virginia, to the land she left as a teenager. She and her sister (who also lives in New Jersey) still own their childhood home amid three wooded acres.

On a visit to Cartersville not long ago, Mollie took me to their house, where an elderly aunt was living. Adjoining the property still is the grammar school Mollie attended, and next door to the school New Hope Baptist Church, where her father was assistant pastor. When Mollie was young, there was a juke joint on a rise just down the road from the church. During the week, the jukebox—or "piccolo," as Mollie calls it—blared the sweet soul and blues of Louis Jordan, Muddy Waters, "all the old guys." Weekend nights would feature live music. "Man that joint used to *jump*," Mollie says, her fingers snapping. "And sometimes they'd set up a tent in the field and show a movie or play music, and we'd sneak in under the tent."

The joint was razed long ago, the surrounding land converted to a cemetery where Mollie's parents are buried. Her mother died in 1964, her father a decade later. Asked if she, too, would be buried there, she is quick with an answer: "They better not put me in no dirt up there in New Jersey. Bring me back home, brother."

Toward the close of 1999, two and a half years after she had encouraged me to return someday to Matamoros, I took up Balbina Duque on her invitation. She, too, dreams of returning to her ancestral home, to the clear high-desert air of Monte Bello, where she could raise her children in a calm, safe place. But there is no work around Monte Bello for her, no future there for her children.

She is more concerned with the immediate future of her job. I tell her that since I last saw her, I had paid my respects to the company's dead and dying plants in Arkansas and Mississippi. She asks if I knew that MagneTek had transferred the bulk of the Mississippi operations not to Matamoros but sixty miles upriver to Reynosa (where the company opened a plant in January 1998). The union is weaker there, she says, the wages lower. In Reynosa, she reminds me, there is no strong labor leader, no Agapito Gonzalez, no *espinazo*—backbone.

In reality, the era of a union strongman, and indeed the era of state-controlled unions, was fading. Fidel Velázquez Sánchez, who headed the authoritarian labor confederation for fifty years, defied skeptics in mid-1997 and finally died. He was ninety-seven years old. With his passing, and with the national governing party, the PRI, on the verge of splintering after seventy years of monopoly rule, has emerged a formidable, politically independent labor movement. Though it has yet to make inroads in Matamoros, the movement has forged cross-border organizing alliances with unions from the United States, which themselves have reawakened in the course of the 1995 takeover of the AFL-CIO by the John Sweeney–led slate from the somnolent leadership of Lane Kirkland. "We're finding a new vision among trade unionists in the United States," says Benedicto Martínez Orozco, a leader of the independent Authentic Labor Front. "They're showing more interest in understanding what we're up against in Mexico: the control, the manipulation, the gangster tactics. And we're learning about the problems they face: the firings, the factory shutdowns."

Yes, I tell Balbina, I am aware of MagneTek's expanded operations in Reynosa. I add that I'd heard recently that the company already had a thousand employees there, that it was gearing up to start a second shift, and that it had just opened an on-site day-care center.

I ask if she would consider transferring to Reynosa if the company relocated her job there.

"And what if they were to move again?" she replies. "Maybe to Juárez or Tijuana? What then? Do I chase my job all over the world?"

Acknowledgments

Most authors come to depend on the kindnesses, small and great, of strangers. That dependence came early in the preparation of this book—before I'd scrawled a single word in my reporter's pad. On a white-hot Sunday morning a few Augusts past, I was in Arkansas, puttering north along Interstate 30 in a balky Ford barely younger than its driver. Somewhere between Hope and Arkadelphia—en route to Paterson from my home in Texas—the radiator rebelled, overheating like a Mexican soap opera. I was stranded on the searing highway shoulder when a passing long-haul trucker, a card-carrying Teamster, swept me up into his air-conditioned cab and deposited me at a service station. What do I owe you? I asked. "Not a damn thing," he said, handing me a soft drink. "Just write it up that a Teamster lent a helping hand." Amen, brother, you're first on the list.

Next on the list is Mollie James, who welcomed me into her life and her home. For four months, whether over morning coffee or the evening news, Mollie endured a steady barrage of questions with an unfailing generosity of spirit and time that I will never be able to repay.

My other great debt in Paterson is to Sol Stetin, who grew up with Archie Sergy on Water Street and whose own life merits a biography. Sol has had an extraordinary career spanning six decades in the American labor movement, during which he rose to the presidency of the Textile Workers Union of America. He serves as president emeritus of the invaluable American Labor Museum/Botto House National Landmark in Haledon, New Jersey. A gifted raconteur and a devoted correspondent, Sol took me under his wing, introduced me to others of Archie's boyhood friends, and showed me how tiring it can be traipsing around after an octogenarian.

Many others helped, too many to name. In Paterson, let me at least thank Laird Coates for his companionship and guidance; Flavia Alaya for her scholarship and culinary skills; Michael Stein, a nephew of Archie's and Universal's last remaining link to MagneTek; and Archie's three sons, Sam, Alan, and Bruce Sergy, for their unflagging interest and many courtesies.

Let me also mention Michael Bober; Morris Paer; Giacomo De Stefano of The Paterson Museum; Margit and David Linforth; Jerry Nathans of the Jewish Historical Society of North Jersey; Edward A. Smyk, the Passaic County historian; and Billy Carnemolla of the Park Avenue Service Center.

In Washington, thanks to John McCabe; Rand Wilson of the International Brotherhood of Teamsters; Carol Cipolari of the International Brotherhood of Electrical Workers; and David A. Taylor of the American Folklife Center, which in 1994 produced the fine study "Working in Paterson."

In Mississippi, I am deeply grateful to Siegfried Steinberger, on whom I came to lean heavily, and who regaled me for many well-spent hours in his chamber of commerce roost atop Mendenhall City Hall; to Dorothy Carter for making time for me when she had none; and to Joe White of the *Clarion-Ledger,* a Mendenhall native and resident who schooled me in the ways of his hometown and the wonders of Thai food in Jackson. Thanks also to Margaret Downing, who opened the *Clarion-Ledger*'s door to me, and to Susan Garcia, the newspaper's librarian.

In Magee, I appreciate the help of Budgie Wallace, who worked for Universal for twenty-nine years, and of Forrest Hailey of the *Magee Courier.* Thanks also to Tami J. Friedman, a keen student of Mississippi labor history, who graciously steered me toward state archives and background reading from which I benefited greatly.

In Brownsville and Matamoros, my first and foremost debt is to

Christina Lowery, a documentary filmmaker who dropped out of her own busy life for a month to act as translator, map reader, researcher, running buddy. For advice and encouragement at every step along the border, I thank Domingo González, the inspiring environmental activist. I also thank Fidencio Guerrero Garcia, *presidente de los presidentes* of a thirteen-*colonia* association in Matamoros, who provided a guided tour of his domain, including *Colonia Vista Hermosa,* where I met Balbina Duque. I am deeply grateful to Balbina for believing she had a story to tell, for having the courage to tell it, and for trusting me to report it accurately; I hope I have done so.

I'm also appreciative of the editorial staff of the *Brownsville Herald,* particularly Tony Vindell and Henry Krausse, for sharing their insights and clip files. Thanks also to Aurora de la Garza, district clerk of Cameron County, for providing me with helpful contacts on both sides of the border, and to Ed Krueger and Maria Guadalupe Torres Martinez, who work with the American Friends Service Committee Maquiladora Project and the pathbreaking *Comité Fronteriza de Obreras,* Border Committee for Working Women.

The idea of a book describing the narrative history of a job grew out of conversations with my friend and former editor Anton Mueller. The decision to focus on Universal was suggested by an acquaintance at Teamsters headquarters in Washington, who was passingly familiar with the company due to the Local 945 connection and who had read about Universal in the *Philadelphia Inquirer.* The company's journey from Paterson to Matamoros was described in a sidebar to the first of a nine-part series in the *Inquirer* by the distinguished reporting team of Donald L. Barlett and James B. Steele. The series, "America: What Went Wrong?" ran in October of 1991 and was expanded into their 1992 book of the same title.

I am grateful for the research facilities and assistance offered by the staffs of the following: the local history room of the Paterson Public Library; the local history room of the University of Texas at Brownsville; the Mississippi Department of Archives and History, Jackson; the Rio Grande Valley Historical Collection, Pan American University, Edinburg, Texas; Coalition for Justice in the Maquiladoras, San Antonio, Texas; Documentation Exchange, Austin, Texas (which publishes the indispensable biweekly digest *Mexico NewsPak*); International

Union of Electrical Workers (IUE) Archives, Special Collections and University Archives, Rutgers University Libraries, New Brunswick, New Jersey; National Archives and Records Administration, Southeast Region, East Point, Georgia.

For timely and generous financial support, I thank the Dick Goldensohn Fund, which underwrote an extended visit to Mississippi, and Carol Bernstein Ferry, who supported my research in Mexico at a critical juncture.

Relations and friends sustained me in various ways over the course of this book. Thanks to Lani and Tim for the locker-room privileges; and to Rumby and Sherri, and the Schultz clan for their Brooklyn hospitality. My gratitude also to Rick Levy and the entire "Talkin' Union" staff; the *Texas Observer* regulars; Mary Hall Rodman and Scott Campbell, who endowed the writer-in-residence program at the HighLife Cafe; John Dugan, Suzanne Hershey, the family Hobart, Charlotte Katzin, Mark Kyle, Rich Lee, Bill Lewellen, Russell Lewis, Jere Locke, Jim and Hester Magnuson. Thanks, too, to Julia Carol and Len Casey of ANR in Berkeley, who offered a visiting writer office equipment and technical and moral support, and to Marisel Brown for eleventh-hour translation services.

I owe a special debt to my dear and ever-steadfast agent, Geri Thoma, who was there when I needed her, as she has always been. I was fortunate to have as my editor Lisa Drew, whose enthusiasm, forbearance, and sure judgments greatly enhanced this book.

The sweetest debt of all is to my bride, Robin. Without her love, patience, and many, many indulgences, I'd still be out there, figuratively—a *little* figuratively—broke down south of Arkadelphia.

Selected Bibliography

American Social History Project, the City University of New York. *Who Built America?* Vol. 2. New York: Pantheon, 1992.

Barlett, Donald L., and Steele, James B. *America: What Went Wrong?* Kansas City, Mo.: Andrews and McMeel, 1992.

Bluestone, Barry, and Harrison, Bennett. *The Deindustrialization of America.* New York: Basic Books, 1982.

Boyer, Richard O., and Morais, Herbert M. *Labor's Untold Story.* New York: United Electrical, Radio and Machine Workers of America, 1955.

Branch, Taylor. *Parting the Waters: America in the King Years, 1954–63.* New York: Simon & Schuster, 1988.

———. *Pillar of Fire: America in the King Years, 1963–65.* New York: Simon & Schuster, 1998.

Bright, Arthur A. *The Electric-Lamp Industry.* New York: Arno Press, 1972.

Brill, Steven. *The Teamsters.* New York: Pocket Books, 1979. (Paperback ed.; originally published 1978.)

Brooks, John. *The Go-Go Years.* New York: Weybright and Talley, 1973.

Brown, Peter G., and Shue, Henry, eds. *The Border That Joins.* Totowa, N.J.: Rowman and Littlefield, 1983.

Browne, Harry, with Sims, Beth, and Barry, Tom. *For Richer, for Poorer: Shaping U.S.-Mexican Integration.* Albuquerque, N.M.: Resource Center Press, 1994.

Bruck, Connie. *The Predators' Ball.* New York: Penguin Books, 1989. (Paperback ed.; originally published 1988.)

Cagin, Seth, and Dray, Philip. *We Are Not Afraid.* New York: Bantam, 1991. (Paperback ed.; originally published 1988.)

Cobb, James C. *The Selling of the South.* 2d ed. Urbana and Chicago: University of Illinois Press, 1993.

Cox, James A. *A Century of Light.* New York: The Benjamin Co./Rutledge Books, 1979.

Dittmer, John. *Local People: The Struggle for Civil Rights in Mississippi.* Urbana and Chicago: University of Illinois Press, 1995.

Dubofsky, Melvyn. *We Shall Be All: A History of the Industrial Workers of the World.* Chicago: Quadrangle Books, 1969.

Elkins, Stanley, and McKitrick, Eric. *The Age of Federalism: The Early American Republic, 1788–1800.* New York: Oxford University Press, 1993.

Fairfield, Roy P., ed. *The Federalist Papers.* Garden City, N.Y.: Anchor Books, 1961.

Fernandez, Raul A. *The United States–Mexico Border.* Notre Dame, Ind.: University of Notre Dame Press, 1977.

Flynn, Elizabeth Gurley. *I Speak My Own Piece.* New York: Masses and Mainstream, 1955.

Foner, Philip S. *History of the Labor Movement in the United States.* 2d ed. Vols. 1–7. New York: International Publishers, 1975.

Fromson, Brett Duval, ed. *The Gaga Years: The Rise and Fall of the Money Game, 1981–1991.* New York: Carol Publishing, 1992.

Gelernter, David. *1939: The Lost World of the Fair.* New York: Avon Books, 1995.

Golin, Steve. *The Fragile Bridge: Paterson Silk Strike, 1913.* Philadelphia: Temple University Press, 1988.

Green, Howard L., ed. *Words That Make New Jersey History: A Primary Source Reader.* New Brunswick, N.J.: Rutgers University Press, 1995.

Greider, William. *One World, Ready or Not.* New York: Simon & Schuster, 1997.

———. *Who Will Tell the People?* New York: Touchstone, 1993. (Paperback ed.; originally published 1992.)

Guerrero-miller, Yolanda, Alma, and Ayala, César Leonel. *¡Por Eso!* Matamoros, Tamaulipas, Mexico: Centro de Investigacion Multidisciplinaria de Tamaulipas, 1993.

Harrison, Helen A., ed. *Dawn of a New Day: The New York World's Fair, 1939/40.* The Queens Museum, New York: New York University Press, 1980.

Havard, William C., ed. *The Changing Politics of the South.* Baton Rouge: Louisiana State University Press, 1972.

Haywood, William D. *Bill Haywood's Book.* New York: International Publishers, 1977. (Paperback ed.; originally published 1929.)

Herbst, John A., and Keene, Catherine. *Life and Times in Silk City: A Photographic Essay of Paterson, New Jersey.* Haledon, N.J.: The American Labor Museum, 1984.

Howe, Irving. *World of Our Fathers.* New York: Schocken Books, 1989. (Paperback ed.; originally published 1976.)

Jackson, Kenneth T. *Crabgrass Frontier: The Suburbanization of the United States.* New York: Oxford University Press, 1985.

James, Ralph C., and James, Estelle Dinerstein. *Hoffa and the Teamsters.* Princeton, N.J.: D. Van Nostrand, 1965.

Kennedy, Robert F. *The Enemy Within.* New York: Popular Library, 1960.

Kornbluh, Joyce, ed. *Rebel Voices: An I.W.W. Anthology.* Ann Arbor: University of Michigan Press, 1964.

Kozol, Jonathan. *Savage Inequalities.* New York: Crown, 1991.

La Botz, Dan. *Democracy in Mexico.* Boston: South End Press, 1995.

Leuchtenberg, William E. *The Perils of Prosperity, 1914–32.* Chicago: The University of Chicago Press, 1958.

Lewis, Belle, ed. *Our Paterson Jewish Heritage.* West Paterson, N.J.: Jewish Historical Society of North Jersey, May 1986.

Lichtenstein, Nelson. *The Most Dangerous Man in Detroit: Walter Reuther and the Fate of American Labor.* New York: Basic Books, 1995.

Lukas, J. Anthony. *Big Trouble.* New York: Simon & Schuster, 1997.

Maas, Peter. *The Valachi Papers.* New York: Bantam, 1968.

Madrick, Jeff. *Taking America.* New York: Bantam, 1987.

McCullough, David. *Truman.* New York: Simon & Schuster, 1992.

McElvaine, Robert S., ed. *Down & Out in the Great Depression: Letters from the Forgotten Man.* Chapel Hill: University of North Carolina Press, 1983.

———. *The Great Depression: America, 1929–1941.* New York: Times Books, 1984.

Mitchell, Broadus. *Alexander Hamilton.* 2 vols. New York: Macmillan, 1957–1962.

Moldea, Dan E. *The Hoffa Wars.* New York and London: Paddington Press, 1978.

Mollenhoff, Clark R. *Tentacles of Power: The Story of Jimmy Hoffa.* Cleveland: World Publishing, 1965.

Morrison, Joan, & Zabusky, Charlotte Fox. *American Mosaic: The Immigrant Experience in the Words of Those Who Lived It.* New York: E. P. Dutton, 1980.

Moskin, J. Robert. *Mr. Truman's War.* New York: Random House, 1996.

Nelson, William. "Alexander Hamilton in New Jersey." An address before the Washington Association of New Jersey, at Morristown, February 22, 1897. Washington: The Daniel A. P. Murray Collection, 1818–1907, Library of Congress.

Nelson, William, and Shriner, Charles A. *History of Paterson and Its Environs.* New York and Chicago: Lewis Historical Publishing Co., 1920.

Norwood, Christopher. *About Paterson: The Making and Unmaking of an American City.* New York: Harper Colophon, 1975. (Paperback ed.; originally published 1974.)

Oshinsky, David M. *"Worse Than Slavery": Parchman Farm and the Ordeal of Jim Crow Justice.* New York: The Free Press, 1996.

Pastor, Robert A., and Castaneda, Jorge G. *Limits to Friendship: The United States and Mexico.* New York: Knopf, 1988.

Piven, Frances Fox, & Cloward, Richard A. *Regulating the Poor: The Functions of Public Welfare.* New York: Vintage Books, 1972.

Rosenstone, Robert A. *Romantic Revolutionary: A Biography of John Reed.* New York: Knopf, 1975.

Roth, Philip. *American Pastoral.* Boston: Houghton Mifflin, 1997.

Ruggiero, Greg, and Sahulka, Stuart, eds. *The New American Crisis.* New York: The New Press, 1995.

Salter, John R., Jr. *Jackson, Mississippi: An American Chronicle of Struggle and Schism.* Hicksville, N.Y.: Exposition Press, 1979.

Sanders, Ronald. *Shores of Refuge: A Hundred Years of Jewish Emigration.* New York: Holt, 1988.

Schlesinger, Arthur M., Jr. *The Crisis of the Old Order, 1919–1933.* Boston: Houghton Mifflin, 1957.

Scranton, Philip B., ed. *Silk City: Studies on the Paterson Silk Industry, 1860–1940.* Newark: New Jersey Historical Society, 1985.

Sheridan, Walter. *The Fall and Rise of Jimmy Hoffa.* New York: Saturday Review Press, 1972.

Sherrill, Robert. *Gothic Politics in the Deep South.* New York: Ballantine Books, 1968.

Shriner, Charles A. *Paterson, New Jersey: Its Advantages for Manufacturing and Residence.* Paterson: The Press Printing and Publishing Co., 1890.

Silver, James W. *Mississippi: The Closed Society.* New York: Harcourt, Brace & World, 1963.

Sklair, Leslie. *Assembling for Development: The Maquila Industry in Mexico and the United States.* San Diego: Center for U.S.-Mexican Studies, University of California, San Diego, 1993.

Sloane, Arthur A. *Hoffa.* Cambridge, Mass.: The MIT Press, 1992.

Stewart, James B. *Den of Thieves.* New York: Touchstone, 1992. (Paperback ed.; originally published 1991.)

Syrett, Harold C., et al., eds., *The Papers of Alexander Hamilton.* 27 vols. New York: Columbia University Press, 1961–1981.

Thernstrom, Stephan, and Sennett, Richard, eds. *Nineteenth Century Cities: Essays in the New Urban History.* New Haven: Yale University Press, 1969.

Trumbull, L. R. *A History of Industrial Paterson.* Paterson, N.J.: Carleton M. Herrick, 1882.

Whalen, Charles and Barbara. *The Longest Debate: A Legislative History of the 1964 Civil Rights Act.* Cabin John, Md.: Seven Locks Press, 1985.

Williams, William Carlos. *Paterson.* New York: New Directions, 1995. (Paperback ed.; originally published 1946.)

Zinn, Howard. *A People's History of the United States.* 2d ed. New York: HarperCollins, 1995.

Source Notes

Archive Abbreviations
IUE-A: IUE Archives, Special Collections and University Archives, Rutgers University Libraries, New Brunswick, N.J.
MDAH: Mississippi Department of Archives and History, Jackson, Miss.

Newspaper Abbreviations
BR: Bergen Record
C-L: Clarion-Ledger (Jackson, Miss.)
MC: Magee Courier
JDN: Jackson Daily News
NYT: New York Times
NJH&N: North Jersey Herald & News
PMC: Paterson Morning Call
PEN: Paterson Evening News
PN: Paterson News
SCN: Simpson County News
WSJ: Wall Street Journal

Introduction: The End of the Line

Sources

Newspaper Article
"Brilliante Inauguración de MagneTek Matamoros," *El Bravo,* June 12, 1988.

Interviews
Balbina Duque Granados, Mollie James, William J. Landry, Charles E. Peeples, Hector J. Romeu Jr.

Notes
going-native: Opening ceremonies were described by Romeu, Peeples, and Landry, and in *El Bravo,* June 12, 1988.
"If MagneTek grows": MagneTek press release (translated from Spanish), June 10, 1988.

Chapter One: Dimples Takes a Ride

Sources

Books
American Social History Project, *Who Built America?*

Newspaper Articles
E. A. Smyk, "Investor's Gamble Paid Off for Theater," *NJH&N,* October 25, 1992.
"Sixtieth Anniversary Mid-Century Edition," *PEN,* July 15, 1950.

Documents
U.S. Bureau of the Census, *Census of Population, 1940,* vol. 2, *Characteristics of the Population,* part 4, Minnesota–New Mexico, p. 932.
U.S. Bureau of the Census, *Census of Population, 1950,* vol. 2, *Characteristics of the Population,* part 30, New Jersey, pp. 30–71.

Interviews
Arnold Berger, Phil Chase, Vincent J. Cortese, William Dolan, Arthur Holloway, Mollie James, Bunny Kuiken, Edward A. Smyk.

Notes
Come they did: American Social History Project, pp. 240, 300.
next four decades: Ibid., p. 513.

heart of downtown: Edward A. Smyk, the Passaic County historian, provided vivid detail of the shopping district, and especially of Meyer Bros., where his parents, who were fellow employees, met.

"asking price leaped": Smyk column, October 25, 1992.

"it was known": The de facto segregation was described by Chase and Holloway.

overall population shrank: Bureau of the Census, *Census of Population, 1940* and *Census of Population, 1950.*

largest employer: For more on Wright, see "Sixtieth Anniversary Mid-Century Edition," *PEN,* July 15, 1950.

"dropped their aprons": Ibid.

"Some guy named Randolph": American Social History Project, pp. 451–452.

CHAPTER TWO: THE GOLDEN LAND

Sources

Books

American Social History Project, *Who Built America?;* Dubofsky, *We Shall Be All;* Elkins and McKitrick, *The Age of Federalism;* Fairfield, ed., *The Federalist Papers;* Flynn, *I Speak My Own Piece;* Golin, *The Fragile Bridge;* Green, ed., *Words That Make New Jersey History;* Haywood, *Bill Haywood's Book;* Howe, *World of Our Fathers;* Kornbluh, ed., *Rebel Voices;* Lukas, *Big Trouble;* Mitchell, *Alexander Hamilton;* Morrison and Zabusky, *American Mosaic;* Nelson and Shriner, *A History of Paterson and Its Environs;* Norwood, *About Paterson;* Rosenstone, *Romantic Revolutionary;* Sanders, *Shores of Refuge;* Scranton, ed., *Silk City;* Shriner, *Paterson, New Jersey;* Syrett et al., eds., *The Papers of Alexander Hamilton;* Thernstrom and Sennett, eds., *Nineteenth Century Cities;* Trumbull, *A History of Industrial Paterson;* Williams, *Paterson.*

Newspaper Articles

Vincent D. Waraske, "A Tale of River Street in Yesteryear," *PN,* June 21, 1971.

Mel Most, "The Silk Strike Terror of 1913," *BR,* September 30, 1973.

Newsletters, Pamphlets, and Journal Articles

Bulletin of the Passaic County Historical Society, vol. 4, no. 6, June 1956.

"Stories of New Jersey," Work Projects Administration, *Bulletin No. 7,* 1941–1942 series.

Herbst and Keene, *Life and Times in Silk City.*

Lewis, ed., *Our Paterson Jewish Heritage.*

Robert H. Zieger, "Robin Hood in the Silk City," *Proceedings of the New Jersey Historical Society,* n.d.

Speeches

Nelson, "Alexander Hamilton in New Jersey," an address before the Washington Association of New Jersey, at Morristown, February 22, 1897. Washington: The Daniel A. P. Murray Collection, 1818–1907, Library of Congress.

Documents

U.S. Department of Justice, "Petition for Naturalization" for Sam Gutin, no. 44680; "Petition for Naturalization" for Ida Sergey, no. 31052; "Certificate of Arrival" for Ida Sergei, no. 2507324, April 9, 1937; "Declaration of Intention" for Ida Sergey, no. 36619, June 22, 1937. The above are on file at the Passaic County Courthouse, Paterson, N.J.
City of Paterson, Division of Health, Office of Vital Statistics, death certificate for Samuel Sergey, June 7, 1929.

Interviews

Arnold Berger, Esther Gerber, Meyer Horwitz, Bunny Kuiken, Anne Morganstein, Jerry Nathans, Morris Paer, Alan Sergy, Bruce Sergy, Sam (Sandy) Sergy, Sol Stetin, Irving Stillman, Sylvia Streit, Seymour Wolfe.

Notes

"howling wilderness": Description is from a pamphlet written by Abraham Clark at the end of the Revolutionary War, reprinted in Green, ed., p 69.

"excellent grog": The scene is described in the diary of Colonel James McHenry, who was aide-de-camp to the Marquis de Lafayette. Quoted in Norwood, p. 30.

"great manufacturing center": Williams, p. 70.

"these thousand years": Quoted in Nelson and Shriner, p. 317.

"mobs of great cities": Quoted in Norwood, p. 34, from John C. Riker, *The Works of Thomas Jefferson*, vol. 13, p. 406.

Hamilton proposed: The report is published in Syrett et al., eds., vol. 10, pp. 230–340. For synopses, see Elkins and McKitrick, pp. 258–263, and Nelson and Shriner, pp. 318–321.

"finest site anywhere": *Bulletin of the Passaic County Historical Society*, vol. 4, no. 6, June 1956, p. 36.

nation's first tax abatement: Nelson and Shriner, p. 320.

named its new city: Ibid., p. 322.

"far surpass[ing] anything": Ibid., pp. 328–329.

"child will be a Hercules": Ibid., p. 330.

felled by a bullet: Biographical information on Hamilton is from two principal sources: Mitchell, and Nelson, "Alexander Hamilton in New Jersey."

workforce won acclaim: Gutman, p. 106, in Thernstrom and Sennett, eds., "The Reality of the Rags-to-Riches 'Myth': The Case of the Paterson, New Jersey, Locomotive, Iron, and Machinery Manufacturers, 1830–1880." The eminent historian draws an invaluable portrait of industrial Paterson in the middle years of the nineteenth century. His thesis was that the city's manufacturers of that era came from humble origins and grew their businesses, as *Sci-*

entific American writer Gutman quotes put it, "as the quicksilver expanded in his purse." In Paterson, as Gutman saw it, the rags-to-riches stories were more reality than "myth."

Rogers Locomotive: Gutman, p. 105.

"Engine No. 119": Norwood, p. 42.

John Ryle: "Stories of New Jersey," prepared for use in the public schools by the New Jersey Writers' Project, Work Projects Administration, *Bulletin No. 7,* 1941–1942 series.

"They pushed me": Howe, p. 63.

Ten million people: American Social History Project, p. 17.

thirst for workers: Norwood, p. 40.

"obvious advantages": Fenner was vice president of the Paterson Board of Trade. His article, "The Progress of Paterson," is included in Shriner, p. 28. The prophecy from L. R. Trumbull, the contemporary of Shriner's referred to in the footnote, is in Trumbull, p. 5.

"in everybody's mouth": Howe, p. 27.

"famous land": Biographical material on Sam Sergy is drawn from interviews with Gerber, Paer, Stillman, Wolfe, and from Sergy's death certificate and his sister Ida's naturalization papers, including her "Petition for Naturalization" and "Declaration of Intention."

"into my casket": Morrison and Zabusky, p. 68.

"couldn't see the sky": Author's notes of Ellis Island exhibit.

"mud puddle"; "rocking like a seesaw"; "could drive anyone insane": Newman is quoted in Morrison and Zabusky, p. 9; the unnamed passengers are quoted in Sanders, p. 67.

"Who cared?": Ibid.

"if they sent me back": Author's notes of Ellis Island exhibit.

"Where's your money?": Howe, p. 44.

"distinctly bad": Dubofsky, p. 265.

unsanitary conditions: Berger.

different colored signs: Paer.

experienced textile workers: Herbst and Keene, p. 37.

rewarded accordingly: Flynn, *I Speak My Own Piece,* p. 156.

moving business: Paer, whose father, Louis, was a close friend of Sam's.

Judaism in the Riverside: Information about the Jewish community in early-twentieth-century Paterson is from interviews with Berger, Kuiken, Nathans, Paer, and Stetin, and from Lewis, ed., pp. 4–30.

executive offices: The sketch of the thriving mill and commercial district of the era is drawn from interviews with the above and from Waraske, *PN,* June 21, 1971.

"No Quota Here!": Lewis, ed., p. 8.

Rose was the eldest: Biographical information on Rose is from interviews with Horwitz, Morganstein, Paer, Alan Sergy, Bruce Sergy, Sam (Sandy) Sergy, Stillman, and Sylvia Streit, and from the "Petition for Naturalization" of Rose's brother, Sam Gutin.

three hundred mills: Dubofsky, p. 264.

"steam so thick": Most, *BR*, September 30, 1973.

"less liable to labor troubles": Scranton, ed., p. 137.

four-loom system: For background on the origins of the strike, see especially Golin, the most authoritative and only book-length treatment. Other helpful works include Dubofsky, chapter 11; Haywood, pp. 261–277; Kornbluh, ed., chapter 7; and Scranton, ed.

"working clothes": These are Haywood's words, quoted in Lukas, p. 233.

"One Big Union": For background on the IWW, see Dubofsky, Flynn, Haywood, Kornbluh, ed., and Zieger.

"[coming] out of the West": Zieger p. 184.

"dropped its seed here": Dubofsky, p. 269.

"to starve fighting": Ibid.

"sledge hammer blows": Lukas, p. 220.

"disorderly conduct": Zieger, p. 187.

"Why chief": Dubofsky, p. 277.

"marred by only": Quoted in Golin, pp. 81–82. Other accounts of Flag Day appear in Haywood, p. 262, Kornbluh, ed., p. 201, and Zieger, p. 189.

"War in Paterson": The best account of the pageant and of Reed's involvement with the strikers is his biographer's: Rosenstone, pp. 117–132. Also useful are Flynn's recollections, "The Truth about the Paterson Strike," reprinted in Kornbluh, ed., pp. 214–226, and Golin, pp. 157–178, who takes exception to the historical consensus that the failed pageant undermined the strike. Golin argues that the pageant succeeded by bringing much-needed publicity in New York and that, in turn, "[drew] additional support to the hungry strikers" (p. 177).

more poetic: The quotes from the *Times* and the *World* are included in Kornbluh, ed., p. 212.

"Go to Haywood": Golin, p. 106.

"The latter fervidly": Gregory Mason, "Industrial War in Paterson," *Outlook*, June 7, 1913, p. 286. Cited in Scranton, ed., p. 155, n. 22.

"crust of bread": Kornbluh, ed., p. 221.

"stampede of hungry": Ibid., p. 224.

CHAPTER THREE: HIGH, WIDE AND HANDSOME

Sources

Books

American Social History Project, *Who Built America?;* Leuchtenberg, *The Perils of Prosperity;* McCullough, *Truman;* McElvaine, ed., *Down & Out;* McElvaine, ed., *The Great Depression;* Moskin, *Mr. Truman's War;* Norwood, *About Paterson;* Piven and Cloward, *Regulating the Poor;* Schlesinger, *The Crisis of the Old Order;* Scranton, ed., *Silk City;* Zinn, *A People's History of the United States.*

Newspaper Articles
E. A. Smyk, "Paterson Heralded Hoover's Campaign," *NJH&N,* September 27, 1992.
Smyk, "Hamilton Hotel's Glorious Heyday," *NJH&N,* February 28, 1993.
Smyk, "N.J. Played Role in Radio's Early Growth," *NJH&N,* April 18, 1993.
Smyk, "Area Was Vitalized by WWI," *NJH&N,* November 7, 1993.
Smyk, "Back on the Home Front," *NJH&N,* June 5, 1994.

Documents
City of Paterson, Division of Health, Office of Vital Statistics, death certificate for Samuel Sergey, June 7, 1929.

Interviews
Arnold Berger, Irving (Zeke) Bromberg, Phil Chase, Milton Cohen, Charles Conti, Hattie Beck Feit, Richard Florio, Esther Gerber, Ruby Goldstein, Abe Jaffee, Stanley Kushner, Morris Paer, Elsie Lesnick Poppe, Sol Stetin.

Notes:
"We covered the entire": Kushner interview and letter to the editor of *NYT,* August 16, 1997.
"easy, quick, adventurous": Quoted in Leuchtenberg, p. 269.
Unemployment had decreased: Zinn, p. 373.
other heavily industrial: Leuchtenberg, p. 179.
stocks surged 110 points: Ibid., p. 243.
"roulette wheel": Schlesinger, p. 68.
"Quit knocking": Norwood, p. 59.
"rush down the street": Smyk column, April 18, 1993.
Paterson's smart set: Smyk column, February 28, 1993.
"unsightly lot": The description is from a 1921 prospectus cited in Smyk, op cit.
"magnificent building": Ibid.
industrial production: Leuchtenberg, p. 179.
"fundamentally unsound": Zinn, p. 377.
only 7 percent: Schlesinger, p. 112.
silk industry: For further reading on the decline of silk in Paterson, see Scranton, ed.
Great Depression: For a good account of the era, see McElvaine, ed., *The Great Depression,* and its companion, *Down & Out in the Great Depression.*
feelish feverish: Biographical material on Sam Sergy's last weeks is drawn from interviews with Berger, Gerber, Goldstein, and Paer, and from Sergy's death certificate.
"looked the other way": This source requested anonymity.
tunnel operations: Others who discussed Prohibition in Paterson with the author included Berger, Florio, and Jaffee.
double the figure: Schlesinger, pp. 171, 248.
"telephone rates": McElvaine, ed., *Great Depression,* p. 79, and Schlesinger, pp. 173–174.

value of the city's: Only a few years earlier, during a whistle-stop tour in September 1928 in his presidential campaign against the Democratic governor of New York, Alfred E. Smith, Hoover enjoyed an enthusiastic reception in Paterson. A crowd of more than fifteen thousand turned out at the county courthouse, where the candidate was presented with a large, locally woven silk flag. (Smyk, September 27, 1992.)

apple sellers: Quoted in American Social History Project, p. 319.

In lieu: Piven and Cloward, p. 109.

"a quicker way": Quoted in McElvaine, ed., *Down & Out*, p. 43.

"always desperate": Biographical material on Lesnick was drawn primarily from interviews with Poppe and Bromberg, as well as from interviews with Jaffee and Cohen.

"Mrs. Average Citizen": *PEN*, July 15, 1950.

"Rubber scrap": Smyk, June 5, 1994.

New York Times: Cited in Moskin, p. 345.

"Lipstick-smeared": *PEN*, July 15, 1950.

National Manufacturing: Bromberg.

Lesnick pointed out: Cohen.

CHAPTER FOUR: THE WORLD OF TOMORROW

Sources

Books
American Social History Project, *Who Built America?*; Bright, *The Electric-Lamp Industry*; Cox, *A Century of Light*; Gelernter, *1939: The Lost World of the Fair*; Harrison, ed., *Dawn of a New Day*.

Film
The World of Tomorrow, narrated by Jason Robards. Buffalo, N.Y.: Media Study, 1986.

Magazine Articles
"The Show Goes on at New York," *Business Week*, April 29, 1939. p. 17.
"What Shows Pulled at the Fair," *Business Week*, November 4, 1939, p. 22.

Newspaper Articles
"Cosmic Rays Start Brilliant Display," *NYT*, May 1, 1939.
"President Opens Fair as a Symbol of Peace," *NYT*, May 1, 1939.

Newsletters and Pamphlets
Focus on GE Stock, June 1997.
100 Years of Progress for People Worldwide: GE, 1878–1978, in the author's possession courtesy of General Electric corporate communications, Fairfield, Conn.

Documents

United States of America v. *General Electric Company et al.*, Civil Action no. 2590, *Complaint*, December 9, 1942.
Hearings Before the Committee on Patents, U.S. Senate, 77th Cong., 2d sess., on S. 2303 and S. 2491, Government Printing Office, Washington, D.C., part 9, August 18, 1942.

Notes

"number 1 hit": Gelernter, p. 25. See also pp. 11, 34 for more on Futurama.
to serve mankind: Harrison, ed., p. 36.
"soundly sold": *Business Week*, November 4, 1939, p. 22.
"as bright as day": "Cosmic Rays Start Brilliant Display," *NYT*, May 1, 1939.
"Fair's major contributions": *Business Week*, April 29, 1939, p. 17.
"Visible for miles": Cited in Harrison, ed., p. 46.
"cornerstone of control": Bright, p. 458.
"increasingly close relations": Cited in *100 Years of Progress for People Worldwide*, p. 6.
General Electric epitomized: Material on the company's origins is from *100 Years of Progress*, p. 10; Bright, pp. 11–12; *Focus on GE Stock*, June 1997; and American Social History Project, p. 167.
"cold and like sunlight": Bright, p. 384.
"too small": Cox, p. 66.
First commercial rendering: For a clear, concise explanation of the electrical process, see Bright, pp. 395–396.
confidential memo: *Hearings before the Committee on Patents*, Walker Exhibit No. 80, pp. 4943–4946.
"Council of War": *Hearings*, Walker Exhibit No. 21, p. 4848.
"hold down inflation": Ibid., p. 4784. Bone also pointed out (p. 4781) that here was big business assuming the traditional role of labor by opposing technological change. "I hope this is not lost on the public," Bone said, adding, "although these records, like many others, will probably be duly enshrined in libraries and forgotten until earnest souls and diligent seekers after truth dig them up."
"very much disturbed": *Hearings*, Walker Exhibit No. 11, p. 4824.
"[GE] should specifically": Bremicker letter to J. E. Mueller, chairman, Lighting Sales Committee, Edison Electric Institute, May 16, 1939. *Hearings*, Walker Exhibit No. 31, pp. 4855–4856.
"We will oppose": *Hearings*, Walker Exhibit No. 22, pp. 4848–4849; **The GE release:** *Hearings*, Walker Exhibit No. 23, p. 4849.
"an old saying": *Hearings*, Walker Exhibit No. 23, p. 4773.
"dramatic differences": *Hearings*, Walker Exhibit No. 49, pp. 4916–4917.
already being withdrawn: "If it is the one I have in mind," Harrison wrote, "it was loaned temporarily for the Fair exhibit and is already being returned to our Exhibit Shop." Letter of June 1, 1939. *Hearings*, Walker Exhibit No. 50, p. 4917.
Sylvania's share: Figures are from Bright, p. 405.

GE struck back: For more on the suit, see Bright, pp. 418–423.
entered the fray: The antitrust division of the Justice Department brought suit against GE four months later. See U.S. District Court for the District of New Jersey, *United States of America* v. *General Electric Company et al.,* Civil Action No. 2590, *Complaint,* December 9, 1942.
"power shortage": *Hearings,* p. 4766.
"We are threatened": Ibid.
Wartime studies: Bright, pp. 430–431.
sales of the lamps: Ibid., p. 410.

CHAPTER FIVE: EIGHT DAYS A WEEK

Sources

Books
Jackson, *Crabgrass Frontier;* Roth, *American Pastoral;* Williams, *Paterson.*

Newspaper Articles
"Fair Lawn Is One of Fastest Growing Municipalities in State, County," *PEN,* July 15, 1950.
"Meyner Picks Pashman for Superior Court," *PEN,* August 18, 1961.
E. A. Smyk, "Restaurant Exists Just in the Lick of Time," *NJH&N,* September 13, 1992.

Documents
State of New Jersey, Department of Law and Public Safety, Division of State Police, State Bureau of Identification, cumulative arrest record of Archie Sergy, June 22, 1965.
Certificate of Incorporation of UMC, File No. 85147, Passaic County, N.J., Clerk of Court, March 31, 1947.
Paterson Directory: 1948, 1952, 1954. Paterson, N.J.: Price and Lee; *Directory of Major Malls,* 18th ed. Spring Valley, N.Y.: Directory of Major Malls, 1997.

Interviews
Irving (Zeke) Bromberg, Laird Coates, Milt Cohen, Armando DeMauro, Paul H. Einhorn, Ruby Goldstein, Harold Harris, Mollie James, Belle Meyers, Morris Pashman, Joe Santelli, Jules Schwartz, Alan Sergy, Bruce Sergy, Sam (Sandy) Sergy, Joel Steiger, Michael Stein, Sam Stein, Siegfried Steinberger, Irving Stillman, Harold Streit.

Notes
"lid was off": Roth, p. 40.
"Arrested 8-15-32": Sergy's rap sheet from the Paterson Police Department, in the author's possession.

"They went broke": Biographical material on Pearl Sergy is from Sam Stein and his son, Michael Stein.

wire-making machinery: Recollections of Goldman from Cohen, Stein, and Bromberg.

might complicate: Pashman.

"always thought big": Pashman, and Certificate of Incorporation of UMC, March 31, 1947.

"rack job": Santelli, Stillman, and Streit.

Einhorn's blunt manner: Bromberg and Santelli.

"Why don't you look": Harris.

not just his friends: The population decreased from 139,658 in 1940 to 139,423 in 1950. *Paterson Directory: 1952,* p. 16.

the population swelled: *PEN,* July 15, 1950.

"on the nickel": Ibid.

Cape Cod–style: Alan, Bruce, and Sam Sergy

thirty-seven locals: *Paterson Directory: 1952.*

"big sad poppa": From a letter to William Carlos Williams in *Paterson,* p. 211.

celery fields: Author interview with the veteran north Jersey journalist Laird Coates. For the years the malls opened, see *Directory of Major Malls;* for more on suburbanization and its toll on urban America, see especially Kenneth Jackson's superb *Crabgrass Frontier.*

grew at ten times: Cited in Jackson, p. 238.

"Well, come on!": Cohen.

"Who ordered": Cohen.

career in politics: *PEN,* August 18, 1961.

"We're going home": Belle Meyers. Other biographical material on Rube Pashman prior to his days at Universal is from his brother, Morris Pashman, and his brother-in-law, Milt Cohen.

"You would wonder": Edward M. Graf quoted in Smyk, *NJH&N,* September 13, 1992.

hot pumpernickel: Steinberger and Santelli.

"red-carpet life": Meyers.

wined and dined: Among those who described Archie's penchant for entertaining were Sam Stein, Harris, Cohen, and Morris Pashman.

"Don't ask me": Schwartz.

CHAPTER SIX: FARRELL DOBB'S VISION

Sources

Books

American Social History Project, *Who Built America?;* Boyer and Morais, *Labor's Untold Story;* Brill, *The Teamsters;* Foner, *History of the Labor Movement in the United States;* James and James, *Hoffa and the Teamsters;* Kennedy, *The Enemy*

Within; Lichtenstein, *The Most Dangerous Man in Detroit;* Moldea, *The Hoffa Wars;* Mollenhoff, *Tentacles of Power;* Sheridan, *The Fall and Rise of Jimmy Hoffa;* Sloane, *Hoffa.*

Magazine Articles

Paul Jacobs, "The World of Jimmy Hoffa—I," *The Reporter,* January 24, 1957, p. 13.
Paul Jacobs, "The World of Jimmy Hoffa—II," *The Reporter,* February 7, 1957, p. 10.
Lester Velie, "Six Days That Reshaped the Labor World," *Reader's Digest,* March 1958, p. 116.
A. H. Raskin, "Why They Cheer for Hoffa," *NYT Magazine,* November 9, 1958, p. 15.
"Pretty Simple Life," *Time,* August 31, 1959, p. 14.

Newspaper Articles

"Hoffa Men Begin a Drive to Purge His Foes in Union," *NYT,* October 1, 1957.
"Coast Delegates Switch to Hoffa," *NYT,* October 2, 1957.
"Hoffa's Machine Is Well-Heeled," *NYT,* October 2, 1957.
"Teamsters Convention Rejects Labor's 'Indictment' of Hoffa," *NYT,* October 3, 1957.
"Hoffa Is Elected Teamsters Head; Warns of Battle," *NYT,* October 5, 1957.
"Labor Suspends Teamsters Union; Insists Hoffa Go," *NYT,* October 25, 1957.
"AFL-CIO Ousts Teamsters Union by Vote of 5 to 1," *NYT,* December 7, 1957.

Notes

"I cannot remember": Sheridan, p. 47 (The McClellan Committee hearings began on February 26, 1957, and continued through March 1960. The record includes fifty-eight volumes of testimony and seven reports.)
"dangerous influence": Moldea, p. 81.
"well-nigh incalculable": *Time,* August 31, 1959, p. 14.
"prerequisite" for "advancement": Ibid., p. 15.
"unrefuted . . . evidence": Sloane, p. 88
"personal profit": Moldea, p. 77.
"I'm not afraid": *NYT,* October 3, 1957.
free coffee: *NYT,* October 2, 1957.
"straight to hell": *NYT,* October 1, 1957.
his acceptance speech: The text is printed in *NYT,* October 5, 1957.
recommendation of expulsion: *NYT,* October 25, 1957.
"conspiracy of evil": Kennedy, p. 159.
"bonds of unity": Foner, vol. 2, pp. 141–142.
two Teamsters organizations: For concise histories of the formation of the IBT, see Moldea, pp. 18–19; Brill, pp. 372–373; James and James, pp. 13–17; and Sloane, pp. 10–12.
"tough days": The member was Frank Fitzsimmons, who, like Hoffa, rose from Local 299 to the presidency of the IBT. He is quoted in Moldea, p. 21.

Ford Hunger March: Lichtenstein, pp. 31–32.

thirty-two cents an hour: Material on Hoffa's boyhood is drawn from Sloane, pp. 3–9, and Brill, p. 23.

twenty-two-year-old rabble-rouser: Moldea, pp. 23–24, and Sloane, p. 14.

single small local: Brill, p. 374.

"a union button": Jacobs, *The Reporter,* January 24, 1957, p. 16.

"island of truckdrivers": Ibid. This and the following quotation are excerpted by Jacobs from a Local 574 newspaper.

"leapfrogging": The technique is described in Jacobs, ibid.; Sloane, p. 19; and Brill, pp. 376–377. The membership figures are cited in Sloane, p. 19. For more on Dobbs, see his memoir, *Teamster Politics* (New York: Monad Press, 1975).

described as "rubbish": Jacobs, ibid.

"rather small potatoes": The scene is drawn from a composite of details provided by Boyer and Morais, p. 292, and American Social History Project, pp. 378–379. For a further account of the convention, see Melvyn Dubofsky and Warren Van Tine, *John L. Lewis: A Biography* (New York: Quadrangle, 1977), pp. 217–221.

decisive blow: Boyer and Morais, p. 295.

successfully emulated: For more on Beck's background, see Jacobs, *The Reporter,* January 24, 1957, p. 16. The IBT average annual membership figures from 1903 to 1965 are compiled in James and James, p. 14.

final ignominy: American Social History Project, p. 435, and Moldea, p. 33.

"Treat 'em right": Raskin, *NYT Magazine,* November 9, 1958, p. 79.

In Seattle: Moldea, p. 70.

rigged his election: Sloane, p. 91.

$20,000 payoff: Mollenhoff, p. 248. Mollenhoff, a reporter for the *Des Moines Register,* won a Pulitzer Prize for his inquiry into labor racketeering. It was he, according to a letter from Robert F. Kennedy reprinted in the book, who "more than anyone else [was] responsible" for the McClellan Committee's subsequent investigation of Hoffa.

"strategic importance": Mollenhoff, p. 243.

"dispensed with supplication": *NYT,* December 7, 1957.

"bell the cat": *Reader's Digest,* March 1958.

"call the roll": Ibid.

"didn't build us": *NYT,* December 7, 1957.

CHAPTER SEVEN: "ALL HELL BROKE LOOSE"

Sources

Books
Brill, *The Teamsters;* Maas, *The Valachi Papers;* Moldea, *The Hoffa Wars;* Sloane, *Hoffa.*

Magazine Articles
Paul Jacobs, "The World of Jimmy Hoffa—I," *The Reporter,* January 24, 1957, p. 13.
James P. Quigel Jr., "Charged with Electricity: The IUE Archives Project," *Journal of the Rutgers University Libraries,* vol. 57, nos. 1 and 2, pp. 40–63.

Newspaper Articles
"Union Favors Cited in Jersey Inquiry," *NYT,* January 28, 1959.
"Teamsters Threatened Children, Jersey Scanveger Tells Inquiry," *NYT,* January 29, 1959.
"Jersey Judge Seeks Arrest of Unionist," *NYT,* March 3, 1959.
"Teamster Secty-Treas. Disappears," *PEN,* June 9, 1961.
"Castellito Case Recalls Clifton Man's Disappearance," *PEN,* June 9, 1961.
"Police Arrest Four in Duralite Flare-Up," *PMC,* September 7, 1961.
"Duralite Pickets, Police Clash . . . ," *PMC,* September 8, 1961.
"Duralite Strike Flames into Riot; Scores Hurt," *PMC,* September 14, 1961.
"IUE Denies Red Charge by Duralite," *PMC,* September 18, 1961.
"1,200 Attend Dinner for Universal Workers," *PMC,* November 9, 1961.
"AFL-CIO Votes to Continue Ban on Hoffa's Union," *NYT,* October 11, 1961.
"Strike Vote by Teamster Local Is Set," *PMC,* January 19, 1962.
"Teamsters, Universal Agree on New Contract," *PEN,* January 29, 1962.
"City of Hope Cites Ardis Tonight," *BR,* October 28, 1967.

Documents
"The Duralite Story—Your Questions Answered," undated pamphlet on file at IUE-A.
Leaflets circulated during the Duralite and Universal campaigns are on file at IUE-A.
"Organized Crime Links to the Waste Disposal Industry," *Hearing before the Subcommittee on Oversight and Investigations of the Committee on Energy and Commerce,* 97th Cong., 1st sess., U.S. Government Printing Office, Washington, D.C., serial no. 97-32, May 28, 1981.

Interviews
Michael Ardis Jr., Burt Caplan, Phil Chase, Paul H. Einhorn, Wallace Eisenberg, Mollie James, Nicholas Kourambis, Angelo Landron, Joe Santelli, Sigfried Steinberger, Sol Stetin.

Notes
independent union: A framed copy of the Local 945 charter is displayed at the union hall in Wayne, New Jersey.
turf battles: Jacobs, *The Reporter,* January 24, 1957, p. 14.
"What we want": Ibid.
under threats: *NYT,* January 29, 1959.
"keep on his good": *NYT,* January 28, 1959; and "Organized Crime Links" hearing, May 28, 1981, p. 16.

black Cadillac abandoned: *NYT,* March 3, 1959; and *PEN,* June 9, 1961.

"stability and security": Quoted in "Organized Crime Links" hearing, p. 16.

Vito Genovese's crime family: For more on the "family" and the Cosa Nostra of the era in New Jersey and New York, see Maas.

taking bribes: Ibid., and Moldea, p. 112.

"nothing to eat": *BR,* October 28, 1967. Other biographical material on Ardis is from an interview with his son, Michael Ardis Jr., and newspaper articles published after Ardis's disappearance in June 1971.

Duralite was originally located: For the chronology of Duralite's move from the Bronx to Clifton, the author relied principally on a letter of January 17, 1962, titled "Statement of Facts," that IUE Local 485 counsel Irving Abramson wrote to James Carey, IUE international president. The letter is on file in IUE-A.

"having trouble": Affidavit of Sol Stetin filed in October 1961 in support of charges before the National Labor Relations Board by IUE Local 485 against Duralite and Teamsters Local 945. On file in IUE-A.

"shopping around": Stetin.

"not interested": Stetin.

"asking for trouble": Affidavit of Joseph Opilla filed September 19, 1961, in support of charges before the National Labor Relations Board by IUE Local 485 against Duralite and Teamsters Local 945. On file in IUE-A.

"All the employees": Leaflet reproduced as Exhibit A in support of charges before the National Labor Relations Board by IUE Local 485 against Duralite and Teamsters Local 945. This and all other IUE leaflets cited in this chapter are on file in IUE-A.

"Not wanted": IUE leaflet of September 7, 1961.

Strollo reassigned: Brill, p. 133 (Brill includes a chapter on Provenzano, pp. 121–154); **"soldier" to *capo*:** Moldea, p. 112.

"puffed eyelids": Quoted in Brill, p. 129.

"capable of atrocities": Brill, p. 11.

one of the largest: Sloane, p. 167.

"paper locals": Brill, p. 134.

"Hoffa himself feared": Sloane, p. 365.

under indictment: "Organized Crime Links" hearing, p. 16, and Moldea, p. 112.

three jobs together: Brill, p. 135.

ordered the murder: Castellito's disappearance and background were reported in *PEN,* June 9, 1961. For more on Provenzano's involvement, see Moldea, p. 114, and Brill, pp. 137–138.

Provenzano was indicted: Sloane, p. 397.

"accident-prone": Brill, pp. 131–132.

"all hell broke": Description of the riot is drawn from Eisenberg and from *PMC,* September 14, 1961.

"Communist-dominated": *PMC,* September 18, 1961.

rich irony: *Journal of the Rutgers University Libraries,* p. 48.

"IUE News": Leaflet of July 18, 1961.

"the bosses' union": IUE leaflet of July 19, 1961.
Wages at Universal: *PEN,* January 29, 1962.
"do-nothing dues": IUE leaflet of August 8, 1961.
"Were they in Universal": Ibid.
"Again today": IUE leaflet of September 7, 1961.
"hoodlum tactics": IUE leaflet of September 8, 1961.
"These animals": IUE leaflet of September 11, 1961.
"$1000 Reward": IUE leaflet of October 23, 1961.
"False Victory": Teamsters leaflet of October 26, 1961. All Teamsters leaflets cited are also on file at IUE-A.
"LEARN THE TRUTH!": Teamsters leaflet, undated.
"IN GOOD COMPANY": IUE leaflet, undated.
"RED FOR BREAD": IUE leaflet, undated, most likely distributed on October 30 or October 31, 1961.
printed verbatim: *PMC,* November 9, 1961.
"You can bet": The Teamster spoke on the condition of anonymity.
"disorganizing the organized": *El Observador,* November 11, 1961, on file in IUE-A.
Meany remained firm: *NYT,* October 11, 1961.
"Negro Union Head": *NYT,* November 12, 1961.
"Any impartial observer": Teamsters leaflet of November 13, 1961.
"get these benefits": *PMC,* January 19, 1962.
came to terms: *PMC,* January 29, 1962.

CHAPTER EIGHT: BISCUITS AND BOND ISSUES

Sources

Books
Branch, *Parting the Waters;* Cobb, *The Selling of the South;* Dittmer, *Local People;* Havard, ed., *The Changing Politics of the South;* Oshinsky, *Worse Than Slavery;* Salter Jr., *Jackson, Mississippi;* Sherrill, *Gothic Politics in the Deep South;* Silver, *Mississippi: The Closed Society;* Whalen, *The Longest Debate.*

Newspaper Articles
"Selling Segregation," *WSJ,* December 4, 1957.
"Refinery Said Triumph for Race Segregation," *JDN,* September 18, 1961.
"Two Industries Coming South," *C-L,* February 24, 1962.
"Mississippi's Industrial Climate," *Chicago Daily News,* December 20, 1962.
"U.S. Court Denies Negro-Voter Suit," *NYT,* April 2, 1963.
"Looking Back over the Years," *MC,* March 21, 1974.
"Stanley Berry: Simpson County's Living History," Orley Hood column, *C-L,* March 13, 1996.

Speeches

"Balancing Agriculture with Industry," the address of Hon. Hugh L. White before the annual convention of the Mississippi Press Association at Gulfport, June 12, 1936. BAWI subject file, MDAH.

Governor Barnett's address to the Agricultural and Industrial Board of February 8, 1962. Minute Book No. 70, Mississippi Agricultural and Industrial Board, RG 76, Nos. 103 and 104, MDAH.

Documents

"Traffic Survey, Mendenhall, Mississippi," prepared by the Traffic and Planning Division, Mississippi State Highway Department, February 15, 1959. MDAH.

Mississippi, an industrial recruitment booklet of the Mississippi Agricultural and Industrial Board. Undated, but published during the Barnett administration, 1960–1964, MDAH.

State of Mississippi, Sovereignty Commission Files, Report of Robert C. Thomas, investigator, July 19, 1960. Document No. 2-90-16, MDAH.

U.S. Bureau of the Census, *Census of Population, 1960,* vol. 1, *Characteristics of the Population,* part 26, Mississippi, pp. 26–13.

U.S. District Court, Southern District of Mississippi, Jackson Division, *Fiering et al.* v. *Universal Manufacturing Corporation et al.,* Civil Action No. 3682 (J)(C), Deposition of Reuben Pashman, April 14–15, 1965.

Interviews

Irving (Zeke) Bromberg, Paul Einhorn, Archie Magee, G. O. Parker Jr., Carl Reiter, Mrs. Murray Reiter, Frank Smith, Siegfried Steinberger.

Notes

"another milestone": *C-L,* February 24, 1962.

"long and prosperous": *SCN,* December 19, 1963. Further description of the opening ceremonies is drawn from interviews with Steinberger and Frank Smith, and from *MC,* December 12 and December 19, 1963.

"Balance Agriculture": Unless otherwise noted, material on the early years of BAWI is drawn from Cobb, a superb account of the history of Southern industry. For more on prewar Mississippi, see especially chapter 1.

"efficient and intelligent": White's remarks are excerpted from his address to the Mississippi Press Association, "Balancing Agriculture with Industry," June 12, 1936, pp. 6–12.

"Instead of utilizing": Cobb, pp. 42–43.

"a mind relatively innocent": Silver, p. 43.

"bone dumb": Sherrill, p. 199.

"Fish and Game": Ibid., p. 200.

"Negro is different": Ibid., p. 189.

"no one's surprise": Silver, p. 44.

took Barnett's bait: Background on Reiter is from Mrs. Murray Reiter, Carl Reiter, and Frank Smith.

"six- or eight-feet": Pashman deposition, April 14–15, 1965, p. 49.

especially female labor: Pashman said the consultant's report discussed the "availability of female labor" because that was "the biggest item for us." Pashman deposition, p. 147.

mock advertisement: Oshinsky, pp. 233–234.

"breach of the peace": Ibid., p. 234.

"destination doom": For a brief discussion of Faulkner's view of Parchman, see Oshinsky, pp. 226–232.

"killed before breakfast": *WSJ,* December 4, 1957.

"Consider him instead": Cobb, p. 92.

"Mr. White": Bromberg and Einhorn described Barnett's visit to Paterson.

"Who says segregation": *JDN,* September 18, 1961.

"prudent businessman": *Chicago Daily News,* December 20, 1962.

"won't consider expanding": Cobb, p. 135.

"rapid industrial": Barnett described his standard practice in recruiting sessions in a speech before the Agricultural and Industrial Board of February 8, 1962.

"native-born": *Mississippi* industrial recruitment booklet, p. 36.

"Strongly ingrained": Ibid.

well connected: The Highway Commission member: John Smith; the state senator: Jack Pace; the governor's former roommate: G. O. Parker, pastor of First Baptist Church, Magee. Parker's son, G. O. Jr., was editor of the *Magee Courier.*

Mendenhall enjoyed: For capsule versions of the county's history, see: "Looking Back over the Years," *MC,* March 21, 1974; "Traffic Survey, Mendenhall, Mississippi," February 15, 1959; and "Stanley Berry: Simpson County's Living History," *C-L,* March 13, 1996.

Mendenhall reigned supreme: Bureau of the Census. *Census of Population, 1960.*

"With the support": *MC,* March 8, 1962.

"Roi-Tans": G. O. Parker Jr. also provided details of the trip.

"greatest opportunity": *MC,* April 26, 1962; SCN, April 26, 1962.

"blue chip"; "I can remember": *SCN,* May 3, 1962.

"only the beginning": *MC,* May 24, 1962.

"overjoyed": The telegram was reproduced on the front page of *SCN,* May 17, 1962.

voting-age white population: *NYT,* April 1, 1963.

"There's a fire": Branch, *Parting,* p. 723.

"trampling on the rights": *NYT,* April 2, 1963.

"I shall stand": Ibid.

imprisoned since Friday: Branch, *Parting,* p. 721.

bric-a-brac: Material on the sit-in and the Jackson movement is drawn from Dittmer, pp. 161–163, and Salter Jr., chapter 7.

"just and moral": Branch, *Parting,* p. 822.

"heart of the question": Whalen, p. xx.

off-the-record: Steinberger. A note in Havard, ed., p. 483, also mentions that the BAWI program made these agreements with "many of the new industries coming into towns."

a sniper's rifle: Branch, *Parting*, p. 825.
NEGRO KILLED: *SCN*, November 9, 1961.
"helps the whites": State Sovereignty Commission report of July 19, 1960.
"I doubt if": Ibid.
Few blacks even tried: Ibid.
"Sergy got a better": Johnson made the remark at Universal's dedication ceremonies. *MC*, December 19, 1963.
'DREAM COME TRUE': *SCN*, December 12, 1963.

CHAPTER NINE: WORKING FOR THE RAILROAD

Sources

Book
Brooks, *The Go-Go Years*.

Documents
Philadelphia & Reading Corp. annual reports for 1961–1967.

Magazine Article
"Finding the Right Combination," *Business Week*, August 21, 1965, pp. 49–52.

Interviews
Henry Berenstein, Robert C. Courboin, Paul Einhorn, Chestina Hughes, Howard A. (Mickey) Newman, Alan Sergy, Bruce Sergy, Sam (Sandy) Sergy, Siegfried Steinberger.

Notes
Aaronson lived: Biographical material on Aronson is from his son-in-law, Henry Berenstein, along with Alan Sergy, who worked briefly in Aronson's brokerage house.
P&R's ledger: *Business Week*, August 21, 1965.
The younger Newman: Newman.
"ingesting whatever": Brooks, p. 155.
Newman had dug: Philadelphia & Reading Corp. annual report for 1963.
"favorable opportunities": Ibid.
sale barely registered: *WSJ*, January 6, 1964.
"Our joining": *SCN*, January 16, 1964.
earnings had plummeted: *Business Week*, August 21, 1965.
"We just purchased": Hughes.
"fight 'em": Courboin.

CHAPTER TEN: HANDBILLS FROM HEAVEN

Sources

Books
Branch, *Pillar of Fire;* Cagin and Dray, *We Are Not Afraid;* Silver, *Mississippi: The Closed Society;* Whalen, *The Longest Debate.*

Magazine Articles
"Organizing in Mississippi," part 1, *The Electrical Workers' Journal,* March 1965; part 2, April 1965.
"Move Ahead Goal Met in Mississippi," *The Electrical Workers' Journal,* November 1966.

Documents
U.S. District Court, Southern District of Mississippi, Jackson Division, *Fiering et al.* v. *Universal Manufacturing Corporation et al.* Civil Action No. 3682 (J)(C), Deposition of Reuben Pashman, April 14–15, 1965.
National Labor Relations Board: Decision, Order, and Direction of Second Election, Universal Manufacturing Corporation of Mississippi and International Brotherhood of Electrical Workers, AFL-CIO-CLC, Petitioner. Case No. 15-RC-3061, February 14, 1966.
U.S. District Court, Southern District of Mississippi, Jackson Division, *E. C. Fiering, Wallace G. Wickliff et al.* v. *Universal Manufacturing Corporation of Mississippi et al.,* Civil Action No. 3682 (J)(C), January 20, 1965.
"Investigation of the racial situation in Simpson County and Rankin County." State of Mississippi, Sovereignty Commission Files, Report of A. L. Hopkins, investigator, September 15, 1965, Document No. 2-90-41, MDAH.

Interviews
Mildred Andrews, Dorothy Carter, Louis Carter, Robert C. Courboin, Archie Magee, G. O. Parker Jr., Lenon Smith, Siegfried Steinberger, Lloyd Stephens, Frank Thames, Wallace G. Wickliff.

Notes
"By God": Wickliff.
"danger is real": Silver, p. 78.
"even further liberalism": Ibid.
"captive-audience": The meeting is discussed in the Pashman deposition, pp. 102–104, and the substance of Steinberger's remarks was corroborated by Courboin in an interview with the author.
"if the union came in": *Electrical Workers' Journal,* April 1965, p. 19.
"free slice": *MC,* March 19, 1964.
"kind of greenhorns": Pashman deposition, p. 82.

"it's not Christmas": *MC,* March 26, 1964.

"EMPTY, NO JOBS": Ibid.

"until trouble": *Electrical Workers' Journal,* April 1965, p. 20.

questioned about their attitude: Ibid.

threatening employees: NLRB decision, p. 1461, f. 3, February 14, 1966.

Goldwater positively buried: *MC,* November 5, 1964.

half the Northern: Branch, *Pillar of Fire,* p. 522.

"the first Inauguration": Ibid., p. 563.

The three-count complaint: *Fiering, Wickliff et al.* v. *Universal Manufacturing Corporation et al.,* complaint, pp. 6, 9, and *Electrical Workers' Journal,* April 1965, p. 21.

"being invaded": Andrews.

"handbills from heaven": Jewel C. Roberts, *Electrical Workers' Journal,* November 1966.

"scorned, shunned": Ibid.

"several carloads": *Electrical Workers' Journal,* April 1965, p. 21.

sheriff's investigation reached: Ibid.

"faith in the future": *MC,* March 18, 1965.

"Thank you for calling": Affidavit of Julia B. Chadwick, n.d., *Fiering, Wickliff et al.* v. *Universal Manufacturing Corporation et al.*

"red carpet": Pashman deposition, p. 114; **"strictly kosher":** ibid, p. 120; **"don't dislike unions":** ibid., p. 68.

thirty cents an hour: Ibid., p. 150; **"Slight variances":** ibid., p. 152.

"exorbitant" wage demands: *MC* editorial, April 8, 1965.

"production-wise"; "too much confusion": Pashman deposition, p. 55; **"Girls sitting next":** ibid., p. 109.

"What do you want": Steinberger.

IT'S TIME TO THINK!: *MC,* April 15, 1965.

"Have you asked": Excerpts from the leaflets were printed in the NLRB decision, p. 1465.

WHO AIN'T TELLING: *MC,* April 22, 1965.

"laboratory conditions": The union's charge and the regional director's findings were cited in the NLRB decision, pp. 1459–1466.

County News **buried:** *SCN,* February 24, 1966.

Greenwood closed: Branch, *Pillar of Fire,* p. 389.

CLOSED IN DESPAIR: Cagin and Dray, p. 379.

"Frustration reigns supreme": *SCN,* July 9, 1964.

"not one Negro": Mississippi Sovereignty Commission, document No. 2-90-41, September 15, 1965.

Title VII: For the best account of the legislative history of the Civil Rights Act of 1964, see Whalen.

"automatic submarines": *SCN,* December 12, 1963.

CHAPTER ELEVEN: BORDER DREAMS

Sources

Books
Bluestone and Harrison, *The Deindustrialization of America;* Brown and Shue, eds., *The Border That Joins;* Brown et al., *For Richer, For Poorer;* Fernandez, *The United States–Mexico Border;* La Botz, *Democracy in Mexico;* Pastor and Castaneda, *Limits to Friendship.*

Documents
Patricia Wertman, Congressional Research Service Report for Congress, "Tariff Items 907.00 and 806.30 and the Mexican Maquiladoras." Library of Congress, June 8, 1967.
Octaviano Campos Salas, "Inaugural Speech of the Tenth Home Fair, Tijuana, Baja California, August 6, 1965." Included in *"El Sentido Dinamico de El Mexico Economico de Nuestros Dias"* (1965). Obtained from the Benson Latin American History Collection, University of Texas, Austin.

Interviews
Dorothy Carter, Mollie James.

Notes
"did not have enough": For further background on the bracero program, see Garcia Y Griego, "The Importation of Mexican Contract Laborers to the United States, 1942–1964: Antecedents, Operation, and Legacy," chapter 3, pp. 49–98, in Brown and Shue, eds. The quote is from p. 73.
"oust any alien": Ibid., p. 53.
"stop deporting": Ibid., p. 64.
1956 study: Ibid., p. 75. Galarza himself published two books that may be of interest: *Barrio Boy* (Notre Dame, Ind.: University of Notre Dame Press, 1971), an autobiographical account of his boyhood journey from Mexico to the United States; and *Merchants of Labor: The Mexican Bracero Program* (Charlotte/Santa Barbara: McNally and Loftin, 1964).
"When wages": *NYT,* December 9, 1964.
one final reprieve: *NYT,* January 30, 1963.
"stave off": Brown and Shue, eds., p. 76.
Large-scale agriculture: Browne et al., p. 98, n. 17.
second biggest oil exporter: Ibid.; Pastor and Castaneda, p. 218.
Díaz fled: For a concise history of the U.S. role in undermining the post-Díaz government, see Pastor and Castaneda, pp. 29–30.
formed PEMEX: La Botz, p. 53. Chapter 3, "From Mexican Revolution to One-Party State," is a fine introduction to the conditions leading to the return of foreign investment to the country.

Cárdenas retired: Browne et al., p. 12.

"intended to promote": La Botz, p. 55.

"The farm problem": *WSJ,* November 12, 1964.

"a meal, a girl": *WSJ,* January 21, 1964.

"a new phase": *NYT,* July 26, 1965.

"alternative to Hong Kong": *WSJ,* May 25, 1967.

"cordial cooperation": *NYT,* July 26, 1965.

free-trade conditions: For more on the legal structure of the BIP, see Fernandez, p. 135.

"export-platforms": For a thorough history of these tariff items, see Wertman, Congressional Research Service Report for Congress, June 8, 1967. For a cogent analysis of the impact of these tariff items during the 1960s and 1970s, see Bluestone and Harrison, pp. 132, 171–172.

obra barata": From Campos Salas's "Inaugural Speech of the Tenth Home Fair, Tijuana, Baja California, August 6, 1965," p. 78. The speech is reprinted in *"El Sentido Dinamico de El Mexico Economico de Nuestros Dias"* (1965). Obtained from the Benson Latin American History Collection, University of Texas, Austin.

"potential of cheap labor": *WSJ,* May 25, 1967.

"Inexhaustible labor supply": The pamphlet was published by the Development Authority for Tucson's Expansion and cited in *WSJ,* February 21, 1969.

up and running: Figures are from Fernandez, p. 134.

CHAPTER TWELVE: LEVERAGED LIVES

Sources

Books

Barlett and Steele, *America: What Went Wrong?;* Bruck, *The Predators' Ball;* Fromson, ed., *The Gaga Years;* Madrick, *Taking America;* Stewart, *Den of Thieves.*

Magazine Articles

"The Last Fundamentalist?" *Forbes,* November 27, 1989, p. 132.

"They Do Repair Jobs on Small Companies," *Business Week,* February 17, 1973, p. 50.

Documents

Northwest Industries Inc., annual reports for 1968–1979.

"Organized Crime Links to the Waste Disposal Industry," *Hearing Before the Subcommittee on Oversight and Investigations of the Committee on Energy and Commerce,* 97th Cong., 1st Sess., U.S. Government Printing Office, Washington, D.C., serial no. 97-32, May 28, 1981.

MagneTek, Inc. Prospectus, June 3, 1986. Filed with the Securities and Exchange Commission, Washington, D.C.; MagneTek SEC Form 10-K, 1987.

Interviews

Irving (Zeke) Bromberg, Louis Carter, Carmelo Colon, Paul Einhorn, William Farley, Andrew G. Galef, Harold Harris, J. Ira Harris, Ben W. Heineman, Michael Himmel, Chestina Hughes, Mollie James, William J. Lyons, Otto Payonzeck, Joe Santelli, Sam (Sandy) Sergy, Siegfried Steinberger.

Notes

union also won: *PMC,* October 30, 1968.

"going to fold": *PMC,* September 28, 1967.

cardiac arrest: Einhorn, Santelli, Sam Sergy, and Archie's obituary, *PEN,* November 5, 1968.

"We're all working": Bromberg.

"offset the weaknesses": *Time,* June 23, 1967.

more than $300 million: *NYT,* September 19, 1967.

an "excellent reflection": *WSJ,* September 19, 1967.

"broad policy": Quoted in the Northwest Industries annual report for 1977, a ten-year retrospective.

another banner year: Northwest annual report for 1979.

"no criminal record": The report, "Portrait of a Corrupt Union—Teamster Local 945," was prepared by PROD, a Teamsters dissident group, and introduced by Lt. Col. Justin Dintino of the N.J. State Police into the record of the "Organized Crime Links" hearing. For the reference to Campisano, see p. 17.

Cariello joined Local: Ibid.

"a long line": Ibid.; **appointed to his job:** Dintino testimony, "Organized Crime Links" hearing, p. 24.

police believed: Stated in "Portrait of a Corrupt Union," "Organized Crime Links," p. 19.

several arrests: Dintino testimony, "Organized Crime Links," pp. 24–25.

"clutching her throat": Cited in "Portrait of a Corrupt Union," "Organized Crime Links," p. 16.

"gangland-execution style": "Organized Crime Links," p. 24.

racketeering, soliciting and receiving: For a lengthy investigative report on the scheme, see *WSJ,* September 14, 1977, p. 1. For details on the indictment, see *WSJ,* October 6, 1978. For the conviction, see *WSJ,* May 7, 1979, and *NYT,* May 6, 1979.

avoided jail: For more on Franconero's dealings, see *WSJ,* September 14, 1977; for his plea bargain and death, see *PN,* March 3, 1981, and March 10, 1981.

"don't want to hear": *PN,* October 17, 1980.

"I got two kids": *PN,* October 22, 1980.

Rizzo was a nephew: Dintino testimony, "Organized Crime Links," p. 24.

"ongoing probe": *PN,* October 22, 1980.

"We're glad": *PN,* October 25, 1980.

"they don't matter": *SCN,* February 19, 1981.

"My Fellow Employees": Reprinted in *SCN,* February 12, 1981.

"quit the campaign": *BR,* October 25, 1983.

"very fair": *BR,* October 30, 1983.

"agreed in principle": *NYT,* June 27, 1984.

"corporate dinosaurs": Herb Greenberg, "Conglomerates Going to Pieces," *Chicago Tribune,* January 20, 1985.

"full circle": Ibid.

"wonderful thing": *NYT,* May 7, 1984.

"golden parachute": *NYT,* May 25, 1984.

fifty dollars a share: *NYT,* September 21, 1984.

"terminated": *NYT,* September 27, 1984.

"hell with it": *NYT,* January 29, 1985.

stock plunging: On January 9, the stock dropped $3.87 to close at $47.50. *NYT,* January 10, 1985.

Buffett bought: *Chicago Tribune,* March 22, 1985.

leading lights: His role in the Esmark buyout was cited in *NYT,* May 25, 1984.

adoring splash: For an exemplary specimen, see "Bill Farley Has a Dream Machine," *Fortune,* May 27, 1985. Other stories from which are drawn the lines of Farley's thumbnail biography: "Northwest Industries: The Acid Test for Bill Farley's Offbeat Style," *Business Week,* September 9, 1985; "The Buyout Man," *U.S. News & World Report,* January 26, 1987; "Look Who Wants to Be President," *Fortune,* November 23, 1987; and "Taking Over in a One-Company Town," *NYT,* March 5, 1989.

"distinctly minor league": "Taking in Each Other's Laundry," *Forbes,* November 19, 1984.

"We get up at four A.M.": Quote cited in James Grant, "Junk Debunked," *Grant's Interest Rate Observer,* September 24, 1984, and reprinted in Fromson, ed., p. 31.

"almost literally buy": "Pyramid Power," *Forbes,* January 27, 1986.

"right product": "Taking in Each Other's Laundry," *Forbes,* November 19, 1984.

"pay the price": Bruck, p. 11.

Farley Industries went from: *Fortune,* May 27, 1985.

1984 sales: *NYT,* April 11, 1985.

"At only forty-two": *Fortune,* May 27, 1985.

"pinch myself": Ibid.

"great respect and affection": *Chicago Tribune,* April 11, 1985.

"exciting time": *NYT,* April 11, 1985.

lion's share: *Business Week,* September 9, 1985.

"Greed is all right": The quotation was first reported in the *San Francisco Chronicle,* May 19, 1986, and cited in Stewart, p. 261.

Milken did not originate: For more on Drexel's early use of LBOs, see Bruck, pp. 99–100.

"a failure": Biographical material from *Forbes,* November 27, 1989.

"turnaround specialist": *Business Week,* February 17, 1973.

Litton devoured: Madrick, p. 37.

"Magnetics Group": The transaction merited little coverage. On July 10, 1984, the *Wall Street Journal* mentioned it in three brief paragraphs deep inside the paper; the *Los Angeles Times* on July 7 published a single forlorn sentence in its "Business in Brief" digest of corporate press releases.

spare him nearly: *Chicago Tribune,* January 15, 1986.

"did what Milken": Stewart, p. 122.

received advisory fees: MagneTek, Inc. Prospectus, June 3, 1986, p. 29.

piggy bank: Ibid., pp. 28–29.

"unaffiliated parties": Ibid., p. 29.

highest-paid: *Forbes,* November 27, 1989.

bought a house: When Galef was seeking to acquire Warnaco, he granted a rare interview at home to the *Los Angeles Times,* which reported on April 15, 1986, the details of his house and neighborhood. The *Forbes* profile of November 27, 1989, also addressed his grandiose surroundings, but Galef did not speak to the magazine's reporter, other than a terse "I don't give interviews. The record speaks for itself."

filled the walls; tooling around town: *Galef* v. *Galef,* Further Judgment on Reserved Issues, Case no. D191067, Los Angeles County Superior Court, November 30, 1988.

"first-class hotels": The material is from Billie M. Galef's 1987 divorce petition and was reported in Barlett and Steele, p. 33.

added title: MagneTek, Inc. SEC Form 10-K, 1987.

CHAPTER THIRTEEN: "ON THE BORDER, BY THE SEA"

Sources

Books
Browne et al., *For Richer, for Poorer;* Sklair, *Assembling for Development.*

Magazine Articles
"In the Shadow of the Maquiladoras," *Business Week,* September 7, 1992.
Louis Dubose and Karen Olsson, "Border Games," *Civilization,* August/September 1997.

Documents
"Commerce Department's Promotion of Mexico's Twin Plant Program," *Hearing Before the Subcommittee on Economic Stabilization of the Committee on Banking, Finance and Urban Affairs, House of Representatives,* 99th Cong., 2nd Sess., U.S. Government Printing Office, Washington, D.C., serial no. 99-105, November 25, 1986.
"Department of Commerce's Program to Promote Relocation of U.S. Industry," *Hearing before the Subcommittee on Commerce, Transportation, and Tourism of the Committee on Energy and Commerce, House of Representatives,* 99th Cong., 2nd Sess., U.S. Government Printing Office, Washington, D.C., serial no. 99-181, December 10, 1986.

District Court of Cameron County, Texas, 107th Judicial District, *Juan and Alma Alvear et al.* v. *AT&T Microelectronic and/or AT&T Technologies, Inc., et al.,* Deposition of Charles E. Peeples, August 25, 1994.

Newspaper Article
"Brilliante Inauguración de MagneTek Matamoros," *El Bravo,* June 12, 1988.

Interviews
Domingo Gonzales, Mollie James, William J. Landry, Deanna McComb, Sally Miller, Charles E. Peeples, Lindsey Rhodes, Hector J. Romeu Jr.

Notes
"Should this occur": Letter of June 13, 1988, to Local 945 secretary-treasurer Anthony Rizzo, in the author's possession.
outside influence: For an insightful, colorful history of the Bermudez dynasty, see Dubose and Olsson, "Border Games."
"land of mañana": *Brownsville Herald,* February 4, 1970.
More big names: Sklair, p. 120.
"extraordinary business opportunities": Quotes from the brochure were cited in "Commerce Department's Promotion of Mexico's Twin Plant Program," p. 2.
full-page ads: Sklair, p. 181.
windshield wipers: "Commerce Department's Promotion of Mexico's Twin Plant Program," p. 3, and Sklair, pp. 122–123.
"quid pro quo": "Commerce Department's Promotion," p. 14.
"unbelievably low wages": Ibid., p. 15.
"We collect taxes": Ibid., p. 19.
"bunch of crap": Ibid., p. 22.
"a crisis unparalleled": *Detroit News,* November 21, 1983.
Carr lectured Good: "Commerce Department's Promotion," p. 22.
"tax-deductible expense": Ibid., p. 23.
"For that matter": Ibid., p. 43.
peso plummeted: See Sklair, p. 40, for a table of peso-to-dollar exchange rates from 1948 to 1988, and p. 41 for a discussion of the effects of the devaluation on the Texas-Mexico border.
MagneTek broke ground: Ibid., p. 40.
global bottom-fishers: See Sklair, p. 120, for a table on the growth of the industry from 1970 to 1988.
coil-manufacturing business: The company, National Electric Coil, was formerly owned by McGraw Edison Power Systems. *Brownsville Herald,* January 18, 1987.
"Buy some bulk": Cited in Browne et al., p. 34.
"union avoidance": "Union Avoidance in Twin Plants," *Twin Plant News (TPN),* July 1988; **vacation tips:** "Not Just for the Birds," *TPN,* October 1996; **meet and greet:** "My Amigos," *TPN,* March 1994; **"maquila wives":** *TPN,* December 1989.
Built to accommodate: *Business Week,* September 7, 1992.

Blytheville native: Biographical material on Peeples is drawn from interviews with the author and from a deposition he gave in *Alvear et al.* v. *AT&T Micro-electric,* August 25, 1994, pp. 15–25.

CHAPTER FOURTEEN: THE LUCKY ONES

Sources

Books
Browne et al. *For Richer, for Poorer;* Guerrero-miller and Ayala, *¡Por eso!;* Sklair, *Assembling for Development.*

Documents
U.S. District Court, Southern District of Texas, Brownsville Division, *USA* v. *Jose Guillermo DeLeon Moreno,* Indictment, Criminal No. B-92-234, October 27, 1992. Judgment in a Criminal Case, March 5, 1993.

Interviews
Agapito Gonzalez Cavazos, Balbina Duque Granados, Elsa Duque Granados, Juana Granados, Teresa DeLeon Moreno, Charles E. Peeples, Fred J. Quintana.

Notes
"Tamale-puss": *Texas Observer,* May 28, 1999. The article is also the source for Clements's dismissive description of Bustamante.
"100 kilograms": Judgment in a Criminal Case, *USA* v. *Jose Guillermo DeLeon Moreno,* March 5, 1993.
"support those investments": Browne et al., p. 49.
"between the hammer": Sklair, p. 135.
forced the "resignation": Ibid.
"no further labor problems": Browne et al., p. 49.
maquilas **came knocking:** Biographical material on Gonzalez comes from his interview with the author and from *¡Por eso!* a Spanish-language history of the SJOI by Guerrero-miller and Ayala.
"We can't afford": *Brownsville Herald,* November 8, 1990.
"not practical, not legal": Ibid.
Quintana declared: Interview with author.
"inflationary situation": *Brownsville Herald,* January 9, 1990.
"out of competition": *Brownsville Herald,* November 8, 1990.
"Imposible": *Brownsville Herald,* January 30, 1992.
"real crime": William Greider, "The Perfect Dictatorship," *Utne Reader,* January/February 1993. (First published in *Rolling Stone,* September 3, 1992.)
"South Africa, or Korea": *Brownsville Herald,* February 11, 1992.
"something better": Ibid.

new contract: *Brownsville Herald,* February 13, 1992.
"still the struggle": Ibid.
"relative tranquility": *Brownsville Herald,* November 9, 1992.
"None older": A union official showed the author the letter, dated January 28, 1997.

Chapter Fifteen: Sleeping with the Elephant

Sources

Books
Greider, *One World, Ready or Not;* Greider, *Who Will Tell the People?;* Ruggiero and Sahulka, eds., *The New American Crisis.*

Magazine Articles
Matthew Cooper, "Fools and Their Money," *The Washington Post National Weekly Edition,* January 29–February 4, 1996. p. 25.
Debbie Nathan, "Death Comes to the Maquilas: A Border Story," *The Nation,* January 13–20, 1997.
John Ross, "Memories of 'La Crisis,' " *Texas Observer,* January 27, 1995, p. 13.
Nadav Savio, "The Hard Sell: Mexico Lobbies for NAFTA," *Multinational Monitor,* May 1993.

Interviews
Rolando González Barrón, Inez Barrajas Cruz, Andres Cuellar, Domingo Gonzalez, Balbina Duque Granados, Elsa Duque Granados, Fernando Montemayor Lozano, Teresa DeLeon Moreno.

Notes
"engine of global growth": Clinton's speech of February 26, 1993, was cited in Greider, *One World,* p. 195.
"sleep with the elephant": *Los Angeles Times,* June 11, 1990.
steep price: *NYT,* October 27, 1993.
"booty of privatization": Ibid.
Burson-Marsteller: *Multinational Monitor,* May 1993.
"coordinate speaking": Ibid.
"Democracy is held captive": Greider, *Who Will Tell the People?,* p. 39.
"A Better Mexico": *Multinational Monitor,* May 1993.
presidential pork: *NYT,* November 19, 1993.
"planes, trains and bridges": Ibid.
"really clinched": Ibid.
Mount Rushmore: Both the *Time* and *Economist* quotes are from Cooper, *Washington Post National Weekly Edition,* January 24–February 4, 1996, p. 25.
"death sentence": *NYT,* December 29, 1994.

working Mexicans . . . had lost: Dick J. Reavis, "A Murder in Tijuana," *NYT* Op-Ed, March 26, 1994.
"Those who applauded": Marc Cooper, "Starting from Chiapas," *The New American Crisis,* pp. 127–128.
allegedly raked in: Cooper, p. 25.
"I'm quite calm": *NYT,* December 22, 1994.
"Economic Emergency": *Los Angeles Times,* January 8, 1995.
"¡Basta Ya!": Ross, *Texas Observer,* January 27, 1995, p. 21.
"pothole along the road"; "Mexico's future": *Boston Globe,* January 5, 1995.
rate of occurrence: Figures were compiled by the nonprofit Coalition for Justice in the Maquiladoras and cited in *Dallas Morning News,* June 25, 1997.
"something terrible happened"; "These were atrocities": *Baltimore Sun,* January 19, 1992.
"can't ignore the obvious": *Dallas Morning News,* June 25, 1997.

EPILOGUE: "THANK GOD FOR NAFTA"

Sources

Book
Kozol, *Savage Inequalities.*

Documents
International Brotherhood of Teamsters, In the Matter of: Emergency Trusteeship of Local 945, IBT, Findings and Recommendations of Trusteeship Hearing Panel, May 1, 1995; and Notice to Officers and Members of Local Union 945, October 6, 1995.

Interviews
Bobbie Ainsworth, Dorothy Carter, Louis Carter, Balbina Duque Granados, Mollie James, Deanna McComb, Benedicto Martínez Orozco, Siegfried Steinberger.

Notes
"I've given MagneTek": *C-L,* October 11, 1997.
"No city boasts": *NJH&N,* July 3, 1992.
lives in poverty: Bureau of the Census figures cited in City of Paterson Application for Designation of New Jersey Urban Enterprise Zone, April 22, 1994;
Unemployment is high: *NJH&N,* July 25, 1996.
one elementary school: Kozol, p. 160.
"this quiet moment": *NJH&N,* July 13, 1996.
"affordable and market-priced": Rod Allee, "Paterson Wasteland Could Become Thriving Community," *Bergen Record,* July 23, 1999.

Index

AFL (American Federation of
    Labor), 47, 99, 102–3, 105,
    107–8, 113, 115
AFL-CIO:
    civil rights positions of, 134,
        189
    Clinton's NAFTA support criti-
        cized by, 291
    cross-border organizing alliances
        of, 312
    no-raiding policy of, 113,
        116
    on Southern industrial tax breaks,
        143
    on suppression of Mexican labor
        leader, 283
    Teamsters expelled by, 99, 101–3,
        109–11, 113
agribusiness, migrant labor
    employed by, 209–11
Ainsworth, Bobbie, 308
Alexander Hamilton Hotel, 25, 56,
    310
Allen, Gracie, 25

American Federation of Labor
    (AFL), 47, 99, 102–3, 105,
    107–8, 113, 115
    see also AFL-CIO
American Light Alloy, 23–24
Anco (Automotive Necessities Com-
    pany), 63–68
Andrews, Mildred, 182–83, 190,
    199, 201
anencephaly, 298–99
Arcelay, Louis, 229
Ardis, Michael A., 171
    background of, 114–15
    disappearance of, 225, 226
    in IUE-Teamster conflict, 118,
        124, 127, 128, 133, 135
    as Local 945 president, 115, 116,
        219, 225
    progressive racial views of, 126–7,
        133
    in Universal negotiations,
        135–36, 151
Ardis, Michael A., Jr., 127n
Arguelles family, 14

Arguelles Gutierrez, Sergio, 259, 260, 264

Aronson, Bernard, 167, 169

Asia, manufacturing plants in, 207, 211

Authentic Labor Front (FAT), 312

Automotive (Aeronautic) Necessities Company (Anco), 63–68

Balance Agriculture with Industry (BAWI) program, 141–42, 143, 146, 147, 149, 154, 155, 162, 203

Banco Mexicano, 293

Barnes, H. F., 77

Barnett, Ross:
    background of, 144, 152
    industrial development promoted by, 140, 145, 146, 151
    segregationist policies of, 144–45, 150, 159, 162, 165
    Universal plant welcomed by, 139, 140, 149–50, 151, 153

Barrajas Cruz, Ines, 300–301

BAWI, *see* Balance Agriculture with Industry program

Beatrice Foods, 235

Beck, Dave, 100, 101, 108, 109

Bel Geddes, Norman, 71

Berger, Arnold, 29, 30, 43, 54, 58

Bermudez, Antonio J., 257, 259

Bermudez, Jaime, 257, 259

Bieber, Owen, 283

Bimson, John, 48

Birmingham, Ala., civil rights movement in, 160

birth defects, 298–99, 304

Black, Leon, 236–37, 238

blacks:
    Northern migration of, 20, 22–23, 27
    see also racial and ethnic issues

Bloom, Sender, 57, 60–61

Blytheville, Ark., Universal/Magne-Tek facilities in, 253, 254–55, 264, 266, 305–7, 308

Boesky, Ivan, 241

Bone, Homer T., 77, 79

bootleggers, 58–59

Border Industrialization Program (BIP), 215–17, 256–57, 258, 278

Border Patrol, U.S., 210, 273, 276

Boudinot, Elisha, 36–37

Boyd, Frederick Sumner, 48

bracero program, 209, 210–11, 213, 214, 256

Bremicker, C. T., 77

Breslin, Jimmy, 118

Briggs, Roger T., 235–36, 240, 242

Bright, Arthur, 73, 74

Brill, Steven, 105, 118–19

Bromberg, Irving (Zeke), 64, 65, 66, 67–68, 84, 155–56

Brotherhood of Sleeping Car Porters, 27, 134

Brown, Anna, 21, 22

Brown, Lorenzo (Renza), 21, 23

Brownsville, Tex.:
    birth defects in, 298, 299
    Matamoros economic development linked with, 257–58
    Mexican day laborers hired in, 275
    prostitution in, 303

Brown v. *Board of Education of Topeka*, 144–45, 162, 163

Bruck, Connie, 238

Buffett, Warren, 236

Bullock, Joe, 149–50

Bureau of Prisons, U.S., 276

Burns, George, 25

Burson-Marsteller, 290

Bush, George, 288, 291

Bustamante, Jorge, 274n

Bywater, William, 246n

Campisano, Joseph, 225, 226, 227, 228–29

Campos Salas, Octaviano, 209, 211, 214–15, 216

Canada, industrial assembly products
  from, 215
Caplan, Burt, 122, 130
Cárdenas, Lázaro, 213
Carey, James, 110
Cariello, Vito, 225–26
Carr, Bob, 261–62
Carr, Fred, 246
Carter, Dorothy Black, 193
  background of, 195
  employment history of, 195, 307
  homes of, 202, 203, 208
  labor globalization and, 207, 209,
    286
  on racial issues, 199, 202
  Universal jobs of, 196–97, 200,
    208, 307
Carter, Louis, 194–95, 196–97,
    199–200, 201–3, 208, 231,
    307
Cartersville, Va., 21, 311–12
Castellito, Anthony (Three Fingers
  Brown), 119
Centers for Disease Control, U.S.,
  298
Chaney, James E., 181
Chase, Phil, 26, 28, 120, 128, 129–31
Chestnut, Flen, 226, 227
Chiapas, Mexico, anti-NAFTA
  protests in, 292
CIO (Congress of Industrial Organi-
  zations), 99, 107, 112, 113, 115
  see also AFL-CIO
Citizens Council of America, 144,
  145, 149, 150, 163
Ciudad Juárez, Mexico, industrial
  development in, 256–57, 264
Civil Rights Act (1964), 180, 193–94
civil rights movement, 147–49,
  159–61, 180, 181, 183, 189
  see desegregation
Clements, Bill, 274
Clinton, Bill, 288, 290–91, 293
COBRA, 305
Cohen, Milt, 92, 96–97
Cohen, Sidney, 251

Coleman, Mozelle, 23, 24, 30
Coleman, Turner, 23, 24
Colon, Carmelo, 227, 228
Colonia Vista Hermosa, 274, 277,
  295–98, 300
Colt family, 59–60
Commerce Department, U.S.,
  260–63
Componentes Mecánicos, 286
Coney Island, 55
Confederation of Mexican Workers
  (CTM), 277–82, 283, 285, 289
Congress, U.S.:
  civil rights legislation enacted by,
    165, 180
  free-trade agreement passed by,
    287–88, 290–91
  Hamilton's industrialization pro-
    posal to, 34–35, 36
  on Mexican border industries,
    260–63
  on migrant farmworkers in U.S.
    agribusiness, 209, 211, 213,
    256
  Teamster corruption investigated
    by, 99–101
Congress of Industrial Organizations
  (CIO), 99, 107, 112, 113, 115
  see also AFL-CIO
Congress of Racial Equality (CORE),
  128, 194
Connor, Eugene (Bull), 160, 161
Constantine, John, 66
Conti, Charles, 59
Conti, Sam, 61
corporate mergers, 168–70, 221–22
Cortese, Vincent J., 24
Cosa Nostra, 114
Costello, Frank, 109
cotton industry, 37, 38
Coughman, Royce, 176, 190
Courboin, Robert C., 171–72, 175,
  182
Cowley, Malcolm, 55
crime, organized, *see* organized
  crime

CTM, *see* Confederation of Mexican
    Workers
Cuellar, Andres, 297

Dalitz, Moe, 109
Dalvito, Frank, 95
Davis, Sidney, 170
Delco, 259
DeLeon Moreno, Guillermo, 274–76
DeLeon Moreno, Teresa, 277, 286,
    300
Deltronicos, 286
Deluxe Reading, 169, 170, 182
DeMauro, Armando, 84
DeMauro, John, 84
democracy, financial interests vs., 290
Depression, Great, 57, 60, 63, 70,
    71, 209
desegregation, 160–61
    school, 144–45, 194
Detroit, Mich., 262
    labor movement in, 104–5
Diaz, Margaret, 298
Díaz, Porfirio, 211, 212, 213
Díaz Ordaz, Gustavo, 213–14
Dioguardi, John, 100
Doak, William, 209
Dobbs, Farrell, 106–7, 108, 109
Doherty and Company, 46–47
Dolan, William, 24
Donahue, Thomas R., 283
Donaldson, Lufkin & Jenrette, 233
Donigan, William, 230
Dorfman, Paul, 109
Drexel Burnham Lambert, 236–37,
    238, 239–40, 242, 243, 244,
    245, 246, 247
drug offenses, U.S. prosecution of,
    276
Duer, William, 36
Du Pont Company, 55n, 259
Duque Granados, Balbina, 268–77,
    300
    family background of, 270–72
    living conditions of, 295–98, 303,
        304

marriage of, 275–76, 295
Matamoros jobs of, 15, 269, 273,
    274, 275, 286, 294–95, 301–2,
    304, 312, 313
Monte Bello home of, 268–70,
    271–72, 276, 312
motherhood of, 268, 269, 271,
    272–73, 275, 277, 295, 296
at union hiring hall, 277, 284,
    285, 286
wages paid to, 15, 275, 294–95,
    303
Duque Granados, Elsa, 277, 284,
    285, 286, 295, 296, 304
Duralite Co., 113, 115–18, 119,
    120–22, 124, 125, 147, 149

Edison, Thomas, 73, 74
Einhorn, Paul H.:
    on company ownership changes,
        169, 170, 171
    on customer service, 96
    financial management by, 85–86,
        89, 94, 171
    in management team, 89, 91, 93,
        94
    Mississippi expansion plan and,
        146, 147, 151, 167
    retirement of, 223, 225, 227
    on unions, 112
    as Universal president, 222–23,
        224–25
Einstein, Albert, 72, 75
Eisenberg, Wallace, 120, 121, 131,
    134–35
Eisenhower, Dwight D., 152
electric lighting, history of, 73–80
Electronic Control Corporation,
    258
Ellis Island, 41, 45
Employment Security Commission,
    179
Enfield, William L., 74
English, John, 102, 110
environmental problems, 290, 296,
    297–99, 303–4

Equal Employment Opportunity
    Commission, 194
Esmark, 235
Essex Wire, 221
ethnic issues, *see* racial and ethnic
    issues
Evers, Medgar, 163
Executive Life Insurance Company,
    246
Exide Corporation, 247
Expo Maquila '86, 260, 261, 262*n*

Fabian, Sy, 90
Fabian theater, 25, 26, 310
Fair Lawn, N.J., 29, 87
Fair Standards Labor Act (1938),
    105
Fantus Factory Locating Service,
    147
Farley, William F., 236–41, 242–44,
    245–46
Farley Industries, 237, 239
Farley/Northwest Industries, Inc.,
    240
farmworkers, 209–11, 213–14
Fath, Creekmore, 78, 79
Faulkner, William, 148
Federalist Papers, The, 34
Federal Trade Commission, 245
Fenner, William G., 38–39
Fiering, E. C. (Red), 175, 178, 179,
    180
Finsa Group:
    industrial park developments of,
        14, 259–60, 261, 274, 277,
        282, 286, 296, 297, 300–301
    MagneTek cultivated by, 14, 256,
        264
Fisher-Price, 259
fluorescent lights, 12, 31, 69, 73,
    74–80
    ballasts in, 75, 80, 83, 94, 95–98,
        200–201
Flynn, Elizabeth Gurley, 48, 51
Ford, Henry, 104–5, 262
Ford Motor Company, 43

Fortenberry, Harmon F., 193
Francis, Connie, 227
Franconero, George A., 227
Franklin, Benjamin, 33
Freedom Riders, 147–48
free trade:
    in Mexican-U.S. border zone, 215
    NAFTA establishment of, 287–92,
        295, 306
Fuentes, Carlos, 291
Furniture Workers Union, 115

Galarza, Ernesto, 210
Galef, Andrew G., 243–48, 251, 254,
    307
Galef, Billie, 248
Garret Mountain Reservation, 26
Geller, Herman, 61, 62
General Battery Corporation, 241
General Electric (GE), 71–78, 79,
    86, 89, 94, 96–97, 217, 250
General Motors (GM), 71, 72, 217,
    256, 259–60, 263, 282, 286
Genovese, Vito, 109, 114
Genovese family, 118, 119, 226, 229,
    230
Gerard, Mickey, 65
Gifford, Walter, 60
Ginsberg, Allen, 87
Glenn, John, 136, 139
Glockner, Walter, 120
GM, *see* General Motors
Goldman, Al, 62, 63, 68, 69, 83, 84
Goldsmith, Sir James, 236
Goldstein, Ruby, 59, 61, 62, 82
Goldwater, Barry, 180
Gompers, Samuel, 102, 103, 104
Gonzalez, Domingo, 299, 301
González Barrón, Rolando,
    299–300, 302
Gonzalez Cavazos, Agapito, 279–80,
    281, 282–83, 284, 285, 312
Good, Alexander, 260, 261, 262
Goodman, Andrew, 181
Gore, Al, 291
Graham, Benjamin, 167

Graham-Newman Corporation, 167, 168

Graves, Frank X., Jr., 232–33

Great Falls, 33, 34, 35, 37

Great Migration, 20, 22

Greenberg, David, 87

Greenwood, Miss., voter registration in, 159–60

Greider, William, 290

Grisanti, Frank A., 244

Gutin, Ida, 45

Gutin, Sam, 45

Hamilton, Alexander, 33, 34–35, 36–37, 38, 42

Harris, Harold, 97, 249–50

Harris, J. Ira, 236–37, 239–40

Harrison, Ward, 76, 78

Harvey, F. M. (Crip), 164

Haywood, William D. (Big Bill), 47–48, 49, 50

health insurance, 305, 306–7

Heineman, Ben W., 221–22, 224, 233, 234–35, 236–38, 239–40

high-intensity discharge (HID) ballasts, 253, 254, 255, 264

Hightower, Jim, 274n

Himmel, Michael, 227

Hoffa, James R., 100–103, 105, 108–11, 113, 114, 119, 133n, 187

Holloway, Arthur, 29

Hoover, Herbert, 60

Horwitz, Meyer, 158

House of Representatives, U.S.: NAFTA vote in, 290–91 *see also* Congress, U.S.

Howe, Irving, 41

Hudson, Henry, 32

Hughes, Chestina, 170–71, 222

Hutcheson, William, 107

IBEW, *see* International Brotherhood of Electrical Workers

IBT, *see* International Brotherhood of Teamsters

immigration, 22, 38, 39–42

industrial economy, agrarianism vs., 33–34

Industrial Workers of the World (IWW), 47–51

Ingalls Ironworks Shipyard, 142

insider trading, 36, 241n

Institutional Revolutionary Party, *see* PRI

International Brotherhood of Electrical Workers (IBEW), 209, 218–19, 225, 230–31, 306 Mississippi plant representation gained by, 173–93

International Brotherhood of Teamsters (IBT): civil rights movement supported by, 187 criminal links with, 99–101, 108–9, 114, 118–20, 128, 225–27, 229–30 history of, 103–7 in jurisdictional union rivalry, 113, 115–35, 136, 147, 149, 209 Local 945 of, 112–15, 116, 122, 150–51, 225–30, 232, 255 1957 AFL-CIO expulsion of, 99–100, 101–3, 109–11 regional contracts developed by, 108 at Universal, 112–13, 122–25, 127–36, 147, 150–51, 218–19

International Transformer Corporation, 68–69, 83–85, 90, 220

International Union of Electrical Workers (IUE), 110, 115, 116–18, 120–25, 127, 129, 130–36, 147, 149, 225, 246

ITT, 223, 224, 233, 235, 256, 259

IWW, *see* Industrial Workers of the World

Jaffee, Abe, 62, 63, 65

James, Anita, 31

James, David, 31

financial management of, 85–86, 89, 151, 170–71, 222
growth of, 89, 94, 151, 167, 223
hiring policies at, 31, 88–89, 139, 158, 162–63, 193, 196
incorporation of, 85, 90
management style at, 89–94, 171, 200–201, 203, 220–21, 223–25, 230–33, 248–52
Mexican facilities of, 217; *see also* MagneTek, Inc., Mexican facilities of
Mississippi operations of, 15, 136, 139–41, 143–44, 146, 149–52, 153–56, 162–63, 164–65, 167, 171–93, 195–203, 216, 219, 230–32, 253, 305
numbers-running with workers at, 128
ownership changes of, 12, 16, 166, 167–71, 220–25, 231, 233–34, 235, 236, 241, 242–44, 245–46, 247, 248–52
Paterson factory of, 11–13, 86–87, 136, 167, 185, 225, 227–30, 232–33, 248–49, 253, 254, 255
plant operations of, 85, 86, 89–90, 200–201
profitability of, 12, 85, 93–94, 220, 223, 242
quality commitment of, 98, 220
racial concerns at, 162–63, 193, 196–203
sales force of, 97
union activities at, 112–13, 122–25, 127–36, 147, 149, 150–51, 171–93, 199–200, 201–2, 209, 218–19, 220, 225–33
wages paid by, 13, 31, 135–36, 182–83, 185, 186, 196, 216, 219, 229, 230, 231, 233, 253–54
walkouts at, 218, 219, 228–29, 231, 232

Varner, Howard, 178, 179, 180
Velázquez Sánchez, Fidel, 278, 279, 280, 282, 283, 285, 289, 312
Velsicol Chemical, 233
Vento, Bruce, 261
Villa, Francisco (Pancho), 212
voting rights, 159–60, 164, 189, 194, 196

Wachner, Linda J., 247
W Acquisition Corporation, 247
Wagner Act (1935), 105
Warnaco, Inc., 247, 248
Washington, George, 32–33, 34
Waters, Frank, 305–6
Weir, Paul, 170–71
Westinghouse, 72, 74, 76, 77, 78, 198
Whalen, Grover, 71, 72
White, Alton, 155
White, Hugh L., 141–42, 145
Wickliff, Wallace, 174, 175, 178, 179, 180, 181–82, 184, 185, 186, 189
Wilkins, Roy, 134
Williams, Don, 223–24
Williams, William Carlos, 33
Wilson, Baxter, 146
WODA, 56
World War II:
business opportunities in, 63–64, 66
migrant farmworkers employed in, 209–10
rationing in, 65–66, 79
Wright Aeronautical Company, 27–28, 55, 66

Young, Coleman, 262
Young Men's Hebrew Association (YMHA), 45

Zager, Annie Sergy, 40, 42
Zager, Nathan, 42, 43, 52
Zapata, Emiliano, 212, 270
Zedillo Ponce de Léon, Ernesto, 293–94
Zenith, 258–59, 260, 278, 279

James, Etta, 31, 208
James, Florence, 22
James, Mollie Brown, 19–24
  assembly-line jobs of, 11, 286
  on dismantling of Paterson plant,
    253, 254
  final Universal workday of, 11–13
  homes of, 13, 23, 29, 208, 309,
    311
  Mexican industrial growth and,
    209
  on Mississippi move of Universal,
    136
  Mississippi workers trained by,
    264
  motherhood of, 31, 207–8
  on 1983 strike settlement, 232
  Northern move of, 15, 19–20,
    21–22, 23, 311
  after Paterson plant closure,
    308–9
  on quality commitment, 98
  second full-time job of, 113, 208,
    228, 232
  severance pay received by, 308
  on union leaders, 115, 227–28
  as union steward, 11, 112–13
  on Universal employee relations,
    93, 98, 220
  on Universal ownership changes,
    16, 248–49
  Virginia background of, 15,
    19–20, 21–22, 311–12
  wages of, 13, 20, 30, 31
James, Sam (father), 22–24, 29, 31,
    208
James, Sam (son), 31
James, Vivien (father), 22
James, Vivien (son), 22
J. C. Todd Machine Works, 37
Jefferson, Thomas, 33–34
Jefferson Electric, 245
Jews, east European, emigration of,
    39–42
Johnson, Lyndon B., 180, 193, 199,
    234

Johnson, Paul B., Jr., 140, 163, 164
Josephson, Matthew, 73
Juárez, Mexico, industrial develop-
    ment in, 256–57, 264
junk bonds, 238, 240, 242, 244,
    246n, 247

Kackley, Leila, 306
Kaja, Jim, 255
Kelly, Briggs & Associates, 235–36,
    240
Kelly, Donald P., 235–36, 238, 239,
    240, 242
Kennedy, John F., 100, 127, 136
  civil rights policies of, 145, 159,
    160, 161, 163, 211
  on Southern industrial develop-
    ment, 143
Kennedy, Robert F., 145, 160
  in Hoffa investigation, 100, 103,
    127
King, Martin Luther, Jr., 134, 160,
    161, 187, 189
Kirkland, Lane, 291, 312
Kourambis, Nicholas, 123, 125–28,
    129, 130, 131, 134, 135
Kozol, Jonathan, 310
Kramer, Lawrence F., 219
Ku Klux Klan, 183, 198, 201
Kushner, Stanley, 55

Labor Department, U.S., unemploy-
    ment programs of, 306
labor force:
  black, 22, 185, 193–94
  immigration and, 22, 38
  Mexican, 209–11, 213–14;
    see also Mexico, industrial
    workers of
  of migrant farmworkers in U.S.,
    209–11
  of 1920s, 57
  organized crime used against,
    64–65
  racial issues in, 185–86, 189,
    193–94, 199–203

labor force *(cont.)*
  retraining programs for, 306
  in Southern states, 140, 143, 149,
    151–52, 193–94
  after U.S. plant closures, 305–9
  working conditions of, 277,
    282–83, 295, 299–302
labor unions, 103–8
  Communist sympathies and, 121,
    131–32, 189, 191
  crime connections among leaders
    of, 100–103, 109–10, 114,
    118–20, 128, 225–27, 229–30
  cross-border alliances of, 312
  federal legislation on, 105, 107
  global competition and, 260–63,
    288
  industrywide organization by,
    106–8
  jurisdictional rivalry in, 113,
    115–35
  leapfrogging tactics of, 106–7
  and organizing Universal's Missis-
    sippi workers, 173–93
  trade policy and, 288
La Botz, Dan, 213
LaFalce, John, 261, 262–63
La Guardia, Fiorello, 71
Landry, William J., 264
Lansky, Meyer, 109
LaPlaca, Peter, 226
Lardiere, John (Johnny Coca-Cola),
    226
LBOs (leveraged buyouts), 235–37,
    239–40, 242, 244–46, 247
Lefkowitz, Joseph, 25
Lehman, Herbert, 71
L'Enfant, Pierre-Charles, 36
Lesnick, Frank, 62–65, 66–67,
    68–69, 84, 86
Lesser, Bert, 116, 121
leveraged buyouts (LBOs), 235–37,
    239–40, 242, 244–46, 247
Lewis, John L., 107–8
lighting technology, history of,
    73–80

Lindbergh, Charles, 27, 55
Lipps, William, 298
liquor industry, bootlegging in,
    58–59
Lithuania, czarist rule in, 40
Litton Industries, 245, 246
locomotive factories, 37–38
Lone Star Steel, 233, 235, 241
López Mateos, Adolfo, 214, 257
Lowrey, Grosvenor P., 73
Luciano, Charles (Lucky), 109
Lukas, J. Anthony, 48*n*
Lyons, William J., 227–28, 229, 230,
    232

McBride, Andrew F., 48
McClellan, John L., 100, 101
McClellan Committee, 100–101,
    110
McComb, Deanna, 254, 306–7
McLean, Colin M., 56
Madero, Francisco, 212
Magee, Archie, 154, 197
Magee, Miss., 152, 153
MagneTek, Inc.:
  Blytheville operations of, 254–55,
    264, 266, 305–7, 308
  board of directors of, 246–47
  employee relations at, 251–52,
    267, 301–2, 305–6, 307
  executives of, 266
  labor policies of, 254, 255, 267,
    285, 305–6, 308
  management style of, 249–52,
    301–2, 307
  Mexican facilities of, 14, 254,
    255–56, 263, 264, 266–67,
    277, 282, 285, 286, 296, 298,
    299, 312, 313
  Mississippi operations of, 263,
    305, 307–8, 312
  origins of, 244, 245
  Paterson plant of, 248–49, 252,
    264, 308–9
  sexual harassment at, 301–2
  toxic pollution from, 298, 299

Universal Manufacturing bought by, 12, 243, 245–46, 247, 248–49

U.S. ballast plants closed by, 11–13, 305–9, 312

wages paid by, 254–55, 264, 267, 277, 282, 302–3, 306, 307

working conditions maintained by, 277, 300–302

Mancone, Angelo, 92, 97

Mandela, Nelson, 291

maquiladoras, 15, 216–17

Commerce Department support of, 260–63

Martínez Orozco, Benedicto, 312

Matamoros, Mexico:

agricultural region of, 14, 256, 259

Brownsville development effort tied to, 257–58

city dump of, 299, 303–4

factory workforce of, 14, 15, 265–67, 282–86, 295–304

Finsa industrial park in, 14, 259–60, 261, 274, 277, 282, 286, 296, 297, 300–301

interior migration to, 265–66, 268–69, 272–74

MagneTek operations in, 13–15, 254, 255–56, 263, 264, 266–67, 277, 282, 285, 286, 296, 298, 299

pollution problems in, 296, 297–99, 303–4

population of, 256, 265–66

residential areas of, 265, 266–67, 295–98, 300, 302–4

Reynosa vs., 312

unemployment rate of, 264

U.S. industries moved to, 258–60, 263

Matamoros Maquiladora Association:

on abusive management behavior, 299–300

MagneTek executives welcomed by, 256

on wages, 280–81, 282, 283–84, 302

Maygors, Lois, 189

Meany, George, 99, 101, 102–3, 110–11, 113, 133*n*, 189

Mendenhall, Miss., 152, 153, 307–9

Menger, Paul, 178

Meredith, James, 145, 163

mergers, 168–70, 221–22

Mexico:

agriculture in, 212, 213–14

border redevelopment program of, 214–17, 256–57, 259–60

Commerce Department support of *maquila* industry in, 260–63

currency fluctuations in, 263, 267, 278, 292–93, 294–95

economic nationalism in, 212–13

environmental damage in, 290, 297–99, 303–4

financial bailout of, 293–94

free-trade agreements established with, 215, 287–92

industrial parks near border of, 14–15, 257, 258–60

interior villages of, 268–70, 271–72

migrant labor from, 209–11

oil industry of, 212, 213, 257

PRI political dominance in, 277–78, 281–82, 284*n*, 288, 300, 312

privatization in, 289

revolutions in, 211, 212, 270

state-run development programs in, 211–17

U.S. industry moved to, 15, 214–17, 256–60, 289, 312

wealth distribution polarized in, 289, 292

Mexico, industrial workers of:

abuse of, 299–300

age requirements for, 285

assembly-line jobs of, 15

job placement system for, 277, 284–86

Mexico, industrial workers of *(cont.)*
  living conditions of, 265, 266–67,
    295–99, 302–4
  PRI links with, 277–78
  second income required by, 303
  sexual harassment of, 301–2
  union activities of, 216, 263,
    277–81, 282–84, 312
  U.S. employment threatened by,
    260–63
  wage levels of, 15, 216, 253–54,
    263, 264–65, 267, 277, 280–81,
    282–84, 294–95, 302–3
  working conditions of, 277,
    282–83, 295, 299–302, 313
Meyer Bros., 24–25, 88
Meyner, Robert B., 90
Milken, Michael, 12, 238–39, 240,
    241–42, 243, 244, 245, 246
Miller, Sally, 254–55
Mississippi:
  industrial development efforts in,
    140, 141–43, 146–47, 149–50,
    151–52, 153–55
  racial concerns in, 145, 147–49,
    150, 159–64, 193–203
  unions discouraged in, 149,
    151–52, 173–93
  Universal/MagneTek plant opera-
    tions in, 15, 136, 139–41,
    143–44, 146, 149–52, 153–56,
    162–63, 164–65, 167, 171–93,
    195–203, 216, 219, 230–32,
    253, 263, 305, 307–8, 312
  workforce in, 140, 149, 307, 308
Mississippi, University of, 145
Mississippi Agricultural and Indus-
    trial Board, 146, 149, 151–52
Mississippi Industrial Commission,
    142
Mississippi Power & Light Company,
    146, 147, 149, 153, 196
Mississippi Sovereignty Commission,
    148–49, 164, 194
Mitsubishi, 256
Mohn, Einar, 110

Moldea, Dan, 104
Monte Bello, San Luis Potosí, Mex-
    ico, 268–70, 271, 312
Montemayor Lozano, Fernando, 297
Moses, Robert, 160

NAFTA (North American Free Trade
    Agreement), 287–92, 295, 306
National Action Party (PAN), 300
National Association for the
    Advancement of Colored Peo-
    ple (NAACP), 128, 129, 134,
    163, 194
National Labor Relations Board
    (NLRB), 105, 174, 179, 183,
    187n, 190, 191–92
Negro Committee for Participation
    in Government, 29
New Hope Baptist Church, 21, 311
Newman, Howard A. (Mickey), 167,
    168, 169, 170, 221, 222
Newman, Jerome, 167, 168
New York Stock Exchange, 55, 56,
    236
New York World's Fair, 70–73,
    76–77, 78
Nixon, Richard M., 220
NLRB (National Labor Relations
    Board), 105, 174, 179, 183,
    187n, 190, 191–92
North American Free Trade Agree-
    ment (NAFTA), 287–92, 295,
    306
North American Philips, 86, 89
Northwest Industries, Inc., 221–22,
    224, 233–37, 238, 239–41, 242
Norton Simon, Inc., 235

O'Dea, Richard, 56
Opilla, Joseph, 116
organized crime:
  union leaders' connections to,
    100–103, 109–10, 114,
    118–20, 128, 225–27, 229–30
  used against labor force, 64–65
  see also specific individuals

Paer, Louis, 43
Paer, Morris, 54, 59
Palmeri, Ernest, 226, 227, 229
PAN (National Action Party), 300
P&R, *see* Philadelphia & Reading
  Corporation
Parker, G. O., Jr., 152, 154, 176, 177,
  184, 188, 190
Parks, Rosa, 147
Pascrell, William J., Jr., 309
Pashman, Belle Cohen, 91
Pashman, Morris, 85, 89, 90, 91, 92,
  95
Pashman, Reuben (Rube), 89–94
  background of, 90–91
  in company ownership changes,
    169, 170
  death of, 222
  on labor policy, 186, 187, 192
  management style of, 89–90,
    91–92, 93, 94, 96–97
  Mississippi expansion plan and,
    146, 147, 151, 156, 165
  Simpson County business commu-
    nity and, 176–77
Passaic River, 33, 42
Passaic Rolling Mill, 37
Paterson, N.J.:
  black community of, 26, 28–29
  as commercial center, 24–25,
    44–45, 56, 87–88, 310
  contemporary decline resisted in,
    309–11
  cultural activities in, 25–26, 56,
    310
  Depression era in, 60
  history of, 32–33, 35–39, 55–57
  as industrial center, 35–39,
    42–43, 46–51, 60n, 309
  Jewish population of, 29, 39, 40,
    42–45, 54, 59, 62, 87
  job opportunities in, 26–28,
    30–31, 42–43, 309
  1913 strike action in, 47–51, 57
  population levels in, 38, 87,
    309
residential areas of, 29–30, 310,
    311
  segregation in, 26–28, 128
  silk industry in, 38, 39, 42–43, 44,
    46–51, 57, 216
  Universal/MagneTek facilities in,
    86–87, 136, 167, 185, 225,
    227–30, 232–33, 248–49, 252,
    253, 254, 255, 264, 308–9
Paterson, William, 35
Paterson (Williams), 33
Payonzeck, Otto:
  background of, 223, 224, 233
  as CEO of Universal, 223–25,
    241, 242, 248
  retirement forced on, 251–52
  Steinberger fired by, 250, 251
  union relations with, 230–32, 233
  Universal acquisition attempted
    by, 233–34, 235, 236, 242–44
PCB (polychlorinated biphenyl),
    95–96
Peeples, Charles E., 14, 266–67, 282
PEMEX, 213, 257
pension plans, corporate raiding of,
    246n
Perna, Frank (MagneTek president),
    251–52
Philadelphia & Reading (P&R) Cor-
  poration:
  history of, 167–68
  labor relations policies of,
    171–72, 175, 182, 192
  Northwest Industries acquisition
    of, 221–22, 240
  Universal Manufacturing pur-
    chased by, 166, 169–71, 220
Politinsky, Max (Grubby), 52, 54
polychlorinated biphenyl (PCB),
    95–96
Poppe, Elsie Lesnick, 63, 65
Popular Merchandise, 208, 228, 232
Porfiriato, 212
Preakness Hills Country Club, 59,
    61
Predators' Ball, 242, 243

President's Organization on Unemployment Relief (POUR), 60
PRI (Institutional Revolutionary
Party), 213, 277–78, 281–82,
283, 284*n*, 288–89, 292, 293,
300, 312
Price, Leontyne, 180
Pritzker family, 236
Programa Nacional Fronterizo
(PRONAF), 214, 257
Prohibition, 58
prostitution, 303
Provenzano, Anthony (Tony Pro):
background of, 118
in IUE-Teamsters jurisdictional
disputes, 116, 120, 124, 125,
127, 128, 130
Local 945 presidents appointed
by, 114, 115, 225
organized crime and, 114,
118–20
on racial issues, 126–27, 129
as Teamsters official, 114, 118,
119
violent tactics used by, 118–20,
124
Pucillo, Anthony J., 14–15

Quaker Oats, 259
Quintana, Fred J., 280, 281, 283,
284

racial and ethnic issues:
civil rights activism and, 147–49,
159–61
desegregation and, 144–45,
160–61, 194
federal legislation on, 165, 174,
180, 193–94
in job market, 26–28, 129,
162–63, 193–203
in North vs. South, 20–21, 26,
157
in Paterson, 26–29
in railroad accommodations, 20,
23

in Southern politics, 144, 145,
150, 163, 180
union campaigns on, 126–27,
129, 133–34, 184–85
at Universal's Mississippi plant,
162–63, 193, 196–203
voting rights and, 159–60, 164,
194, 196
Rancho Viejo, 255–56
Randolph, A. Philip, 27–28, 134
Rauh, Joseph, 28
RCA, 217, 259
Reagan, Ronald, 260, 288
Reed, John, 49, 50
Regent theater, 25
Regula, Ralph, 262
Reiter, Murray, 145–46, 149
"Report on the Subject of Manufac-
tures" (Hamilton), 34–35
Reuther, Walter, 110
Revolutionary War, 33
Reynosa, Mexico:
birth defects in, 298
MagneTek operations begun in,
312, 313
union activities quashed in,
278–79, 312
Rhodes, Lindsey, 257–60
Riesel, Victor, 100
Riverside Iron & Metal, 52
Rizzo, Anthony, 229, 232
Robert E. Lee Hotel, 194
Roberts, Jewel, 183
Robinson, Jackie, 20
Robinson, Sugar Ray, 20
Rogers Locomotive Works, 37–38
Rohrbach, Edward, 115–16
Romeu, Hector, Jr., 13–14, 256, 259
Roosevelt, Franklin D., 27–28, 65,
66, 71, 106, 108, 132
Roth, Philip, 81
Ryle, John, 38

Salinas de Gortari, Carlos, 281–82,
283, 287, 288–90, 291–93, 294
Salinas de Gortari, Raul, 293

Salomon Brothers, 236–37
Santelli, Joe, 83, 85, 92, 93
school desegregation, 144–45, 194
Schwartz, Jules, 89–90, 96
Schwerner, Michael, 181
Sciapani, Joseph, 229
SCLC (Southern Christian Leadership Conference), 134, 194
Sears Tower, 237
Securities and Exchange Commission (SEC), 241n, 247
Senate, U.S.:
    Teamsters investigated by, 99–101
    see also Congress, U.S.
Sergeant, Richie, 128
Sergy, Alan, 87, 166–67
Sergy, Annie, 40–42
Sergy, Archie:
    childhood of, 54–55, 58–61
    death of, 219–20, 222
    entrepreneurial abilities of, 61–62, 63, 68–69, 75, 80, 83, 84–85, 97–98, 309
    fatherhood of, 166–67
    jobs of, 59, 60, 61–62, 115
    labor relations and, 112, 124, 135, 147, 149, 150–51, 171, 184, 188–89, 218, 219
    management style of, 12, 85–86, 88–89, 91–94, 97, 171, 220
    Mississippi plant operations and, 136, 140–41, 146–47, 149–52, 153–54, 155–56, 162, 164, 165, 176, 184, 199, 216
    Paterson operations and, 86–87, 112, 136
    personnel policies of, 31, 88–89, 92–94, 97, 159, 165, 220
    prison sentence served by, 81–82, 84
    racial discrimination opposed by, 199
    relatives employed by, 84, 88, 158, 166, 220
    as salesman, 94–95, 97
    suburban residence of, 87

    Universal sold by, 166–67, 169, 170, 220–21, 248
Sergy, Bessie, 39–40
Sergy, Bruce, 87, 167
Sergy, Ida, 40n
Sergy, Mary, 58, 85n
Sergy, Morris, 39–40
Sergy, Pearl Eisman, 82, 87, 91, 220
Sergy, Rose Gutin, 45–46, 51–52, 53, 57–58, 61
Sergy, Sam (Sandy), 87, 88, 92–93, 166
Sergy, Samuel, 39–43, 45, 46, 51–52, 53, 57, 58, 59, 60
Sergy, Sylvia, 58, 85
Serratelli, John V., 114, 225, 229
Sharp, Howard M., 78
Shea, Cornelius P., 104
silk industry, 38, 39, 42–43, 46–47, 57, 216
Silver, James, 145
Simmons, William, 145
Simpson County, Miss.:
    bond issue for industry in, 140, 153–55, 196
    industrial employment in, 139, 202–3, 308
    MagneTek closure of ballast plant in, 305, 307, 308
    organized labor efforts in, 173–93, 209
    racial issues in, 160, 163–64, 175, 193–203
    town rivalries in, 152–53
    Universal welcomed in, 140, 154–55, 176–77, 184, 195–96, 203, 307
Sinclair, Upton, 49
SJOI (Union of Industrial Workers and Day Laborers), 277, 279–80, 284, 285
Sklair, Leslie, 278
Smith, Frank (business executive), 146, 147, 149, 152, 154
Smith, Frank (union official), 226
Smith, Lenon, 197, 198, 200–201, 202

Smith Act (1940), 109n
SNCC (Student Nonviolent Coordi-
nating Committee), 160, 194
Society for Establishing Useful Manufactures (SUM), 35–37, 43n
Southern Christian Leadership Conference (SCLC), 134, 194
Spectrum Group, Inc., 244–45,
246–47, 251
spina bifida, 299, 304
Spirit of St. Louis, 55
Stalin, Joseph, 106n
Standard Oil of Kentucky, 150, 151
Steiger, Joel, 94
Stein, Michael, 93
Stein, Sam, 82, 83, 86
Steinberger, Siegfried, 92, 166
background of, 156–58, 162
corporate ownership changes
and, 170, 172, 175
on labor policies, 124, 171, 175,
179, 180, 182, 184, 186, 187,
188, 192, 199, 228, 231
as Mississippi plant administrator,
162, 165, 171, 179, 184, 187,
197–98, 200–201, 250, 307
on racial discrimination, 157,
159, 160, 161–62, 165, 198,
199, 200–201, 203, 250
retirement forced upon, 250–51,
307
Simpson County life of, 250,
307–8
on Universal executives, 89, 91, 93
Stephens, Lloyd, 203
Stetin, Sol, 115–16
stock market, 55, 57, 168
Strollo, Tony, 118
Student Nonviolent Coordinating
Committee (SNCC), 160,
194
SUM, *see* Society for Establishing
Useful Manufactures
Supreme Court, U.S., school desegregation ruling of, 144–45
Sweeney, John, 312

swimming pools, racial segregation
of, 26, 194
Sylvania Hygrade, 78–79

Tariff Code, U.S., 215
Teamsters, *see* International Brother-
hood of Teamsters
Texas Center for Policy Studies, 299
Textile Workers Union of America,
115–16
Thames, Frank, 178
Tijuana, Mexico, industrial develop-
ment in, 256, 257
Tisch, Laurence A., 221
Tobin, Daniel J. (Big Dan), 104, 106,
107, 108, 109n
Torres, Jose, 133
Traxler, Annie Mae, 182
Tresca, Carlo, 48
Triad-Utrad, 245
Trico Products Corporation, 261
Trotsky, Leon, 106n
trucking industry, 106
Truman, Harry S, 66
Trumbull, L. R., 39n

Union of Industrial Workers and Day
Laborers (SJOI), 277, 279–80,
284, 285
Union Underwear, 240
United Auto Workers, 27, 110, 260,
262, 283
Universal Citizens Advisory Committee, 176–77, 178, 180–81, 184,
185, 186–87, 192
Universal Manufacturing Company:
Arkansas plant of, 253, 254–55,
264, 266, 305–7
ballasts produced by, 12, 31, 69,
89, 95–98, 200, 234, 253
closing of, 11–13, 305–9
customer service of, 94–97, 220,
250
disappearance of, 249, 252, 253
employee relations at, 92–94,
97–98, 198–202, 220, 242